# The Islamic Marriage Contract

## Case Studies in Islamic Family Law

## Harvard Series in Islamic Law

# The Islamic Marriage Contract

## Case Studies in Islamic Family Law

Edited by

Asifa Quraishi
Frank E. Vogel

Published by the
Islamic Legal Studies Program, Harvard Law School
Distributed by Harvard University Press
Cambridge, Massachusetts
2008

Library of Congress Control Number: 2008939958


Printed in the United States of America
ISBN 978-0-674-02821-0

# CONTENTS

## PART ONE

## THE LEGAL DOCTRINE OF MARRIAGE CONTRACTS IN COMPARATIVE PERSPECTIVE

## PART TWO

## THE MARRIAGE CONTRACT IN MUSLIM HISTORY

## PART THREE

## MODERN PRACTICE AND REFORM

PART FOUR

## THE MUSLIM MARRIAGE CONTRACT IN WESTERN
## SECULAR LEGAL SYSTEMS

# AUTHOR BIOGRAPHIES

Kecia Ali is an Assistant Professor of Religion at Boston University where she teaches a range of classes in Islamic Studies. She received her undergraduate degree in history from Stanford University (1993) and her Ph.D. in religion from Duke University (2002). After working as a research analyst with the Feminist Sexual Ethics Project (www.brandeis.edu/projects/fse), she spent a year as a visiting researcher at the Women's Studies in Religion Program at Harvard Divinity School, followed by two years as a Florence Levy Kay postdoctoral fellow at Brandeis University.

Ali is the author of *Sexual Ethics and Islam: Feminist Reflections on Qur'an, Hadith, and Jurisprudence* (Oneworld, 2006), and the co-author of *Islam: The Key Concepts* (Routledge, 2008). She has also contributed articles to a variety of journals and edited volumes on topics ranging from the example of the Prophet as a husband to the depiction of veiled figures in newspaper cartoons. In addition to her research on marriage in early Islamic jurisprudence, she is working on a biography of the jurist al-Shāfiʿī.

Zainah Anwar is the Executive Director of Sisters in Islam (SIS), a non-governmental organization working on the rights of Muslim women within the framework of Islam. Sisters in Islam, founded in 1987, is at the forefront of the women's movement that seeks to end discrimination against women in the name of religion. The group's activities in research, advocacy, legal services, and public education help to promote the development of Islam that upholds the principles of equality, justice, freedom, and dignity within a democratic state.

Her other work experience includes: Chief Programme Officer, Political Affairs Division, Commonwealth Secretariat, London; Freelance Writer; Senior Analyst, Institute of Strategic and International Studies, Kuala Lumpur; Political and Diplomatic Writer, The New Straits Times, Kuala Lumpur. Her book, *Islamic Revivalism in Malaysia: Dakwah Among the Students* has become a standard reference in the study of Islam in Malaysia. She was a member of the Human Rights Commission of Malaysia from April 2000–April 2004. She was educated at the Fletcher School of Law and Diplomacy, Boston University, and the MARA Institute of Technology, Malaysia, in the fields of international relations and journalism.

Ali Asani was born in Nairobi, Kenya, and is currently Professor of Indo-Muslim and Islamic Religion and Cultures at Harvard University. After completing his high school education in Kenya, he attended Harvard

College, with a concentration in the Comparative Study of Religion, graduating summa cum laude in 1977. He continued his graduate work at Harvard in the Department of Near Eastern Languages and Civilizations, receiving his Ph.D. with high distinction in 1984. Since then he has been on the faculty at Harvard providing instruction on Islam in India, Pakistan, and Bangladesh, Islamic mysticism, and the study of literature and the arts in Muslim societies. He also offers instruction in various South Asian and African languages.

Professor Asani is the author of many scholarly articles and several books on the devotional literatures of Muslim communities in South Asia, including *The Bujh Niranjan: An Ismaili Mystical Poem, The Harvard Collection of Ismaili Literature in Indic Languages: A Descriptive Catalog and Finding Aid, Celebrating Muhammad: Images of the Prophet in popular Muslim poetry, Ecstasy and Enlightenment: The Ismaili Devotional Literatures of South Asia, Let's Study Urdu*, and *An Infidel of Love: Exploring Muslim Understandings of Islam*. He has contributed chapters to various books as well as articles to *The Encylopedia of Religion, The Oxford Encylopedia of the Modern Islamic World, Encylopedia of South Asian Folklore*, and *The Muslim Almanac*. In 2002 he was awarded the Harvard Foundation Medal for his contributions to improving intercultural and interracial relations.

Charles Donahue, Jr., is the Paul A. Freund Professor of Law at Harvard Law School and immediate past-president of the American Society of Legal History. Among other books, he is the co-author or co-editor of *Select Cases of the Ecclesiastical Courts of the Province of Canterbury, c. 1200–1301; Year Books of Richard II: 6 Richard II, 1382–1383; The Records of the Medieval Ecclesiastical Courts*, and *Cases and Materials on Property: An Introduction to the Concept and the Institution*. He is also the author of more than 70 articles in the fields of ancient, medieval, and early modern legal history.

Donahue teaches legal history in both the Law School and the Faculty of Arts and Sciences at Harvard and has taught at the University of Michigan, the London School of Economics, the Vrije Universiteit te Brussel, Columbia University, the University of California at Berkeley, Boston College, and Cornell University. Donahue is vice-president and literary director of the Ames Foundation and a councillor of the Selden Society (UK). He is a life member of the American Law Institute and the Medieval Academy of America, a Fellow of the Royal Historical Society, and a previous Guggenheim Fellow. His most recent study, *Law, Marriage and Society in the Later Middle Ages: Arguments about Marriage in Five Courts*, was published by Cambridge University Press in December 2007.

Christina Jones-Pauly has done field research and published numerous articles on Islamic law in African and Asian countries. She taught and researched at German universities in comparative and Islamic laws for over a decade. She taught Islamic law in Africa at the Harvard Law School and was a Radcliffe Fellow. She is now Research Associate at the Faculty of Law, University of Oxford, and a legal adviser and consultant for multilateral international organizations on law, gender, religion, and development.

Richard Freeland was called to the Bar in England in 1997, and in 2000 spent some time as a Visiting Researcher at Harvard's Islamic Legal Studies Program. Between 2001 and 2006 Richard worked in legal publishing, spending the last three years as editor of The Legal 500.

Martin Lau is a Reader at the Department of Law of the School of Oriental and African Studies, University of London, and a Barrister at Essex Court Chambers in London. His research interests include South Asian law, comparative constitutional law, and modern Islamic law. Recent publications include *The Role of Islam in the Legal System of Pakistan* (Brill, 2006) and the *Yearbook of Islamic and Middle Eastern Law*, co-edited with Eugene Cotran.

Brinkley Messick is Professor of Anthropology at Columbia University. He is the author of *The Calligraphic State: Textual Domination and History in a Muslim Society* (Berkeley, 1993), and a co-editor of *Islamic Legal Interpretations: Muftis and Their Fatwas* (Cambridge, Mass., 1996).

Ziba Mir-Hosseini is a legal anthropologist, specializing in Islamic law, gender, and development, and a Senior Research Associate at the London Middle Eastern Institute, SOAS, University of London. She obtained her B.A. in Sociology from Tehran University (1974) and her Ph.D. in Social Anthropology from University of Cambridge (1980). She has held numerous research fellowships and visiting professorships, most recently Fellow at the Wissenschaftskolleg zu Berlin (2004–05) and Hauser Global Law Visiting Professor at the School of Law, New York University (2002, 2004, and 2006). Her publications include the monographs *Marriage on Trial: A Study of Islamic Family Law in Iran and Morocco* (I. B. Tauris, 1993, 2002), *Islam and Gender: The Religious Debate in Contemporary Iran* (Princeton University Press, 1999; I. B. Tauris, 2000), and (with Richard Tapper) *Islam and Democracy in Iran: Eshkevari and the Quest for Reform* (I. B. Tauris, 2006). She has also directed (with Kim Longinotto) two award-winning feature-length documentary films on contemporary issues in Iran: *Divorce Iranian Style* (1998) and *Runaway* (2001).

Nik Noriani Nik Badli Shah graduated with an LL.B. (Hons) from the University of Malaya (UM) in 1986 and served for ten years (1986 to 1996) in the Judicial and Legal Service, Malaysia. Among the posts she held while in the legal service were the posts of Assistant Parliamentary Draftsman and Deputy Commissioner for Law Revision in the Attorney-General's Chambers. She joined Sisters in Islam (SIS Forum Malaysia), a non-governmental women's group working for the rights of women within the Islamic framework, in 1996. She obtained the degree of Master of Comparative Laws (M.C.L) from the International Islamic University, Malaysia (IIUM) in 1998, and is now a Ph.D. candidate at the International Institute of Islamic Thought and Civilization (ISTAC), IIUM. She has written several books and articles relating to family law. Her publications include *Marriage and Divorce under Islamic Law* (International Law Books Services, Kuala Lumpur, 1998), *Marriage and Divorce: Law Reform within Islamic Framework* (International Law Books Services, Kuala Lumpur, 2000) and "Marriage, Polygyny and Divorce within the Malaysian Muslim Community," in *(Un)tying the Knot: Ideal and Reality in Asian Marriage*, ed. Gavin W. Jones and Kamalini Ramdas (Asia Research Institute, National University of Singapore, 2004).

Amira Sonbol specializes in the history of modern Egypt, Islamic history and law, and women, gender and Islam, and is the author of several books including *The New Mamluks: Egyptian Society and Modern Feudalism; Women, the Family and Divorce Laws in Islamic History; The Creation of a Medical Profession in Egypt: 1800–1922; The Memoirs of Abbas Hilmi II: Sovereign of Egypt; Women of the Jordan: Islam, Labor and Law*; and *Beyond the Exotic: Muslim Women's Histories.* Professor Sonbol is editor-in-chief of *HAWWA: The Journal of Women of the Middle East and the Islamic World* published by Brill and co-editor of *Islam and Christian-Muslim Relations*, a quarterly journal co-published with Selly Oak Colleges (UK). She teaches courses on the History of Modern Egypt, Women and Law, and Islamic Civilization.

Suzanne Last Stone is Professor of Law at Cardozo School of Law and Director of its Program in Jewish Law and Interdisciplinary Studies. In 2006–07, she was a visiting professor at Columbia University Law School and at the Hebrew University Law School. In 2004–05, she held the Caroline Zelaznik Gruss and Joseph S. Gruss Visiting Chair in Talmudic Civil Law at the Harvard Law School. She also has taught Jewish Law at Haifa Law School and Tel Aviv Law School as a Cegla Scholar in Residence. In the fall of 2007 and 2008, she will be the Gruss Professor of Talmudic Civil Law at University of Pennsylvania Law School and, in addition, she will be teaching Jewish Law at Princeton University. In addition to teaching courses on Jewish Law, Professor Stone teaches Civil Procedure, Federal Courts, and Law, Religion and the State. A graduate of Princeton University and Columbia University Law School, Professor Stone also was a Danforth Fellow in Jewish History and Classical Religions at Yale University. Before joining the Cardozo faculty, Professor Stone clerked for Judge John Minor Wisdom of the Fifth Circuit Court of Appeals and then practiced litigation at Paul, Weiss, Rifkind, Wharton and Garrison.

Professor Stone is the co-editor-in-chief of *Diné Israel*, a peer-reviewed journal of Jewish law, co-edited with Tel Aviv Law School. She is also on the editorial board of the *Jewish Quarterly Review*. She is co-curator of the Jews and Justice Series at the Center for Jewish History and a member of the boards of the Jewish People Policy Planning Institute, the Center for Ethics of Yeshiva University, and the International Summer School in Religion and Public Life. Professor Stone writes and lectures on the intersection of Jewish legal thought and contemporary legal theory. Her publications include: "In Pursuit of the Countertext: The Turn to the Jewish Legal Model in Contemporary American Legal Theory" (Harvard Law Review); "The Jewish Conception of Civil Society," in *Alternative Conceptions of Civil Society* (Princeton University Press); and "Justice, Mercy and Gender in Rabbinic Thought." Professor Stone's work has been translated into Italian, German, Hebrew, and Arabic. In 2004 she was chosen, along with five other path-breaking scholars in the field of Jewish Studies, to reflect on her scholarly career in the first edition of the revised *Jewish Quarterly Review*.

Judith Tucker (Ph.D., History and Middle Eastern Studies, Harvard University) is Professor of History, Director of the Master of Arts in Arab Studies Program at Georgetown University, and Editor of the *International Journal of Middle East Studies*. She is the author of many publications on the history of women and gender in the Arab world, including *Women in 19th Century Egypt* (Cambridge University Press, 1985) and *In the House of the Law: Gender and Islamic Law in Ottoman Syria and Palestine* (California University Press, 1998), and co-author of *Women in the Middle East and North Africa: Restoring Women to History* (Indiana University Press, 1999). She is the editor of *Arab Women: Old Boundaries, New Frontiers* (Indiana University Press, 1993) and co-editor of *A Social History of Women and Gender in the Modern Middle East* (Westview Press, 1999). In addition, she has authored numerous articles for professional journals and edited volumes. Her research interests focus on the Arab world in the Ottoman period, women in Middle East history, and Islamic law, women, and gender.

L. L. Wynn received her Ph.D. in cultural anthropology from Princeton University in 2003. She has conducted ethnographic research in Saudi Arabia and Egypt on women's issues, social movements and identity politics, nationalism and the uses it makes of history and archaeology, tourism, and transnational movements of people and culture. Her first book, based on 3–1/2 years of dissertation research in Cairo and titled *Pyramids and Nightclubs: A Travel Ethnography of Arab and Western Imaginations of Egypt, from King Tut and a Colony of Atlantis to Rumors of Sex Orgies, Urban Legends about a Marauding Prince, and Blonde Belly Dancers*, was published in 2007 by the University of Texas Press. Her current research examines medical language, public health campaigns, new reproductive health technologies, and cyberIslam. She is an associate lecturer in the Department of Anthropology at Macquarie University in Sydney, Australia.

Amalia Zomeño is currently a Tenured Researcher at Consejo Superior de Investigaciones Científicas (CSIC) in Madrid. She holds a Ph.D. in Arabic philology from Barcelona University and was a postdoctoral fellow at Princeton University from 1998–2000. The main topic of her research is Islamic family law and transmission of property in medieval western Islam. Ms. Zomeño is the author of *Dote y matrimonio en al-Andalus y el norte de África* (Dowry and Marriage in al-Andalus and North Africa) (Madrid: CSIC, 2000). She is currently working on the edition and study of different collections of Arabic documents in the Archives of Granada. She is co-editor of *From al-Andalus to Khurasan: Documents from the Medieval Muslim World* (Leiden: Brill, 2007, with P. M. Sijpesteijn, L. Sundelin, and S. Torallas Tovar).

Mona Zulficar is Senior Partner at Shalakany Law Offices in Cairo, where she heads the Banking and Capital Markets Group at the Firm and is recognized internationally as a leading expert in this field. As a practicing attorney for more than twenty-five years, Mrs. Zulficar is a recognized specialist in major financial, industrial, and other contracts required by some of the most important joint venture businesses in Egypt. She has received a number of awards and has been recognized by various local and international agencies in both the fields of international business law and human rights, and has represented Egypt at many international conferences. She has authored numerous articles and studies in international legal and economic journals on Egyptian law and international transactions and in the field of human rights and is recognized as a leading advocate of human rights, including women's rights.

Ms. Zulficar is a professional member of the Egyptian Bar Association, International Bar Association, the Egyptian Society for Economics, Statistics, and Legislation, and the Egyptian Society for International Law. She also contributes to drafting of major Egyptian economic and social laws, whether as legal adviser to the competent ministry or member of the drafting team, such as the new Capital Market Law and Taker Over Regulations, the new Telecom Law, the new Special Economic Zones Law, the new Banking Law and its regulations, the new NGO Law, the new Divorce and Family Disputes Procedural Law and regulations, the amendments to the Nationality Law and the Family Courts Law. She has been a member of Egypt-US Business Council since 2002 and is also a member of the Council of Advisers to the World Bank for the Middle East and North Africa Region.

Mona Zulficar is a human rights and women's rights activist who has during the last twenty-five years lead NGO initiatives and campaigns that successfully culminated in giving women equal divorce rights, equal rights to give their children the Egyptian nationality, the issue of a new form of a marriage contract, and in general the elimination of discrimination against women. She has also been active in advocating liberalization and democratization of civil society and has continuously been involved in campaigns and projects for legal and judicial reform. She was a member of the National Council for Women from 2000 to 2006, and Chair of the External Gender Consultative Group of the World Bank, Washington D.C. from 2001 to 2006. She is currently a member of the National Council for Human Rights, Chair of Women's Health Improvement Association, Cairo, and Chair of its successful microfinance program El Tadamun. She was previously a member of the International Council of Human Rights, presided by President Carter, and a Board member of PCI, New York, as well as several other distinguished Egyptian and international non-governmental organizations.

# INTRODUCTION

This book focuses on a single legal concept—the marriage contract—for four main reasons. The first reason is that this focus brings to the fore many complex issues of Muslim marriage and divorce that intersect in the framing and implementation of the marriage contract. The substantive doctrines of the marriage contract itself (who negotiates it, the types of consideration it exchanges, the stipulations it allows) have been generally neglected by students of Islamic law in the West. The second main purpose in adopting this focus is that the marriage contract offers a fruitful site, or case-study, for observing the workings of Islamic law in actual legal systems of diverse times and places. It is an area of law that usefully defines observable contexts of practice of the Muslim present and past. And it turns out to offer significant common ground with other religious and secular bodies of law, even of ages long past, enabling meaningful and telling comparisons. The third reason to explore the marriage contract is that, because it reflects how parties choose privately to order their marriage relations, it helps reveal how in practice these parties are affected by and respond to prevailing regimes of legislation and regulation in matters of marriage and the family. As the fourth and final purpose, study of the marriage contract doctrinally and practically illuminates the status of contemporary Muslim women. In particular, we find that in widely diverse contexts worldwide activists for women's rights have chosen the marriage contract as a means to pursue their reforms, sometimes even as an alternative to outright legislative change.

To reap this broad range of potential insights this collection brings together essays from many perspectives—jurisprudential, legal, comparative, sociological, religious, secular, historical and contemporary. The collection is organized into four sections. The first section, "Legal Doctrine of Marriage Contracts in Comparative Perspective," offers three essays presenting doctrinal studies of the law regarding marriage contracts in Islam, Christianity and Judaism, respectively. This section, while eliciting revealing comparisons among the three religious legal systems, also sets the Islamic doctrinal stage for the historical and sociological studies of Muslim marriage contracts throughout the remainder of the book.

Kecia Ali's piece, "Marriage in Classical Islamic Jurisprudence: A Survey of Doctrines," sets out the framework of Islamic legal doctrine governing the marriage contract. Ali performs the difficult, almost impossible, task of concisely summarizing, across a number of schools, the many basic *fiqh* principles and rules relating to the marriage contract. Though inevitably superseded in details by the individual articles to follow, her article is indispensable for setting into Islamic religious and legal context the events, debates, and developments described in later articles. Ali's study is also a useful point of departure for deeper inquiries into the relevant legal doctrines, such as in exploring their comparison with other religious laws; their theological and jurisprudential relationship with the scriptural texts from which they claim to spring (an issue often central to modern reform work); their evolution and variation in different social contexts and across eras and regions; as well as the endless question of whether and how they have been applied in practice.

In the next article in this section, "The Western Canon Law of Marriage: A Doctrinal Introduction," Charles Donahue, Jr. presents basic Christian concepts of marriage, engaging particularly with the notion, often heard, that in contrast to Muslim and Jewish marriage, Christian marriage is a sacrament, not a contract. He presents evidence of the degree to which scriptural texts shaped the development of the canon law of marriage, such as in establishing its character as a sacrament and in giving rise to characteristic doctrines such as monogamy and indissolubility. Donahue's study indicates several aspects of similarity between Muslim and Christian marriage contracts (for example, the centrality of mutual consent and the neglect of ritual or ceremony), showing how ripe the subject is for further comparative study.

Concluding this first section, Suzanne Stone's "Jewish Marriage and Divorce Law" provides important insights from the Jewish law sphere into the interaction of religious and secular systems of marriage law, pointing out especially the difficulty in Jewish law of distinguishing between man-made law and God-made law. Her description of marriage law in the Halakha articulates the distinction between laws that govern the relations of human beings among themselves and those that govern the relations between human beings and God, and where marriage falls in that distinction. In all of her descriptions, the reader will find many parallels to Islamic law.

The next section of the book, "The Islamic Marriage Contract in Muslim History," consists of four studies using extant records of Muslim marriage contracts to draw conclusions about the doctrine and practice of marriage contracts in historical periods. Together, these essays suggest in broad outlines the spectrum of variation of Islamic marriage law and practice across the regions of the Muslim world and over time. Moving from doctrine into the application of Islamic marriage contract law in history, Amira El-Azhary Sonbol's essay, "A History of Marriage Contracts in Egypt," succeeds in the ambitious goal of tracing and comparing the practice of Egyptian marriage contract in three disparate ages: pre-Islamic Egypt, the Ottoman era (her chief focus), and the contemporary age of national family law codes. She juxtaposes research in Ottoman-era court records—which both record litigation proceedings and serve as a registry of documents including marriage contracts—with briefer references to both pre-Islamic and post-colonial Egyptian norms and practices. The records show the surprising extent to which Egyptian women were able to shape the legal framework for their marriage relationships by creative contractual terms, and how ready they were to litigate to defend their rights. As does the third article in this section, Sonbol's piece offers striking concrete examples of pervasive and powerful use of contractual terms to protect various interests of spouses, particularly wives, examples going far beyond anything routinely encountered in contemporary Muslim law and practice. Sonbol points out how modern nationalist codifications inspired by the laws of colonial powers greatly narrowed the legal options of Egyptian women by rendering binding, by legislative reference, the rules of classical Hanafi *fiqh*, rules that in Egypt had long before been rendered more flexible both by evolution of the Hanafi school itself and by affording an option to invoke other schools' views when desired.

In "Questions of Consent: Contracting a Marriage in Ottoman Syria and Palestine," Judith Tucker tackles the controversial question of a woman's right to consent to marriage in relation to the right of her parent or guardian to contract a marriage for her. Surveying court records and fatwa collections, Tucker highlights the elements of the Islamic legal tradition that support a woman's right to choose her marriage partner. She reviews important *fiqh* doctrines on spousal suitability (*kafāʾa*) and as to the stages by which a woman attains majority, tracing the practical legal and social consequences of these rules. She explains how the courts became a refuge of women seeking to mitigate the consequences of culturally entrenched patriarchy.

Amalia Zomeño's essay, "The Islamic Marriage Contract in al-Andalus (Tenth-Sixteenth Centuries)," takes us to medieval Muslim Spain through the few remaining court documents of Muslim marriages found in Spain. Through a study of registered marriage contracts, notarial handbooks, and fatwa collections, Zomeño gives insights into how marriages were contracted in Andalusia from the tenth through the sixteenth centuries. She shows how some parts of these contracts were standardized but others changed with changes in economic conditions, social conventions and Maliki legal norms. Her presentation reveals a tension between social customs and muftis' views, particularly concerning *mahr* (dower) payment and other property transfers. Andalusian records show a divergence in local practice regarding stipulations in the contract: in some localities, contracts nearly always included certain standardized clauses as to monogamy, spousal abuse, location of marital home, and spousal absence, while in other regions contracts tended to include no stipulations at all.

The last piece in the historical study of Muslim marriage contracts comes from Brinkley Messick whose "Interpreting Tears: A Marriage Case from

Imamic Yemen" provides a case study of a marriage contracted in Yemen during the most recent historical period for which its Shariʿa law remained uncodified. Messick's piece views Islamic marriage contract law, and gender relations under it, through the lens of the efforts of a young woman to annul an alleged marriage contract made for her during her childhood. Messick reviews Zaydi rules as to contracts made during a girl's minority and the rights over her marriage wielded by her father and other male guardians, demonstrating how these rules impact the case. He gives excerpts from notarial manuals and analyzes their relationship to *fiqh* doctrine on the one hand and social practice on the other. As with all the essays in this section, his piece suggests new ways to think about how Islamic legal doctrine shapes and is shaped by social custom and convention.

The next section of this book, "Modern Practice and Reform," addresses the contemporary age, and the realities of Muslim marriage contracts in contemporary nation states under modern family or personal status codes. Again covering various geographical areas, the essays in this section address the impact of such legislation on prior Shariʿa doctrine (especially with regard to women's rights) and investigate the reform efforts of Islamic traditionalists and Muslim feminists. In the first piece, Nik Noriani Nik Badli Shah addresses the evolving Malaysian law of marriage and divorce. Her essay, "Legislative Provisions and Judicial Mechanisms for the Enforcement and Termination of the Islamic Marriage Contract in Malaysia," argues for the reinterpretation of Islamic legal principles from the original sources of the Qurʾan and Sunna, suggesting new codifications in order to engender greater equity and justice for women. Her piece, an example of Muslim modernist reform work, proposes ways to equalize rights of divorce between husband and wife, redefine the doctrine of disobedience (*nushūz*) to apply to both spouses, and establish breach of marriage contract stipulations as a valid, non-statutory ground for divorce.

L. L. Wynn provides a view into the lives of Muslim families during the period of negotiation immediately before a marriage contract is finalized. Based on her personal interactions and interviews with Saudi Arabian women, her "Marriage Contracts and Women's Rights in Saudi Arabia: *Mahr, Shurūṭ*, and Knowledge Distribution," investigates anthropologically how Saudi families in fact negotiate a Muslim marriage contract today, paying close attention to where belief and practice converge and diverge. Her piece exposes how well the marriage contract (especially as to crucial elements like dower and additional stipulations) can serve as an Islamically-sanctioned mechanism to gain certain rights for women. She shows how women are using this mechanism to legitimate gradual shifts in their roles in that society, such as using marriage contract provisions about the *mahr* to enhance women's economic independence.

Ziba Mir-Hosseini's essay, "A Woman's Right to Terminate the Marriage Contract: The Case of Iran," takes up the question of the formal inequality inherent in the classical Islamic law's grant of unconstrained unilateral divorce rights to the husband while allowing the wife to divorce only with his permission or that of the court. She undertakes a study of the opinions of contemporary Iranian religious scholars to determine to what extent, given their views, this inequity could one day be overcome from within Islamic legal doctrine. She discovers that in Iran—where the marriage contract has been a central mechanism for negotiating gender inequalities under classical Islamic law and where women's rights have been a central issue for jurisprudential debate in religious centers—there are in fact important new strands of thought about gender equality emerging in religious law circles. Specifically, she presents and contextualizes two juristic arguments by respected scholars that represent a radical break from established Islamic divorce doctrine.

In contemporary Egypt as well, the marriage contract in its effect on women's rights is a matter of vigorous religious and public debate. In her essay, "The Islamic Marriage Contract in Egypt," Mona Zulficar traces the experience of Egyptian women in their campaign to create a statutorily-approved model Islamic marriage contract. After reviewing the laws of marriage under Egyptian personal status and family law codes and women's proposals for their liberalization (often grounded on reinterpretation of Shariʿa), Zulficar presents an inside view of the experience of one activist project, its motivations, challenges, and ultimate dilution through religious and secular political maneuvering. Concluding, Zulficar emphasizes the potential of the marriage contract for empowering Muslim women, but also the need to educate women locally about its use to counterbalance governmental resistance.

Zainah Anwar provides another inside view of Muslim women's activist work, this time in Malaysia. Her contribution, "Advocacy for Reform in Islamic Family Law: The Experience of Sisters in Islam," focuses on the efforts of her own organization, Sisters in Islam (SIS), to respond to the social and legislative campaign by traditionalist Muslim groups to "Islamize" Malaysian law. She reviews recent Islamic-revivalist changes to the Malay Islamic Family Law (regarding divorce, maintenance, and polygamy provisions, including many involving the marriage contract) and summarizes SIS's responses to these changes, responses arguing that these recent codifications dishonestly mutate original Islamic laws and principles that protect women's rights and directly criticizing the exhibited gender bias of Malaysian Shariʿa courts.

Finally, in the last article in the section, "Improving the Status of Women Through Reforms in Marriage Contract Law: The Experience of the Nizari Ismaili Community," Ali Asani describes the law of Nizari Ismaili Muslim communities on matters of marriage and the marriage contract, explaining the varying ways in which Ismaʿili personal law interacts with various legal systems. The former and present Agha Khans, who represent for the community the final authority in matters of doctrine, have promulgated extensive changes to Ismaʿili personal law to remedy gender inequities in marriage and divorce law. Yet, in an example of the difficulty of top-down legal change, patriarchal social customs inimical to the reforms have yielded only slowly.

The final section of the book, entitled "The Muslim Marriage Contract in Western Secular Legal Systems," takes on the topic of how Muslim marriage contracts are treated under the laws of western countries, a topic of growing prominence for global Islamic family law. This section examines how Muslim marriage contracts are understood and applied in the West. The essays in this section address the situation of Muslim minorities in Germany and the United Kingdom, western secular societies where the distinction between the religious and the secular (an awkward distinction in Islamic law) is central. The pieces ably present attempts by Muslims to preserve basic principles of Islamic marriage law in the private realm, and the consequent challenges the local legal systems face in trying to apply such arrangements within the context of local laws and institutions. The first essay, by Christina Jones-Pauly, "Marriage Contracts of Muslims in the Diaspora: Problems in the Recognition of *Mahr* Contracts in German Law," presents the various approaches taken by German courts in dealing with Muslim marriage contracts, particularly in understanding the exact nature of *mahr*. In seeking to understand the *mahr* these courts have employed analogies to a host of German doctrines (including debt, action for non-community property dissolution, post-divorce maintenance, and action for contractual performance), none of which are wholly satisfactory to those with a deeper grasp of Islamic marriage contract law. Most often, dower is treated as post-divorce maintenance, with the result that German courts often reduce the contracted dower amount to the standard maintenance amount of the time and place—a direct infringement of a woman's dower rights under classical Islamic doctrine. Jones-Pauly's essay points out the pitfalls facing well-intentioned secular courts when litigation arises as to Islamic institutions such as the marriage contract, and emphasizes the need (and potential) for mutual education between these legal systems.

The next article describes litigation involving Muslim marriages in the United Kingdom, which, because of a divergence in conflicts of law principles between English common law and the civil law systems of the continent, presents outcomes in strong contrast to those of Germany. In their piece "The Shariʿa and English Law: Identity and Justice for British Muslims," Richard Freeland and Martin Lau summarize English matrimonial law, its recognition of the law of religious minorities, and the potential for Muslim marriage law to be recognized in British courts. Reviewing court opinions in cases adjudicating Muslim marriages, they show how certain aspects of Islamic marriage law have been recognized (such as the *mahr* as a contractual right), not as an application of Islamic law per se, but indirectly through already established English legal doctrines (such as the principle of enforcing contractual terms as long as they do not offend public policy). Freeland and Lau also describe the informal systems of matrimonial dispute resolution that have evolved inside British Muslim communities, noting both the advantages and disadvantages of these systems.

This volume is the culmination of several studies of the Islamic marriage contract by the Islamic Legal Studies Program at Harvard Law School. In May 1997 the Program convened a small workshop, gathering a handful of activists and academics to share their thoughts on the subject and to determine its utility and importance for an international conference. The extraordinary success of that workshop led the Program to organize a three-day international conference on January 29–31, 1999, again at Harvard Law School, to address the topic in much more depth. This conference convened over twenty panelists and an audience of more than 100 participants. As the conference closed, we concluded that among the papers presented there was material both weighty and coherent enough to produce a valuable book on the Islamic marriage contract. From the many excellent conference papers, we selected those that more directly highlighted the legal aspects of the subject and otherwise served the varied objectives pursued in this volume. Those essays eventually became the collection you see here, each piece offering a vital contribution to the overall goal.

This volume is the result of the dedicated work of many people. We would like to thank all who participated in the 1997 workshop and 1999 conference, since the knowledge, insights and inspiration shared at those events shaped and enriched the final essays gathered here. Next, of course, we extend our thanks to the authors of the pieces here published. We thank them not only for their superb contributions but also for their patience. Some of them completed their contributions five or more years ago and have had to wait patiently during a long delay before their pieces have appeared—a delay that (frankness requires us to mention) has been more often the fault of one of the editors than that of the authors. Next we extend our thanks to Peri Bearman, the Associate Director of the Islamic Legal Studies Program. Without her subtle but insistent pressure to respect both deadlines and the highest standards this volume would not have taken its present form. Another recognition is owed to our student copyeditors, Emily Thompson and Levi Bjork, who have helped make this volume read as a coherent whole. Finally, we thank the Harvard University Press for supporting this project and bringing it to the public, where we have long known it belongs.

Asifa Quraishi
Frank E. Vogel

# *Part One*

## THE LEGAL DOCTRINE OF MARRIAGE CONTRACTS IN COMPARATIVE PERSPECTIVE

# One

## MARRIAGE IN CLASSICAL ISLAMIC JURISPRUDENCE: A SURVEY OF DOCTRINES

Kecia Ali

According to Muslim jurists, marriage is a contract (*ʿaqd*), established by bilateral agreement. Some considered marriage to be in part an act of worship (*ʿibāda*) and not purely a worldly transaction (*muʿāmala*).[1] The Qurʾan has much to say about marriage that is not purely regulatory in effect, and the Prophet Muḥammad reportedly stated that those who marry have fulfilled half of their religion.[2] In legal writings, however, the contractual dimensions of marriage take precedence over its broader religious significance or ethical merit.

This essay sets out the basic rules governing the marriage contract in classical Islamic jurisprudence (*fiqh*) as presented in legal treatises and related writings produced by Muslim jurists (*fuqahāʾ*, sing. *faqīh*), from the tenth century CE (third century AH) up to the fifteenth century CE (ninth century AH).[3] Focusing on the four extant schools of Sunni jurisprudence[4] (Hanafi,[5] Maliki,[6] Shafiʿi,[7] and Hanbali),[8] with some attention to the Jaʿfari[9] school followed by the Twelver Shiʿa, I summarize key doctrines, point out noteworthy differences between these legal schools (*madhāhib*, sing. *madhhab*), and highlight minority views when these are particularly significant.[10] Standard school doctrines are fixed by the latter part of the era, and in many cases significantly earlier; these views are quoted as authoritative down to today in many cases, although the practice of following a living jurisprudent, known as a *marjaʿ al-taqlīd*, makes the Jaʿfari case somewhat different.

This essay does not address modern laws and legal reforms or the multi-faceted controversies surrounding them.[11] Nor does it deal with the application of law by judges throughout Muslim history. The legal treatises that comprise its source material are not historical records; although they reveal some of the social circumstances in which they were composed, one must not rely on them for an accurate portrait of women's lives or even of judicial practice. Sympathetic judges and customary court practice often mitigated doctrines outlined in the jurists' manuals that were disadvantageous to women. On the other hand, rights guaranteed in texts might be flouted in reality. Historians have made significant strides, particularly for the Ottoman period, in assessing the application of law to matters of marriage, divorce, and custody, challenging views of Islamic law as unremittingly patriarchal or uniformly oppressive to women.[12]

Although it is impossible to determine past legal practice from evidence in these treatises, it is not stretching the bounds of plausibility to assume that the frequency with which certain types of stipulations, for instance, appear in the texts reflects their centrality in ongoing legal debates and in practical negotiations between spouses. These doctrines have been implemented and contested in myriad situations. The close case studies that comprise the remainder of this volume illustrate the diverse and complex ways in which jurisprudence on marriage has affected women's and men's lives throughout Muslim history.

## Rights and Duties in Marriage

Marriage (*nikāḥ*)[13] makes sex licit,[14] establishes the husband's paternity of any children his wife bears,[15] creates mutual rights of inheritance,[16] "obliges each spouse to treat the other well,"[17] and gives rise to a variety of gender-differentiated but interdependent claims (*ḥuqūq*, sing. *ḥaqq*). The spouses' claims are interconnected: what is a duty for (*ʿalā*) the husband is a right for (*li-*) the wife, and vice-versa.

The wife's claims[18] include dower[19] and lodging,[20] as well as food,[21] clothing,[22] and possibly domestic service, the amount and quality of each of these varying with her status and/or his means. The Sunni jurists allot each wife an equal share of the husband's time if he has more than one wife,[23] but the Jaʿfari position allows him a certain amount of discretion once each wife receives a minimum of one in four nights.[24] This right to a turn does not include equality in sexual contact.[25] A wife's sexual rights are affirmed, but enforcement mechanisms are scarce.[26] She is universally agreed to have the right to divorce for impotence but only so long as the marriage has not been consummated.[27] Most agree that a wife must consent to the use of coitus interruptus as a method of birth control, as it could interfere with her pleasure or her right to progeny.[28]

The husband's main right is to derive sexual enjoyment from his wife,[29] and to that end, he may exercise control over her mobility.[30] He may enjoy her whenever he wishes "so long as he does not harm her,"[31] although penetration is forbidden during menstruation.[32] In order to obtain his due from her, he may compel her to perform ablution after her menstruation;[33] may take her with him when he travels;[34] and may forbid her from leaving his home,[35] although the Malikis hold that she must be allowed to visit her close kin.[36] The jurists differ over whether a wife has an obligation to nurse her offspring or to perform household service, with the majority holding that she does not have a legal obligation to undertake these duties.[37]

The schools vary greatly in the validity they accord to various types of contractual stipulations (*shurūṭ*, sing. *sharṭ*) specifying or altering these basic rights of the spouses; these will be discussed at some length below. This essay discusses divorce primarily as it pertains to enforcing stipulations; a full treatment of divorce would require a separate study.[38]

## Essential Elements of Marriage

Apart from the absence of impediments to marriage between the bride and groom, the only element of marriage uniformly agreed to be absolutely necessary to conclude a valid marriage is offer and acceptance (*ījāb* and *qabūl*). The spouses may or may not conclude the contract themselves. Other items often listed as essentials of marriage include witnesses, a marriage guardian (*walī*), and dower. But jurists differ over whether witnesses must observe the contracting event and what qualifications they must have, when the consent of one or both spouses is required, whether a female in her majority can contract her own marriage or must have a guardian do so on her behalf, and what impact the lack of a valid dower has on the contract.

A valid contract requires the absence of impediments to marriage between the would-be spouses, either permanent such as kinship[39] or temporary such as a woman's post-divorce waiting period (*ʿidda*).[40] Sunni jurists permit a Muslim man to marry a Christian or Jewish woman,[41] though often disapprovingly, as do a minority of Jaʿfaris; the dominant Jaʿfari view prohibits such a marriage.[42] Marriage between a Muslim woman and a non-Muslim man—whether he is polytheist, unbeliever, or *kitābī* ("person of the Book," i.e., Christian or Jewish)—is not considered valid by any group of jurists.[43]

### (1) *Offer and Acceptance*

It is standard practice for the offer of marriage to be made from the bride's party to the groom's party, though this sequence is not a condition for the validity of the marriage according to Hanafi,[44] Maliki,[45] Shafiʿi,[46] and Jaʿfari[47] doctrine. For Hanbalis, the acceptance must follow the offer.[48] Both offer and acceptance should be stated in the past tense to confirm the parties' intent to contract a marriage at that time rather than to make a (non-binding) promise of future matrimony, although pronouncing the acceptance alone in the past tense may suffice for validity.[49] To accept, the Hanbali jurist Ibn Qudāma suggests the statement "I have accepted this marriage," but allows the single word response "*qabiltu*," i.e., "I have accepted,"[50] as does the Jaʿfari scholar Ḥillī.[51] Additionally, some Hanafi[52] and Shafiʿi[53] texts specify that acceptance must closely follow the offer in time to prevent confusion. According to the Hanbalis, the acceptance may follow the offer so long as the parties have not separated, nor become occupied with some other matter; either event voids the offer.[54] Unlike in sales, once offer and acceptance have occurred in marriage, there can never be *khiyār al-majlis*, the option to void an agreement so long as the parties have not separated.[55]

According to Shafiʿi,[56] Hanbali,[57] and Jaʿfari[58] doctrines, the offer and acceptance must be made using derivatives of the terms "marriage" or "espousal" (*nikāḥ* or *tazwīj*), while Maliki[59] and Hanafi[60] jurists also allow metaphorical terms such as gift (*hiba*), charity or "free will offering"[61] (*ṣadaqa*), transfer of ownership (*tamlīk*), and sale (*bayʿ*). The Hanafis specifically disallow use of the terms hire (*ijāra*), permissibility (*ibāḥa*), and making lawful (*iḥlāl*).[62] If the parties speak Arabic, the offer and acceptance should be done in Arabic to avoid any potential ambiguity.[63] For those who do not speak Arabic, equivalent expressions in other languages are valid.[64] For Sunnis, an offer and acceptance made in jest constitute a binding valid marriage.[65]

An agent (*wakīl*) may contract a marriage, though only one who has the power to contract the marriage may appoint a *wakīl* to act on his (or her) behalf.[66] Agency (*wakāla*), which is commonly used in business transactions of all types, is similarly permitted in divorce, as will be seen below.[67]

A guardian-representative (*walī*) often has a role in contracting a marriage, usually on behalf of the bride but sometimes on behalf of a minor groom. Maliki,[68] Shafiʿi,[69] and Hanbali[70] schools insist that a female must always be married off by a guardian; though a woman can conclude other contracts, she may not conclude a marriage contract. The dominant Hanafi view is that a guardian is required for the marriage of a minor female but merely recommended for a female past majority,[71] a view shared by Jaʿfari authorities,[72] though dissenting opinions in both schools hold that such a marriage contracted by a woman without the intervention of her *walī* is either altogether void or suspended until he approves it or a judge does so.[73]

(2) *Qualifications of the Guardian*

A Muslim bride's *walī*—who is usually a member of her agnatic kin—must be a legally responsible adult Muslim; Malikis,[74] Shafiʿis,[75] and Hanbalis[76] hold that he must be male while the Hanafis allow for female guardians under certain circumstances.[77] Jaʿfaris reject the ascription of *wilāya* to the mother or other female relatives, but if a mother marries off her child, they consider the marriage valid if the offspring assents; otherwise it is void.[78]

Jurists differ over whether freedom, probity, and intellectual maturity (*rushd*) are requirements for guardianship.[79] Malikis affirm that Islam, majority (*bulūgh*), and maleness are required, and while Mālik himself holds that intellectual maturity is required, most other jurists of the school do not.[80] One Shafiʿi manual states that a *walī* must be male, legally responsible (*mukallaf*), Muslim, upright (*ʿādil*), and of sound judgment (*tāmm al-naẓar*), but notes that later scholars do not require uprightness, holding that an immoral man (*fāsiq*) may serve as a guardian.[81] The Hanbali Ibn Qudāma lists eight qualifications for a *walī*: reason (*ʿaql*), freedom, maleness, majority, sameness of religion,[82] probity (*ʿadāla*), agnatic kinship, and the absence of a more closely related *walī*.[83] According to the Hanafi text *al-Hidāya* slavery, minority, and insanity disqualify potential guardians; positive qualifications are majority, reason, and being an heir (i.e., a close enough relative to inherit from the woman in question).[84] The *Radd al-Muḥtār*, another Hanafi text, explicitly permits immorality (*fisq*) in a guardian, but notes disagreement over whether agnatic kinship is required.[85] Jaʿfaris do not view immorality as a disqualification,[86] though insanity and slavery do disqualify.[87]

In the three schools that consider a *walī*'s involvement necessary for a female's marriage, the refusal of a bride's closest *walī* to marry her to a suitable[88] groom of her choice can cause conflicts. According to the Hanbalis,[89] she can seek to have a less closely-related *walī* marry her off, or have a judge intervene on her behalf. According to Shafiʿi[90] and Maliki views,[91] she should seek judicial intervention, with the judge potentially serving as marriage guardian himself. If there is conflict between her and her guardian as to which of two suitable grooms she will marry, the Shafiʿis hold that the guardian's choice prevails if he has the right of compulsion; otherwise "the one she selects takes precedence."[92]

As noted, the dominant Jaʿfari[93] and Hanafi[94] position is that a female who has attained majority[95] does not require a *walī*, regardless of whether she has been previously married. Not only does she not need a *walī*'s permission, she may contract her own marriage just as she may conclude other contracts.[96] Yet Hanafis place some limitations on a woman's right to marry independently: a *walī* may have the marriage dissolved with the judge's intervention if the bride marries an "unsuitable" groom.[97] Maverick Maliki scholar Ibn Rushd departs from the doctrine of his school and comes to a similar conclusion: "[A] woman has the right to contract her own marriage and the guardians have the right to revoke it if it is not in conformity with her status."[98]

### (3) *Suitability*

The *walī*'s power to revoke a marriage to an unsuitable groom brings into focus the importance of the various jurisprudential discussions of "suitability" (*kafāʾa*). Suitability is a consideration of varying importance; among the Sunnis, it is least important for the Malikis[99] and most important for the Hanafis,[100] and it exists in only a very limited form in Jaʿfari law. Rules of suitability function to prevent a mismatch between the bride and the groom who is her inferior. Suitability is primarily an issue in two cases: first, if a *walī* wants to marry a bride off without her consent, the groom's unsuitability may be grounds for objection by the bride or her other guardians, or, in some cases, the public judicial authority (the "sultan"), who will prevent or annul the marriage if he finds the objection valid.[101] Second, when the bride wants to marry herself off against the wishes of her *walī*, unsuitability is grounds for objection by the *walī*, who may refuse to marry her off (Shafiʿi)[102] or may seek to have the marriage annulled, if she has contracted it herself (Hanafi).[103] Otherwise, if her *walī* refuses to marry her to a suitable groom, she can seek to have the marriage concluded over his objections.[104] If a woman and her *walī* (or, in some views, all of her *walī*s on his level of closeness to her) agree to her marriage to an unsuitable groom, most jurists agree that there is no legal obstacle to such a marriage,[105] though a contested Hanbali doctrine holds that such a marriage can never be valid, even if the parties agree.[106] The Jaʿfari school notably holds that if she marries herself off to an unsuitable man, the marriage is binding.[107] Notably, suitability is only a consideration with regard to the groom; there are no regulations in any school to prevent a competent male in his majority from marrying an unsuitable bride.[108] The Hanafi *al-Hidāya* sums up the universal sentiment: "[I]t is not necessary that the wife be the equal of the husband, since men are not degraded by cohabitation with women who are their inferiors."[109]

What makes a groom unsuitable? Crucial elements of suitability for Sunni jurists include lineage, morality, and freedom: a slave is generally not a suitable match for a free female,[110] nor is a non-Arab for an Arab woman—although Maliki doctrine allows a match between a respectable freed client and an Arab,[111] nor an immoral (*fāsiq*) man for a virtuous (*ʿafīfa*) woman.[112] For Jaʿfaris, non-Arabs are suitable matches for Arabs and all Arabs are suitable for one another regardless of lineage.[113] Suitability also comprises freedom from physical defects that would permit annulment of the marriage.[114] Shafiʿi[115] and Hanafi[116] jurists include means of livelihood or profession as an element of suitability, comparing the bride's father's profession with that of the groom. Jaʿfaris deny any relevance to profession, even if it is lowly.[117]

Jurists disagree as to whether wealth is to be taken into account and, if it is, whether only the groom's ability to support the bride is relevant or also his ability to pay her fair dower. Most Shafiʿis hold that wealth is not a relevant criterion in determining suitability.[118] Maliki authorities agree that fair dower is not part of suitability but that the husband's ability to support his wife is to be considered.[119] Hanafi authorities disagree on exactly how the groom's finances are taken into consideration. Abū Ḥanīfa and Muḥammad al-Shaybānī hold that dower and sufficient means to maintain a wife are both necessary elements of suitability; if either is lacking, the groom is not suitable.[120] According to the view attributed to Abū Yūsuf, however, only maintenance is taken into consideration, since the groom's father can be expected to help provide the bride's dower.[121] Jaʿfaris consider relevant only his ability to maintain the bride to be relevant.[122]

Religion (*dīn*) is frequently mentioned as a criterion of suitability,[123] though the Jaʿfaris cite "equality of faith": "It is not allowed for a believing woman to marry someone who is not a believer even if he is a Muslim."[124] Equality in religion does not mean simply that the groom must be Muslim if the bride is, for this is a prerequisite for the validity of the marriage; rather, it refers to how long a groom's family has been Muslim: a recent convert is not a suitable match for a woman whose father or both father and grandfather were Muslim.[125]

(4) *Witnesses*

The Jaʿfaris[126] consider witnessing of the marriage contract recommended but not a condition for the contract's validity, but Sunni jurists generally hold that the statements of offer and acceptance must be made in the presence of qualified witnesses.[127] The Malikis, focusing on the need for public acknowledgment of the marital bond, allow for post-facto witnessing, at the time the marriage is to be consummated.[128] The Maliki,[129] Shafiʿi,[130] and Hanbali[131] schools require two adult, male, Muslim witnesses, and hold that these witnesses must be upright (*ʿādil*); this probity is assumed in the absence of specific indications to the contrary.[132] The Hanafis allow either two men or one man and two women to serve as witnesses.[133] These witnesses must be "Muslim, free, major and sane,"[134] but not necessarily upright.[135]

While it is common practice to memorialize marriage contracts in writing, and include signatures of the witnesses, Muslim jurists do not require that any contract be written. When properly witnessed, the oral agreement of the contracting parties or of their agents constitutes a valid contract.[136]

(5) *Consent and Coercion*

Classical jurisprudence grants some guardians the power to marry off certain females as well as minor males without their consent. Whether consent is needed for a particular marriage depends on three factors: the identity of the marriage guardian (*walī*), whether the bride is a major (*bāligha*)[137] or a minor (*ṣaghīra*), and whether she is a virgin (*bikr*) or a non-virgin (*thayyib* or *ayyim*).

**Minors**

In keeping with shared presumptions about kinship and paternal authority, all legal schools allow fathers[138] to marry off their minor virgin[139] daughters without their consent and even against their will. In some schools this power extends to paternal grandfathers[140] and occasionally, as in the view of the Hanbali Ibn Taymiyya,[141] to the bride's brother or paternal uncle.[142] This power is referred to as *ijbār* or *ilzām*, compulsion.[143] When a *walī* with the power of compulsion (*walī mujbir*) contracts the marriage of a minor, that child has no option to dissolve the marriage on reaching majority.[144]

Compulsion applies equally to male and female offspring so long as they are minors.[145] When a male thus married attains majority, however, he has the option of unilaterally repudiating his wife by *ṭalāq*, thus immediately ending the marriage.[146] A daughter, on the other hand, cannot automatically obtain divorce, making the question of her consent more significant.

The schools differ as to whether a *walī* aside from the *walī mujbir* may marry off minors. The Maliki and Shafiʿi schools do not generally permit the marriage of minors by anyone but the father (or paternal grandfather), while he lives, or someone appointed by him.[147] The Jaʿfari school discourages some such marriages,[148] but holds that in other cases such marriages may be validated by the minors themselves when they reach majority.[149] Hanafis[150] and some Hanbalis[151] allow such marriages to be contracted by other agnatic relatives or, in the Hanafi case, the mother if the father was deceased. In these cases the child's consent is still not sought, but the child may have an option to annul the marriage on attaining majority (*khiyār al-bulūgh*).[152] Those Hanbalis who hold that marriages of minors by other than the father are permissible generally do not support a right of option at majority, effectively granting these *walī*s the power of *ijbār*. According to the dominant Hanafi view, both male and female minors have the right of option if married off by a *walī* such as an uncle, though a minority view holds that there is no such right, thus effectively extending the power of compulsion beyond the father and grandfather.[153] A minor child married off by his or her mother, however, retains the option at puberty.[154]

## Major (*bāligh*) Persons

While male and female offspring are equally subject to *ijbār* as minors, when males of sound mind reach majority no guardian can compel them to marry and they may contract marriage without the involvement or consent of a *walī*.[155]

In the case of a female virgin[156] in her majority, there is disagreement over whether she may be compelled to marry and whether she may contract her own marriage. Maliki,[157] Shafiʿi,[158] and some Hanbali[159] jurists hold that the paternal power of compulsion continues when a female reaches majority so long as she remains a virgin. Thus, if her father marries her off, she need not be consulted. However, the Shafiʿi position, echoed by those Hanbalis who allow compulsion in this case, is that such consultation is strongly recommended.[160] This recommendation carries only ethical weight; failure to consult a daughter or heed her rejection of the marriage has no effect on a marriage's validity.

Maliki doctrine allows a father to emancipate his mature virgin daughter by *tarshīd*, a declaration that she has reached intellectual maturity (*rushd*).[161]

In such a case, he loses his power to compel her to marry, and her spoken consent is necessary for any marriage he wishes to contract for her.[162]

Other Hanbalis[163] along with the Jaʿfaris[164] and Hanafis[165] hold that a virgin female who has reached majority may not be married off without her consent, even by her father. In later Hanafi texts, this distinction is explicitly justified in terms of reason (*ʿaql*). When a daughter reaches majority, she becomes like the male youth (*ghulām*): "Her capacity for being free with respect to marriage is just like her freedom to undertake transactions in her wealth."[166] In order for her consent to be valid, her *walī* must specify and describe the groom, so that she is fully informed as to the particulars of the marriage to which she is giving her consent.[167]

Jurists agree that a virgin in her majority can be married off by a guardian other than her father, but only with her consent.[168] This consent need not be spoken; a virgin's silent acquiescence (or laughter) is construed as permission.[169] According to Hanafi doctrine, which requires consent of all major females even when married off by a father, silence constitutes consent, as does laughter unless it is sarcastic; silent weeping does not constitute rejection of the marriage, but loud crying may express "annoyance and disapproval" which would indicate lack of consent.[170] Jaʿfaris agree that silence, if it is not accompanied by indications of rejection or dislike, suffices as consent.[171]

Finally, a non-virgin female (*thayyib* or *ayyim*) who has reached majority cannot be compelled to marry and her spoken consent is required for her marriage to be valid, regardless of who serves as her *walī*.[172] Any marriage contracted without her prior consent is either void or invalid; there is disagreement over whether subsequent consent is sufficient to retroactively authorize the marriage.[173]

(6) *Dower*

Dower is obligatory in all Muslim marriages. Paid from the groom to the bride, the dower belongs exclusively to her, although jurists may treat approvingly a customary practice where a portion of the dower is expended to provide the bride's trousseau.[174] The substance of the dower itself can be any item that may be lawfully bought and sold,[175] although some schools set a minimum amount.[176] Rules governing usurious[177] or speculative[178] commercial transactions also generally apply to dower, which is often discussed as analogous to the price in a purchase. However, while a sale would be automatically cancelled due to a problem with the price, marriages with defective dowers are generally held valid and dower problems rectified by substitution of a similar item, payment of its price, or payment of the wife's fair dower, about which I will say more below.[179]

When a dower has been fixed but the marriage is dissolved before consummation[180] the wife will be due only half the dower amount.[181] If the dower has not been fixed, she will be due a compensatory payment (*mutʿa*).[182] The jurists agree on these basic provisions, which can be found in summary form in Qurʾan 2:236–237.[183]

Though dower is a necessary element of marriage, the dower need not be specified at the time of the contract in order for the marriage to be valid.[184] Even in the case that it is stipulated at the time the contract is made that no dower is to be paid, the marriage is valid and the wife is owed a dower if the marriage is consummated according to Hanafi,[185] Shafiʿi,[186] and Hanbali[187] schools. The Malikis agree that a dower is due, but hold that the marriage must still be dissolved.[188] If no dower is specified and the parties fail to agree on a specific amount later, jurists agree that the wife is due her fair dower (*mahr al-mithl*) if the marriage has been consummated. If the marriage has not been consummated, and no agreement on dower has been reached, then a compensatory gift is all that is required in case of divorce.[189] In contrast to the situation where the dower was simply left unsettled, where it was stipulated instead that the dower would be decided independently by either of the spouses or by a third party, the Malikis allowed for dissolution (without divorce or any financial penalty) if an agreement could not be reached between the spouses and consummation had not taken place.[190]

A woman's fair dower is used as a yardstick and default amount in various contexts, analogous to fair market value in the law of contracts and torts. A fair dower is determined on the basis of her status, and is calculated in relation to the dowers received by her female paternal relatives, particularly if they live in her hometown. Her own qualities, such as beauty, intelligence, wealth, virginity, and refinement (*adab*), can be taken into account in adjusting that amount upward or downward.[191]

The jurists disagree as to whether a woman may agree to marry for less than her fair dower against the wishes of her marriage guardian. Maliki,[192] Shafiʿi,[193] Hanbali,[194] and Jaʿfari[195] doctrines hold that a female in her majority who wishes to marry for less than her fair dower is permitted to do so if she is considered competent to control her own financial affairs. Whatever restrictions are placed on her with regard to marrying herself off do not affect her control over her finances, which belongs to her alone as a legally competent adult. The Hanafi jurists disagree over whether, if a woman is marrying herself off without her *walī*, the marriage guardian may object to the marriage on the grounds of the reduced dower as he could if the groom was unsuitable.[196]

There is disagreement over whether anyone has the right to marry off a minor girl or an adult virgin for less than her fair dower. The Maliki jurists hold that only a father (or, as is typical in these cases, a paternal grandfather) may marry off his virgin daughter (regardless of her age) for less than her fair dower, but only if it is in her best interest.[197] Hanbali jurists hold that a father may marry off his minor virgin daughter for whatever dower he chooses.[198] The Hanafi authorities are split again: Abū Ḥanīfa holds that it is permissible for a minor girl's father to marry her off for less than her fair dower, while Abū Yūsuf and Muḥammad al-Shaybānī disagree.[199] The Shafiʿi jurists take the strongest position against this practice, holding that no one can compel a woman or girl to marry for less than her fair dower, since no *walī* has the right to spend her assets without her permission. Nor can a minor consent to a reduced dower, since she is not qualified to make financial decisions.[200] However, if such a marriage is contracted, it is not invalidated; rather, the bride receives her fair dower. The Jaʿfari view is that "neither an agent nor a *walī* may marry a woman off for less than her fair dower."[201]

Dower may be entirely "prompt" (due and payable immediately); divided between a prompt portion and a deferred portion; or entirely deferred, although some prefer payment of at least a token amount before consummation.[202] Indefinite deferral of either part or all of the dower is allowed by Shafiʿi[203] and Hanafi[204] jurists, but there is disagreement as to whether the bride must allow consummation of the marriage before the deferred portion is paid.[205]

When the husband proves unable to pay the dower, Maliki,[206] Shafiʿi,[207] and Hanbali[208] jurists allow the wife to dissolve the marriage before it is consummated.[209] However, Hanafi doctrine does not, granting the wife instead a continued right to be supported by her husband while withholding herself sexually until her dower is paid.[210]

**Stipulations in the Contract**

Muslim women through history have employed stipulations in the marriage contract to protect their rights, with varying degrees of practical success.[211] The enforceability of stipulations depends on many variables and differs significantly from school to school; court practice may also diverge from textual prescriptions.[212] Some stipulations void contracts, some are themselves void but without effect on the contract, and others may be enforceable with various penalties for non-compliance. Generally speaking, the Hanbali school allows the widest scope for stipulations to be enforced, including those against polygyny or relocation of the wife; breach of these stipulations usually gives a wife the right to opt for divorce even if divorce is not explicitly mentioned as a consequence of such breach.[213] Those who follow other Sunni schools can achieve similar effects through divorce-based enforcement mechanisms—essentially contingent divorces—discussed in the following section.

Certain stipulations that contravene the basic purpose(s) of marriage always void the contract, including that the groom will divorce the bride after "making her lawful" for a previous husband who had repudiated her triply[214] and those that state a time for the marriage to end,[215] although the latter creates a valid *mutʿa* marriage under Jaʿfari law.

Jurists disagree over the effect of other stipulations that contravene the basic purpose of marriage—such as that the spouses will not engage in intercourse, or that the husband will repudiate the wife. Their effect ranges from invalidating the marriage in the Shafiʿi view[216] to voiding the stipulations while allowing the marriage to remain in force in the Hanbali approach.[217] In an "exchange marriage" (*shighār*), where two *walī*s stipulate that each will marry his ward (often a daughter or a sister) to the other, both thus avoiding paying dower, some consider the marriage void while others hold the marriages valid but insist on payment of fair dower to each bride.[218]

The enforceability of other stipulations that do not void or invalidate the marriage contract depends upon the school. The Hanbali school, which has a more flexible approach to contract law in general, deems valid most stipulations that receive the most attention in manuals. Hanbali jurists view these stipulations as benefiting women and protecting their interests, citing a prophetic statement that the best of stipulations are those that make sexual relations lawful.[219] A husband who binds himself contractually to remain monogamous can nonetheless contract a second valid marriage, but his first wife has the option to dissolve (*infisākh*) her own marriage.[220] The same is the case for stipulations that the wife will be able to remain in her hometown, or in a particular house. The Hanbali jurists disagree only as to whether she must go before a judge to claim her right to dissolution or whether she may effect the dissolution herself.[221] Hanafi,[222] Maliki,[223] and Shafiʿi[224] jurists hold, by contrast, that stipulations as to monogamy or place of residence are void; nonetheless the marriages to which they are attached are valid.

A number of other stipulations seek not to alter particular rights of spouses but to attach financial penalties to particular actions. One common issue concerns the right of a wife to receive either a higher dower if it turns out the husband has another wife already or to be compensated if he later takes one, or removes her from her hometown. One type of controversial stipulation does not seek to manage rights so much as to compensate women for less desirable circumstances, allowing women to augment their bargaining positions in ways other than by preserving an option to divorce. Thus, a dower that varies according to conditions (e.g., one thousand dinars if the man has no other wife, two thousand if he has already another wife; five hundred dinars if he never takes her from her hometown, doubled if he does so later) was subject to disagreement.[225]

Other stipulations that seek to specify, eliminate, or otherwise alter claims that would normally exist between the spouses are themselves void and have no effect on the validity of the marriage, because they are infringing upon default rights that are already set out by divine text.

According to Shafiʿi,[226] Hanbali,[227] and Hanafi[228] doctrine, stipulations waiving the wife's right to maintenance or to a portion of her husband's time if he has more than one wife are void and the marriage valid. The dominant Maliki view, on the other hand, is that the party that would have benefited by such a stipulation has the option to annul the marriage contract if he or she learns that the stipulation is unenforceable before the marriage has been consummated. Thus, a husband who learns he would be obligated to maintain his wife despite his stipulation to the contrary, has the choice of remaining married, with the obligation to maintain her, or annulling the marriage without the half-dower obligation that would result if he were to divorce her. If the marriage has been consummated, however, there is no option of annulment.[229] In this case, the Malikis join the other schools and hold that the stipulation is void and the marriage is valid.[230]

Stipulations concerning matters such as which family members will live with the couple or the amount of maintenance that the wife is to receive, are more likely to be held valid by jurists from all schools.[231] Many jurists discuss the issue of the residence of the wife's minor children from another marriage and their support.[232] Maliki jurists allow the wife to stipulate that she will be allowed to receive visits from family members not otherwise automatically permitted to visit among other conditions in her favor.[233] Finally, Maliki jurists, who are unique in providing for the husband some role in restricting his wife's ability to dispose of her personal assets, allow her to stipulate full and sole control over said assets.[234]

## Divorce-Based Mechanisms for Enforcing Stipulations

Although Maliki, Hanafi, and Shafiʿi jurists deem stipulations binding husbands to monogamy or non-relocation void, wives can use certain divorce-based mechanisms to obtain release from marriage if their husbands do not comply. (Hanbalis can use these mechanisms as well, but have less need to do so as they consider such stipulations valid.) In essence, the otherwise void stipulations are attached to divorce pronouncements and thus are governed by the more stringent rules regarding oaths: if the specified action or condition, such as the husband taking an additional wife, occurs, the *ṭalāq* takes place automatically (conditional or contingent[235] divorce) or, alternately, the wife gains an option to pronounce herself divorced (contingent delegated divorce).

Before proceeding to discuss these stipulation enforcement mechanisms, a brief survey of the main regulations surrounding divorce is necessary. Divorce is generally of three types: (1) repudiation by the husband (*ṭalāq*), (2) divorce for compensation (*khulʿ*),[236] which requires the consent of both husband and wife according to the vast majority of jurists,[237] and (3) judicial divorce for cause (*faskh, firāq*, or *taṭlīq*).[238] Aside from certain defects that are grounds for one spouse to opt for annulment before consummation,[239] the degree to which the different schools allow women to initiate divorce for cause varies tremendously. The grounds range from being nearly non-existent in the Hanafi school (limited to such things as long-term abandonment, until the husband would have reached the end of his presumed life-span) to extensive in the Maliki school (including abandonment, non-support, and "harm" or injury, which can be broadly interpreted) with the Shafiʿi and Hanbali schools falling in the middle of the spectrum.

Far more common means as of marital dissolution is repudiation (*ṭalāq*, literally "release"). As a contract (*ʿaqd*), marriage requires the consent of two parties; by contrast, *ṭalāq* falls into the category of unilateral acts (*īqāʿāt*, sing. *īqāʿa*) and is undertaken by the husband alone. Like manumission of a slave by its owner, to which the jurists frequently likened it, *ṭalāq* is a "performative utterance"; the pronouncement of the "correct words in the correct form can produce a change in the status of others."[240] *Ṭalāq* can be revocable (*rajʿī*) or irrevocable (*bāʾin*). If the repudiation is revocable, the husband may unilaterally choose to resume marital relations during the waiting period (*ʿidda*) that follows all consummated marriages.[241] He may take his wife back without her consent and does not owe her a new dower since the original marriage contract is still in force.[242] There is debate[243] over what is necessary to effect a return, including whether it can be done by intercourse[244] or must involve a formal declaration;[245] likewise, the jurists disagree as to whether witnesses are required.[246] If her waiting period expires without revocation, or if no waiting period was necessary because the marriage was never consummated, the repudiation is irrevocable.[247]

In irrevocable repudiations, the husband has no right to take the wife back unilaterally. To reunite after an irrevocable repudiation or another form of irrevocable divorce such as divorce for compensation or judicial divorce, a new marriage, with a new dower, must be contracted. Also, if the husband has repudiated his wife twice previously, taking her back during her waiting periods, then the third repudiation is "absolute," meaning that a complete bar to remarriage arises between the spouses. The couple can remarry only if the ex-wife marries another man, consummates that marriage, and then that marriage ends in either divorce or the husband's death.[248] These details about irrevocability of divorce matter because the effectiveness of stipulations in a marriage contract may depend on ensuring that a husband cannot take a wife back without her consent after a single, revocable divorce.

(1) *Contingent Repudiation*

A husband's extensive power over repudiation allows him to attach conditions to a repudiation (*taʿlīq*).[249] Legal texts give examples of *ṭalāq* pronouncements used as threats to control women's behavior: "If you leave the house without my permission, you are divorced."[250] *Ṭalāq* may also serve as a penalty on an oath to restrict a husband's behavior: "If I ever drink wine again, my wife is divorced." In such repudiations, once the specified condition occurs, *ṭalāq* takes effect automatically.[251] The husband's power of repudiation can potentially be used in ways beneficial to wives. Both delegated divorce and contingent divorce can be used to restrict the husband's behavior in ways similar to stipulations. Although the classical texts do not primarily serve as guidelines for how to achieve those aims, one can reason by analogy from the texts to create outlets for women, e.g., "If I ever hit you, you are divorced," and there is some historical evidence, from fatwas and court archives, that women have done so.[252]

Shafiʿi,[253] Hanbali,[254] and Jaʿfari[255] jurists hold that oaths of repudiation can be validly made only after marriage has taken place. In contrast, Maliki[256] and Hanafi[257] jurists allow for a variety of divorce oaths to be made even before marriage. For Maliki jurists, such oaths must be specific in some way; thus: "Any woman I marry is repudiated" is not valid, but "Any woman I marry from tribe X is repudiated" is valid.[258] Hanafi jurists, on the other hand, hold that both specific and universal oaths preventing marriage are binding.[259] Such oaths cannot be expiated but will render any marriage the man attempts to contract void.[260]

Under Maliki[261] and Hanafi doctrine, then, a man may make oaths that bind him to monogamy more effectively than a contractual stipulation not to take additional wives does in Hanbali doctrine, where the wife gains only the right to dissolve her own marriage: he can automatically and irrevocably repudiate any future wife by declaring "Every woman I marry while (name of current wife) lives is triply [i.e. absolutely] repudiated."[262] A wife desiring to protect herself by having her husband pronounce such an oath would have to make sure not to inadvertently leave any loopholes that would allow the divorce of a co-wife to be revocable, thus allowing her husband to take her back without incurring the divorce oath.[263]

(2) *Contingent Delegated Divorce*

When a husband pronounces a contingent *ṭalāq*, a divorce takes place automatically if and when a specified event, such as the husband taking an additional wife, occurs. With a contingent delegated divorce, the occurrence of the specified event grants the wife a choice regarding divorce. Contingent divorce, delegated or not, is the standard way in which Maliki jurists allowed a restriction on the husband against polygyny or relocation.[264] Yet there are significant limitations to the duration and scope of delegated divorce; the wife's power varies considerably depending upon the language used in the original declaration and the doctrine of the relevant school.

All agree that a husband's power of repudiation includes the ability to allocate some portion of his authority to another individual, male or female. He can do so through a relationship of agency (*wakāla*), which may or may not be considered a subtype of delegation (*tafwīḍ*).[265] The power of divorce may also be delegated to the wife, allowing her to "divorce herself" under certain circumstances.[266] Jurists disagree about whether such a delegation can be made at the time of or only after conclusion of the marriage contract[267] and whether the wife's delegated authority extends to a triple (absolute) divorce or only a single divorce and, if the latter, whether it is irrevocable[268] or revocable. Jurists also debate whether the husband's intentions or the specific wording of his remarks determines the scope of the wife's powers and whether certain pronouncements constitute oaths or grants of agency.[269] These factors affect whether the wife's right is valid indefinitely, until she utilizes or relinquishes it, or until it is withdrawn by the husband; or whether it is valid only for the session where it is granted; as well as which of her actions may extinguish her capacity to opt for divorce. Delegated divorce allows for slightly broader options as well: Hanafi doctrine permits a husband to grant his wife an option to divorce "when" or "whenever" she likes[270] which persists beyond the session where it is granted but exhausts itself after she pronounces one repudiation. With his declaration "You are divorced as often as (*kullamā*) you like," she may pronounce successive repudiations up to three, but not all at once.[271]

Two basic forms of delegated divorce exist: *tamlīk* and *takhyīr*. *Tamlīk* means to transfer ownership or control, in this case of the marriage tie, and is most commonly set in motion when a man informs his wife that "Your affair is in your hands." *Takhyīr*, or the related term *ikhtiyār*, means giving a choice or option; in this form of delegated divorce a man usually states "Choose" or "Choose yourself"; the command "Divorce yourself" may sometimes be understood also to fall under this category.[272] The regulations governing *tamlīk* and *takhyīr* may be quite firmly distinguished (as in the Maliki or Hanafi[273] view) or overlap to a large extent (as in the Shafiʿi view).

The Hanbali doctrines governing delegated divorce are representative in terms of complexity: The main Hanbali view considers *tafwīḍ* (the delegation from the husband of the power to "divorce yourself") a type of agency, giving the wife a right to divorce herself singly, unless a greater number of divorces is explicitly stipulated or intended by the husband.[274] The same holds true for the statement "Your affair is in your hands," elsewhere defined as *tamlīk*.[275] She may divorce herself whenever she wishes until he revokes the right. However, a minority view is that the wife's choice only exists for that session (*majlis*). *Takhyīr*, for the Hanbalis, involves slightly different language ("Choose," *ikhtari*), but again, the wife may not choose more than a single divorce unless explicitly stated or intended by the husband. There is one key difference: unlike in *tafwīḍ*, in *takhyīr* the wife's right of choice only persists for the session.[276] In both cases, the husband may verbally rescind the delegation before she uses it to divorce herself, as with a grant of agency (*tawkīl*) to an unrelated individual.[277] If he has sex with her, it automatically constitutes a revocation of the *tafwīḍ*, as he is demonstrating his desire to retain her.[278]

**Islamic Law in the Contemporary World**

The legal doctrines discussed in the treatises and manuals referenced here do not precisely reflect what was implemented in pre-modern courts in practice. They served as the basis for judges to make rulings, but judicial practice was also influenced by local custom and considerations of public interest, both supplementary sources of law in some views. In majority-Muslim nation states in the modern period, legislated codes have mostly taken the place of the classical system of jurisprudence. Commercial and criminal law have become secular and marriage law has become codified and bureaucratized, with standardized contracts supplanting individually drafted agreements designed to protect women's interests. Legislators formulating modern family laws have used *ikhtiyār*—a right, asserted by rulers such as the Ottomans, to choose among doctrines of the classical schools according to their utility—and *talfīq*, pasting together doctrines from different schools and scholars.[279] Advocates for women's marital rights in countries where "Muslim laws" are applied have, like lawmakers, drawn selectively from classical doctrine to advocate for women's interests.[280] It is not surprising that the textual tradition gains attention on the basis of its contemporary relevance to these reform projects. Nonetheless, the voluminous heritage of Islamic jurisprudence, of which I have only scratched the surface here, merits investigation for its own sake as well.

NM

NOTES

I would like to thank Asifa Quraishi and Frank Vogel for their comments on earlier drafts of this essay. I take full responsibility for any errors of fact or interpretation.

1 See, e.g., al-Zaylaʿī 2000, 2:444.

2 See, e.g., Ḥillī 1999, 3:414 for a citation of this statement. On marriage in the Qurʾan, see also Ali 2005; Motzki 2001.

3 For ease of consultation by non-specialists who may wish to explore further, I have cited English translations of legal texts in the notes where these are available and generally reliable; the Arabic editions I consulted in such cases are also included in the bibliography. Where texts are available in parallel English-Arabic editions, I have cited these. However, most important texts remain untranslated, and therefore Arabic texts are cited, as they are where translations are unreliable on a given point. Where quotations appear and the English citation is given, I have used that translation unless otherwise noted. All other translations, including from European languages, are my own. Any attempt to render precise legal terminology into another language and conceptual system is fraught with peril; I have opted usually for more rather than less explanation and for repetition of Arabic terminology where essential for clarity.

[4] For an historical account of the early development of these schools, see Melchert 1997; see also Hallaq 1997, 2001.

[5] For Hanafi doctrines I draw primarily on *al-Hidāya* of al-Marghīnānī (al-Marghīnānī 2006), recently translated by Nyazee (though I make occasional reference to the idiosyncratic English version by Charles Hamilton, *The Hedaya* [al-Marghīnānī [2]1975]); the *Radd al-muḥtār*, composed by Ibn ʿĀbidīn (Ibn ʿĀbidīn 1994), often summarizing doctrines found in earlier works; the *Mabsūṭ* of al-Sarakhsī (al-Sarakhsī 2001); and the *Tabyīn al-ḥaqāʾiq* of al-Zaylaʿī (al-Zaylaʿī 2000). Early texts such as the *Kitāb al-Ḥujja* (al-Shaybānī 1965), *al-Muwaṭṭaʾ* (al-Shaybānī 1997), *al-Jāmiʿ al-saghīr* (al-Shaybānī n.d.), *al-Jāmiʿ al-kabīr* (al-Shaybānī 1967), and *Ikhtilāf Abī Ḥanīfa wa-Ibn Abī Layla* (Abū Yūsuf 1938), attributed to Abū Hanīfa's main disciples Muḥammad al-Shaybānī and Abū Yūsuf Yaʿqūb, are discussed in Ali 2002.

[6] Maliki doctrines are primarily drawn from the *Mukhtaṣar* of Khalīl ibn Isḥāq (an abridged and sometimes unreliable English version is available in F. X. Ruxton's summary of the French translation, hereafter Khalīl 1980; the Arabic version is cited as Khalīl 2004). I also use Ibn Rushd's *Bidāyat al-Mujtahid* (very competently translated into English as *The Distinguished Jurist's Primer*; Ibn Rushd 1994–1996), which also gives usually accurate comparative treatment of other schools' doctrines; *al-Kāfī fī fiqh ahl al-Madīna al-mālikī* (Ibn ʿAbd al-Barr 1987); and *Muʿīn al-ḥukkām* (Ibn ʿAbd al-Rafīʿ 1989). I also draw on earlier works such as Saḥnūn's *Mudawwana* (Saḥnūn al-Tanūkhī 1323H) where relevant; for more on this text and Mālik's *Muwaṭṭaʾ*, see Ali 2002. Those interested in specifically Maliki doctrines may also consult Santillana 1925.

[7] I draw upon two Shafiʿi manuals: *Minhāj al-ṭālibīn* (rendered into English from the French by Howard, and cited here as al-Nawawī 1977) and Ibn al-Naqīb al-Miṣrī, *ʿUmdat al-sālik* (translated into English by Nuh Keller as *Reliance of the Traveller* and published with parallel Arabic text, cited as Ibn al-Naqīb al-Miṣrī 1999). I occasionally cite the early texts *Mukhtaṣar al-Muzanī* (Muzanī 1993) and al-Shāfiʿī's *al-Umm* (al-Shāfiʿī 1993); see Ali 2002 for more on these texts.

[8] I use two works by Ibn Qudāma, *al-Kāfī fī fiqh Aḥmad b. Ḥanbal* (Ibn Qudāma 1994), and his *ʿUmda fī aḥkām al-fiqh*, translated into French by Henri Laoust as *Le précis de droit d'Ibn Qudāma* (Ibn Qudāma 1950); and the *Mukhtaṣar* of al-Khiraqī (al-Khiraqī 1982). I make occasional reference to *al-Fatāwā al-kubrā* (Ibn Taymiyya 1948). Selections from the *Masāʾil* of third/ninth century-school eponym Aḥmad b. Ḥanbal have been usefully edited and translated by Susan Spectorsky as *Chapters on Marriage and Divorce* and appear here occasionally (Spectorsky 1993).

[9] Here, I rely on ʿAllāma Ḥillī's *Taḥrīr al-iḥkām al-sharʿiyya ʿalā madhhab al-imāmiyya* (hereafter Ḥillī 1999), with occasional reference to the M.A. thesis by Sachiko Murata (Murata 1974).

[10] For broader comparative studies, see De Bellefonds 1965 and Bakhtiar 1996, which adapts and abridges two standard modern Arabic comparative works: *Fiqh ʿalā l-madhāhib al-arbaʿa* and *Fiqh ʿalā l-madhāhib al-khamsa*. Both Bakhtiar's work and the latter Arabic treatise include discussion of the Jaʿfari school of law. Ibn Rushd 1994–1996 is itself a work of *ikhtilāf*, or different opinions among classical Sunni jurists.

[11] On modern laws, see Esposito with DeLong-Bas 2001 and An-Na'im, ed., 2002.

[12] For the historical application of law, see Sonbol, ed., 1996; Tucker 1998; and works cited in Rapoport 2005, 3nn12–17.

[13] My analysis here focuses on standard marriage or *nikāḥ*. Jaʿfari doctrine also recognizes the contract of "temporary" (*mutʿa*) marriage as legitimizing intercourse and establishing paternity, though not inheritance or certain other rights. On *mutʿa*, see Ḥillī 1999, 3:519–526; see also Murata 1974. For discussion of *mutʿa* contemporary Iranian contexts, see Haeri 1989, 1996. *Mutʿa* differs in key ways from *nikāḥ*, with different and lesser mutual claims and no divorce necessary to effect dissolution; I will discuss it herein only in passing.

[14] Classical jurists agree that a man's exclusive ownership of an unmarried female slave also entitles him to sexual access; see Ali 2002 and Ali 2006, 39–47. Such ownership is referred to as *milk al-yamīn*, "ownership by the right hand."

[15] This presumption of paternity is rebuttable only through the practice of *liʿān*, mutual cursing, outlined in Qurʾan 24:6–9. In *liʿān*, a husband swears four times that his wife is guilty of adultery; then he swears that God's curse will be upon himself if he is lying. The wife then swears four times that she is not guilty, and then that God's curse will be upon herself if she is lying. In this way, the husband is not liable to punishment for bringing a false accusation (Qurʾan 24:4), and the wife is not liable to punishment for adultery (Qurʾan 24:2). Following *liʿān*, the couple is permanently separated and the husband is divested of any and all rights and duties associated with paternity. The child is linked to the mother alone and has no legal father. See, e.g., Ibn Rushd 1994–1996, 2:140–149; Ibn al-Naqīb al-Miṣrī 1999, 572–574; al-Khiraqī 1982, 97–98; Ḥillī 1999, 3:471; al-Marghīnānī n.d., 2:23–26.

[16] Inheritance, where both spouses are free and Muslim, is reciprocal although the proportions inherited by the spouses differ. If the wife is non-Muslim, there are no inheritance rights, as inheritance does not cross confessional boundaries. Slavery also constitutes a bar to inheritance. Because the aim of this chapter is to summarize the main doctrines bearing on the Muslim marriage contract, I have left out most references to slaves as parties to the marriage contract; unless otherwise specified, my discussion refers to doctrines that apply to free Muslims. For a discussion of slave marriage in early Islamic jurisprudence (ca. ninth century CE), see Ali 2002.

[17] Ibn al-Naqīb al-Miṣrī 1999, 538 (I have slightly modified Keller's translation); similar sentiments are expressed by other jurists.

[18] Food and clothing are often discussed under the single rubric of *nafaqa*, support, which can also encompass things such as domestic service. See, e.g., Ḥillī 1999, 4:29 for one listing of component elements of *nafaqa*, which can usually be paid in kind or in cash. On *nafaqa* broadly, see al-Marghīnānī n.d., 2:39–42; Ibn Rushd 1994–1996, 2:63–65; Khalīl 2004, 108–109 (Khalīl 1980, 147–148); Ibn al-Naqīb al-Miṣrī 1999, 539–540; Ibn Qudāma 1950, 191–193.

[19] For more discussion of dower, see the section on Dower, below.

[20] The quality of the lodging according to the Shafiʿis relies only on the wife's standards; further, "If she had servants in her father's house, the husband is obliged to provide servants for her" (Ibn al-Naqīb al-Miṣrī 1999, 538); see also Ḥillī 1999, 3:587 and 4:12. In discussing the wife's accommodations, the jurists also treated matters related to polygyny. "If he has two wives, he may not join them in a single lodging without their consent" (Ibn Qudāma 1994, 3:85); the

same view is expressed in Ibn al-Naqīb al-Miṣrī 1999, 538; Ḥillī 1999, 3:591; Khalīl 2004, 88 (Khalīl 1980, 119).

[21] Ibn al-Naqīb al-Miṣrī 1999, 542–543; al-Khiraqī 1982, 102; Ḥillī 1999, 3:587.

[22] Ibn al-Naqīb al-Miṣrī 1999, 544–545; al-Khiraqī 1982, 102; Ḥillī 1999, 3:587.

[23] On division of time (*qasm*), see al-Marghīnānī 2006, 1:545–546; Ibn Qudāma 1994, 3:85, al-Khiraqī 1982, 90; Khalīl 2004, 88 (Khalīl 1980, 118).

[24] That is, if he has two or three wives, he may choose with whom to spend the night or nights left over after he allocates one night of four to each woman. Ḥillī 1999, 3:588 (but Ḥillī 1999, 3:595 mentions only equality in division).

[25] Khalīl 2004, 88 (Khalīl 1980, 118); Ibn Qudāma 1994, 3:88, with the recommendation of equal distribution; al-Khiraqī 1982, 90; Ḥillī 1999, 3:589; see also Ali 2002, chapter 3.

[26] Al-Marghīnānī 2006, 1:579. By contrast, most jurists agree that a concubine has no right of sexual enjoyment (*istimtāʿ*) or division of time. Ibn Qudāma 1994, 3:89. The *Reliance of the Traveller* does not make reference to these points, but Keller's translation includes a relevant selection from al-Ghazālī (Ibn al-Naqīb al-Miṣrī 1999, 525). Hanbalis hold that he must have sex with her once every four months if he has no legitimate excuse, but his failure to do so does not give her grounds for divorce (Ibn Qudāma 1994, 3:85). Ḥillī 1999, 3:426 states "It is not allowed for a man to abandon having sex with his wife for more than four months except under extenuating circumstances (*ilā li-ḍarūra*)." For a fuller exposition of early doctrine on these vows, see Hawting 1994.

[27] Ibn al-Naqīb al-Miṣrī 1999, 531; al-Marghīnānī n.d., 2:26; Khalīl 2004, 83 (Khalīl 1980, 104–105); al-Khiraqī 1982, 87; Ḥillī 1999, 3:532.

[28] Al-Marghīnānī 2006, 1:533 (implicitly; the discussion focuses on an enslaved wife); Khalīl 1980, 103; Ibn Qudāma 1994, 3:84. The Shafiʿis hold that her consent is not required (Ibn al-Naqīb al-Miṣrī 1999, 526). Jaʿfari opinion diverges as to whether it is forbidden or merely reprehensible to practice withdrawal without the wife's permission when no stipulation regarding the practice has been made in the contract (Ḥillī 1999, 3:426). See Musallam 1983, especially chapter 2, for a broader exploration of contraception.

[29] Ibn al-Naqīb al-Miṣrī 1999, 545 refers to "al-istimtāʿa bihā"; Ḥillī 1999, 3:587 refers to "tamkīn min al-istimtāʿa." Ḥillī discusses the connection between support (*nafaqa*) and its two prerequisites: the contract and the "complete *tamkīn* of the wife." See also Ḥillī 1999, 4:12; al-Marghīnānī 2006, 1:522.

[30] See, e.g., al-Zaylaʿī 2000, 3:301, 303. Terms such as *ḥabs/iḥtibās* reflect the notion of control. Al-Marghīnānī 2006, 1:522; al-Marghīnānī n.d., 2:39.

[31] Quote from Ibn Qudāma 1994, 3:83; similar sentiments are expressed in Ibn al-Naqīb al-Miṣrī 1999, 525.

[32] Ibn Qudāma 1994, 3:83; see also Ibn al-Naqīb al-Miṣrī 1999, 525; Ḥillī 1999, 3:528; al-Marghīnānī 2006, 1:61.

[33] Ibn Qudāma 1994, 3:82; see also Ibn al-Naqīb al-Miṣrī 1999, 526; Ḥillī 1999, 3:482.

[34] Khalīl 1980, 119 (with an exception if the journey is perilous). See also Ibn Qudāma 1994, 3:82; Ibn al-Naqīb al-Miṣrī 1999, 526; Ḥillī 199, 3:595; al-Marghīnānī 2006, 1:546, 522.

[35] Ibn Qudāma 1994, 3:82 (making an exception for going out for what is absolutely necessary to her); Ibn al-Naqīb al-Miṣrī 1999, 538; Ḥillī 1999, 3:587, 593; al-Marghīnānī 2006, 1:522 (implicitly, as it forbids him from doing so until he pays the entire dower).

[36] Khalīl 1980, 148.

[37] Ibn Rushd 1994–1996, 2:66; Khalīl 1980, 147; Ibn al-Naqīb al-Miṣrī 1999, 543.

[38] Spectorsky's introduction to *Chapters on Marriage and Divorce* deals extensively with the types of divorce pronouncements in Ibn Ḥanbal's thought and includes some comparative discussion of Maliki and Shafiʿi examples. Spectorsky 1993. For another discussion of early jurisprudence on divorce, see Ali 2002, chapter 4.

[39] Close kinship between the spouses creates a permanent impediment to marriage. This kinship may be actual or the result of milk-fosterage, which generally creates the same barriers as blood relationship. See Van Gelder 2005, 93–96, for a brief treatment of the issue. Another impediment is a prior marriage between one of the intended spouses and a child or parent of the other (though whether this marriage was consummated may have an effect). See, e.g., Ibn al-Naqīb al-Miṣrī 1999, 527–529. On blood kinship and affinal ties, see Ibn ʿAbd al-Barr 1987, 239–240; on blood kinship, see al-Khiraqī 1982, 83; on affinal ties and milk-fosterage, see idem at 84; Ḥillī 1999, 3:445–446 on blood kinship, and idem at 3:447–460 on milk fosterage and at 3:460–467 on ties created by marriage.

[40] Other temporary impediments include the existence of a marriage tie between the groom and a woman who cannot be combined in marriage with the prospective bride (e.g., her sister or aunt) and the husband having already four wives. See Ibn Rushd 1994–1996, 2:37–58 for discussion of these rules; see also Ibn ʿAbd al-Barr 1987, 240–243; Ibn Qudāma 1950, 175–178, al-Khiraqī 1982, 83–84; Ibn al-Naqīb al-Miṣrī 1999, 529; al-Muzanī 1993, 9:181; Ḥillī 1999, 3:472 (on two sisters), 474 (on having four wives).

[41] Al-Nawawī 1977, 294–295; Ibn al-Naqīb al-Miṣrī 1999, 529; al-Marghīnānī 2006, 1:483; Ibn Qudāma 1950, 182; al-Khiraqī 1982, 84; Ibn ʿĀbidīn 1994, 4:125–136, including extensive editor's notes; Ibn Rushd 1994–1996, 2:51; Khalīl 1980, 103; Ibn ʿAbd al-Barr 1987, 244. See also al-Muzanī 1993, 9:182. Most held that a *majūsiyya* was not among "the people of the book" (*ahl al-kitāb*) with whom intermarriage was permitted. On intermarriage, see also Friedman 2003.

[42] Ḥillī 1999, 3:481 ("*al-mashhūr taḥrīmuhunna*"), but mentioning two views as to whether it is permissible to contract *mutʿa* with them; on 3:522 *mutʿa* with *kitābiyyas* is declared permissible; the distinction is revisited on 3:543, with the prohibition of "permanent" marriage with them viewed as stronger, likewise the permission with regard to *mutʿa*. Nonetheless, the validity of such a marriage is implicit in the discussion of division of time (*qasm*) when one wife is *kitābiyya* and the other Muslim. Ḥillī 1999, 3:590, setting twice as long for the Muslim wife, in contrast to the standard Sunni rule of equality. This case might relate to that of the *kitābī* who converts to Islam and is allowed to retain his Christian or Jewish wife. Idem, 3:481, 483, 491.

[43] Most classical legal texts do not even state this rule, taking it for granted. See Ibn al-Naqīb al-Miṣrī 1999, 529, where this point appears only in the clarifying comments of a modern Muslim scholar. Discussing *mutʿa*, Ḥillī specifies that a Muslim woman may only contract it with a Muslim man. Ḥillī 1999, 3:522. See

also the discussion of suitability, below. For a brief discussion of contemporary Muslim thought on intermarriage between Muslim women and *kitābī* men, see Ali 2006, 14–21. Muhammad 2008, 2:397 suggests that "some imams now permit such marriages as long as there is a prenuptial agreement guaranteeing the wife freedom from coercion to convert."

[44] Ibn ʿĀbidīn 1994, 4:69; al-Marghīnānī 2006, 1:475.

[45] Khalīl 1980, 92.

[46] Al-Nawawī 1977, 283; Ibn al-Naqīb al-Miṣrī 1999, 516; al-Muzanī 1993, 9:179.

[47] Ḥillī 1999, 3:428.

[48] Ibn Qudāma 1994, 3:21; see a twist on this rule in al-Khiraqī 1992, 83.

[49] Al-Marghīnānī 2006, 1:475; Ibn ʿĀbidīn 1994, 4:69; Ḥillī 1999, 3:428.

[50] Ibn Qudāma 1994, 3:20. The offer and acceptance can also be phrased as questions, provided the questions themselves are in the past tense and are answered with "yes"; see Ḥillī 1999, 3:428.

[51] Ḥillī 1999, 3:427.

[52] Ibn ʿĀbidīn 1994, 4:76.

[53] Ibn al-Naqīb al-Miṣrī 1999, 517; al-Nawawī 1977, 283.

[54] Ibn Qudāma 1994, 3:21.

[55] See, e.g., Khalīl 1980, 92.

[56] Al-Nawawī 1977, 283; Ibn al-Naqīb al-Miṣrī 1999, 517 (in parallel Arabic text). This Shafiʿi view is noted in al-Marghīnānī 2006, 1:475.

[57] Ibn Qudāma 1994, 3:20 (also explicitly forbidding the use of *iḥlāl*); see also Ibn Qudāma 1950, 170.

[58] Ḥillī 1999, 3:427, also explicitly forbidding the use of *hiba, ṣadaqa, bayʿ, ijāra*. Contracts of *mutʿa* marriage may use the terminology of hire or lease (*ijāra*) according to Murata 1974, but Ḥillī rejects the use of the term (along with *hiba, tamlīk*, and *ʿāriya*) in favor of *nikāḥ* or *mutʿa*. Ḥillī 1999, 3:520.

[59] Ibn Rushd 1994–1996, 2:3; Khalīl 2004, 76.

[60] Al-Marghīnānī 2006, 1:475; the *Mabsūṭ* allows for *hiba, ṣadaqa*, and *tamlīk*. Al-Sarakhsī 2001, 5:56.

[61] Nyazee's translation of *ṣadaqa*; al-Marghīnānī 2006, 1:475.

[62] Nor can the term *iʿāra*, "commodate loan" (Nyazee's term) be used. Al-Marghīnānī 2006, 1:475.

[63] According to the Shafiʿis, however, it will be valid if done in a foreign language even by those who speak Arabic. Ibn al-Naqīb al-Miṣrī 1999, 517; for the Jaʿfaris, Ḥillī disagrees. Ḥillī 1999, 3:428.

[64] Ibn Qudāma 1994, 3:21; Ḥillī 1999, 3:428.

[65] See, e.g., Ibn Qudāma 1994, 3:21.The Jaʿfari school differs. Bakhtiar 1996, 402.

[66] Al-Marghīnānī 2006, 1:504–506; Ibn Qudāma 1994, 3:14–15; Ibn Qudāma 1950, 171; al-Khiraqī 1982, 81; Ibn Rushd 1994–1996, 2:14; Ibn al-Naqīb al-Miṣrī 1999, 521; Ibn ʿAbd al-Barr 1987, 229; Khalīl 1980, 95.

[67] For a general discussion of agency, see Ibn Rushd 1994–1996, 2:363–367.

[68] Ibn Rushd 1994–1996, 2:9–10; see also Khalīl 1980, 92.

[69] Al-Nawawī 1977, 284–285; Ibn al-Naqīb al-Miṣrī 1999, 518.

[70] Ibn Qudāma 1994, 3:9; al-Khiraqī 1982, 81.

71 Generally, maturity corresponds to legally responsible adulthood (*mukallafa*). The rationale for the dominant view presented in the *Ḥidāya* "is that she has undertaken an act that pertains purely to her personal right, and she possesses the legal capacity to do so being sane and in possession of discretion." Al-Marghīnānī 2006, 1:491.

72 Ḥillī 1999, 3:430.

73 Ibn ʿĀbidīn 1994, 4:154; al-Marghīnānī 2006, 1:491. Within the Hanafi school, Abū Ḥanīfa is always said to hold that a major female contracting her own marriage is valid. Abū Yūsuf is sometimes said to agree entirely with him (al-Marghīnānī 2006, 1:491) and sometimes said to hold that the marriage is suspended (*mawqūf*) until it is ratified by the guardian (Abū Yūsuf Yaʿqūb 1938). This same position is attributed to Muḥammad al-Shaybānī in some texts, e.g., al-Marghīnānī 2006, 1:491, while in others, e.g., the *Muwaṭṭa'*, he is said to hold such a marriage to be void (al-Shaybānī 1997, 177).

74 The question of maleness of the *walī* usually is assumed and only arises in directly polemical contexts, where the Hanafi view is being contested; Khalīl 1980, 94 (with regard to marriage of her slave); see also Ali 2002, chapter 1.

75 Ibn al-Naqīb al-Miṣrī 1999, 518.

76 Al-Khiraqī 1982, 81 does not point out the necessity of the guardian's being male but simply lists male relatives in order of preference.

77 Al-Marghīnānī 2006, 1:496, disallowing a mother's power of compulsion (*ijbār*) but implicitly allowing her to act as *walī*; femaleness is also absent from the Hanafi list of disqualifying factors for guardians, and maleness is not listed as a requirement. Idem, 498–499.

78 Ḥillī 1999, 3:438.

79 See general discussion in Ibn Rushd 1994–1996, 2:13–14.

80 Ibn Rushd 1994–1996, 2:13.

81 Ibn al-Naqīb al-Miṣrī 1999, 518–519.

82 That is, if the bride is a Muslim, the guardian must be also. Al-Khiraqī 1982, 81.

83 E.g., when the bride's father is available, her paternal uncle should not serve as her *walī*. Ibn Qudāma 1994, 3:12–13. See a slightly different list in Ibn Qudāma 1950, 171–172.

84 Al-Marghīnānī 2006, 1:498–499. Abū Ḥanīfa is sometimes said to have held that a male slave could be a guardian. See Ibn Rushd 1994–1996, 2:13.

85 Ibn ʿĀbidīn 1994, 4:153; al-Marghīnānī 2006, 1:498–499, including discussion of Abū Yūsuf's slightly different views.

86 Ḥillī 1999, 3:346.

87 Ḥillī 1999, 3:347.

88 See discussion below on suitability.

89 Ibn Qudāma 1994, 3:13, also noting a minority view that she must go to the sultan (Ibn Taymiyya 1948, 4:61).

90 Ibn al-Naqīb al-Miṣrī 1999, 521.

91 Khalīl 1980, 95; Ibn Rushd 1994–1996, 2:17.

92 Ibn al-Naqīb al-Miṣrī 1999, 523. On compulsion, see the discussion below.

93 Ḥillī 1999, 3:430.

94 Ibn ʿĀbidīn 1994, 4:155; al-Marghīnānī 2006, 1:491. See also, e.g., al-Marghīnānī 2006, 1:478. This Hanafi doctrine conflicts with a *ḥadīth* that the

other schools use to bolster their doctrines that "There is no marriage without a *walī*," or "The marriage of any woman who marries without a *walī* is void (*bāṭil*)." Some versions of these traditions state, more emphatically, "void, void, void." See, e.g., Ibn Qudāma 1994, 3:9.

95 Hanafi texts use the term *bāligha* (e.g., al-Marghīnānī 1:196), while Jaʿfari texts use *rāshida*, or *rāshida bāligha* (e.g., Ḥillī 1999, 3:430, 433).

96 However, Ḥillī recommends that she ask her father's permission and that, if he is deceased, she appoint her brother as her agent for the contract. Ḥillī 1999, 3:438. On contracting *mutʿa*, see idem, 525, she can conclude it for herself if she is *bāligha rāshida* even if a virgin, but in that case, it is reprehensible for her to do so without her father's permission. Idem, 523. The debate as to whether the father's permission is required for a virgin to contract *mutʿa* remains a live issue for contemporary Jaʿfari scholars; see Haeri 1996.

97 Al-Marghīnānī 2006, 1:491–492; Ibn ʿĀbidīn 1994, 4:156. The Hanafi jurists disagree over whether the guardian may intervene where she marries herself off for less than her fair dower. Al-Marghīnānī 2006, 1:503.

98 Ibn Rushd 1994–1996, 2:11–12.

99 Khalīl 1980, 98; see also Zomeño 1997.

100 See Siddiqui 1996 and, more generally, Ziadeh 1957.

101 Ibn Rushd 1994–1996, 2:17–18; Ibn al-Naqīb al-Miṣrī 1999, 523 (requires the bride's agreement and "the acceptance of all who can be [her] guardians"), 524. Abū Ḥanīfa allows a father to marry off his minor daughter to a slave, while Abū Yūsuf and Muḥammad al-Shaybānī disallow it. Al-Marghīnānī 2006, 1:504. *Al-Mabsūṭ* declares the permissibility of this action without giving disagreement (al-Sarakhsī 2001, 5:116), but notes a parallel disagreement concerning low *mahr* (idem, 4:248). Ibn Qudāma 1994, 3:22 presents two views in the case of a bride married to an unsuitable groom. If she does not consent or some of her *awliyāʾ* do not, one view holds that the marriage is void. The other view is that the marriage is valid but those who object can seek to have it annulled (*faskh*), even the brothers if both the father and the bride agree. Ḥillī states that "if the *walī* marries her off to an unsuitable man, she has the right to dissolution (*lahā al-faskh*)." Ḥillī 1999, 3:441.

102 Ibn al-Naqīb al-Miṣrī 1999, 523.

103 Al-Marghīnānī 2006, 1:501.

104 Khalīl 1980, 95; Ibn Rushd 1994–1996, 2:17; see the discussion below.

105 Al-Sarakhsī 2001, 5:25; Ibn al-Naqīb al-Miṣrī 1999, 524; al-Nawawī 1977, 288.

106 Al-Khiraqī states "If she is married to someone unsuitable, the marriage is void" (1982, 82), and Ibn Qudāma makes a similar statement in *al-Kāfī* (Ibn Qudāma 1994, 3:2; I read the text without the period placed between *lam yuṣiḥḥ* and *wa-in raḍū bihī*). The two Arabic manuscripts used by the French translator of Ibn Qudāma's *ʿUmda* (*Précis de droit*) show the dispute; one states simply that "No *walī* may marry a woman to an unsuitable groom"; the other adds "without her consent." Ibn Qudāma 1950, 173. See also Ibn al-Naqīb al-Miṣrī 1999, 524; al-Nawawī 1977, 288.

107 Ḥillī 1999, 3:441.

108 However, jurists do discuss the question of a minor boy or an adult male who is not legally competent. Shafiʿis hold that a *walī mujbir* may not marry a minor

boy to a slave or a woman with defects permitting annulment of the marriage. al-Nawawī 1977, 289. Abū Ḥanīfa allows such a marriage, though his disciples do not. Al-Marghīnānī 2006, 1:504.

[109] Quoted from Hamilton's translation, al-Marghīnānī ²1975, 1:110; see al-Marghīnānī 2006, 1:500–501.

[110] Al-Marghīnānī 2006, 1:501–502, but see idem, 504, where Abū Ḥanīfa permits a father to override considerations of suitability to marry his minor daughter to a slave.

[111] Al-Marghīnānī 2006, 1:475; Ibn al-Naqīb al-Miṣrī 1999, 523. There is disagreement as to whether lineage is a consideration among non-Arabs (al-Marghīnānī 2006, 1:501) as well as whether all Arabs are suitable matches for other Arabs, or whether tribal and clan differences are also taken into account. Further, the Egyptian Maliki authority Ibn al-Qāsim is said to have held that an (Arab) slave was a match for an Arab woman; Mālik, citing Qur'an 49:13, allowed marriage "between the Arabs and the clients" (Ibn Rushd 1994–1996, 2:18). See also Ibn ʿAbd al-Rafīʿ 1989, 167–168; Khalīl 1980, 98.

[112] Ibn al-Naqīb al-Miṣrī 1999, 523–524; al-Nawawī 1977, 288–289; Ibn Qudāma 1994, 3:21; Ibn Rushd 1994–1996, 2:18; Ibn Qudāma 1950, 173; al-Marghīnānī 2006, 1:502 (which reports that in the *Muwaṭṭaʾ al-Shaybānī*, this is only the case where his bad conduct is public and notorious). Ḥillī finds it reprehensible to marry a *fāsiq*. Ḥillī 1999, 3:528.

[113] Idem.

[114] Ibn Rushd 1994–1996, 2:18; Ibn al-Naqīb al-Miṣrī 1999, 523–524; Ibn ʿAbd al-Barr 1987, 168.

[115] Al-Nawawī 1977, 288–289; Ibn al-Naqīb al-Miṣrī 1999, 524.

[116] Al-Marghīnānī 2006, 1:503, which attributes two opposing views about the relevance of profession to Abū Ḥanīfa; Abū Yūsuf holds that the husband's occupation only matters if it is one of the "lower professions like those of the cupper, weaver, and the tanner."

[117] Ḥillī 1999, 3:528.

[118] Ibn al-Naqīb al-Miṣrī 1999, 524; al-Nawawī 1977, 289. However, his inability to pay dower or support his wife is grounds for marital dissolution under certain circumstances. Ibn Rushd reports that under Shafiʿi law, if a father marries his daughter without her consent to a man unable to support her, the marriage can be dissolved (Ibn Rushd 1994–1996, 2:18).

[119] Idem. The husband's poverty is one of the few grounds on which a mother may intervene and object to a particular match for her daughter. Khalīl 1980, 98.

[120] Al-Marghīnānī 2006, 1:502. Likewise, in the case of a very wealthy woman, the groom should be of the same status; Abū Yūsuf disagrees, though, holding that he need only be able to provide for her.

[121] Al-Marghīnānī 2006, 1:502.

[122] Ḥillī 1999, 3:441, 527 (mentioning it as one view but not an essential condition of suitability).

[123] Al-Khiraqī 1982, 82 mentions only "religion and lineage." See also Ibn Rushd 1994–1996, 2:18.

[124] Ḥillī 1999, 3:527. The text continues, "It is allowed for a believing man to marry whom he wishes among Muslim women, but it is recommended for him to marry a believing woman." See also idem, 3:441.

[125] Hanafi jurists are split as to whether one or two generations where necessary, but agreed that a man who was the first in his family to be Muslim was not a suitable match for a woman born into Islam. Al-Marghīnānī 2006, 1:501–502.

[126] Ḥillī 1999, 3:430. A marriage may be contracted secretly whether the spouses themselves or their *walīs* are parties to the contract but witnessing is recommended. Idem, 3:423.

[127] Ibn ʿĀbidīn 1994, 4:93; al-Marghīnānī 2006, 1:476.

[128] Ibn ʿAbd al-Barr 1987, 229. Some early Maliki authorities make a limited exception in the case of a "lowly" woman, and allow an unwitnessed marriage contract to stand provided that it was publicly celebrated. Saḥnūn al-Tanūkhī 1323H, 2:170; see also idem, 2:166 on the role of the *walī* in such a case. But see Khalīl 1980, 90.

[129] Ibn Rushd 1994–1996, 19–20; Khalīl 1980, 92.

[130] Al-Nawawī 1977, 283–284; Ibn al-Naqīb al-Miṣrī 1999, 518. Freedom is an additional qualification here, along with knowing the language of the contracting parties and good hearing; the *Reliance* lists sight as a qualification, but the *Minhāj* records dispute on that point.

[131] In *al-Kāfī*, Ibn Qudāma (1994, 3:16–17) lists seven specific qualifications: reason, hearing, speech, majority, Islam, probity (*ʿadāla*), and maleness (though the possibility of one man and two women is considered). Freedom and sight are not required. Although Ibn Qudāma lists witnesses among the essentials of marriage, it is related from Aḥmad [Ibn Ḥanbal] that after manumitting Ṣafiyya, Muḥammad married her "without witnesses," because it is an *ʿaqd muʿāwaḍa* and witnesses are not stipulated, like in a sale. By contrast, Ibn Qudāma's *ʿUmda* notes only that "two Muslim witnesses" are required (Ibn Qudāma 1950, 171), likewise in al-Khiraqī 1982, 81.

[132] Ibn al-Naqīb al-Miṣrī 1999, 518. In *al-Fatāwā al-kubrā*, Ibn Taymiyya opines, without stating his reasoning, that even in a case where the *walī* knows the witnesses to be immoral, the marriage will be valid so long as they are outwardly known as upright. Ibn Taymiyya 1948, 4:72.

[133] Al-Marghīnānī 2006, 1:476–477; Ibn ʿĀbidīn 1994, 4:90–91. The *Mabsūṭ* points out that four women may not serve (al-Sarakhsī 1991, 5:35).

[134] Al-Marghīnānī 2006, 1:476. In a case where the bride is a Christian or Jew, Abū Ḥanīfa and Abū Yūsuf allow the witnesses to be *dhimmīs* also; Muḥammad al-Shaybānī disagrees. Al-Marghīnānī 2006, 1:477; Sarahksī 1991, 5:33.

[135] Al-Marghīnānī 2006, 1:477; the rationale here is that an immoral person nonetheless possesses *wilāya* and can give testimony. Ibn ʿĀbidīn 1994, 4:93.

[136] Wakin 1972, 6.

[137] *Bulūgh* or majority is different from modern understandings of adulthood, and is linked to the onset of puberty for girls. According to most jurists, females reach legal majority with the onset of menstruation, and the exact age therefore varies according to the individual. However, the Hanbalis hold that nine years is the age at which a girl becomes an adult (Ibn Qudāma 1994, 3:20; Ibn Taymiyya 1948, 4:67) In *al-Radd al-muḥtār*, Ibn ʿĀbidīn (1994, 4:18) states the Hanafi view that a nine-year old female is not automatically considered major, but if a female and her guardian differ as to whether she is bāligh, her word is accepted if she is at least nine. For boys, puberty (*iḥtilām, ḥulum*) also marks legal majority (idem).

The relevant physical criterion for boys is generally nocturnal emission, with fifteen years given as the upper limit for when a boy attains majority. See Ibn Rushd 1994–1996, 2:4n4. In the Jaʿfari view, a man is prohibited from consummating a marriage with his wife until she has reached the age of nine. Ḥillī 1999, 3:467–468 (with discussion of potential consequences).

[138] In the case of the fatherless child (*yatīm/yatīma*), another may sometimes act in the father's stead. In some cases a testamentary guardian (*waṣī*) may compel a charge to marry. Khalīl 2004, 76 (Khalīl 1980, 92). Where I refer to fathers, these instances are included.

[139] The jurists disagree about the minor non-virgin, with some holding that she can be compelled to marry if minority rather than virginity or in addition to it is a sufficient cause for compulsion. See Ibn Rushd 1994–1996, 2:5–6; Khalīl 1980, 92 (2004, 76); Ibn ʿAbd al-Rafīʿ 1989, 219; Ibn al-Naqīb al-Miṣrī 1999, 522 (this discussion appears only in the Arabic text); Ibn ʿĀbidīn 1994, 4:154; al-Marghīnānī 2006, 1:493–495; al-Sarakhsī 2001, 4:242; Ibn Qudāma 1994, 3:19; Ḥillī 1999, 3:433, 435. There is disagreement as to whether any act of intercourse suffices to change the status of a female from virgin to non-virgin or whether this intercourse must take place within a legal marriage. There is likewise disagreement as to whether privacy between spouses that creates the presumption of intercourse and obliges the payment of dower changes her status, as well as whether the loss of the hymen due to something other than intercourse does so. See, e.g., Ibn Rushd 1994–1996, 2:6, 25–26; Ibn Qudāma 1994, 3:20; al-Marghīnānī 2006, 1:493–494; Ibn Taymiyya 1948, 4:64, 104; Ḥillī 1999, 3:433. Discussions in the text here refer only to the issue of legal status as virgin or non-virgin.

[140] The jurists disagree over the extent of power wielded by the paternal grandfather, with some jurists even holding that he may marry off a minor while the father is living. Allowing *ijbār* by the paternal grandfather, see al-Marghīnānī 2006, 1:496; Ibn al-Naqīb al-Miṣrī 1999, 522; Ḥillī 1999, 3:433; see also Ibn Taymiyya 1948, 4:60.

[141] Ibn Taymiyya 1948, 4:65.

[142] Ḥillī explicitly rejects this (1999, 3:435).

[143] Ibn Rushd 1415 [1995], 3:17; Ibn ʿĀbidīn 1994, 4:159. The Jaʿfari Ḥillī makes a distinction between *wilāyat al-ijbār* and *wilāyat al-ikhtiyār* (1999, 3:439).

[144] This is taken for granted; most texts do not explicitly discuss it but rather exclude the *walī mujbir* or *walī* with the right of compulsion from their discussions of whether a marriage may be dissolved when contracted by one who is not *mujbir*. The Malikis do not discuss an option of majority, as they disallow contracting by someone who does not have the power of *ijbār*. For the Hanbali view, see Ibn Qudāma 1994, 3:18–19.

[145] Al-Marghīnānī 2006, 1:496; Ḥillī 1999, 3:433–434. (Except in the case of the minor non-virgin in Shafiʿi doctrine.)

[146] Of course, a half-dower obligation exists in this case. See below. As for the right to pronounce divorce upon arriving at majority, the *Hidāya*'s statement is typical: "The divorce pronounced by any husband is valid if he is sane and major" (al-Marghīnānī 2006:–1:565). Ibn al-Naqīb al-Miṣrī adds the qualification, important for non-Hanafis, that the husband must pronounce it voluntarily. Ibn al-Naqīb al-Miṣrī 1999, 556; see also Ibn Rushd 1994–1996, 2:97.

[147] Ibn ʿAbd al-Barr 1987, 213; on the testamentary guardian or *waṣī*, see above and Khalīl 1980, 95.

[148] Ḥillī 1999, 3:434, noting the view that a testamentary guardian may not marry off a ward, whether male or female, and if female, whether a minor or in her majority.

[149] Idem, 3:437.

[150] Al-Marghīnānī 2006, 1:496.

[151] Ibn Qudāma 1994, 3:18–19; al-Khiraqī 1982, 82 holds that this power is only for the father.

[152] On marriage of minors, the guardianship of mothers, and the option at majority in Ottoman practice, see Yazbak 2002; see also Motzki 1996 and Tucker 1998, chapter. 5. On minors more generally, see Sonbol 1996a.

[153] The dominant view is attributed to Abū Ḥanīfa and Muḥammad al-Shaybānī and the minority position identified with Abū Yūsuf. Al-Marghīnānī 2006, 1:496; Ibn ʿĀbidīn 1994, 4:184–185.

[154] Al-Marghīnānī 2006, 1:496.

[155] This point is taken for granted and thus not usually stated explicitly, although Ibn Rushd notes the agreement of jurists "about the stipulation of the consent and acceptance of men who had attained puberty, were free, and were in charge of their own affairs" (1996, 2:4). In other texts, their ability to contract this marriage becomes clear by contrast with the exceptional cases of those who retain diminished legal capacity at adulthood, such as an insane man (*majnūn*), an imbecile (*maʿtūh*), someone interdicted, or even a slave. See, e.g., Ibn Rushd 1994–1996, 2:4; Ibn al-Naqīb al-Miṣrī 1999, 524; al-Khiraqī 1982, 82; Ḥillī 1999, 3:443.

[156] That is to say, who is legally considered to be a virgin.

[157] Ibn Rushd 1994–1996, 2:4.

[158] Al-Nawawī 1977, 284; Ibn al-Naqīb al-Miṣrī 1999, 522.

[159] Ibn Qudāma 1994, 3:19; Ibn Qudāma 1950, 172; al-Khiraqī 1982, 82.

[160] In addition to Ibn al-Naqīb al-Miṣrī 1999, 522, see al-Shāfiʿī 1993, 5:29.

[161] For a Hanbali treatment of *rushd*, see Ibn Taymiyya 1948, 4:96–97.

[162] Khalīl 1980, 92. There is disagreement as to whether a father can subsequently revoke this declaration and reassert the power of compulsion over his daughter. Ibn ʿAbd al-Rafīʿ 1989, 218–219.

[163] Ibn Taymiyya 1948, 4:96; Ibn Qudāma 1994, 3:19; Ibn Qudāma 1950, 172.

[164] Ḥillī 1999, 3:435.

[165] Al-Marghīnānī 2006, 1:492; Ibn ʿĀbidīn 1994, 4:155, 159.

[166] Al-Marghīnānī 2006, 1:492. At this time, if she is still a virgin her father can receive her dower with her consent, but not over her objection. On who can lawfully take possession of the dower in general, see al-Marghīnānī 2006, 1:493; for a Maliki view, see Ibn ʿAbd al-Barr 1987, 172.

[167] However, he need not specify the dower she is to receive (al-Marghīnānī 2006, 1:493).

[168] Except for the paternal grandfather, where he also wields the power of *ijbār* (which obtains past majority only in the Maliki, Shafiʿi, and one Hanbali view). See, e.g., Ibn Taymiyya 1948, 4:96.

[169] Khalīl 1980, 93; Ibn Rushd 1994–1996, 2:3; Ibn al-Naqīb al-Miṣrī 1999, 522, noting that the virgin's silence is permission when discussing the recom-

mendation that the father or paternal grandfather ask her permission; al-Nawawī 1977, 285. (However, Ibn Rushd characterizes the Shafiʿi doctrine differently: she must express consent verbally where her *walī* is someone other than her father [Ibn Rushd 1994–1996, 2:3]. This view is expressed in the Hanafi texts; see next note.) Silence also constitutes consent of a mature virgin when sought by a father for those schools in which the father must obtain her consent. Ibn ʿĀbidīn 1994, 4:160; al-Marghīnānī 2006, 1:492–493.

170 Al-Marghīnānī 2006, 1:492–493. See also, Messick, this volume, pp. 156–179, on the application in practice of an analogous rule.

171 Ḥillī 1999, 3:435.

172 That is, whether it is her father or anyone else, Ibn Rushd 1994–1996, 2:4; Ibn al-Naqīb al-Miṣrī 1999, 522; al-Nawawī 1977, 285; al-Marghīnānī 2006, 1:493; Khalīl 1980, 94; Ibn Qudāma 1950, 172–173; Ḥillī 1999, 3:435.

173 Ḥaṣkafī 1992, 34–35. *Al-Mabsūṭ* presents the view that (silent) consent is valid in the case of the *bikr* (al-Sarakhsī 2001, 5:9). Implicitly, silence is not consent in the case of the non-virgin, although her spoken consent would validate the marriage (idem, 5:10).

174 On the social phenomenon of women's being endowed by their families in Andalusia, see Zomeño 2000a, and her chapter in this volume, pp. 141–144. See also Rapoport 2005.

175 Ibn al-Naqīb al-Miṣrī 1999, 533; Ḥillī 1999, 3:543 defines it slightly differently as anything that can be "validly owned." Items that have no legal sale price, such as wine or pork, may not serve as dower for Muslims (e.g., al-Marghīnānī 2006, 1:518; Ibn al-Naqīb al-Miṣrī 1999, 563 [discussing compensation in *khulʿ*]; al-Khiraqī 1982, 88; Khalīl 1980, 106; Ibn Rushd 1994–1996, 2:31–32; Khalīl 1980, 106; Ḥillī 1999, 3:543 [even if the husband alone is Muslim; in one view, though not the preferred one, this voids the marriage]). For a discussion of problem cases, see Ibn Rushd 1994–1996, 2:31–34. On the wife's right to dower in the Hanafi *Fatāwā ʿĀlamgīrī*, see Siddiqui 1995.

176 The legal schools disagree over whether a minimum dower is required. Maliki doctrine requires three dirhams or one-fourth of a dinar (Khalīl 1980, 109; see also Saḥnūn al-Tanūkhī 1323H, 2:223 [discussed at more length]), while the Hanafis require ten dirhams (al-Marghīnānī 2006, 1:507; see an early discussion in al-Shaybānī 1965, 3:218). Early texts link the minimum dower to the minimum amount for which the hand is amputated in theft. The *Hidāya* justifies this amount on the basis that the dower is God's imposition and not the woman's right. The Shafiʿi view is that no minimum dower is required, as there is no minimum price set in a sale; a woman may agree to any amount she wishes (Ibn al-Naqīb al-Miṣrī 1999, 533; see also al-Shāfiʿī 1993, 7:376). Hanbali jurists likewise set no minimum dower (Ibn Qudāma 1950, 186), though al-Khiraqī 1982, 88, does specify that it should be something with a value that can be halved. Jaʿfari doctrine likewise sets no minimum dower (Ḥillī 1999, 3:547).

177 I.e., *ribāwī*. On *ribā*, see Vogel and Hayes 1998.

178 *Gharar*, or hazard, appears when lack of knowledge or future contingencies impinge on a transaction. See idem, 63–64, 87–93.

179 Al-Marghīnānī 2006, 1:516–519; Ibn al-Naqīb al-Miṣrī 1999, 533–534; al-Khiraqī 1982, 88. For a discussion of how early Hanafi, Maliki, and Shafiʿi jurists dealt with these issues, see Ali 2002, chapter 1.

[180] There is a dispute as to whether intercourse is required or whether the full dower becomes due with the occurrence of valid privacy (*khalwa ṣaḥīḥa*) between the couple. See, e.g., Ibn Rushd 1994–1996, 2:25–26; al-Marghīnānī 2006, 1:510–511.

[181] Ibn Rushd 1994–1996, 2:26.

[182] Idem, 2:30–31; al-Marghīnānī 2006, 1:412. Some consider this also recommended or even obligatory alongside the dower in case of divorce after consummation (al-Khiraqī 1982, 89).

[183] Ibn Rushd 1994–1996, 2:26; Ibn al-Naqīb al-Miṣrī 1999, 534, in the case of annulment for cause, see idem, 531.

[184] Al-Marghīnānī 2006, 1:507; Ibn al-Naqīb al-Miṣrī 1999, 533; al-Nawawī 1977, 305; Ibn Rushd 1994–1996, 2:30; Khalīl 1980, 110; Khalīl 2004, 85 notes that the omission of a dower amount must not be accompanied by a declaration that the bride is "giving" herself to the groom, something explicitly permitted in the Qur'an to Muḥammad alone. Ibn Qudāma 1950, 188; al-Khiraqī 1982, 89. Ḥillī 1999, 3:546 sums up the general stance: "Mentioning the dower in the contract is not obligatory but it is recommended."

[185] Al-Marghīnānī 2006, 1:507; al-Shaybānī 1969, 3:215.

[186] Al-Shāfiʿī 1993, 5:88; al-Muzanī 1993, 9:194.

[187] Ibn Qudāma 1994, 3:40.

[188] Ibn Rushd 1994–1996, 2:36; see also Saḥnūn al-Tanūkhī 1323H, 2:238.

[189] Al-Marghīnānī 2006, 1:509; Ibn al-Naqīb al-Miṣrī 1999, 536; Khalīl 2004, 85–86.

[190] Saḥnūn al-Tanūkhī 1323H, 2:238; Ibn Rushd 1994–1996, 2:30, 34.

[191] Ibn Rushd 1994–1996, 2:34; Ibn al-Naqīb al-Miṣrī 1999, 534–535; al-Nawawī 1977, 310; al-Muzanī 1993, 9:195. The *Hidāya* qualifies these relatives as her sisters, paternal aunts, and daughters of her paternal uncles (al-Marghīnānī 2006, 1:520–521).

[192] Ibn Rushd 1994–1996, 2:19; with regard to the emancipated daughter, see Khalīl 1980, 110.

[193] Al-Shāfiʿī 1993, 5:91.

[194] Ibn Qudāma 1994 3:71.

[195] Ḥillī 1999, 3:528.

[196] Al-Marghīnānī 2006, 1:503.

[197] Ibn Rushd 1994–1996, 2:18; Ibn ʿAbd al-Rafīʿ 1989, 166–167.

[198] Ibn Qudāma 1950, 187.

[199] Al-Marghīnānī 2006, 1:503; al-Shaybānī n.d., 171–172; al-Sarakhsī 2001, 4:248. The authorities hold parallel views as to whether a father may agree to a dower larger than her fair dower for his minor son's bride.

[200] Ibn al-Naqīb al-Miṣrī 1999, 533; al-Nawawī 1977, 308–309; al-Shāfiʿī 1993, 5:103–104. But see an incorrect assertion to the contrary at Ibn Rushd 1994–1996, 2:18–19.

[201] Ḥillī 1999, 3:435.

[202] Deferral of the entire dower to death or divorce was usually considered by very early jurists to be impermissible (see Rapoport 2000) although some, including Mālik, permitted a delay for a specified term such as one or two years. Ibn Rushd 1994–1996, 2:25; Ibn ʿAbd al-Rafīʿ 1989, 169ff.; Khalīl 1980, 109.

[203] al-Nawawī 1977, 306; Ibn al-Naqīb al-Miṣrī 1999, 534.

[204] Al-Marghīnānī 2006, 1:522.

[205] In his discussion of the wife's right to refuse her husband access to herself until he pays the dower, al-Marghīnānī (2006, 1:522) assumes the permissibility of dividing the dower into prompt and deferred portions and even deferring the entire dower. The dominant Hanafi doctrine holds that a woman whose entire dower is deferred does not have the right to refuse her husband based on non-payment. For an exploration of this position in early legal texts, see Ali 2002, chapter 2.

[206] Ibn ʿAbd al-Rafīʿ 1989, 175. Saḥnūn al-Tanūkhī 1323H–, 2:253; Khalīl 1980, 108.

[207] Ibn al-Naqīb al-Miṣrī 1999, 535; see also al-Shāfiʿī 1993, 5:132–133.

[208] Bakhtiar 1996, 445.

[209] She retains this right after consummation in Jaʿfari thought (Murata 1974); Hanbali doctrine likewise allows for dissolution even after consummation "provided she had no knowledge of his inability [to pay dower] before the marriage" (Bakhtiar 1996, 445–446).

[210] Al-Shaybānī n.d., 183; al-Marghīnānī 2006, 1:522.

[211] For discussion of the use of conditions historically, particularly in the Ottoman period, see Sonbol, ed., 1996.

[212] The legal texts are not straightforward guides to implementing the stipulations; more guidance here is available in legal formularies. See the discussion of Ṭaḥāwī's formulary in Wakin 1972.

[213] See Spectorsky 1993.

[214] See, e.g., Ibn al-Naqīb al-Miṣrī 1999, 530. However, if the groom merely intends to divorce her at a specified time or after making her lawful, and does not expressly stipulate this in the contract, the marriage is valid in many though not all views, although the husband's behavior is unethical. See also Ḥillī 1999, 3:478; Ibn ʿAbd al-Barr 1987, 238–239; Ibn Rushd 1994–1996, 2:68.

[215] Al-Marghīnānī 2006, 1:487–488; Ibn al-Naqīb al-Miṣrī 1999, 530; Khalīl, 1980, 96; Ibn ʿAbd al-Barr 1987, 238; Ibn Rushd 1994–1996, 2:68.

[216] Al-Nawawī 1977, 308.

[217] Ibn Qudāma 1994, 3:39–42.

[218] The Hanafis consider the marriage valid, and the remedy is to determine a fair dower for each woman (al-Marghīnānī 2006, 1:512). The Shafiʿis consider the marriage not valid: Ibn al-Naqīb al-Miṣrī 1999, 530; this Shafiʿi view is noted in al-Marghīnānī 2006, 1:512. *Shighār* also voids the marriage according to the Malikis, though a compensatory dower will be due if intercourse has transpired (Ibn ʿAbd al-Barr 1987, 238; Khalīl 1980, 109–110). See also Ḥillī 1999, 3:431, 478–479; Ibn Rushd 1994–1996, 2:67.

[219] Ibn Qudāma 1950, 183–184; al-Khiraqī 1982, 83.

[220] Ibn Taymiyya 1948, 2:175–176.

[221] Idem, 4:65–66.

[222] Al-Shaybānī 1969, 3:210–212. However, unrelated to the issue of stipulations, the *Hidāya* also states that a husband should not move his wife beyond a certain distance from her kin (al-Marghīnānī 2006, 1:523). This is an ethical guideline, not a legal restriction.

[223] Ibn Rushd 1994–1996, 2:69.

[224] Al-Nawawī, 1977, 308.

[225] Al-Muzanī 1993, 9:195–196; Ibn Rushd 1994–1996, 2:33–34; Ibn ʿAbd al-Rafīʿ 1989, 188; Khalīl 2004, 84 (Khalīl 1980, 109). The *Hidāya* allows this with a range of positions attributed to Abū Ḥanīfa and his two disciples (al-Marghīnānī 2006, 1:515–516).

[226] Al-Nawawī 1977, 308.

[227] Ibn Qudāma 1994, 3:40. Ibn Qudāma lists other stipulations which likewise have no effect on the marriage, such as that the wife will not be due dower or will return the dower to her husband, or that the husband will practice coitus interruptus (*ʿazl*, "withdrawal") or will apportion his time to her without giving her co-wife her due.

[228] Al-Shaybānī 1965, 3:210–212.

[229] Ibn ʿAbd al-Rafīʿ 1989, 277.

[230] A variant Maliki view, however, holds that the marriage is dissolved either before or after consummation, because the irregularity is basic to the contract. Ibn ʿAbd al-Rafīʿ 1989, 176. About dissolution on the basis of certain stipulations, Ibn Rushd says, "The consternation within the school over these matters is extensive" (Ibn Rushd 1994–1996, 2:70).

[231] See, for example, Ibn Taymiyya 1948, 4:70 where a husband proves unable to live up to his promise not to lodge his wife in his father's house.

[232] On the stipulation that a husband will support his wife's minor child, see Ibn ʿAbd al-Rafīʿ 1989, 205. According to the doctrine presented there, his agreement to do so is acceptable after the marriage, but not enforceable if it is attached to the marriage contract itself because of the uncertainty of what type of financial obligation he is agreeing to. The attention devoted to this topic suggests that rules prescribing that a mother who remarries automatically loses custody (*ḥaḍāna*) of her children were not always followed in practice; see Tucker 1998.

[233] Khalīl 1980, 111.

[234] Ibn ʿAbd al-Rafīʿ 1989, 203–204.

[235] I borrow the term "contingent" from Nyazee's usage in Ibn Rushd 1994–1996.

[236] Jurists have sometimes distinguished between *khulʿ* and other types of "ransoming" where the payment is more or less than the exact dower received, such as *ṣulḥ*, *fidya*, or *mubāraʾa*, defining *khulʿ* as a divorce where the wife returns the precise dower she received (or its value); *ṣulḥ* when she returns less than the full amount, *fidya* when she pays more, and *mubāraʾa* when she forgoes a claim she has against him or when the spouses mutually relinquish all claims on one another. See Ibn Rushd 1994–1996, 2:79. However, on other occasions they are held to be synonymous. Ibn Qudāma 1994, 3:95 defines *khulʿ* as "a husband separating from his wife for a countervalue," and Ibn al-Naqīb al-Miṣrī (1999, 562) includes a similar definition. Khalīl (2004, 90) includes its extrajudicial nature in his definition: "repudiation with a countervalue and without a judge (*bilā ḥākim*)." As to whether a khulʿ can be contracted without compensation, there has been disagreement. The dominant Hanbali view is that *khulʿ* without compensation but where *ṭalāq* is mentioned is a revocable *ṭalāq*. Al-Khiraqī holds that *khulʿ* is valid without a countervalue (1982, 91); see also Ibn Qudāma 1994, 3:95).

[237] Ibn al-Naqīb al-Miṣrī 1999, 562–563; this point is mostly taken for granted. Both Pakistan (1961) and Egypt (2000) allow a wife to obtain *khulʿ* without her

husband's consent by applying to a judge and returning her dower. See Esposito with DeLong-Bas 2001.

[238] *Faskh* may also be annulment, as with discovery of an impediment to marriage between the "spouses" or a significant defect in bride or groom.

[239] These defects typically include diseases such as leprosy and conditions in either party's sexual organs that make intercourse impossible. See al-Nawawī 1977, 299–300; Ibn Rushd 1994–1996, 2:59–60; Ibn Qudāma 1950, 184–185; Ibn Taymiyya 1948, 4:59–60, 86, 91; al-Muzanī 1993, 9:189, 191; Ibn ʿAbd al-Rafīʿ 1989, 222–223, 228–231; Ḥillī 1999, 3:531–540.

[240] See Calder 1988, 216.

[241] The post-divorce *ʿidda* is to determine if the wife is pregnant. If she is pregnant, it ends with her giving birth. Otherwise, it normally lasts three menstrual cycles or, in a female too old or young to menstruate, three months. On the *ʿidda*, see, e.g., Ibn al-Naqīb al-Miṣrī 1999, 566–571. A widow's normal waiting period is four months and ten days. In case of pregnancy, jurists disagree over whether the widow's *ʿidda* ends with birth or whether she must observe the full term in any case.

[242] Ibn Qudāma 1994, 3:148; al-Khiraqī 1982, 95; Ibn al-Naqīb al-Miṣrī 1999, 564–565.

[243] See Ibn Rushd 1994–1996, 2:101–103 for an overview.

[244] According to Ibn Qudāma, intercourse effects a return whether or not the husband intends to take back his wife (Ibn Qudāma 1994, 3:149).

[245] Ibn al-Naqīb al-Miṣrī 1999, 565; al-Khiraqī 1982, 95.

[246] Witnesses are not required for validity by the Shafiʿis (Ibn al-Naqīb al-Miṣrī 1999, 565). Ibn Qudāma reports two opposing views on whether witnesses are necessary (1994, 3:148). Al-Khiraqī prefers the view requiring witnesses but reports a second view of Ibn Ḥanbal that witnesses are not necessary (1982, 95). Generally, on taking back a wife, see al-Marghīnānī 2006, 2:6–8.

[247] This is so well known that it is not usually stated in these terms. For an exception, see Ibn Qudāma 1994, 3:147. In an unconsummated marriage the husband has no right to take her back following a single repudiation (*ṭalāq*) but she need not contract and consummate an intervening marriage for remarriage to the original husband to be lawful.

[248] The requirement of remarriage is Qurʾanic; the requirement that the intervening marriage be consummated is usually attributed to Sunna. For a summary, see Ibn Rushd 1994–1996, 2:103–104.

[249] For a basic discussion of contingent repudiation, see, e.g., Ibn Qudāma 1950, 203–205; al-Marghiīnānī 2006, 1:607–613; Ibn Rushd 1994–1996, 2:93–97.

[250] This example is from Ibn al-Naqīb al-Miṣrī 1999, 561. Shafiʿis make an exception for forgetfulness or compulsion (e.g., if a husband declares a *ṭalāq* if he does a certain act and then performs it unthinkingly).

[251] For a controversial minority Maliki view in which certain contingent *ṭalāq* oaths become effective immediately, see Ibn Rushd 1994–1996, 2:94–95.

[252] See Zomeño in this volume.

[253] Al-Muzanī 1993, 9:202.

[254] Ibn Qudāma 1950, 203. This poses less of a problem for women attempting to attach stipulations to their marriage contracts under Hanbali law since it is generally favorable to stipulations.

[255] Ḥillī 1999, 4:53. Ḥillī also stresses that *ṭalāq* takes effect only in valid marriages; if the marriage is irregular (*fāsid*), then dissolution happens without *ṭalāq*.

[256] Ibn Rushd 1994–1996, 2:100.

[257] Al-Marghīnānī 2006, 1:607; see also al-Shaybānī 1965, 3:289–298, 305. However, the Hanafi authorities do not allow future delegation (*tafwīḍ*); see Ibn ʿĀbidīn 1994, 4:98. The Hidāya does not discuss future *tafwīḍ*.

[258] Only the fear of fornication if a man is unable to marry serves to release him from this type of oath. Ibn ʿAbd al-Rafīʿ 1989, 195.

[259] Al-Marghīnānī 2006, 1:607. See al-Shaybānī 1965, 3:289–293, which has section titles including "The man says, 'Every woman that I marry from such-and-such tribe is triply, absolutely repudiated"; 293–298, "The man says, 'Every woman I marry alongside you is absolutely repudiated"; 305, "The man says, 'Every woman I marry while so-and-so lives is absolutely divorced."

[260] The man in such a case cannot simply pay *kaffāra* and keep the new wife; the new marriage would be void.

[261] Al-Shaybānī 1965, 3:305. Ibn ʿAbd al-Rafīʿ 1989, 195.

[262] This would be true even if he divorced his current wife. This is the case unless the man swears that by his oath he only intended to bind himself while remaining married to his current wife; in that case, his word is accepted and the oath is not binding on him. Ibn ʿAbd al-Rafīʿ 1989, 195.

[263] For example, according to Maliki doctrine, if a wife induces her husband to swear that if he marries again she will be divorced, she will in fact be divorced if he marries another woman. But the divorce will only be single, and he may take her back, even without her consent. Moreover, the effect of the oath has been expended, and besides remaining married to the second woman, he may even marry additional wives. This is the case unless the original oath included language to the effect of "every time" he married again. See Ibn ʿAbd al-Rafīʿ 1989, 198.

[264] Saḥnūn al-Tanūkhī 1323H, 2:197. Ibn ʿAbd al-Rafīʿ 1989, 189, 190–191, 201.

[265] See, e.g., Ḥillī 1999, 4:51–52. On agency in divorce in general, see Ibn al-Naqīb al-Miṣrī 1999, 557.

[266] An extensive form of this right, setting forth for the wife a permanent and unabridgeable right to divorce herself as part of the marriage contract, has become known colloquially as *ʿiṣma* and is legally allowed in Egypt and elsewhere. *ʿIṣma* is a means of obtaining a wife-initiated divorce outside of the *khulʿ* and *faskh* mechanisms, giving a wife an efficient way out of a marriage that she no longer wants. It essentially equates husband and wife with regard to divorce—she has *ʿiṣma*, he retains the right of *ṭalāq*—and for this reason it is disallowed by those (few) early jurists who discuss the concept at all. In her article "Rethinking Women and Islam," Amira Sonbol states that the Qurʾan talks about the *ʿiṣma* or marriage bond, knot, or tie being held in someone's hand in Qurʾan 2:237 (the citation to 3:237 is a typographical error) (Sonbol 2001, 129). The Qurʾanic phrase here is *ʿuqdat al-nikāḥ*; the term *ʿiṣma* appears, with a similar meaning, in the plural in Qurʾan 60:10. When medieval commentators and legists debated the meaning of the phrase "the one in whose hand is the marriage 'tie'," they were not attempting to ascertain whether it was the husband or the wife but rather the husband or the

wife's father (e.g., al-Khiraqī 1982, 89, identifying it as the husband). For mention of *ʿiṣma* in modern Egypt, see Shaham 1999; Human Rights Watch 2004, 16–19; Ahmed 1999, 132 (mentioning that one of her mother's cousins negotiated an *ʿiṣma* clause in her marriage contracts and used it twice); Badran 1995, 130 (but curiously relating it to polygyny). For the Sudan, see Badri 1989.

[267] The Malikis place limits on the wife's scope of action with regard to the number of divorces she may pronounce and their revocability, as they do with delegated divorce in general. A wife has more protection if the contingent delegated divorce is pronounced as part of the marriage contract and if it explicitly states that she is allowed to repudiate herself absolutely or however much she wishes. According to the *Muʿīn al-ḥukkām*, if the contingent delegated divorce is included in the contract and the wife is allowed to repudiate herself absolutely or however much she wishes, her husband may not later deny the number of divorces on the grounds that he intended to grant her control over a limited number of divorces. However, if he has voluntarily agreed to the contingent delegated divorce at some point after the conclusion of the original contract, then he may deny her the right to any repudiation over one. Thus, if he has not repudiated her twice in the interim, then her divorce of herself will be revocable at his discretion. Ibn ʿAbd al-Rafīʿ 1989, 190–191.

[268] In most cases, delegated divorces are irrevocable in Hanafi doctrine. See, e.g., al-Marghīnānī 2006, 1:594. There are a number of nuances surrounding the precise formulae involved; see idem, 594–596.

[269] Hanafis consider the husband's command "Divorce yourself" an oath (*yamīn*) and therefore not subject to being withdrawn by the husband before the wife acts; the wife retains the right until the end of the session (al-Marghīnānī 2006, 1:600). This is unlike the grant of agency to an unrelated individual, where the agency can be withdrawn before it is used (idem, 1:601); it also differs from a man giving one wife the delegated power to divorce another of his wives (idem, 1:600).

[270] Idem, 1:600–601, 603.

[271] Idem, 1:603–604; see also broader discussion of "kullamā" in oaths at 1:608.

[272] Al-Marghīnānī 2006, 1:593.

[273] The *Hidāya* has an extensive discussion of dealing with *ikhtiyār, takhyīr*, putting her "affair in her hand," *mashīʾa* (divorce at will), and the relationship of these forms to *wakāla* or agency. Al-Marghīnānī 2006, 1:593–600. Idem, 1:596–599.

[274] Ibn Qudāma 1994, 3:118.

[275] Al-Khiraqī 1982, 93.

[276] Ibn Qudāma 1994, 3:118.

[277] Idem, 3:119.

[278] Idem, likewise where her affair is placed in her hand; al-Khiraqī 1982, 93.

[279] Hallaq 1997, 210–211; An-Na'im 2002; Esposito with DeLong-Bas 2001; see also Hallaq 2004.

[280] Women Living Under Muslim Laws (www.wluml.org) is an important transnational organization; see Shaheed 1994. The Malaysian group Sisters in Islam has been influential both nationally and internationally.

# *Two*

## THE WESTERN CANON LAW OF MARRIAGE: A DOCTRINAL INTRODUCTION

Charles Donahue, Jr.

I have been handed an impossible brief.[1] I have been asked to summarize the legal doctrine concerning marriage in western canon law, in ten pages. The notion is—and it is a notion with which I heartily agree—that the readers of this book might obtain comparative insights from such a summary. The problem, however, is that although the readers of this book are all interested in marriage in Islam, the range of topics in which they are interested is breathtakingly wide. Some are interested in history, some in a wide variety of contemporary situations. Some are interested in doctrine, be it legal or religious or both; some in praxis. Some are interested in understanding historical or contemporary praxis, some in reforming contemporary praxis. Parallel sets of interests and topics exist in the study of marriage in Christianity and of the canon law of marriage, each one of which might prove fruitful for comparative discussion, but if I attempted to deal with the law as it was, as it is, as it was applied, as it is applied, and as it might be reformed, I would have exhausted my space in this volume before I had covered even half of the first topic.

So I will have to make a leap: My impression is that the most frequently made comparative statement about the Christian law of marriage, on the one hand, and the Islamic (about which I must confess to know very little) or the Jewish (about which I know some, but not much, more), on the other, is that marriage is a sacrament in Christianity but it is not in Islam or Judaism. The statement is usually made by those who want to argue that comparative work of this kind is fruitless, and the statement is made on both sides of the equation. The student of Christian marriage will say that he or she need not look to Islam or Judaism (except perhaps to the latter as a forerunner of Christianity), because marriage is a sacrament in Christianity and not in Islam or Judaism, and the student of marriage in Islam or Judaism will say the same thing only in reverse. I have already said that I disagree with the result of that position; I do not think that the sacramentality of marriage in Christianity means that fruitful comparisons cannot be made between marriage in Christianity and marriage in Islam, but I will not argue that position here. What I will do instead is to try to be a bit more precise about what Christians have meant in the past (and, to the extent that they still say it, mean today) when they say that marriage is a sacrament and to try to sketch briefly what effect that might have had on the development of the canon law of marriage. It will be for the reader to decide whether these differences make the canon law of marriage an inappropriate topic for comparative study.

Even this topic is too broad. Many Protestants today deny the sacramentality of marriage, and some deny that they have a canon law. I cannot pursue the effect of those denials. The facts, however, that the first seems to have had relatively little effect on the canon law of those Protestant churches which retained a canon law and that neither denial seems to have radically affected the functional equivalent of canon law in those churches that deny that they have a canon law is part of the reason for my belief that the sacramentality of marriage does not mean that it is useless to compare marriage in Christianity with marriage in those religions that do not have the concept of the sacramentality of marriage. Perhaps an even more important exclusion is that I cannot pursue the question of the practical or religious effect of the doctrines that I will be discussing. From all periods in Christian history there is some evidence as to those effects; for the recent periods the amount of evidence is truly massive. Those who are interested in praxis would find much here of comparative interest, but what I cover in this essay is, I believe, an essential prerequisite for making the comparison.

## Marriage in the New Testament

So what do Christians mean when they say, to the extent that they do say, that marriage is a sacrament? They have meant different things at different times. There is little doubt, however, that the application of the word "sacrament" to marriage can be traced back to a passage in a letter to the Ephesians attributed to St. Paul that is one of the books in what Christians call the New Testament (Eph 5:21–33). In its general outlines this passage has many parallels, not only in Paul (Col 3:18) but also in the letter ascribed to Peter (1 Pet 3). While Peter and Paul both preached the fundamental freedom and fundamental equality of all Christians, they also preached obedience, of all to civil authority, of slaves to masters, and of wives to husbands. In the case of slavery and of civil authority there are a few hints, but only a few, that the counsel was one of prudence. But there are no such suggestions in the case of husband and wife. What we get instead is a set of parallel but not quite equal obligations: wives be subject to your husbands, husbands love your wives. Only in one place, in Ephesians, does Paul, or one of his disciples, go further. "He who loves his wife," the author of Ephesians tells us, "loves himself. For no one ever hates his own body, but he nourishes it and tenderly cares for it, just as Christ does for the church, because we are members of his body." Here he ties the obligation of obedience and love into the passage in Genesis (2:24) about the relation of husband and wife: "For this reason a man shall leave his father and mother and be joined to his wife and the two will become one flesh." "This is a great mystery," our writer continues, "and I am applying it to Christ and the church."

The source of this extraordinary analogy between the relationship of husband and wife and the relationship of Christ and church is the Hebrew Bible. Israel is the bride of the Lord in much prophetic writing (e.g., Hosea 1:2; Isaiah 62:5). But the author of Ephesians goes quite a bit further: just as the bride is bathed before marriage, so a Christian is baptized to become the bride of Christ. Just as Christ sacrificed himself for the church to make her holy, so the husband should sacrifice himself for his wife. Just as the church obeys Christ, so the wife should obey the husband. Just as Christ loves the church, so the husband should love the wife. The union of husband and wife, our author then tells us, is a great mystery, but he is saying that it applies to Christ and the church. The word that I have translated as "mystery" was translated into Latin as *sacramentum*, "sacrament," something that came to be important when Christians began to define what were the sacraments of the church. (I am not saying that this was a mistranslation. The eastern church, which keeps the word *mystérion* in the original Greek, developed a theology of the mysteries substantially parallel to the theology of the sacraments in the west.)

## The New Testament on Divorce

Before we get to the subsequent development, however, we must look at what else the New Testament has to say about marriage. The synoptic gospels, three New Testament books that summarize the life and teachings of Jesus, report a saying (*logion* to use the technical vocabulary) of Jesus about divorce. The saying occurs once in Mark and Luke and twice in Matthew (Mk 10:11–12; Lk 16:18; Mt 5:32; Mt 19:9) in various forms, but the base textual form seems to be "A man who divorces his wife and marries another is guilty of adultery." The first letter of Paul to the Corinthians, which is earlier than any of the Gospel texts, does not quote the *logion* but says something quite close, "A man must not send his wife away," and says that the statement is "from the Lord." (1 Cor 7:11.) Now what can we make of this as historians? This base text is probably as close as we are going to get to what Jesus said. There seem to have been oral and then written collections of "sayings of the Lord" compiled in the very early church. The presence of this saying in all three synoptics and its reflection in First Corinthians make it virtually certain that this was among those early sayings.

If this is the saying, what could it have meant to Jesus's hearers? Nothing less than a prohibition of divorce. In Jewish law, only the man could initiate a divorce, and adultery could only be committed by one who was married. The saying must mean that the divorce is invalid, for only then could the man's remarrying be adulterous.[2]

What did the early church do with this saying? First, and perhaps most notably, it applied it to women. The application to women is found in all our sources, including Paul, though the way in which it is applied varies: Paul (1 Cor 7:10–11): "A wife must not leave her husband—or if she leaves him, she must either remain unmarried or else make it up with her husband—nor must a husband send his wife away." We are still quite close here to the Jewish context. There is no suggestion here that a woman could give a bill of divorce. There is, however, a suggestion that in certain circumstances, unstated, separation without remarriage is permissible, at least for women. Mark (10:12): "If a woman divorces her husband and marries another she is guilty of adultery too." Mark's is generally thought to be a gospel for non-Jews. In the pagan world women could obtain a divorce and the *logion* is extended to them. Matthew 5 and Luke work the parallelism a bit differently (Mt 5:32; Lk 16:18). Both of them add that a man who marries a divorced woman is guilty of adultery too. Here, it is the man who is doing the divorcing (closer to the Jewish context), but the statement about adultery is applied to both the man who remarries and the man who marries the divorced woman.[3]

Matthew 5 and 19 also contain except clauses: "except for the case of fornication" (Mt 5:32) and "I am not speaking about fornication" (Mt 19:9). What do these clauses mean? The tendency among Protestants and Orthodox has been to take them literally as meaning that under some circumstances of which adultery is one, divorce and remarriage are permissible. I must be careful because I am committed to a tradition that does not read it this way, but if I think as an historian and not as a Roman Catholic, I can say three things about this: (1) We find the passage in the context of a story (of which more shortly) in which the question is posed: "Is it lawful for a man to divorce his wife for any cause?" (Mt 19:3; cf. Mk 10:2). If the answer to be taken is no, only for adultery, this is certainly an odd way of putting it. (2) *Porneia*, the Greek work translated as fornication, does not mean adultery. It is a general word for sexual immorality. In the Greek Bible it translates the Hebrew *zenût*, which can mean "adultery" but is also a generalized term for sexual immorality. It is at least possible that this clause is to be taken as referring to marriages that are invalid because they are incestuous, or are not marriages because they are concubinages. (3) Whatever the phrase means, the author of Matthew depicts the disciples as being shocked. If this is what the rule is, they say, then it is better not to marry (Mt 19:10). This is then followed by a *logion* in which Jesus says that there are those who make themselves eunuchs for the sake of the kingdom.

In order fully to understand what is going on in this passage about divorce we have to say a bit more about the context. Both Matthew and Mark put the *logion* in the context of a question posed by the Pharisees.

Matthew, a gospel generally thought to have been written for a community that contained large number of Jewish Christians, gives us more of the Jewish context. "Is it lawful for a man to divorce his wife for any cause?" (Mt 19:3). This was not the first time that that question had been posed. The *Mishna*, the collection of rabbinical rulings on the Jewish law, composed around 200 CE, tells us that the school of Shammai and the school of Hillel debated this question,[4] the school of Shammai taking the position that the only grounds for divorce were adultery and the school of Hillel, it would seem, taking the position that a man could give a bill of divorce for any fault that he found in his wife. Matthew is depicting the Pharisees as trying to see which side of the debate Jesus would take. He takes neither side. He says that what God has joined man must not divide, citing Genesis in preference to Deuteronomy, where the bill of divorce is authorized (Dt 24:1). "For this reason a man must leave his father and mother and cleave to his wife, and the two will become one flesh. So then, what God has united, man must not divide." (Mt 19:5–6.) Now if the except clauses in Matthew meant that divorce for adultery were permissible, there would have been nothing particularly notable about Jesus' ruling. He would simply have been taking Shammai's position in the debate. That he did not, but took a much more radical position, seems clear from the passage and its context.

There is one more passage in the New Testament on divorce: "If a brother has a wife who is an unbeliever, and she is content to live with him, he must not send her away [...]. However, if the unbelieving partner does not consent, they may separate; in these circumstances the brother or sister is not tied: God has called you to a life of peace" (1 Cor 7:12, 15). What this shows is that despite the univocal teaching of Jesus on the topic, Paul thought that he could create an exception. Whether the exception involves both divorce and remarriage or simply separation is hard to know. In favor of the former interpretation is the fact that divorce in the ancient world implied the freedom to remarry, so that when Paul means separation without remarriage,[5] he says so. On the other hand, Paul does not specifically say remarriage here, and the context of the passage focuses on whether it is possible for the Christian spouse to live with the pagan or Jewish spouse in peace. To say that Paul is speaking of the inherent dissolubility of non-sacramental marriages in favor of the faith is certainly to be anachronistic, but marriage in the Lord is a Pauline concept, as is the marked contrast between the flesh and the spirit. An interpretation of the *logion* to apply only to Christian marriages is not what Paul offers, but such an interpretation is consistent with Pauline thought.

## Marriage in Later Christian Writings

Although one could see how these passages might be used to develop a religious conception of marriage, they are far from giving one a full-scale law of marriage. For the first thousand years of the church's history no one, so far as we know, attempted to do so. Rather, Christian principles, such as indissolubility, at least under most circumstances, and certain religious rituals were grafted onto the secular law and customs of marriage, wherever the church happened to find itself.

These thousand years, of course, saw Christian writing about marriage. One author, in particular, St. Augustine of Hippo (d. 430), was to prove particularly influential on this topic, as on so many others. Perhaps Augustine's most important contribution to the theology of marriage (for he was not a lawyer in the modern sense and influenced the law only indirectly) was his development of the notion of the three "goods," as he called them, of marriage: *fides*, *proles*, and *sacramentum*, fidelity, offspring, and sacrament.[6] None of these goods is easy to define, but we probably would not be too wide of the mark if we associated the first both with monogamy and the prohibition of adultery, which by this time had been made gender-neutral in Christian thought; the second with the duty of parents to be open to children and to care for them if they came; and the third with the prohibition of divorce. The "sacrament" of marriage in Augustine's thought is associated with the indissoluble bond between husband and wife, at least if the husband and wife were baptized Christians. It is also clear in Augustine's thought that one could have one of the goods of marriage without the other two. In particular, the sacrament remained in a childless marriage in which the spouses were not faithful to each other.

A full-scale Christian law of marriage was developed in the twelfth century, when the church courts acquired exclusive jurisdiction over issues of the formation and dissolution of marriage. How this came about is a complicated story that I cannot tell here. It is to be connected with the reform movement of the eleventh century, with the revival of the study of Roman law and of canon law in Bologna at the beginning of the twelfth century, and with the fact that the church developed an up-to-date and, for its time, efficient set of tribunals. The result was an outpouring of legal literature and rulings on legal issues by the popes, particularly Alexander III (1159–1181) and Innocent III (1198–1215). In particular, Alexander III, after some hesitancy, issued a series of rulings on the topic of the formation of marriage that may be distilled into the following three rules.

First, present consent, freely given between parties capable of marriage, made a valid marriage. This marriage was indissoluble so long as the parties lived. This rule applied even if the marriage was unconsummated. While Alexander seems to have recognized a number of exceptions to the rule for unconsummated marriages, there ultimately came to be only one: An unconsummated present consent marriage was dissoluble if one of the parties to such a marriage wished to enter the religious life. Although theologians throughout the middle ages suggested that the Church had the power to dissolve unconsummated present consent marriages, it was not until the fifteenth century that the pope, hesitantly, began to grant dispensations from such marriages, and such dispensations were not at all common until after the council of Trent in the mid-sixteenth century.[7]

Second, future consent, freely given between parties capable of marriage, made an absolutely indissoluble marriage, if that consent was followed by sexual intercourse between the parties. The two ways of forming a valid marriage were combined, at least in doctrine, by the notion that intercourse following future consent raised a *de jure* presumption of present consent.

Third, with minor exceptions, any Christian man was capable of marrying any Christian woman provided: (1) that they both were over the age of puberty,[8] (2) that they were not too closely related to each other,[9] and (3) that neither had taken a solemn vow of chastity and that the man was not in major orders.[10] The rules about relationship were complicated, extending as they did to blood relatives, affines and spiritual relatives, but recent research would suggest that they were not so important practically as had once been thought.[11]

The most important thing about these rules is not what they require but what they do not require. Although couples were strongly encouraged to have their marriages solemnized, no solemnity or ceremony was necessary for the validity of marriage at any time between Alexander III in the late twelfth century and the council of Trent in 1563. Further, in an age characterized by arranged marriages and by requirements in the secular law that lords consent to the marriages of their vassals and serfs, classical canon law required the consent of no one other than the parties themselves for the validity of a marriage. Finally, in an age of class-consciousness, classical canon law imposed no barrier of status to marriages across classes.[12]

## Impact of Sacramentality on the Development of Canon Law

Now what, if anything, does all of this have to do with the sacramentality of marriage? Students of the history of canon law debate that question even today. The range of answers given varies from "virtually everything" to "virtually nothing." I cannot rehearse the debate here. Rather, I would like to give you the strongest form of the argument that I think is warranted by the evidence for the proposition that the development by Alexander's contemporaries and immediate predecessors of the idea of the sacramentality of marriage was a necessary, if not a sufficient condition, for the legal doctrine to have developed in the way that it did.

In the first place, it is an undeniable fact that we owe the notion that marriage is one of the seven sacraments of the church to Peter Lombard, a theologian who wrote about a decade before Alexander III became pope. Peter may not have been the first to state this doctrine, but he incorporated it in his *Sentences*, a basic textbook of theology that was used throughout the middle ages and into the early modern period. Peter also espoused the doctrine that marriages are made by present consent alone.[13] We cannot prove that Alexander knew Peter's work, but he certainly could have known it, and his espousal of a present consent doctrine in his marriage rulings is more likely to have been derived from Peter rather than to have arisen coincidentally.[14]

The question is what does this doctrine of the formation of marriage by present consent have to do with the sacramentality of marriage? To answer this question we should look at the work of Hugh of St. Victor, who wrote about a decade before Peter and whose work was known to Peter and perhaps to Alexander. Hugh writes:

> "Let a man leave his father and mother and cleave to his wife," [quoting Genesis 2:24] so that putting aside the old for the new that follows, he may come from the beginning through love and may rest in the end through love. You see now what sort and how great a sacrament conjugal love is, that in it the rational soul may learn to choose without end the consort of its end and cleave to that undivided bond of mutual love and that equality of individual love. This was the first cause of marriage, on account of which God instituted that leaving his father and mother, a man might choose to become sole and singular partner with his wife in an everlasting and undivided love. Afterwards he enjoined a duty on this partnership by reason of a sure and reasonable sacrament for the sake of multiplying future generations, not that marriage might consist of this, but so that from this, marriage might grow in worth and appear more fruitful in abundance of offspring. Rightly therefore is it said: "Let a man leave his father and mother and cleave to his wife and the two will be one flesh," so that as he cleaves to his wife there might be a sacrament of the invisible partnership that is to be made in the spirit between God and the soul, but so that as the two will be one flesh there might be a sacrament of the invisible communion that is made in the flesh between Christ and the Church. This therefore is a great sacrament, "the two will be one flesh," the sacrament of Christ and the Church, but this is a greater sacrament, "he two will be one heart, one love," the sacrament of God and the soul.[15]

What is Hugh's notion of a sacrament? Clearly, he is taking his definition from the false etymology that was current in his time. A sacrament is a *sacrum signum*, a holy sign. Hugh is less interested than were later theologians in what the effect of this sign was. (The council of Trent's definition of a sacrament, summing up theology from the thirteenth to the sixteenth century is that a sacrament is "a visible sign instituted by Christ to give grace.")[16] What Hugh is interested in is what marriage is a sign of. It is, of course, a sign of the union of Christ and the church. He has to say that: St. Paul had said it in the letter to the Ephesians. But quite daringly Hugh assumes that it is possible to add to the sacrament of Christ and the church proclaimed by St. Paul, another sacrament, one that is in some sense greater. Marriage is also the sign of the mutual love of God and soul. Hence, Hugh expounds an idea of the double sacramentality of marriage. That idea was to have considerable influence in the Middle Ages, and it finds striking echoes in some recent Christian theological writing on marriage.

What is the effect of this doctrine on the law? Here we must enter the realm of the speculative, but it seems relatively clear that a theology that sees in marriage a sign of the mutual yearning of the soul for God and of God for the soul would tend to emphasize, as Hugh does, the element of choice in marriage, and would tend to exclude the choice of anyone else as being relevant to the question of the formation of marriage. We can also see how if one divides, as Hugh does, the two phrases in the Genesis chapter into two sacraments, one might argue that leaving one's father and mother and joining with one's wife (particularly if one took the latter verb as not being a euphemism for sexual intercourse) might have one set of legal consequences, and that becoming one flesh might have another set of legal consequences. Finally, Hugh is speaking of a sacrament of the church. While he recognizes that the institution of marriage long antedates Christianity, it is relatively easy to see how those who followed his views could say that only those who had been baptized could be signs either of the yearning of God for the soul or the union of Christ and the church.

Theological thought on marriage went off in other directions in the succeeding centuries, and the law developed quite independently of it. But at this crucial moment in the mid-twelfth century, the theologians and the lawyers were still talking to one another. The consequences are with us to this day. The Code of Canon Law of the Roman Catholic Church of 1983 holds that a marriage exists between a couple capable of marriage if they presently consent to each other (though if they are Catholics, they normally have to do this in the presence of a priest and two witnesses). The consent of no one else is required. (Alexander's second way of forming a marriage—future consent plus intercourse—was abolished by the council of Trent.) Today, a marriage between baptized Christians is a "ratified marriage," but that marriage may be dissolved if it is not consummated. A marriage between the non-baptized which has been consummated is not a ratified marriage and may be dissolved, at least in some circumstances.

But, as canon 1141 says, "a ratified and consummated marriage cannot be dissolved by any human power or for any reason other than by death."

## Conclusion

The doctrine of the sacramentality of marriage probably did affect the development of the canon law of marriage. It can be seen in the emphasis that that law places on the consent of the couple, in the distinctions drawn between consummated and unconsummated marriages and between ratified and unratified marriages, and in the doctrine of the indissolubility of marriage. All of these doctrines, however, have other possible explanations, and I think it would unwise to conclude that the sacramentality of marriage provides a full explanation for them. For comparative purposes, the major doctrinal differences between the canon law of marriage and the Islamic would seem to be (to put it in terms of the canonic doctrines) monogamy, the prohibition of divorce, and the relative unimportance of the marriage contract (as opposed to the marriage itself), the family, and anything concerning property. Whether these major doctrinal differences make comparative study a fruitless exercise, or whether they make the possibility of comparative study even more interesting, is, as I suggested at the start, for readers to decide. I would hope that at least some of them will take a crack at it.

NOTES

[1] Although I have provided some references and made some stylistic changes, I have tried not to alter the tentative and exploratory nature of the lecture that was given at the conference. Hence, the references should be taken more as "suggestions for further reading" rather than exhaustive documentation. Support for much of what is said here (and disagreement with it) with substantial references will be found in Brundage 1987; Witte 1997; and Schillebeeckx 1965. Exploration of the modern Roman Catholic understanding of marriage is best begun with chapter 1 of part 2 of the dogmatic consitution on the church in the modern world (*Gaudium et spes*) of the Second Vatican Council (7 Dec. 1965), available in a number of translations (e.g., *Vatican Council II: The Conciliar and Post Conciliar Documents*, in Flannery 1975, 949–957). For the modern Roman Catholic canon law on the topic, see Beal, Coriden, and Green 2000, 1234–1399 (giving both the text and commentary). Support for most of what I say about the Bible can be found in Brown, Fitzmyer, and Murphy 1990. Translations from the Bible are based on the *New Jerusalem Bible* 1990, with occasional minor changes to make the language more familiar.

[2] Note that even here the notion of adultery is extended, since in Jewish law intercourse between a married man and an unmarried woman is not adultery.

[3] Matthew and Luke are generally thought not to be dependent on each other. That raises the possibility that the primitive form of the *logion* contained this statement about the man marrying the divorced woman.

[4] Hillel and Shammai feature prominently in the Mishna. They probably lived about a generation before Jesus. I explore the Jewish context of this passage in a bit more depth in "Genesis in Western Canon Law," in *Jewish Law Annual* 16 (2006), 164–167.

[5] As he clearly does in 1 Cor 7:12.

[6] Augustine's ideas are most easily explored in his *De bono coniugali*, edited and translated, most conveniently, in Walsh 2001.

[7] See Donahue 1976, 252 and n2.

[8] Now sixteen and fourteen under the Code of Canon Law (1983), canon 1083, with considerable discouraging in canons 1071 and 1072.

[9] Today, canons 1091–1092 prohibit the marriages of consanguines and affines in the direct line, siblings, and first cousins. Dispensations may be obtained for such marriages, except for those of consanguines in the direct line and siblings. Spiritual affinity (the relationship between godparent and godchild) has been abolished as an impediment to marriage.

[10] This is essentially the same today under canons 1087–1088.

[11] See, e.g., Helmholz 1974, 77–78.

[12] The closest that the developed classical law came was the impediment of error of person: If one married a serf thinking that he or she was free, the marriage could be annulled. See Donahue 1976, 274 and n82.

[13] Lombard 1971–1981, 421–435.

[14] On the difficult problem of the dating of Alexander's decretals, see Donahue 1982, 70–124, with references.

[15] *De beatae Mariae virginitate* c. 1, in Migne 1880, 176.862–864.

[16] This is a catechism definition that summarizes Council of Trent, sess. 7 (1547), *Canones de sacramentis in genere*, canons 1–12, in, e.g., Alberigo 1982, 684–685.

# *Three*

## JEWISH MARRIAGE AND DIVORCE LAW

Suzanne Last Stone

The field of family law provides a rich opportunity to understand a given society because it focuses on how that society conceives of the most fundamental relationships between humans. In a religious society that views law as originating in the revealed word of God, family law takes on additional significance. Here, the relation between husband and wife is often viewed as a mirror or extension of the ideal relationship between God and man. This religious dimension of family law imbues human relationships with symbolic value, but it also heightens the tension that may arise between the ideal religio-legal relation posited by tradition and new social conditions. In the field of family law, no new condition of society has posed so profound a tension between tradition and innovation as the increased awareness of the status of women in the society. "Of all law," it has been said, "family law is the most conservative."[1] Given the tendency toward conservatism of religion as well, one would expect to find that changes in the family law of a traditional religious society, in response to new perceptions of the status of women, will be gradual and slow. Over time, however, these changes often result in a complete transformation of the law. In the case of the Jewish religio-legal tradition, a tradition over two millennia old, adjustments in the laws of marriage and divorce are almost exclusively related to the issue of the status of women. Indeed, these adjustments, taken together over time, have transformed the nature of marriage and divorce. Marriage, originally conceived as the acquisition of the wife, came to be viewed as a contractual relationship rooted in sanctification. Divorce, once the exclusive prerogative of the husband who could banish his wife on whim, became a regime of mutual consent.

These changes in Jewish family law raise two interesting methodological questions. The first is jurisprudential. Is Jewish family law properly characterized as religious law, divinely-mandated, and thus in theory subject only to the limited forms of adaptation and adjustment that the divine law itself countenances, or is it civil law, the customs of a given national entity, and hence, in theory, subject to broad modification? The second is historical. Were the changes wrought in Jewish laws of marriage and divorce natural outgrowths of internal tendencies embedded within the tradition itself or the result of exposure to other cultures and environments? In other words, do changes reflecting increased sensitivity to the status of women or changed conceptions of the nature of marriage, which have parallels in the surrounding societies in which Jews found themselves, "reflect the underlying unity of mankind, which tends to react in similar ways to identical social conditions," or reflect direct cultural exchange?[2] These two methodological issues, the jurisprudential and historical, intersect. For example, even if Jewish family law is secular law, in the sense of the civil law of a given nation, does the national element provide a further ground for resistance to change—to preserve a distinctive national identity? These methodological questions, which I shall address obliquely throughout this essay, are not merely academic. They lie at the core of the controversy raging today over the proper scope and role of Jewish family law in modern secular societies, both in Israel and in the West.

The primary aim of this essay is to acquaint those unfamiliar with the Jewish legal tradition with the broad features of Jewish marriage and divorce law as it has developed over time. Because a full appreciation of the development of Jewish family law is inextricably bound up with the question of the religious, civil, or national status of the various laws, I shall begin with a brief introduction to the mixed nature of the Jewish religio-legal tradition itself, continuing with a description and discussion of Jewish marriage and divorce law. Specifically relevant to this book, I include a discussion of the role of the marriage contract itself in Jewish marriage law. Next, I address in some detail modern complications surrounding classical Jewish divorce law, and reform efforts aimed at these laws. Finally, I conclude with some brief remarks about the contemporary status of and outlook for Jewish family law, given the increasingly secular culture in which it is now set.

## I. The Nature of Jewish Religious Law

One is accustomed in the west to drawing a sharp distinction between religious law, the proper domain of the church, and civil law, the domain of the secular political authority. This sharp distinction is, however, a product of the history of Christianity. Whether an analogous distinction between religious and civil law exists within the Jewish legal tradition is a difficult and important question. The laws of marriage and divorce do have features of both religious and civil law. But it is crucial to understand this point first in terms internal to the tradition, and only then go on to translate that understanding into language employing the terms "civil" and "religious" as defined by western models.

### A. *The Western Idea of the Secular*

The western idea of the secular realm of law derives largely from Christian theology and experience and the legacy of Roman law. The religious, including religious law, is associated with the sacred, numinous realm of the spirit, while the secular governs the mundane and political spheres of life. This distinction is implied by the Christian division between God and Caesar, between the city of God and the city of earth, and between spirit and body.[3] One can trace its genesis to the Jewish-Christian schism over the continued validity of the law as a means to achieve salvation. The Pauline devaluation of performance of the law as the primary means of spiritual expression paved the way for the eventual liberation of large areas of human concern, those of the mundane world, from ecclesiastical regulation. The Protestant Reformation is a logical culmination of this framework. In Martin Luther's division between the heavenly kingdom of grace and faith and the earthly kingdom of sin and death, all law belongs to the earthly kingdom. Law has a "political use," to deter misconduct, and a "theological use," to remind people of their obligations. But faith alone justifies the individual. Hence, the western distinction, entrenched in Anglo-American legal and political philosophy, between the public sphere of law and the private sphere of faith, worship, and conscience.

A second theme is the association of the religious with divine law—the moral, ethical, or ritual precepts that guide right conduct—and the secular with human political activity and coercive institutions. This distinction, fostered by the reintroduction of Roman law into western Christendom is captured in the Roman view: *fas lex divina, ius lex humana est.*[4] The human law, *ius*, is binding law and enforced by human agencies; the divine law, *fas*, is neither enforced nor enforceable by human agencies.

With the Enlightenment, the American and French revolutions, and the rise of the ideology of nationalism, the idea of secular law assumes yet another dimension reminiscent of the ancient distinction between customary and natural law. Each nation has a *lex patriae*, a law that reflects its national, cultural genius and that is a repository of the nation's vision and political ideals.[5] Religion and religious law reflect universal truths; the secular law is the product of a particular culture.

B. *The Judaic Understanding of Law and Religion*

Judaism, in contrast, is an integrated system of religious and national law.[6] The term "religion" is absent from its lexicon. The closest analogue is "*dat*," the feminine form of the word "*din*," meaning custom, law, or judgment. It implies the law given by God to a particular people, Israel. Secular law is simply the law of other nations or polities—whether that law is promulgated by an ecclesiastical or civil body (as, from the perspective of Judaism, ecclesiastical laws are no more divine than laws promulgated by parliaments).[7] In short, the religious is the entirety of Jewish law; the secular is all other forms of law.

In the biblical presentation, God is both king and legislator and man his servant and subject, a form of worship immediately conceived in legal-political terms. The people of Israel enter into a covenant with God, a contractual relationship in perpetuity, the essence of which is Israel's promise to obey the law revealed to them by God at Sinai. Observance of the laws of the Torah are the means by which the people are transformed into a holy nation of priests. To this end, the laws are educative and spiritual as well as mundane and political. They address every aspect of individual, social, and public life, through a system of negative and positive duties owed both to God and to other persons.

Thus, the western distinction between the religious and the secular expressed in terms of two realms, the sacred and the mundane, the spiritual and the temporal, the heavenly and the earthly, or, much later, the private sphere of faith and conscience and the public sphere of law, is combined in the Jewish model under the general concept of law. Laws of property and obligations are laws no different from those prescribing sacrifices, holiday observance, or prayer.

To be sure, the rabbis recognize the subject-matter distinction between laws that govern the relations of persons inter se and laws that govern the relations between God and humans. Although this distinction is used as a classification device, there is no special importance, whether conceptual or methodological, attached to these two categories. Both categories contain laws whose origins are traced to biblical revelation and tradition as well as to rabbinic legislation and judicial development. Legal principles, such as laws of agency, are derived from analysis of the laws of the paschal sacrifice and applied to family law and the law of obligations. Obligations between God and man are formulated as legal norms: defined in juridical terms, in a manner such that the legal subject can perform his or her duties. Thus, as Justice Silberg has written, "both types of law involve the structuring of legal patterns of relationships, whether between man and man or between man and God. As a result of this obliteration of boundaries, the entire range of religious practice is embraced within a network of purely juridical concepts."[8]

Moreover, both categories are enforceable by human agencies. A Jewish court may compel performance of a religious obligation, such as building a tabernacle on the Sukkot holiday, and may punish infractions of religious rules. Not only is the same juridical approach applied to the law of loans applied to the laws of sacrifices, but the same ethical and moral concerns expressed in the talmudic literature are applied to both.[9]

There is also no easy distinction in Jewish law between divine law and human law. The entirety of the Halakha (the body of Jewish law) is divine in that its source is in the divine revelation at Sinai of the written and oral law. The authority to determine, apply, and elaborate the law judicially and legislatively, including the authority to determine the content and meaning of biblical revelation or to temporarily annul biblical law, is given to human authority. This complex interplay between religion and law is particularly evident in the Halakha's relationship to matters of belief. The

Halakha views performance of the commandments as, ideally, undertaken freely and there is a persistent tension in the tradition, beginning in the Talmud, over the validity of a religious act that is coerced. Obedience to the law because it is the command of God is critical for the full realization of the legal obligation; nevertheless, the Talmud rules that the law must be performed even if such intention is lacking. Later authorities argue that this ruling is based on the idea that coercion serves to bring about "inner consent," an internal change in the heart of the person coerced, revealing his or her true desire to achieve religious atonement or remain a member of the religious community.

That such coercion is, in theory, acceptable underscores the national aspect of Jewish law. Until the modern era, the concepts of Jewish people-hood, Jewish governance, and Jewish religion were inseparable. In rabbinic thought, the messianic vision is also political: the restoration of sovereignty to the Jewish people, living as one nation in its land under Torah law. The national aspect of the law is not limited to conventional conditions of sovereignty, however. The biblical theme of Jewish nation-hood is described not only in terms of the establishment of Israel as a divinely ordained polity pursuant to the political and social program of the Torah, but also as the divine reward for Israel's attaining its spiritual goal of becoming a holy nation of priests. From the perspective of the tradition, no Jew can opt out of this collective project. The law does not even recognize conversion as an effective severance of these bonds. And, historically, Jews understood themselves to be a nation even in exile, and their principal means of national expression to be the law.

What, then, is the relationship of Jewish law to the secular law of the nations in which Jews historically have lived? The Bible stresses that the law is the particular inheritance of Israel and only Israel is bound by its precepts. Not only is Jewish law the exclusive province of Jews, obedience to the laws of other nations is generally prohibited as an abhorrence to God and an act of disloyalty. Thus, there is a parallelism between the biblical view of idolatry as the worship of the gods of other nations—an act of disloyalty—and the biblical view that following the laws of other nations is treachery. The biblical view is continued in later rabbinic admonitions to study Jewish law exclusively rather than seek knowledge of non-Jewish jurisprudence and in the rabbinic injunction against litigating in non-Jewish tribunals, even where the laws are substantially the same as Jewish law.[10]

Yet, the attitude of Jewish law to the laws of other polities is not solely negative. Although Jewish law is obligatory only for Jews, Jewish law contains within it a doctrine of universalism that sets forth the legal obligations of non-Jews. Non-Jews are obligated to obey the seven Noahide laws, one of which, *dinin*, consists of the obligation to establish a system of law in order to preserve the social order.[11] Secular law—the legal order of other nations—is thus imbued with a special dignity. Early on, the rabbis adopted the principle that "the law of the kingdom is the law."[12] Jews are obligated, as a matter of Jewish law, to obey the decrees of the foreign, secular authority. According to one rationale, this principle is based on the Noahide obligation to enact a system of civil laws,[13] and it provides a basis not only for accommodation to conditions of exile but also for interaction between Jewish law and the law of other nations. As one authority holds, because the laws of the secular authority are valid instantiations of the Noahide command, non-Jewish "governments may legislate laws and methods of acquisition and they are effective between two Jews."[14]

This principle applies only to a particular class of laws, however. This limitation sheds light on the category of Jewish legal obligation that approximates the western notion of civil law.[15] Jewish law distinguishes between "laws of prohibition and permission," referred to by some as religious command, and *dinei mammona*, monetary law, which generally deals with the legal relationships between private parties. Included in this category are contracts, debts, torts, and the like. With respect to the latter, parties ordinarily may "stipulate out of a law contained in the Torah."[16] In other words, the parties are free to vary even divine biblical law through private ordering. The power to vary such laws is based on the right of a party to forego private claims. "One may waive one's rights, inasmuch as the Torah established such obligations only if desired by the obligee."[17] Many questions that conventional legal systems would classify as civil, however, raise issues of religious prohibition and permission in Jewish law and will not be treated as monetary law. Thus, while the concepts of religious prohibition and permission, on the one hand, and monetary law, on the other, do not coincide with western notions of the religious and the secular, the distinctions that the Halakha itself recognizes between these two categories provides a rough analogy to religious versus civil law.

The question then arises: How extensive is the right of parties to supplant Jewish monetary law with the laws of other nations? Rabbinic authorities have turned to secular law to cure gaps in Jewish law, where fair and equitable in arbitrating the conflicting claims of individual disputants. But the wholesale displacement of Jewish monetary law by foreign law is viewed as tantamount to the destruction of the religio-national core of the law. In short, the duty to preserve the law as a unique national heritage, by avoiding unnecessary resort to foreign law even when technically permissible, is inseparable from the religious obligation to obey the law.

## II. Jewish Marriage and Divorce Law

The laws of betrothal, marriage and divorce are *sui generis* in that they consist of matters of religious prohibition and permission, such as prohibited unions between a Jew and non-Jew or a priest and a divorced woman, as well as monetary matters, laws concerning spousal support and property disposition. In rabbinic terminology, marriage and divorce are matters of prohibition and permission that partly impinge upon monetary law. It is with respect to the institutions of marriage and divorce that the rabbinic view of Jewish law as religious, in contrast to non-Jewish law, which is secular, is most evident. Thus, the talmudic rabbis compare Jewish marriage and divorce to marriage and divorce in the surrounding pagan culture, commenting that in Jewish law marriage and divorce are religious law, whereas in non-Jewish societies such institutions are civil.[18]

A. *Betrothal and Marriage*

Betrothal (*erusin*) is the preliminary and most critical element in the formation of the marriage union. Betrothal has characteristics of both a contractual relationship and an acquisition. It is contractual in that it requires the consent of both parties, but it is effectuated through an act of acquisition of the wife by the husband. In the biblical sources, the acquisition is instantaneous. The father of the groom pays the father of the bride a bride-price (*mohar*), in money or in service. And the act of marriage is simply called a "taking."[19] Although the consent of the bride is required, the families negotiate the marriage and only afterwards seek her consent. In the post-biblical period, however, the contractual element becomes dominant, stressing "the two elements that characterize a contract rather than an acquisition: futurity and consent."[20] The bride-price is transformed into a lien against the husband's property to be paid to the woman either upon divorce or the death of the husband. The extent to which a woman's consent is actual rather than formal, however, varies with time and place. Although it is technically feasible for a father to arrange a marriage for a minor daughter, such arrangements are generally limited to historical periods and situations in which girls of marriageable age are at risk unless affianced.[21] A minor girl may emancipate herself from the marriage until she reaches her majority by declaring "I do not want my husband."[22] Maimonides recognizes the legality of such marriages but instructs that they are in violation of rabbinic precepts.[23] According to him, the daughter must first mature and then declare: "He is the one I want."[24] Finally, the acquisition itself becomes increasingly symbolic.

Although in this period the betrothal takes the form of a contractual relationship, it differs from ordinary contractual understandings in two ways. First, the methods of acquisition for betrothal cannot be varied by the parties. The betrothal must include a formulaic declaration by the bridegroom that the bride is betrothed to the husband in accordance with the laws of Moses and the community of Israel.[25] This betrothal formula must be witnessed by two scrupulously religious Jewish males in accordance with general Jewish testimonial law. The methods of acquisition are detailed in the Mishna, which declares that the woman may be acquired "in three ways . . . by money, by contract, and by intercourse"[26]—that is, through the conveying of something of value to the bride, the writing of a deed, or a single act of cohabitation. Acquisition through payment of money, which the School of Hillel stipulated need be only a penny, recalls the biblical practice of a bride-price, while acquisition through intercourse reflects an ancient custom disapproved of by the rabbinic sages, who viewed it as tantamount to prostitution and deserving of flogging.[27] Indeed, to counter this custom, during the Second Temple period, the rabbis stipulated that a blessing was to be recited at the betrothal "forbidding [to the groom] the betrothed and permitting only the married."[28] Thus, personal relations between the couple could only take place once the actual marriage ceremony took place.

More significantly, the betrothal described here differs from that of the modern conception in that the betrothal is not an agreement to contract a marriage at a future date. The betrothal is part of the marital status. As Zev Falk points out, "the Jewish marriage covenant was instituted by stages and the betrothal can be defined as an 'inchoate' marriage."[29] After the betrothal, the bride is deemed to be the wife of the bridegroom for all purposes of biblical law, both forbidden to any other man and requiring a divorce or death to end the union, even though she may continue to reside in her father's house and is forbidden to cohabit with the groom until the wedding takes place. Betrothal alone does not give rise to the mutual rights and duties that exist between husband and wife, such as financial support as well as cohabitation. The complete change in the personal status of the bride and groom only occurs after the wedding proper, the *nissu'in*. This actual marriage consists of the recital of seven blessings over the couple, who stand under the bridal canopy, and then the withdrawal of the couple into seclusion, which symbolizes consummation. In both the Bible and the Talmud, betrothal and marriage are two distinct temporal stages in the union of the couple. By the eleventh century, betrothal and marriage had become fused into one temporal event, first among the German and French communities, and slowly in nearly all Jewish communities.[30]

As with other *halakhic* institutions, the legal aspects of betrothal and marriage are interwoven with their national and religious dimension. The national dimension is most concretely expressed by the laws of endogamy. Jews may marry only other Jews. Although biblical law is silent on this point, forbidding only unions with Canaanite women,[31] by the time of the prophets Ezra and Nehemiah, Jews were forbidden to marry foreigners. Chronicles record that those returning to Jerusalem from the Babylonian captivity were forced to divorce their foreign wives.[32] The national element is also underscored by the rabbinic attitude to civil marriage between two Jews who may lawfully marry one another under Jewish law. Although rabbinic law recognizes non-Jewish modes of acquisition and contract as valid between Jews, through deployment of the Jewish legal principle "the law of the kingdom is the law,"[33] few rabbinic opinions recognize civil marriage (and none civil divorce). Civil marriage may be retroactively recognized only because cohabitation in circumstances evidencing an intent to marry satisfies the legal standard of acquisition.[34]

Moreover, during the early rabbinic period, as Falk details, "the character of the betrothal act also changed, and instead of being a legal procedure conducted in private, it turned into a religious ceremony of transcendental significance."[35] The rabbinic term for Jewish betrothal, *kiddushin* (literally, "sanctification" or "dedication"), which eventually replaced the earlier biblical term *erusin* (betrothal), may have evolved out of the blessing forbidding intercourse instituted to demarcate between betrothal and marriage, which concludes with the phrase: "Blessed art Thou, O Lord, who sanctifieth Israel." The term *kiddushin* came to signify the ceremony as a whole. This term implies the sanctification or consecration of the woman. In marriage, the wife is exclusively dedicated to the husband in terms of conjugal duties. As the talmudic rabbis explained: "At the beginning he uses the biblical term, while he later employs a rabbinical one. What is the meaning of the rabbinical term? He forbids her to all other males, like *hekdesh* (sacred property dedicated to the sanctuary)."[36] The violation of this exclusive relationship is a grave religious offense. Thus, Maimonides concludes that it is a positive religious commandment to marry a woman with *kiddushin*.[37]

The religious value attributed to the institution of marriage is also evident in the blessings that accompany the legal act of betrothal and marriage. The rabbis envisioned the betrothal "as a continuation of the earlier idea that betrothal is a covenant between the bride and the bridegroom, watched over by God, who adjures them lest this covenant be broken."[38] Moreover, in the Jewish religious imagination, expressed most clearly in the prophetic works, the relationship between God and Israel is analogized to that of husband and wife. God made Israel a people dedicated to Him and for his exclusive possession. Israel's worship of strange gods, the essence of biblical idolatry, is an act of adultery. This imagery, which may have played a role in the eventual rabbinic preference of monogamy over polygamy,[39] imbued the marriage with cosmic significance. Both the marriage blessings formulated by the rabbis and many rabbinic *midrashim* (literary commentaries accompanying legal discussion of the Talmud) emphasize God's participation in the marriage union between the bride and groom. The point of these sources is to emphasize the "the importance of marriage customs as laid down by God Himself."[40]

At the same time, monetary and property rights are triggered by betrothal and marriage. (It is precisely because these property rights flow immediately from the marriage that the formalities of betrothal require a symbolic form of acquisition borrowed, according to one scholarly view, from the formalities recognized as valid in the acquisition of real property.)[41] Most of the monetary aspects of marriage can be varied by private agreement between the parties (such as division of assets, the obligation to support the wife during marriage, or the obligation of the wife to give the husband her earnings), with the notable exception of the minimal amount of maintenance due to the wife upon divorce stipulated in the marriage contract.

B. *The Marriage Contract*

The religious nature of the marriage contract is less clear. The *ketubbah*,[42] or marriage contract, is not the means to effectuate a marriage but rather a document written in Aramaic (although any language may be used)[43] that records the obligations that the husband undertakes toward the wife. These obligations are "conditions enjoined by the court," that are fully enforceable even in the absence of a written *ketubbah*.[44] Thus, the *ketubbah* is merely the record of these obligations. Nonetheless, a *ketubbah* deed must always be written because it is forbidden for the bridegroom to cohabit with the bride until he writes and delivers the deed.[45] It is a positive religious commandment to marry with a *ketubbah*.[46] Moreover, the *ketubbah* must be signed by two witnesses qualified under religious law. The kettubah is read aloud at the marriage ceremony to underscore that the obligations contained in it are a matter of public record.

Most *halakhic* authorities view the obligatory force of the *ketubbah* as talmudic and not biblical.[47] Significantly, the *ketubbah* is a unilateral agreement, binding only on the husband; it is not a mutual marriage contract obligating both parties. The purpose of the *ketubbah* originally seems to have been to provide financial security in a time when women's economic situation was uncertain. But it soon was adapted for another purpose: to create a disincentive for the husband to exercise his biblical right to unilaterally divorce his wife at whim by imposing a heavy financial penalty on divorce.[48] The link between the *ketubbah* rights and marital stability is illustrated by the talmudic discussion of when a wife forfeits her *ketubbah* rights. In cases where the wife is faultless, and the husband initiates the divorce, the husband must fulfill the *ketubbah* obligations. In cases where the wife is at fault, she forfeits her *ketubbah* rights, for example, if she is a recalcitrant wife (*moredet*).[49] If the wife petitions the court for an order of divorce on the basis of the husband's fault and those grounds fall into a class considered grave, the court will order the husband both to give her a divorce and to pay the *ketubbah* financial obligations. In other cases, the wife gains her freedom only at the price of forfeiting the *ketubbah* obligations.[50]

The financial obligation stipulated by the *ketubbah* may be compared to alimony. It must be paid out immediately, however, and not in installments. The *ketubbah* was regarded as adequate support for a wife and children for a single year. Although husbands and wives are free to contract out of many of the financial aspects attendant to the marriage relationship, and may stipulate more financial obligations upon the husband than rabbinic law requires, the husband cannot stipulate that the wife receive less than the prescribed minimum amount of the *ketubbah*.[51] The rabbis "gave this law greater force than biblical law"[52] because it was vital to protect the marital relationship. Nor may the husband insert a clause in the contract avoiding obligations to support, ransom, and care for his wife in the event of illness, kidnapping, or insanity. Thus, while the marriage contract does not relate to matters of religious prohibition and permission per se, it lacks the essential characteristic of a pure monetary matter. This curb on private ordering flows from the special value placed on the marital relationship. One may describe that value as social, moral, or religious, for in the rabbinic worldview the three are inseparable.

C. *Provisions of the Marriage Contract and Other Incidentals*

In general terms, the *ketubbah* constitutes a package of negotiated and agreed upon terms governing the married couple's financial, sexual, and family relationships. The *ketubbah* also represents statutory provisions that are not expressly stated in the actual document. The *ketubbah* is drafted according to standard guidelines, though subjective modifications may be introduced at the discretion of either the husband or the wife. Either party is allowed to insert any additional clause into the *ketubbah*.

In addition to a declaration of marriage, the principal element of the *ketubbah* document is the *mohar*, the purchase price.[53] The *mohar* is likely the oldest formal element of Jewish marriage. *Mohar* was once paid in cash to the bride's father, but during the talmudic period it became a price promised to the wife upon divorce. After this innovation, all the husband's property is made a guarantee for the payment of his wife's ketubbah.[54] The primary motivation for this radical departure from biblical law was to discourage husbands from divorcing their wives.[55] Although most authorities agree that the *mohar* was rabbinically instituted, the *ketubbah* states that it is a debt biblically imposed upon the husband: "And I shall give thee the *mohar* of thy virginity, two hundred silver *zuzim*, Biblically due thee."

Originally, the *mohar* price was 200 *zuzim*, but when that price became too exhorbitant, the rabbis reinterpreted *zuzim* to mean the current currency. Accordingly, the *mohar* price in the United States is 200 dollars.[56] The *mohar* price differs according to the status of the wife as a bride. The standard *mohar* of 200 *zuzim* is generally limited to virgin brides, and non-virgins receive the lower amount of 100 *zuzim*.[57] When the Jewish caste system was intact and rigidly enforced, the priestly class stipulated in their *ketubbot* a *mohar* of 400 *zuzim*, double the usual rate, and other elites did the same.[58]

Voluntary gifts to the wife (*mattan*) are additional monies that a husband owes his wife. *Mattan* appears to have been instituted to provide for the wife's needs after her marriage ends. Though originally given at the time of betrothal, *mattan* is now an additional sum of 100 *zuzim* that the husband is obliged to pay upon divorce. This obligation is stipulated in the *ketubbah*: "And the groom has voluntarily given her in addition [to the *mohar*], out of his own, a hundred *zuzim*." The price is generally set at 100 *zuzim*, though at the discretion of the parties it can increase to much higher amounts.[59] Although the *mohar* obligation is effective immediately upon marriage, the talmud stresses that *mattan* only becomes an effective obligation after the couple has engaged in sexual intercourse.[60] A widow or divorcee must show her *ketubbah* document in order to collect her *mattan*.[61]

The *ketubbah* also records property that the wife brings into the marriage as dowry (*zon-barzel*). Dowry functions to attract suitors and each father is obligated to contribute around one-tenth of his fortune to his daughter's dowry (for this reason, the *ketubbah* is often referred to as *ketubbat b'nin dikrin*).[62] The cash money of the wife's dowry and her other dowry articles are given in tenancy to her husband for the duration of their marriage.[63] Effectively, the husband has title in the sense that the items are considered his property for tax and ritual purposes.[64] The husband's control of the dowry property is restricted by his inability to sell any of the dowry articles without his wife's consent and the mandated future return of the dowry to his wife after the termination of their marriage.[65] Most *ketubbot* contain a clause referring generally to the items brought by the wife into the marriage as dowry and stating that the husband accepts its entire value as 100 *zuzim*. Like the *mohar*, the husband may take possession of the dowry before the marriage is consummated.[66]

In addition to the dowry, Jewish law recognizes the private estate of the wife (*mulug*). Unlike the other property interests, the *mulug* is not entered into the *ketubbah*. This property that the wife acquired before her marriage is subject to specific rules that give expansive rights to her husband and severely constrict her exclusive control. Although the *ketubbah* lacks express provisions regulating the *mulug*, statutory law strictly covers its use. For *mulug*, husbands have the unique right of usufruct, enjoyment of all the advantages of the property (e.g., crops) and neither the husband nor wife may sell the property.[67] Husbands are forbidden from using *mulug* to increase their personal wealth; the *mulug* may only benefit the family unit.[68] If the *mulug* does not yield a sufficient return and the wife does not want to maintain it for sentimental reasons, a court may order that the *mulug* be sold and the money used to buy land, of which, once again, the husband has the right of usufruct.[69] The husband is obligated to care for the *mulug*; if he improves the land, however, he is only reimbursed for his investments and does not share in the profits.[70]

Jewish law presumes complete protection for a wife during the period of her marriage and for all practical purposes, all the wife's property effectively belongs to her husband throughout the marriage (*mohar, mattan, zon-barzel, mulug*, her earnings and findings on the street).[71] Therefore, married women are practically penniless.[72] This system favors husbands by awarding them considerable financial gain, whereas wives are deprived of their property and disadvantaged. There are several ways, however, for a wife to maneuver the laws governing the financial affairs of her marriage to her advantage. As a general rule, a wife interested in obtaining the value of her *ketubbah* is permitted to sell her *ketubbah* rights and to personally keep the proceeds.[73] A wife who sells her *ketubbah* to her husband or another does not lose the benefits imposed by the *ketubbah* as entitlements to her during her marriage (e.g., support and intercourse).[74] A wife may also elect to keep the income from her employment, even though statutory law entitles her husband to her wages.[75] A woman interested in depriving her husband of the rights to her *mulug* can write a "dummy" contract before they are married, stipulating that she conveys the *mulug* property to another at a future date of her choosing.[76]

The *ketubbah* does not mention an express clause specifying the sexual obligations of the spouses, and the obligations are implied by statute. A husband's inability to fulfill his sexual duties is grounds for immediate divorce, and prior to their divorce, the husband has to pay his wife a weekly fine in addition to her *ketubbah* price.[77] A wife is fined more harshly for her refusal to have sex, and the sum of her fines is subtracted from her *ketubbah* until it runs out.[78] A woman who refrains from sex because her husband disgusts her deserves an immediate divorce from her husband, though she forfeits her *ketubbah* rights (excluding the *mulug* and the dowry) and must return all gifts she received from her husband.[79] On the other hand, a wife who refuses her husband's pleas for intercourse in order to torment him is punished. She forfeits her entire *ketubbah* and is deprived of her husband's support during a twelve-month additional period of marriage that by statute must precede their divorce.[80] However, if the wife manages to appropriate her *mulug* and dowry before her husband asserts his exclusive ownership, then she is allowed to keep that property.[81]

At the basic level, a husband must provide his wife with the standards to which she is accustomed; any additional maintenance depends upon the husband's finances.[82] Similar to the rules governing sexual affairs, the *ketubbah* does not mention an express clause for alimony for the wife. The husband must provide his wife with food, spending money, clothing, household goods[83] and medical care.[84] In exchange for supporting his wife, the husband receives her wages.[85] At the husband's discretion, he may divorce his wife instead of paying for her medical care.[86]

In addition to financial and sexual rights, there are several other rights that accrue to a wife upon marriage. According to statute, a husband must redeem his wife if she is taken captive.[87] Post-talmudic authorities forbade husbands from abrogating the ransom obligation with a contrary stipulation in the *ketubbah* because of a community interest that women not be assimilated among gentiles.[88] A husband must also bury his wife,[89] and in exchange for bearing this duty, the husband inherits his wife.[90] In addition, the husband has general domicile rights. However, if a wife wants to move to Israel but her husband does not, then he must agree to move or otherwise divorce her.[91]

In situations where a wife commits adultery or lures the husband into marriage under false pretenses, the wife suffers immediate divorce and forfeiture of her *ketubbah* rights. If a wife is caught committing adultery, then divorce is mandatory and she completely forfeits her *ketubbah.*[92] Once they are married, if a husband discovers his wife to be a non-virgin and he had assumed she was a virgin, then he has a valid reason for immediately divorcing her and retaining the property of her *ketubbah.*[93] A wife who waives her *ketubbah* also bears complete responsibility for her action; she forfeits her *ketubbah* and all its obligations are cancelled.[94]

The *ketubbah* does not directly refer to the procedures of the divorce process, though it is possible to stipulate within it conditions redistributing the rights of divorce. Prior to the enactment that codified mutual consent for divorce, many *ketubbot* contained a clause granting wives equal power to unilaterally divorce their husbands. This clause was commonplace, for example, in Palestinian *ketubbot* of the tenth and eleventh centuries.[95] These *ketubbot* stipulate that the wife can initiate and successfully conclude divorce proceedings against her husband by taking possession of her *ketubbah* money (except for the *mohar*, which could only be collected when her husband subsequently died or divorced her) and leaving her husband's household.[96]

### D. *Divorce*

Jewish divorce, like Jewish marriage, is partly a matter of religious prohibition, affecting religiously prohibited and permitted unions, and partly monetary law, triggering financial dispositions between the parties. A betrothed or married woman who does not receive a Jewish divorce is deemed an adulteress if she cohabits with another man. The product of such a union is a *mamzer* (illegitimate child), who is not permitted to marry a legitimate Jew. A civil divorce has no legal effect in the eyes of the Halakha. (Similarly, a civil marriage ordinarily also has no legal effect and, therefore, those who are married only civilly, need not receive a Jewish divorce.) Divorce lacks the religious ceremonies and religious symbolism that accompany marriage. It is, nonetheless, a positive religious command to divorce in accordance with the procedures of Jewish law.[97] Moreover, the obligation of a husband to divorce his spouse is, in certain circumstances, a religio-moral obligation imposed by rabbinic order rather than an enforceable legal obligation.

The bill of divorce (*get*) is the instrument that dissolves the contractual relationship of marriage. According to biblical law, the husband may privately effect a divorce simply by giving his wife a writ.[98] Although such private divorce protects the parties from public interference by ensuring that a court has no power to dissolve the marital relationship without the husband's act, private divorce poses at least two grave risks for the wife if it should be shown later to have been defective. First, in such an event, the woman is forbidden to any other man. Should she remarry, her children would bear the status of illegitimacy and she would be required to leave her second husband. Husbands occasionally exacted revenge on former wives by casting doubts on the bill of divorce they themselves issued in order to break up the wife's remarriage.[99] Second, without a legal divorce, the wife could be deprived of the financial rights that otherwise accrued to her from her *ketubbah*. Although in the case where a husband abandons his wife, the court supports the wife with property appropriated from her husband, and the court may order the husband to grant a divorce.[100] The talmudic rabbis addressed the question of a defective bill by imposing stringent requirements on the execution of the divorce document. Although the bill theoretically can be written by the husband and is executed by its delivery to the wife, the rabbis stipulated that it must be witnessed in accordance with religious law. The rabbis also introduced numerous formalities into the writing and delivery of the divorce bill, so that it became a virtual necessity to have the divorce supervised by a rabbinic tribunal or by learned representatives of the community. Supervision was not limited to the copying of the divorce document itself; it extended to the manner of delivery and to any conditions that may apply between the parties.[101] Eventually, given expert supervision of the writing and execution of the divorce, the rabbis imposed a ban "that no Jew might question any divorce after it had been issued."[102]

Rabbinic reforms were not limited to matters of form or finality of the divorce. They also sought to address the substantive inequity created by biblical law, that it allowed the husband to divorce the wife at whim. According to biblical and talmudic law, the husband has the legal power to unilaterally divorce his wife at his discretion.[103] The wife cannot divorce her husband because she was acquired by him. As the Mishna summarized: "The woman goes out whether she pleases or not, but the man sends her out only if it so pleases him."[104]

The harshness of substantive biblical divorce law is twofold. It both permits the husband to divorce the wife against her will and, at the same time, denies to the wife the power to divorce her husband should she wish to exit the marriage. The latter dilemma flows from the basic rule, stipulated in the Talmud, that the husband must grant the divorce willingly; as a corollary, he cannot be compelled to execute a divorce.[105] Compulsion includes use or threats of physical force against person or property, such as the imposition of financial penalties.

The talmudic rabbis already sought ways to redress the dilemma of a woman who desires a divorce both by refining what constitutes a compelled divorce and by expanding access to the process of divorce. With respect to the first issue, rabbinic law permits sanctions designed to induce the husband to execute a divorce, provided they are not so stringent as to constitute an overpowering of the husband's will. Sanctions may also be levied based on factors extraneous to the failure to execute the divorce, such as imprisonment for failure to pay child support that would be relieved once a divorce is furnished.[106]

Talmudic law also recognizes a limited number of circumstances in which the wife is entitled to a court order directing the husband to execute a divorce. In cases where, prior to the marriage, the husband swore a religiously binding and irrevocable oath (*shevuah*) to grant a divorce if so ordered by the court, then the court can order a divorce upon the request of the wife; the court is nonetheless unable to enforce the promise due to concerns that under such circumstances the husband would be granting the divorce unwillingly.[107] The court order is effective in cases where husbands hesitate to transgress a religiously binding promise.[108] Furthermore, the court order benefits the wife by obligating the husband to divorce his wife, thereby allowing the wife to demand her *ketubbah* payments before the divorce is granted.[109] Thus, there are times when the husband is under a religio-moral obligation to give a divorce that is purely hortatory and not legally enforceable. In such cases, the court will declare that it is a religious obligation to divorce.

Graver grounds (for example, when the husband is afflicted with boils), however, give rise to an enforceable court order compelling the husband to give a divorce.[110] This court order is, at first blush, inconsistent with the basic legal requirement that the husband execute the divorce willingly. The Talmud simply declares that in such cases the person is forced until he declares: "I am willing."[111] Maimonides rationalizes this paradox by distinguishing between the inner and external intent of the husband. The inner intent of every Jew is to obey religious law. A refusal to do so is the result of an evil disposition that temporarily overpowers his free will. "Duress is therefore applied not to overcome the husband's exercise of will but to remove the impediment that prevents the 'free will' from emerging."[112] Other avenues for redressing the dilemma of the wife who wishes to exit the marriage include annulment and invalidation of the marriage.[113] These and other techniques mitigate the harshness of the law but fall far short of granting to the wife a genuine opportunity to exit the marriage at will—a state of affairs that currently preoccupies the Jewish community.[114]

At the same time, however, rabbinic law moved toward imposing restraints on the husband's right to exit the marriage at will. Indeed, even biblical law evidences some tendency to curb arbitrary divorce by the husband. Biblical law stipulated that a divorced wife who remarried was henceforward forbidden to her prior husband, even if her second husband died or she was divorced, in turn, from him.[115] This law may have had the effect of restraining husbands from divorcing on a whim. The talmudic rabbis also sought to restrain the husband from arbitrarily divorcing his wife by postponing the bride-price from the beginning to the end of marriage. The divorced wife received her marriage portion even "if it meant taking the shirt off [her husband's] back,"[116] a substantial disincentive to divorce for all but the wealthiest husbands. The motivation for this rabbinic rule is spelled out in the Talmud as follows: "so that it should be no light thing in his eyes to send her away."[117] In the medieval period, however, the rabbis finally introduced broad reforms into biblical divorce law to reduce the disparity in the rights of the parties, by making all divorce depend on mutual consent. This innovation granted considerable power to wives by invalidating all divorces that are issued without the wife's agreement and acceptance.

Rabbinic responsa from the ninth century had already begun to grapple with the woman's perspective. These responsa upheld the right of the wife both to insist on receipt of her marriage portion as a precondition to acceptance of the divorce and to advance justifiable grounds for refusing to accept the divorce. These authorities, which presuppose court supervision of divorce, permitted the wife to advance grounds that would impede arbitrary behavior on the part of the husband. Various communal ordinances were also enacted during this period to protect women from arbitrary divorce, such as the directive to impose fines on a husband who divorced his wife without good cause.[118] These reforms culminated in the ban attributed to the recognized head of French-German Jewry, Rabbi Gershom ben Judah Me'or HaGolah (born ca. 960), forbidding divorce without the wife's consent.[119] These legal rabbinic and lay communal enactments (*tekanot*) "introduced a spirit of equality in divorce proceedings and for the most part necessitate that all divorce occur through mutual consent."[120] As one rabbinic authority declared:

> When [Rabbi Gershom] saw how the generation was abusive of Jewish daughters insofar as divorcing them under compulsion, he enacted that the rights of women be equal to those of men, and just as a man divorces only from his own will, so too a woman might henceforth be divorced only willingly.[121]

It remains unclear whether such reforms reflected an inner tendency of the law itself to protect women from arbitrary divorce, already hinted at in biblical and talmudic rules, or, as Falk has argued, a heightened consciousness of the "drawbacks of divorce," stimulated by French-German Jewish exposure to "their Christian neighbors," and by public female outcries against "the traditional order of things."[122] In either case, these reforms represented an important, although incomplete, "amelioration of the status of the Jewish woman."[123]

The amelioration of the status of women in Jewish family law is incomplete because women are still disadvantaged in comparison to men. First, the serious *halakhic* ramifications that follow from a wife remarrying and bearing children without first securing a Jewish divorce do not apply to similar conduct undertaken by a husband. Because biblical law permitted polygamy (later banned for French-German Jewry by a rabbinic legislative order also attributed to Rabbi Gershom ben Judah), a married man who cohabits with an unmarried woman is not an adulterer and the product of such a union is not illegitimate. Furthermore, because polygamy is biblically permitted, the husband is permitted to circumvent the ban requiring the wife's consent to divorce in extraordinary cases. If the wife refuses to accept a divorce where the husband has legal grounds to divorce her, then the court may grant her husband the right to marry another woman.[124] In general, if one hundred rabbis agree, the husband is given permission to remarry even though the first wife never accepted the divorce.[125] Thus, the husband has certain legal avenues for circumventing the wife's veto power over divorce, which the wife does not have. Moreover, despite the power given to women by requiring her acceptance of the divorce in order for it to be valid, men's and women's roles remain substantially disproportionate since it remains the man's exclusive role to initiate divorce proceedings.

## III. Jewish Family Law and the Secular State

The various rabbinic adjustments of Jewish family law over time, responsive to a heightened concern for the status of women and reflective of a general cultural and legal milieu that viewed divorce by mutual consent as permissible,[126] sufficed to keep Jewish family law relevant. The increased secularization of modern society, however, has introduced a new tension between Jewish family law and the general cultural and legal milieu. First, currently society stresses an individualist, contractual model of marriage in which both parties are free to enter and exit relationships at will. This cultural and legal milieu is at odds both with the transformation of Jewish divorce into a regime of mutual consent and with the incomplete amelioration of the status of women under Jewish law. Second, secularization implies emancipation of humans from the religious dimension and from clerical rule, if they so desire. But Jewish law refuses to recognize the validity of a civil marriage or divorce. These new tensions between tradition on the one hand, and changed social conditions on the other, explains why Jewish family law has emerged at the dawn of the new millennium, both in Israel and in the West, as the principal locus of conflict between religious and secular law. I should like to conclude this essay with a brief description of this conflict.

A. *The Case of Israel*

The regulation of marriage in the State of Israel touches on the larger political issue of the role of Jewish law in the contemporary project of Jewish nationalism. If, as described above, one modern conception of secular law is *lex patriae*, the legal genius of a particular nation and a particular people, then the entirety of Jewish law is potentially secular. Indeed, many secular Jewish nationalists anticipating the creation of the state advocated the rejection of all foreign laws that have no connection with the national Jewish spirit. They argued for the reception of Jewish law as the law of the Jewish state. The nationalists were caught between the desire to recapture a precious national and cultural legal heritage on the one hand, and the desire to create a modern, rational, more universally accepted legal system on the other. Religious traditionalists also were caught between two conflicting emotions: the wish to see Jewish law restored to its full glory as the law of the Jewish state and the fear that Jewish law, administered by a secular state, would lose its religious stature and integrity—in short, that the law would be secularized. It is precisely in the area of the regulation of marriage that these debates have been tested by actual Israeli experience.

Israel continues to adhere to the millet system introduced by the Ottoman Empire, which grants recognized religio-ethnic corporate bodies autonomous jurisdiction over matters of personal status. The millet system has survived until now because it comports with both the religious outlook of the traditional elements of Israeli society and the national-political aspirations of the secular Jewish majority in Israel. Although Jewish schools of thought influenced by western Christian models that view Jewishness as a matter of private religion and belief, and not of nationality or ethnicity, emerged in Western Europe and in the United States, this approach did not gain a foothold in Israel. Traditional Eastern European and Sephardi Jews, by far the dominant religious group in Israeli society, continue to view Judaism as both a nationality and a comprehensive religio-legal system. The secular nationalist movement of Judaism, Zionism, defines Judaism primarily as a nationality.[127] In this vision, religious belief and even religious observance is irrelevant to basic Jewish identity. Yet, because it is virtually impossible to abstract a national Jewish identity shorn of religious elements or to separate the religious and secular aspects of Jewish culture, secular Zionists, who are committed to preserving Jewish national identity and Jewish culture, are often allied with Jewish traditionalists in maintaining Jewish religious elements in Israeli public life.

The political decision of the State of Israel to commit the regulation of marriage and divorce to rabbinical jurisdiction satisfied the traditionalists, who were particularly concerned that civil marriage and divorce would lead to a rupture in the unity of the Jewish people living in close proximity in the state. Under Jewish law, it will be recalled, the child of a woman who remarries without obtaining a religious divorce is deemed illegitimate, forbidden to marry a legitimate Jew. Thus, marriage and divorce law is seen as an arena of special communal responsibility and concern, and not solely a matter of individual standards of behavior or individual salvation. The secular Zionists were also concerned with preserving Jewish unity and the ability of Jews to marry one another across the spectrum, albeit for national rather than religious reasons. Moreover, they were inclined to view the Jewish family law of marriage and divorce as a national and cultural law, and thus appropriate for a Jewish state. Thus, they also favored the status quo, emphasizing that the delegation of family law to the rabbinical courts is at the will of the state and ultimately subject to civil legislative control.[128]

Rabbinical court regulation of marriage and divorce has proved to be a very mixed experience. On the one hand, religious jurisdiction over marriage and divorce does preserve a semblance of Jewish unity and also alleviates in some small measure the problems of religious adherents who require a Jewish divorce that would not voluntarily be forthcoming. The rabbinical court has the state's coercive powers at its disposal, including the power to incarcerate recalcitrant spouses who defy the court's order to give a divorce. On the other hand, rabbinical marriage and divorce jurisdiction collides with the interests of those individuals who wish not freedom of religion but freedom from religion. An increasing number of secular Israelis who wish to marry in contravention of Jewish legal standards resent the formalities necessary to obtain either a private marriage or a civil marriage outside the country. Even where the union is permissible under Jewish law, they may have a principled objection to the religious symbolism of the rabbinical courts. Rabbinical jurisdiction, as it is presently formulated, also collides with the interests of those who are allied with nontraditional Jewish sects not yet officially recognized by the state—Reform and Conservative Judaism—whose legal standards differ from traditional Judaism. With respect to the latter, the grant of autonomy to a religious collectivity has devolved into a sectarian schism within the collectivity itself as to who is a proper representative of the group.

Even within the traditionalist camp, there is growing ambivalence toward the delegation of marriage and divorce to rabbinical jurisdiction. First, the prospect of state recognition of Jewish Reform and Conservative religious sects is extremely worrisome to them. Indeed, they see such recognition as defeating the very purpose of state delegation of marriage and divorce to the rabbinical court: the preservation of Jewish unity through adoption of the one standard of Jewish law potentially acceptable to all. Second, there is an increased sensitivity to the negative aspects of state religious coercion. The history of Jewish exile and loss of religious autonomy in the West has perforce created a counterculture within traditional Judaism that views coercive observance of the law as antithetical to its spirit. And the actual experience of government entanglement with religion is increasingly interpreted even by traditionalists as corrosive of religious values and dignity. Finally, many seriously religious people are also products of their time and place, and identify with Western liberal values of freedom of conscience and freedom from religious coercion.

B. *The Case of the United States*

The interaction of Jewish family law with the American legal system is played out primarily in the context of Jewish divorce law.[129] It is in this area, unlike those of marriage, maintenance, or custody, that the Jewish legal system has been most crippled by the loss of Jewish judicial and legal autonomy on the one hand, and the institution of civil marriage and divorce on the other. Thus, the Jewish court can no longer compel husbands to grant divorces through the use of sanctions. Nor do religio-moral exhortations have great force on a largely secular Jewish populace and in a fractured Jewish community lacking social mechanisms of control. The problem is compounded by the fact that spouses can divorce and remarry under civil law, despite their failure to grant or accept a Jewish divorce.

In the absence of comprehensive *halakhic* solutions, the Jewish community has turned to the secular legal system of the United States for assistance. In the United States, there are a variety of civil legislative and judicial avenues available. New York family law, for example, has statutory remedies requiring a petitioner for a civil divorce to affirm that he or she has removed all barriers to remarriage of the spouse, and permitting the judge to take such recalcitrance into account in apportioning equitable distribution of marital assets. Many states recognize contract actions based on express or implied agreements to grant a divorce or to arbitrate the issue of divorce before a Jewish court.[130]

From the perspective of Jewish law, the key question in all these areas is simply to assure that the state does not undermine Jewish legal requirements. The critical issue here is the avoidance of creating a compelled, and hence invalid, divorce. Indeed, some judicial orders—as well as the recent legislation enacted in New York that permits a judge to take the failure to give a Jewish divorce into account in allocating equitable distribution—raise this very specter. This issue aside, rabbinic authorities are not averse to using the secular legal system. Indeed, it is precisely the *halakhic* system's awareness of its limited enforcement powers pursuant to the terms of the modern secular state that leads it to view the secular system of a host state not as a competing authority but, rather, as a potential arm of the Jewish legal system. In an inversion of the liberal state's definition of religious institutions as subsidiary to the state, the Jewish legal system defines itself as the comprehensive polity and the state as a subsidiary institution that can be harnessed for its own purposes. The state simply provides an alternative legal remedy, anticipated and regulated by *halakhic* mechanisms, and harnessed through interest group pluralism.

From the perspective of the civil state, the question is how to justify state action without running afoul of the religion clauses of the United States Constitution. Until now the courts have managed either to avoid this issue or give it very short shrift. On the one hand, there seems to be a tacit understanding by the U.S. judiciary that the state's usurpation of a field historically regulated by ecclesiastical jurisdiction can easily impinge on the ability of the religious system to do justice from within. On the other hand, there is also a powerful sentiment to equalize the rights of men and women to remarry through state manipulation of Jewish divorce law. The result has been that the reasoning of many judicial opinions does violence to both constitutional standards and to Jewish law.[131]

The constitutional issues turn, in part, on whether a Jewish divorce is a religious or secular act. Because the internal Jewish viewpoint is that the western religious-secular divide incorporated into constitutional law is simply inapposite to it, the rabbinic response is appropriately instrumental. Rabbinic authorities assert that the writing of a Jewish divorce is a secular act, from the external perspective of the state.[132] They point to the legal formality of Jewish divorce, which is akin to rescission of a contract; to the lack of reference to the deity in the divorce document; to the fact that divorce is not a product of rabbinic decree but, rather, executed by the husband and effective through the actions of the spouses themselves; and to the irrelevance of the husband's religious beliefs for performance of the act. The comprehensive legal character of the Jewish tradition, when divested of its internal viewpoint, lends itself well to the characterization of Jewish divorce as a "mundane," "secular" act, no different from civil divorce.[133] Moreover, because Jewish divorce is also the national law of Jews, for many centuries the Jewish divorce bill was recognized by foreign law as civilly effective.

There is a strong argument to be made, moreover, that enhancing the ability of a spouse to secure a Jewish divorce serves secular purposes: making remarriage (arguably a fundamental constitutional right) available to all citizens, lessening emotional anguish of persons, discouraging abuse of the marital relationship, and equalizing the status of women embedded in a particular religious and cultural community with those who are not so burdened. Thus, enforcing agreements to give a Jewish divorce can be seen not as an endorsement of a particular set of beliefs but, rather, as a removal of the impediments to remarriage of those who subscribe to a distinct set of beliefs.

Nonetheless, legislative and judicial intervention[134] in Jewish divorce, in the form of special statutory and judicial remedies aimed at enabling a Jewish woman to secure a Jewish divorce, has engendered substantial scholarly criticism. Why, it is argued, should the law carve out a special mechanism to protect Jewish spouses from exploitation or personal anguish caused by their partners? Indeed, such special protective measures challenge the conception of the free and autonomous self that underlies the private choice model driving both American family law and much of First Amendment religion clause jurisprudence. Moreover, the courts and legislatures do risk considerable entanglement with *halakhic* doctrine.[135] The problem is not limited to judicial elucidation of Jewish law, often erroneous, nor to the creation of new problems for the *halakhic* system in the form of compelled and invalid Jewish divorces. Most troublesome is recent judicial rhetoric accompanying decrees. Thus, in the course of invalidating a separation agreement on the grounds that financial concessions were extracted by the husband as the price of granting a Jewish divorce, the court commented that the bargaining chips available to the husband, given Jewish divorce law, conflict with the state's view of "marriage as an institution that should promote equality rather than slavery."[136] Nor are free exercise claims easily dismissed in cases where a spouse states that participation in a Jewish divorce procedure offends his or her freedom of conscience. Indeed, free exercise claims are made not only by spouses who are offended by the notion of having to participate in a Jewish ceremony. They also are asserted, with some merit, by observant Jewish husbands who claim that state implication of an implied agreement to give a divorce drawn from the marriage contract impinges on their actual right under Jewish law not to give a divorce unless so ordered by a Jewish court. The complexity of state interaction with the Jewish legal system in the context of divorce thus raises a larger jurisprudential question: whether the traditional First Amendment framework of the religion clauses, so rooted in Protestant Christian religious and political philosophy with its emphasis on matters of belief and conscience, offers too impoverished a vocabulary for evaluating the interests of individuals embedded in a comprehensive religious legal system that sees itself as a sovereign legal authority, no less authoritative than the state.

In the meantime, the civil state's involvement with Jewish divorce law has spurred efforts to develop internal Jewish legal and social solutions to circumvent the new complications engendered by state intervention. State statutory remedies allowing the judge to impose fines on the husband until he grants a Jewish divorce, and judicial remedies invalidating divorce settlements conditioned on the husband granting a Jewish divorce as the products of duress, raise the question of whether the Jewish divorce that ensues is invalid under Jewish law as the product of compulsion. Recent internal reform is, in part, due to the desire to find remedies within Jewish law itself that do not produce such adverse effects. Indeed, virtually no area of Jewish law has been subjected to the level of communal concern and *halakhic* activity in the modern era as has Jewish family law. Solutions range from special pre-nuptial agreements to renegade calls for the abandonment of Jewish marriage, since foregoing a *halakhic* marriage obviates, in most cases, the need for a *halakhic* divorce. Such extreme proposals are unlikely to garner serious support in the near future. Surely, it would be a sad denouement to the long history of the survival of Jewish law even in exile if exclusively civil marriage and divorce were viewed as the only viable means to assure continued Jewish unity in the modern era.

## IV. Conclusion

Jewish marriage is governed by laws distinguished from the controls and processes of other legal systems. Aside from the laws regulating the procedures of *nissu'in* (wedding rituals) and divorce, most of the marriage laws are embodied by the *ketubbah*. The *ketubbah* is the formal marriage contract representing the obligations between a husband and wife. Although the *ketubbah* expressly lists a number of these obligations such as *mohar* and *mattan*, other duties are imposed by statute, but still referred to as "conditions of the *ketubbah*."[137] Several of these statutory duties are either directly involved with the express provisions of the *ketubbah* (e.g., dowry) or dependant upon the existence and presentation of a *ketubbah* (for example, financial support).

The particular character of Jewish marriage is informed by assumptions that conflict with essential aspects of modernity and secular law (e.g., equality). Throughout history, Jewish lawmakers have endeavored to adapt Jewish law to its surroundings, and though their efforts have been successful, they have not been complete. Jewish law continues to presume that women require the financial, sexual and emotional security of marriage, the *ketubbah* remains the primary means for providing wives with the requisite care, and husbands are therefore forbidden from abrogating the obligations relating to their wives' welfare and security. Under Jewish law, women still lack basic rights and powers that are available to men. Though efforts like the *tekanot* of the medieval period endeavored to equalize the playing field by codifying the requirement of mutual consent, the fact that women cannot initiate divorce proceedings remains a difficult problem for the community. As a result of this fact, women remain overly dependent upon their husbands and the courts. As the key element of Jewish marriage, the *ketubbah* is a fertile source for radical change of the legalities of Jewish marriage (e.g., *shevuah* to divorce upon request; clause granting wives unilateral power of divorce). Subject to minimal restrictions, husbands and wives can subjectively define the contours of their marriages by tailoring the *ketubbah* to fit their particular needs and desires.

NOTES

[1] Falk 1966, xv.

[2] Idem.

[3] See Falk 1981, 13–14.

[4] Isidorus, Origenes, 5, 2, 2, quoted in Cohn 1971, 36.

[5] See Smith 1991, 71–98.

[6] For a comparison of Jewish legal theory and modern legal theory, see Stone 1993.

[7] See generally Cohn 1971.

[8] Silberg 1973, 5.

[9] For example, the obligation to pay one's debts, according to the opinion of one talmudic sage, must be classified as a religious commandment, obligatory on those who achieved the age of religious majority and subject to court compulsion even when the creditor forgoes payment, and not only as a civic obligation that follows from the right of the claimant. Babylonian Talmud, Arakhin 22a. The religious obligation flows, according to one opinion, from the command to honor one's parents, or, according to another, from the command to keep one's word. For a detailed discussion of the interconnection of law and morality in the context of repayment of debts, see Silberg 1973, 66–70.

[10] Hoshen Mishpat, 26:1.

[11] See generally Stone 1991.

[12] Babylonian Talmud, Baba Kamma 113a–b.

[13] Rashi, Babylonian Talmud, Gittin 9b–10b.

[14] H. Hirschenson, Malki BaKodesh, Responsum No. 2.

[15] See Elon 1994, 1:108–109.

[16] Babylonian Talmud, Ketubbot 56a; Maimonides, Mishneh Torah, Laws of Marriage, 6:9.

[17] Nahmanides, Novellae to Babylonian Talmud, Baba Batra 126b. Quoted in Elon 1994, 1:127.

[18] Palestinian Talmud, Kiddushin 1:1 (non-Jewish societies do not have *kiddushin* [sanctification]); Kiddushin 1:5 ("God's name is associated only with the divorces of Jews." "I [God] have given divorce to Jews but not to Gentiles.").

[19] Deuteronomy 24:1.

[20] Dorff and Rosett 1988, 443.

[21] Tosafot, Kiddushin 41a, s.v. Assur l'adam.

[22] Babylonian Talmud, Yevamot 107b–108a; Maimonides, Mishneh Torah, Laws of Divorce 11:1–8.

[23] Maimonides, Mishneh Torah, Laws of Marriage 3:19.

[24] Idem.

[25] Tosafot, Gittin 33a, s.v. Kol.

[26] Mishnah, Kiddushin 1:1.

[27] Babylonian Talmud, Kiddushin 12b.

[28] Babylonian Talmud, Kettubot 7b. For further discussion, see Falk 1966, 40–46.

[29] Falk 1966, 38.

[30] Idem, 43–45.

[31] Deuteronomy 7:3–4.

[32] Nehemiah 13:30.
[33] Babylonian Talmud, Nedarim 28a; Gittin 10b.
[34] See Breitowitz 1993, 71–75.
[35] Falk 1966, 42.
[36] Babylonian Talmud, Kiddushin 2b.
[37] Maimonides, Mishneh Torah, Introduction to Laws of Marriage.
[38] Idem.
[39] For further discussion of the transition from polygamy to monogamy, see Falk 1966, 34.
[40] Idem, 43n1.
[41] See Cohen 1966, 290.
[42] The *ketubbah* is of very ancient lineage. One of the earliest Jewish manuscripts discovered to date is a *ketubbah* from 440–420 BCE belonging to a woman named Mibtahya, and emanating from the Elephantine community of Jewish soldiers and their families that settled in Egypt following the Babylonian exile in 586 BCE. *Ketubbah* fragments have been found in the Dead Sea caves and in the Cairo Geniza dated from approximately 1030. These fragments reveal the varying status of the Jewish woman over time. The *ketubbot*, although essentially formulaic, each contain minor variations or unique conditions and insertions that shed light on the relationship between men and women in their time.
[43] Maimonides, Mishneh Torah, Laws of Divorce 4:11.
[44] Mishnah Ketubbot 4:7; Babylonian Talmud, Ketubbot 16b.
[45] Maimonides, Mishneh Torah, Laws of Marriage 10:7.
[46] Maimonides, Mishneh Torah, Introduction to Laws of Marriage.
[47] Babylonian Talmud, Ketubbot 10a.
[48] Babylonian Talmud, Kiddushin 26a; Ketubbot 95b; Yevamot 89a; Maimonides, Mishneh Torah, Laws of Marriage 10:7.
[49] Mishnah, Ketubbot 5:7.
[50] Babylonian Talmud, Ketubbot 77a.
[51] Babylonian Talmud, Ketubbot 56a–b; Maimonides, Mishneh Torah, Laws of Marriage 12:8; 10:7.
[52] Babylonian Talmud, Ketubbot 56a.
[53] Maimonides, Mishneh Torah, Laws of Marriage 10:7.
[54] Babylonian Talmud, Ketubbot 82b.
[55] Babylonian Talmud, Ketubbot 77a.
[56] For the proposition that all monies of rabbinic law are the current currency, see Mishna, Ketubbot 13:11; Babylonian Talmud, Kiddushin 11a.
[57] Mishnah, Ketubbot 1:2; Babylonian Talmud, Ketubbot 12a.
[58] Babylonian Talmud, Ketubbot 12a–b.
[59] See Babylonian Talmud, Ketubbot 66b, for an example of a *mattan* price numbering a million gold coins.
[60] Babylonian Talmud, Ketubbot 56a.
[61] Maimonides, Mishneh Torah, Laws of Marriage 16:21–22.
[62] Babylonian Talmud, Ketubbot 52b.
[63] Mishnah, Ketubbot 8:6; Babylonian Talmud, Ketubbot 109a.
[64] Babylonian Talmud, Yevamot 66a.
[65] Mishnah, Gittin 5:7.
[66] Babylonian Talmud, Ketubbot 48b.

[67] Babylonian Talmud, Ketubbot 78a–b.
[68] Babylonian Talmud, Ketubbot 80a–b.
[69] Babylonian Talmud, Ketubbot 79b.
[70] Babylonian Talmud, Ketubbot 80a.
[71] Maimonides, Mishneh Torah, Laws of Marriage 12:3.
[72] See Babylonian Talmud, Nazir 24b; Baba Kamma 87a.
[73] Babylonian Talmud, Baba Kamma 89a–b.
[74] Maimonides, Mishneh Torah, Laws of Marriage 17:19.
[75] Babylonian Talmud, Ketubbot 58b; Gittin 12a. See also Ketubbot 70b: if a woman's wages do not sufficiently support her, then her husband must supplement her income.
[76] Babylonian Talmud, Ketubbot 79a.
[77] Mishnah, Ketubbot 5:7.
[78] Babylonian Talmud, Ketubbot 63b.
[79] Maimonides, Mishneh Torah, Laws of Marriage 14:8.
[80] Maimonides, Mishneh Torah, Laws of Marriage 14:9.
[81] Maimonides, Mishneh Torah, Laws of Marriage 14:13.
[82] Babylonian Talmud, Ketubbot 48a; Maimonides, Mishneh Torah, Laws of Marriage 14:13.
[83] Babylonian Talmud, Ketubbot 64b–65b; Maimonides, Mishneh Torah, Laws of Marriage 12:10.
[84] Babylonian Talmud, Ketubbot 52b.
[85] Babylonian Talmud, Ketubbot 58b.
[86] Babylonian Talmud, Ketubbot 51a.
[87] Babylonian Talmud, Ketubbot 51a.
[88] Tosafot, Ketubbot 47b, s.v. Zimnin.
[89] Maimonides, Mishneh Torah, Laws of Marriage 12:2.
[90] Babylonian Talmud, Ketubbot 47a.
[91] Maimonides, Mishneh Torah, Laws of Marriage 13:17–20.
[92] Maimonides, Mishneh Torah, Laws of Marriage 24:18.
[93] Babylonian Talmud, Ketubbot 11b–12a.
[94] Maimonides, Mishneh Torah, Laws of Marriage 17:19.
[95] See Friedman 1980, 1:327.
[96] Idem, 1:312–342 (specifically the comments of Meiri at 325–326).
[97] Maimonides, Mishneh Torah, Introduction to Laws of Divorce.
[98] Deuteronomy 24:1–4.
[99] Babylonian Talmud, Gittin 6b; 23b. Regarding concern for the integrity of divorce, see also Falk 1966, 128–130.
[100] Babylonian Talmud, Ketubbot 106b-107a; Maimonides, Mishneh Torah, Laws of Marriage 12:16. See also Bleich 1984.
[101] See Falk 1966, 122.
[102] Mordecai, Gittin 455.
[103] See Babylonian Talmud, Gittin 90a.
[104] Mishnah, Yevamot 14:1.
[105] Babylonian Talmud, Yevamot 112b; Maimonides, Mishneh Torah, Laws of Marrriage 1:1.
[106] See generally Breitowitz 1993, 20–34.
[107] Shochetman 1995.

[108] Idem, 471–472.
[109] Idem, 472.
[110] Mishnah, Ketubbot 7:10; Babylonian Talmud, Ketubbot 77a.
[111] Babylonian Talmud, Yevamot 106a.
[112] Maimonides, Mishneh Torah, Laws of Divorce 2:20.
[113] For the general principle that the court may abrogate a marriage because all marriages stipulate that they are made at the discretion of the rabbis, see Babylonian Talmud, Gittin 33a. For a general, though critical, discussion of procedures for invalidating a marriage, see Misholov 2001.
[114] For an exhaustive analysis of these techniques, see idem, passim.
[115] Deuteronomy 2:1–4.
[116] Babylonian Talmud, Yevamot 63b.
[117] Babylonian Talmud, Yevamot 63b.
[118] See Falk 1966, 126.
[119] For a comprehensive discussion of the ban and its antecedents, see idem, 113–132.
[120] Breitowitz 1993, 11.
[121] Teshuvot Rosh 42:1.
[122] Falk 1966, 142.
[123] Idem.
[124] Shochetman 1995, 472.
[125] For a fuller discussion, see Breitowitz 1993, 11–14. For an example, see Responsa of Hatam Sofer, Vol. 3, chapter 4, s.v. Yekarto.
[126] This point is developed in Falk 1966, 141.
[127] See Schweid 1996 for a discussion on Zionism and post-Zionism in general.
[128] For a discussion on divorce laws and how they are covered by rabbinical courts, see generally Galanter and Krishnan 2000; Edelman 1994; Baker 1967.
[129] For a general discussion of this topic, see Stone 2000.
[130] For a comprehensive analysis of these mechanisms, see Breitowitz 1993.
[131] Regarding constitutional violations of the Establishment Clause, see Scott 1996. Regarding the problems of judicial intervention affecting the particular constraints of Jewish law, see Bleich 1984. For a summary of the objections on grounds of both Jewish law and American constitutional law, see Zornberg 1995.
[132] See, e.g., Bleich 1984. The author is a recognized *halakhic* scholar. He argues that Jewish divorce is a secular act from the perspective of the secular system.
[133] Idem, 202.
[134] See, for example, N.Y. DOM. REL. LAW § 253 (McKinney 1986); *Avitzur v. Avitzur*, 446 N.E.2d 136 (N.Y. 1983), *cert. denied*, 464 U.S. 817 (1983).
[135] See, for example, Zornberg 1995; Bleich 1984.
[136] *Golding v. Golding*, 581 N.Y. Supp. 2d 4 (N.Y. App. Div. 1992).
[137] Maimonides, Mishneh Torah, Laws of Marriage 12:2.

# *Part Two*

# THE MARRIAGE CONTRACT IN MUSLIM HISTORY

# Four

## A HISTORY OF MARRIAGE CONTRACTS IN EGYPT

Amira El-Azhary Sonbol

A sixteenth-century Egyptian marriage contract reads:

> [At the court of ] the honorable judge (*ḥākim*) al-Mālikī al-ʿIrāqī, the [eminent] merchant (*khawājgi*) al-ʿIlmī Sulaymān [...] married his virgin minor betrothed, the sheltered Saniyya, daughter of the merchant [...] Shaykh of the merchants of Ṭūlūn mosque market [...] for a dower of 170 new gold sultani dinars and a black slave-woman worth 25 dinars of the named gold. [...] Her named father married her to him legally (*sharʿī*) by his power over her (*wilāyat al-ijbār*), and the husband accepted this in the legal way, in accordance with the Hanafi [*madhhab*]. After that [...] the named husband determined as clothing allowance for his bride one new gold sultani dinar per month, per the legally binding amount (*taqdīran sharʿiyyan*), as his responsibility toward her, and her father accepted that for her. Her husband does not demand of her [to consummate the marriage] except when [the full payment of dower] is completed [...] and the husband willingly took upon himself for his named wife (*ʿallaqa ʿalā nafsihi bi-riḍā li-zawjatihi*) that when[ever] he takes another wife after [consummation of their marriage] and when[ever] he takes a slave-woman (*surriyya*), and when[ever] he moves her from the protection (*kanaf*) of her parents [...] and whenever he joins with her another wife under his protection (*ʿiṣma*) after consummation of their marriage, and whenever he joins (*istajmaʿa*) with her a slave-woman, whether by himself, a representative, an unauthorized agent (*fuḍūlī*), or a judge or in any shape or any way or for any reason, and any of this is proven legally, and his named wife is to free him of one dinar from the debt he owes her, then all [women] who entered [his life] after her, and joined her after the consummation of their marriage, will be divorced by a single divorce by which she owns herself, while the honorable wife (*sitta*) remains in his *ʿiṣma*, and the slave-woman who would join in [his] sexual pleasure (*fī l-istimtāʿ*) would be freed for the sake of God.[1]

The first thought that comes to the mind of a researcher reading this marriage contract is, "What do I do with it?" This contract seems odd and out of place when compared with the officially sanctioned marriage contracts in Muslim countries today. In it, the rights reserved by the wife, such as the power to divorce any additional wives her husband may take, have no parallels in contemporary Egyptian marriage contracts. Upon comparison with other contracts in Egypt at the time, however, a researcher finds that it was quite normal to include conditions such as these in marriage contracts. A survey of marriage contracts of the Ottoman period in Egypt provides fascinating evidence of the variety of interests that spouses seek and that may cause them to separate if they fail to achieve them. These records throw light on unanswered questions such as how practical were the conditions and how applicable were they in court? Were these conditions enforceable and how did qadis presiding over Egyptian courts during the Ottoman period treat these conditions, particularly given the fact that qadis belonged to different legal schools? Moreover, even though it is usual to consider conditions as linked to uses of the husband's unilateral power to divorce his wife (by *ṭalāq*), do they not more logically represent demands insisted on by women as a basis for their marriage? This chapter will argue that the traditional assumption that conditions in marriage contracts are merely a delegation of the husband's right to divorce is an inappropriate relic of the historically implicit assumption that marriage in Islam is an unequal relationship in which the man has absolute power and the woman has very little agency. This chapter will illustrate why the marriage contract should not be seen merely as a prenuptial agreement setting the conditions for a couple's separation, but instead as a method by which a couple sets forth the foundation upon which their marriage will be based, continued, or terminated.

Conditions included in marriage contracts give evidence of various interests, of what is desired in marriage, and of what is considered essential for a marriage to persist. The conditions should be seen as the basis upon which the wife is willing to enter the marriage in the first place, as a statement that she wants at least the option not to continue in the marriage in their absence, and as an assurance that she will not lose her alimony if she chooses to enforce them by instigating the divorce herself. Whether they are sometimes constructed using a husband's right to divorce (*ṭalāq*) as a means of enforcement is generally beside the point. This article will touch on the fact that including such conditions was normal for Egyptian society since ancient history and the specifics and fine points included in contracts exhibit significant continuities with the pre-Islamic period. This gives another reason to argue that the exact legal form given these agreements under Islamic law is not determinative of gender relations in marriage. The systems and relations on the ground have mattered more in legal practice than exactly how *fiqh* discourses formulate marriage relations under the Islamic Shariʿa. The disparity between what *fiqh* and various schools of law have to say about Islamic law and the actual practices in court should give us pause to reconsider the idea that what *fiqh*—the leg efforts of various legal schools with their various branches—has to say is synonymous with Islamic Shariʿa.

This chapter about the history of marriage contracts in Egypt draws conclusions regarding continuities and changes in the institution of marriage and suggests a methodology for efforts to change laws dealing with family and gender in Muslim countries today. A basic premise of this method is that social history cannot be understood through literary discourses alone (including *fiqh*) and that doing so is misleading particularly when *fiqh*, presented as God's Shariʿa, is used to establish law. By showing aspects of the actual practice and of the application of law in courts during various periods of Egypt's history, I hope to clearly show the disparities between the theological and jurisprudential discourses on marriage, on the one hand, and actual legal practices regarding marriage, on the other. By connecting law with historical context, *fiqh* discourses will be put in their proper place, as observers' moral opinions and exegetes' Shariʿa interpretations.

It is odd that today Muslim revivalist groups use interpretations of law from various medieval legal schools (sing. *madhhab*, pl. *madhāhib*) as if they constitute "the" Shariʿa, unchanged and unaltered. This is odd because even though *pre-modern* qadis practicing in Shariʿa courts belonged to various *madhāhib*, they considered the *madhhab* to which they belonged as a guide, and not as providing the ultimate ruling. In court they ruled on the specifics of the case in front of them following local custom or *ʿurf* with the *madhhab* as guide. The contract above exemplifies the sort of flexibility qadis employed in applying their *madhhab*'s doctrine to an individual case. Here, the qadi was Maliki but applied Hanafi law, perhaps because the parties requested it or because the rules he was applying would not be acceptable to his school. Quite often qadis would declare that their ruling was based on "whichever school agreed with it."[2] This meant that no single school or corpus of law ruled all cases and none was chosen, whether by the state or the court, as the sole correct "Islamic" interpretation of the Shariʿa. Today, however, conservative traditional practices and existing personal status laws are being defined as "Islamic" and discussions are confined within *fiqh* discourses. This is ironic since medieval *fiqh* was not directed toward determining what is Islamic (a word that does not even commonly appear in literary production until the nineteenth century). In Egypt today, marriage and the family are the focus of efforts to institute what is "Islamic" and this is undertaken in great part through discussions of what different medieval *madhāhib* say about gender relations.[3]

More specifically in regard to women's history, this chapter uses marriage contracts from Egyptian court archives to show that pre-modern Muslim society enjoyed marriage and divorce laws that treated men and women with much greater equality than do contemporary personal status laws. Comparing pre-modern contracts to those from the modern period shows how pre-modern women had much greater ability to negotiate marriage terms and thereby exert some control over their married lives. While both bride and groom could add conditions to the contract, they were more important to a bride, since a husband could get out of a marriage at any time, but a wife, to get out of a marriage, usually had to give up her delayed dower and alimony and sometimes had to pay compensation. However, if a husband were in "breach of contract" for breaking a condition included in the marriage contract, the wife could receive a divorce while preserving her financial rights, she could sue for enforcement of those conditions,[4] or she could renegotiate a new marriage contract after divorce (sometimes in court and sometimes out of court). In renegotiation, new conditions could be added, usually in answer to problems that had plagued the marriage. Also, given the financial issues involved in marital life or in divorce settlements, marriage contracts were an important instrument used by husbands and wives to ensure individual property rights. This social control of marriage changed with historical transformations, particularly the growth in state patriarchal powers with its coercive and hegemonic discourses. These changes are mirrored in the changing nature of marriage contracts in succeeding periods of Egypt's history. For example, modern personal status codes severely curtailed the inclusion and enforceability of conditions to marriage contracts, leading to the absence of detailed conditions in modern marriage contracts.

These modern changes in law literally placed the wife under the "custody" of her husband leaving women with little ability to negotiate their married lives or escape unwanted marriages. Meanwhile traditional *fiqh* ideas of a husband's power of control over wives and children, a husband's unilateral right to divorce at will, and polygamy (up to four wives) remained unquestioned by modern law.

## Pre-Islamic Contracts

> Lately, in accordance with friendly and peaceful disposition, I joined myself to Your Propriety by a giving in legal marriage, based on sound expectations, if God should think best, also for the procreation of legitimate children; and, having found your sacred and secure virginity, I have proclaimed it. Wherefore I have come to this guarantee in writing by which I agree that I owe and am indebted for your wedding gifts or gifts before marriage, agreed upon and pleasing between me and you, for 6 good-quality imperial solidi, less 36 carats, by the scale and standard of Antinoopolis. And I am ready to furnish these to Your Nobility whenever you want, without any neglect or delay, at the risk and wealth and expense of my property,

Levi's – US



general and particular. And I agree no less in addition to support you legitimately and to clothe you in likeness to all my family members of like status and in proportion to the wealth available to me, as far as my modest means will allow; and not to show contempt for you in any way or to cast you out from marriage with me except by reason of unchastity or shameful behavior or physical misbehavior established through three or more trustworthy free men, be they country residents or city residents; and never to leave your marriage bed or to run to other disorder or wickedness, provided however that Your Propriety is obedient to me and preserves all benevolence towards me and sincere affection all fine and useful deeds and words, and is subject to me in all ways that it befits all women of nobility to display toward their own well-endowed and most beloved husbands, without insult or fickleness or any other type of disdain whatever; rather you are to be full-time house-keeper and husband-loving on my account, in keeping with the good and proper disposition that will be displayed to you by me.

But if it should happen that I at some point in time disdain you in the above proclaimed manner, or cast you out without reasonable cause as above written, I, your aforementioned husband Horouonchis, am ready to furnish to Your Propriety, by reason of penalty for the said disdain, 18 solidi, deposited by me on demand without any prevarication or delay of trial or judgment or any pretext or blame or any kind of indisputably legal exception; you, too, however, my aforementioned bride and wife Scholastiia, being liable to the very same penalty if you should disdain me with respect not to invite any inconsequential man home to your presence or to hold a drinking-party in your presence with friends or relatives or anyone else if you are opposed to their presence. And for the security of either party and for our mutual-loving marriage, I have drawn up this agreement of union, or marriage contract, it being authoritative and secure wherever it is produced. And, having been asked the formal question, I have willingly and voluntarily agreed, not overcome by duress or fraud or violence or deceit or compulsion, and I have issued to you for security that which is written below [sic], and for each and every one of the clauses contained in it and for the payment of the penalty (if this should happen), putting under mortgage to you all my property, present and future, by way of pledge and by right of mortgage. And I the aforementioned husband Horouonchis agree in addition that I cannot at any occasion or time introduce other wives above my lawful wife, and if I do so I shall pay the same penalty.[5]

This marriage contract, dated 566–573 CE from the town of Antinoopolis,[6] is from the Roman period, some three-quarters of a century before the Muslim invasion of Egypt. Marriage contracts from ancient Egypt are now becoming better known and many publications are appearing in which historians have undertaken meticulous translations from the hieroglyphics of that period. Modern historians normally do not take ancient history into consideration, and this is particularly true of Muslim historians, since the period before Islam is considered to be a period of *Jāhiliyya* ("ignorance") with little pertinence to Islam. Moreover, historians of the modern period see little significance in the Mamluk or Ottoman periods, and scholars of these latter periods in turn see little relevance for their period in historical material from the Ayyubid or Ikhshidid periods, and so on. This approach is problematic because historical periodization organized according to political events has diverted attention from socio-cultural continuities. Because perceptions of politics are generally patriarchal, this has negatively impacted the appreciation of women's history. It is in the realm of social relations and at the level of day-to-day life that the concrete realities of the lives of most women can be found. Moreover, since gender issues and almost any laws that are placed under the rubric of family are considered to have religious implications, discussions in modern times are almost totally focused on what particular *fiqh* schools of law have to say about the matter, and historical continuities in the practice from one period to another are ignored. Framing gender relations in this way results in an obsession with doctrinal *fiqh* as the method by which to arrive at laws acceptable to Muslim countries today. The critical problem with this exercise is that it is assumed that early *fiqh* discussions took place in a vacuum from the practice, that early *fuqahā'* like Abū Ḥanīfa, Mālik, al-Shāfiʿī and Ibn Ḥanbal were trying to determine in the abstract what God wanted. A more logical way of looking at *fiqh* is this: *fiqh* was produced as a result of efforts to reconcile *ʿurf* (custom) with Qur'anic rules, to formulate laws to be applied in courts of law, and to provide a workable jurisprudence following the takeover of large parts of the ancient world by Arabs at a time when Islamic dogma and traditions were being formulated. It was an effort to conciliate and encompass traditions and practices defining the lives of peoples in the various parts of the new empire created by expanding Arab armies, whose own traditions reflected Arabian tribalism. Reference to *hadīth* (on which *fiqh* is so dependent) was simply part of this effort. The Qur'an was always the starting point, for it presented the law for believers, as it still does today. But the question of how to understand the language of the Qur'an, and more importantly how to apply its general dictates, was articulated by *fiqh* dynamically by thinkers whose effort was to understand the new religion and to successfully apply its dictates within the context of the established cultural and social relations of the societies to which they belonged. These relations then were crucial to the *fiqh* method. Ironically, today the laws that such scholars formulated are considered to be God's Shariʿa, holy and unalterable, and a sacrilege to question.

A look at the pre-Islamic marriage contract above presents us with a model very close to what would later be known as the "Islamic marriage contract." The continuities between the two eras are important, as continuities in their histories of social relations. The details of this marriage contract in turn have similarities to contracts of the pre-Roman period, where it was usual for a groom to promise his wife "fidelity, (loving) attention, the responsibility to provide well for her and their children, to take care of her medically, to take pride in her, and not to treat her as a master treats a servant."[7] Ancient Egyptian marriage contracts, unlike their later Islamic counterparts, concerned themselves solely with financial matters and "were not designed to legitimize the marriage; they were not a prerequisite for marriage nor did they have to be contracted at the time of the union."[8] But the contract detailed what the wife brought into the marriage, the dower or gifts the husband "endowed" her with, his commitment to support and clothe her and their children, and various promises that differed from one contract to the other. The husband took on the responsibility of her financial support and she could sue him if he did not fulfill this responsibility. The similarity between these contracts and marriage contracts from the Islamic period cannot be dismissed. Details of the dower, a declaration regarding the bride's virginity, and expectations of the groom's support and good treatment, are all clauses similar to those included in marriage contracts from the Muslim Ikhshidid and Ottoman periods discussed later in this chapter. Words like *kafā'a, nafaqa, ṭā'a*, the description of marriage as *mawadda wa-raḥma* (companionship and mercy),[9] the husband's responsibility for clothing his wife and housing her as expected of her class or *mathīlatihā*, all have resonance in pre-Islamic contracts. It is also interesting that the requirement for proving fornication (*zinā*) in pre-Islamic contracts was the witness of more than three men, who must be free, to the act. In Shari'a this is translated into the witness of four *'udūl*, i.e., free legally acceptable males. Like its Islamic counterpart later, the marriage contract itself was a written record of a transaction in which the husband asked and the wife or her representative responded "*su'āl/ījāb*" ("offer") and "*qabūl*" ("acceptance"). While it is usual to consider the husband as stating the question, *ījāb*, and the bride as answering, *qabūl*, the contracts are actually a series of *ījāb* and *qabūl*, with the husband often being the accepting party, *qabila li-nafsihi* or other derivatives of the word. Contracts were therefore the recording of a negotiated agreement between two parties "in which Party A spoke to Party B in the presence of witnesses and a [professional] scribe who copied down (and put into legalese) the words of Party A. Although only Party A spoke, Party B had the right to accept or refuse the contract, thus making these agreements bilateral and binding on both parties."[10] Divorce settlements also seemed to be a normal part of marriage contracts in ancient Egypt. There did not seem to be expectations of permanency in marriage; both husband and wife often had children from other marriages and expected to remarry. These traditions were carried on into Islamic Egypt, and even Copts whose Christian beliefs forbade divorce often brought their problems to Shariʿa courts;[11] they recorded their marriages, divorced, and even recorded the buying of slave women and concubines there. The idea of permanence and safeguarding the unity of the marital family was therefore not central to pre-modern marriages even though children were prized.

## Early Muslim Marriage Contracts

Marriage traditions as practiced by Egyptian society before the Islamic period in Egypt became part of what today is referred to as the Islamic marriage contract. At the same time, "Islamic" requirements were added, some remaining constant while others shifted and changed with time. The earliest examples of Islamic contracts available in Egypt date from the middle of the third century AH (ninth century CE).[12] These early contracts were recorded on papyrus, leather, and textiles. From the amount of the dower and occupations of persons involved in the transactions, it would appear that contracts on textiles involved privileged members of society while papyrus and leather were for the more humble. Significantly, conditions included in early contracts allowed women much greater control within the marriage than is seen in later Ottoman contract records. Two papyri contracts from Ashmun dated 256 AH and 279 AH illustrate this:[13]

> 1. [...] promised (*wa-sharaṭa*, lit. "took as condition upon himself") to his wife ʿĀʾisha that he would fear God and treat her well and provide her a good life with him, as ordered by God and according to the *sunna* (example) of the Prophet, to hold with good treatment or to let go in peace (*al-imsāk bi-maʿrūf aw al-tasrīḥ bi-iḥsān*). He [also] added the condition (*sharaṭa*) that if he were to take any other wife, then her [i.e., the new wife's] marriage (*ʿuqdat al-nikāḥ*, lit. "marriage knot") would be in the hands of ʿĀʾisha [...] to divorce her [i.e., the second wife] whenever she wished her to be divorced.[14]
>
> 2. Isḥāq b. Sirrī stipulated (*sharaṭa shurūṭan*) that if he were to marry another woman, Muslim or non-Muslim (*dhimmiyya*), control of her [the new wife's] fate would be in the hands of his wife Hindiyya bint Isḥāq: she can divorce [her] from him any time she wished and he would have to abide by it and any slave-woman that he takes, [...] her sale by her [Hindiyya] would be mandatory to him and he would not deter her from her family's [company] or stop her family from her [...].[15]

In these two contracts we see some of the chief concerns of Muslim women in marriage: good treatment, the fear of a husband's taking a second wife or having sexual relations with his slave-woman/concubine, and a wife's ability to get out of a marriage. The term "good treatment" covered a husband's physical and mental abuse, and the promise "*tasrīḥ bi-iḥsān*" (to let her go in peace) assured her of getting a divorce when things did not work out. As the continued use of such terms in contracts in later eras shows, these conditions must have reflected legal reality, been largely enforceable by law, and presented more than vague, hortatory, or religiously proper words. Most interesting is the term that it would be the wife's right, whenever she wished, to cause the divorce of any other woman whom her husband may marry. That is, she had control over his taking another wife. As already seen in the contracts from ancient Egypt, these demands were usual for Egyptian women, leaving only the specifics up to individual contracting parties.

A thirteenth-century marriage contract written on textiles illustrates the language and procedures involved in a contractual ceremony:

> In the name of God [...] God grant us spouses and descendants who satisfy us and make of us [worthy] examples to believers. Thanks be to God Who commanded and urged [us to] marry, Who secures wealth to whoever strives and works for it, and Who separates between what is allowed and what is forbidden. [...] The learned jurist *faqīh* [and Qurʾan] reciter Najm al-Dīn [...] son of the *faqīh* Burhān al-Dīn [...] son of the *faqīh* Kamāl al-Dīn[16] [...] married (*aṣdaqa*) the woman al-Kāmil, daughter of Nuṣayr, who was previously married to ʿAlī b. Jaʿfar who consummated the marriage then died over nine months ago; her *ʿidda* (post-divorce waiting period) from him being completed four months and ten days ago and she did not marry after him. He [Najm al-Dīn] married her and dowered her [...] a total of 500 dirhams, [...] the *ḥāl* (advanced amount) being 100 dirhams and 400 dirhams *muʾajjal* (delayed) is due her from him in yearly installments, 40 dirhams [per year] without reservations or obstructions. He has to fear God Almighty in her regard, treat her well, and live with her in kindness as God ordered in His Holy Book and according to the Sunna of our master Muḥammad, God's prayers be upon him. [...] He has due to him from her an extra degree (*daraja*) of the same [i.e., kindness and good treatment] as she has due to her from him, as per God's saying, "Men have a degree over them [women] and God is wise." Her full brother [...] was delegated (*wuliya*) to marry her and transact the marriage contract according [to what is mentioned above] as per her permission and consent in the presence of the witnesses, after she was cleared of all legal obstacles [to marriage] according to [so and so] [...] who also

> witnessed that they know the mentioned wife and she is a free adult Muslim woman, in full mental and physical capacity (*ṣaḥīḥat al-ʿaql wa-l-badan*), free from any husbands, or *ʿidda*, or legal obstacles and that she is in her mentioned brother's guardianship (*wilāya*). [...] Thus the mentioned brother properly and legally married her according to the mentioned permission and for the mentioned dower (*mahr*). The mentioned husband expressed his correct acceptance according to the law to be married to her as his lawful wife. The engagement dialogue (*mukhāṭaba*) took place between them in the presence of the witnesses who signed [the marriage contract] willingly on the night preceding the 28th of Jumādā l-Ākhira.
>
> First witness (from the right): "I attended the said contract and accordingly I sign on that date. [Name]
>
> Second witness: "I attended the said contract and signed as a witness to the [acts of the] husband and marrying brother on behalf of his sister."
>
> Third Witness: "I attended the said contract and accordingly I sign on that date [...]."[17]

The contract specifies the details of the dower, involving both a *ḥāl* (advanced) dower of 100 dirhams paid immediately at the time of the marriage and a delayed (*muʾajjal*) dower of 400 dirhams which is to be paid to her in yearly installments.[18]

Conditions included in these early contracts, like their pre-Islamic counterparts, mostly favored the wife, guaranteeing her an honorable dissolution of the marriage if her husband does not abide by her general expectations as well as by specific requirements she considered necessary. Interestingly, the emphasis on good treatment and the expectations of marriage as "living together in kindness," is found in the Qur'an, where marriage is described as "*mawadda wa-raḥma*." Since the Shariʿa gave husbands an unquestionable right to divorce (a right enjoyed by men before Islam), it was natural that husbands were not as interested in adding conditions as were women. But husbands did include conditions, such as the requirement that the wife be obedient and a good housewife (as seen in the ancient Egyptian marriage contract quoted earlier), and treat her husband well (as seen in the above contract from the thirteenth century).

Collectively, marriage contract conditions help us understand a great deal about marriage in Islamic society because they reveal the expectations of a broad spectrum of people. Negotiations between couples, and demands by a wife for dissolution of a marriage, also illustrate the extent of women's agency. In the following section, the most important conditions included by wives before and during the Ottoman period will be discussed.

**Negotiating Marriage in Egypt during the Ottoman Period**

Since marital registration and payment of required fees was mandated by the Ottomans, Ottoman Egyptian archives are wordy and replete with marriage contracts. So we have a rather comprehensive picture of gender relations from the records of Egypt's thirty-seven Shariʿa courts and the sub-courts attached to them. The earliest marriage contract I found in Egypt's Shariʿa court archives is dated 1505, before the Ottoman invasion of Egypt in 1517. Even though it is usual to look at the Ottoman period as representing a watershed break with what came before, this contract is similar to those drafted under Ottoman rule.

Egyptian archives dating from the Ottoman period paint a complex society: very noisy and made up of active and litigious people who quarreled liberally, and who seemed to have a basic understanding of law and court procedures. Women used courts to register land, buy and sell property, sue for divorce, and demand support, alimony, *ʿidda* and *mutʿa* (maintenance) allowances.[19] Far from being secluded in "private" space, women found it natural to come to court and to sell produce and goods in the marketplace. They were often assigned by a court to be *waqf* supervisors. Furthermore, court procedures and legal decisions did not differentiate between men and women; both genders were expected to appear in court in person[20] or through a deputy, and each had to present evidence and witnesses of corroboration.[21] It was quite common for women to sue successfully for divorce because a husband had broken a marriage contract or because a wife had suffered harm (*ḍarar*) caused by the husband. Typical examples of harm included beating, fear of abuse, mistreatment of a wife's family members, lack of financial support, a husband's constant absence from the marital home, and sexual dissatisfaction. A woman could refuse to live with her husband's family and have the qadi order her husband to provide her with a separate residence befitting her social equals (*kafāʾa*). A husband's delegation (*tafwīḍ*) to his wife of his power to divorce a second wife or to sell a concubine became much less frequent in the late Ottoman period.

Common types of divorce seen in the records are divorces obtained by the wife based on her husband's breaching some term of the marriage contract, such as a term about travel, support, or living arrangements. Another type of divorce is *ṭalāq muʿallaq* (suspended or conditional divorce), a divorce based on a husband's taking an oath to do or not do a certain act on pain of his wife's divorce by *ṭalāq* should he breach the oath. This type of divorce comes into immediate effect if the oath is broken.[22] In such an event, it is not left up to the wife to decide whether she wants a divorce or not, the divorce simply occurs, and if the couple wishes to remarry, they must enter into a new contract with the payment of a new dower.

There is yet another type of divorce, known as *ibrāʾ* or *khulʿ*, in which the wife initiates the divorce. In this type she expects to lose financial rights, unlike other forms of divorce discussed above based on the husband's power of *ṭalāq* employed by him or delegated to the wife. The following is an example of the types of rights women are willing to give up in return for their being divorced:

> [...] and then each of the couple declared that neither owed anything to the other, and al-Shamsī [the bride's father and her *wakīl* for this case] added to his declaration that his daughter's divorcer through *khulʿ* (*mukhāliʿuhā*) does not owe her anything else, no rights whatsoever, no demands, no savings, no wishes for any reason or cause, no support, no gold, no money, no copper, no textiles, no furniture, nothing hidden or saved, nothing deposited, no loans taken or given, received or given, nothing pawned [...] no *ṣadāq* nor remaining *ṣadāq*, no *kiswa*, no *nafaqa*, no *mutʿa*, and no reports about such, no type of money, and no rights or any type of general and comprehensive rights.[23]

In contrast to this last form of divorce, in any divorce based on *ṭalāq* (including *ṭalāq* by *tafwīḍ* or *ṭalāq muʿallaq*) the wife receives all her financial rights agreed in the contract (such as delayed support unpaid by husband, or unpaid clothing support within a particular period of time). She may even be able to obtain some form of compensation if the judge considers the divorce abusive. The following appears to be such a case, where a judge orders the husband to pay the wife *mutʿa*, a form of compensation that most schools treat as recommended but not obligatory:

> Al-Ḥājj ʿAlī [...] *wakīl* for his daughter, the woman Zaynab, [...] claimed that her divorcer (*muṭāliquhā*) al-Shihābī [...] divorced her three times and asked for her three compensations (*mutaʿ*) for the three divorces.

In this long case, the ex-husband tried to get out of this by explaining that in the case of the first divorce, his wife had asked for *ibrāʾ*, giving up her financial rights; and that in the second case, her father had come to court and agreed to a non-compensated divorce in front of the Hanbali judge. The qadi asked to see the court records and found that there were no such entries. He then called the wife and she took an oath that she never asked for or agreed to an *ibrāʾ*. The qadi then ordered al-Shihābī to pay her twelve silver dirhams as *mutʿa* for the three divorces. He did so and the wife came to court and made a declaration to that fact.[24]

*Ṭalāq muʿallaq* could be accompanied by an *ibrāʾ*. The following case shows how that works.

> [In front of] the Shaykh Shams al-Dīn al-Kitāmī al-Mālikī, may God support him. After al-Shihābī Aḥmad b. al-Ḥājj Muḥammad,

> known as Karīr al-Ḥarīrī, confessed to what occurred between him and his wife, Fāṭima, the woman, daughter of *al-raʾīs* Muḥammad al-Maghribī, that he was joking around with her five days earlier and said to her that if you would free me (*abraʾtinī*) [from the dower] I will give you yourself (*malaktuki nafsik*). She freed him [from his financial obligations toward her]. She was asked [by the judge], "Did you own yourself by one divorce or more?" She replied one divorce. Al-Shihābī was asked, "Did you mean a triple divorce or other?" He answered that he never intended to divorce at all (*lam yaqṣid ṭalāqan muṭlaqan*) and swore on this. [...] He [the husband?] searched for a solution and chose to take her back [by a new marriage contract]. So the named Fāṭima returned to the *ʿiṣma* of her divorcee al-Shihābī Aḥmad, after one divorce, a legal remarriage according to God's great book and the *sunna* of His noble prophet on the basis of her early *ṣadāq* increased by a gold sultani dinar. She was returned legally to him by the named Maliki judge with her permission and witnessed acceptance. This was accepted by the mentioned husband, a legal acceptance.[25]

Sometimes the conditions included in Ottoman marriage contracts were specific and unique. For example, a woman might include details about the furnishings in the marital home provided by her husband. She could determine where she wanted to live, near her family or not with his family (where a wife's traditional authority would be minimized). She could also require that he not move her far from her family, usually a distance defined by law as greater than the distance that can be traveled in one day (*masāfat al-qaṣr*). Other conditions could indicate the quality of the wardrobe (*kiswa*) he was to provide her with[26] or require the husband to pay the wife certain funds beyond the agreed dower. In one contract a prostitute declared her repentance (*tawba*) and explicitly stated that her husband knew about her past and could not use it against her in the future.[27] These kinds of details included in marriage contracts, therefore, show quite a different picture than the stereotype of a submissive female who follows her husband's orders and goes wherever he decides to go.

How applicable were these conditions? For example, would a court support a wife in her refusal to comply with her husband's wish to move her? The following marriage contract indicates that it was common for wives to insist, enforceable by divorce, on not being moved away from their homes.

> Al-Jamālī ʿAbd Allāh b. Ismāʿīl al-Ṭarābulsī, the traveling merchant (*al-tājir al-musāfir*) dowered (*aṣdaqa*, another word for "married") his adult virtuous virgin (*al-bāligh maṣūna*) betrothed Khadīja, daughter of Shaykh Aḥmadī [or Aḥmad] b. Muḥammad Jamāl al-Dīn al-Khudayr

> al-Ḥanafī, thirty-eight new gold Egyptian dinars. The advanced [dower] to be received before the marriage is consummated (*al-dukhūl bihā*) is twenty-four dinars, the delayed [dower of] fourteen dinars being due on his death or [their] divorce. She was married by her full brother al-Shaykh Zayn al-Dīn ʿAbd al-Muʿṭī al-Khudayr, with her permission and consent as per the witness of al-Surājī [?] ʿUmar al-Ḥinnāwī and al-Ḥājj Shihāb al-Dīn al-Ḥinnāwī. The husband accepted for himself (*qubūl*). She would receive a winter and summer clothing allowance of what is due her equals (*mathīlātihā*). Her mentioned brother accepted this for her, as well as that she not ask him [her husband] for other than what is due her (*istiḥqāqihā*), season by season, and that she eat with him from what he without stinginess provides. [The husband] took upon himself (*ʿallaqa ʿalā nafsihi*), with his consent (*bi-riḍāhi*), that if he were to remove her from her mentioned brother's protection (*kanaf*), or he left her for a period of three months without financial support (*nafaqa*) or legal supporter (*munfiq sharʿī*), or he traveled with her away from Cairo, God's protected [city] (al-Maḥrūsa), to other areas without the approval of her mentioned brother [...], his deputy (*wakīl*), or the judge, or in any other way [...], and any of this be proven, and his wife exempted him from one eighth of a dinar from her advanced dower or one dinar from the delayed dower he still owed her, she would then be divorced one divorce with which she would own herself, with this proven through the witness of his witnesses and the judge (*al-ḥākim al-sharʿī*) without legal action.[28]

Litigation in court regarding husbands' attempts to move their wives illustrates a court's willingness to protect a wife's right to remain in her domicile. In one case, a wife refused to travel with her husband because he beat her. The husband went to court asking that his wife accompany him, asserting that he had married her while she was still a minor but now that she was an adult she had to accompany him to his hometown. She refused, declaring that he beat her and that she would not feel safe with him away from her home. He obligated himself in court not to beat her, [saying that] if she were able to prove that he had, then she could be divorced from him. The woman persisted in her refusal and asked that the judge deal legally with the situation. The judge, referring to the Hanafi *madhhab*, concluded that the husband had no right to move his wife away from where she was secure and that women need protection and security. The court then refused to require the wife to travel with her husband away from the home where he first married her and consummated the marriage.[29]

Socioeconomic conditions also played a role in the shape of these contracts. For example, in some smaller towns such as Manfalut, in Upper

Egypt, marriage contracts did not include any conditions and women accepted that their dowers be paid in installments over ten to twenty years.[30] But in contracts from larger towns such as Assiut or Alexandria, wives tended to add conditions requiring the husband to provide household help, slaves, or jewelry.[31] In other, more socially tribal towns, like the Red Sea port of Qusayr or the Upper Egyptian town of Armant, contracts were generally straightforward, basic documents, without conditions.

A review of these contracts reveal the popularity of certain marriage contract conditions. Perhaps the most important condition wives included in marriage contracts concerned polygamy. Notwithstanding Shariʿa doctrine regarding how many wives a man had the right to take, the courts allowed marital conditions limiting this right, and found the husband in breach of contract when he broke the condition. The second most widely included condition concerned wife-beating. Women, then as now, were at the mercy of husbands who could be abusive. This situation was often exacerbated by the fact that the bride and groom generally did not really know each other before marriage in any way that could forewarn of violence by the husband. The frequent appearance of conditions against wife-beating and abuse shows that concern about abuse was prevalent and that women of all levels of society rejected such treatment through their marriage contracts, giving themselves an option to escape abusive marriages. It is interesting that many contracts that included a condition against wife-abuse were remarriages in which the wife seemed to want to make her remarriage "airtight" and to give herself an immediate way out of the marriage. The following is an example:

> The woman Faraj [...] returned to the *ʿiṣma* of her twice-divorced husband, Sulaymān [...] for a dower of 450 silver sulaymani dinars, 50 *ḥāl* and the rest to be paid over twenty year installments. [...] The named husband determined (*qarara*) 40 *nisf* as her winter and summer allowance, which she legally accepted from him, and the husband took an oath (*wa-ashhada ʿalayhi*) that he would not beat his named wife and would not take another wife and would not travel away from her [...] and if he should do any of these or similar actions and this was proven legally and she cancelled (*abraʾatahu*) the rest of the *nisf*s and her *sadaq* [...] she would be divorced one divorce by which she owned herself.[32]

One prominent obligation in marriage contracts was the husband's responsibility to support his wife and to provide her with an adequate wardrobe (*kiswa*) or a sum of money to cover her clothing expenses. Details of the wardrobe changed according to class and particular needs.

Contracts also included other conditions added by either the groom or the bride and her family that either party considered necessary for his or her marital wellbeing. A husband could state that he expected to live in his wife's house without compensating her. She, on the other hand, might add that she expected him to support her children from another marriage. Contractual agreements stating the husband's responsibility to pay his wife a clothing allowance and be responsible for her food and shelter within his means, and the wife's promise not to demand more of him were pretty typical of contracts from this period and illustrate the detailed nature of such contracts. Breach of contract would allow either party to end the marriage, if they so wished, or sue the other for promises not fulfilled. If the wife opted for divorce, she received her remaining dower, alimony, and *mutʿa* compensation if the husband was the one who broke the contract. If it was the wife who broke the contract, then he could divorce her without giving her any of her financial rights. The following marriage contract should help illustrate these points.

> In front of [the named Hanbali judge] al-Ḥājj ʿAlī [...] married his fiancée, the woman Fāṭima [...] for a dower of five new gold sultani dinars, of which she admitted receiving three in her hands and the rest would be due to her by virtue of death or divorce. She was married [by the named Hanbali judge] accordingly with her permission and consent [...] and in accordance to the end of her *ʿidda* period due to the annulment (*faskh*) of her marriage from her husband Muḥammad. [...] The husband accepted the marriage for himself and determined for her clothing allowance four silver sulaymani *nisf* each month, and she accepted that from him. He took a condition upon himself (*ʿallaqa ʿalā nafsihi*) that if he were to take another wife in any way, or took a concubine from any race whatsoever, and she is able to prove any of this and she freed him of one dinar of the dowry due her, she would then be divorced one divorce by which she would own herself (*tamliku bihā nafsahā*).[33]

In this contract the husband accepts the condition that if he were to take another wife or a concubine, the wife, by coming to court and proving it, would be divorced. *Tamliku bihā nafsahā* means that she is free and without obligation toward the husband, can contract another marriage, and is no longer answerable to this husband.[34] This contract opens the door for her to "re-own herself" if the husband took a step that she disapproved of, such as taking a concubine or another wife. But his taking this action did not force an immediate divorce; rather she would have to take the step of proving his action in court.

According to most Islamic schools of law, a marriage guardian (*walī*) has to be present for the marriage of a woman to be legitimate. Long discussions among the *fuqahāʾ* since the medieval period and until today involve who has priority to act as *walī* for a girl when her father has passed away. Malikis and Shafiʿis insist that any woman who has not been married before, whether virgin, mature (*rashīda*), or having attained legal majority (*bulūgh*, i.e., at the age of menstruation), cannot be married without the presence of a male *walī* to legitimate the marriage. The *walī* should be a family member to act as guardian, and if none is available then the *ḥākim* (judge) can marry her. The Hanafis differ somewhat in that they allow a girl to marry herself once she has reached maturity (*rushd*) or majority (*bulūgh*). The general rule, therefore, is that a *walī* must be present and he must be male. Most marriage contracts follow these rules. But exceptions do exist, and are reflected also in the practice. In the first of the two contracts quoted below, for example, the wife marries herself and receives her own dower without the intercession of any male relation or other guardian. In short, there was no need for a male *walī* to stand with the wife to make a marriage legal. In the second, it is the mother of the bride who has guardianship (*wilāyat al-ijbār*, lit. power to force) in this marriage and delegates a male to officiate in the marriage, but it is she who is the legal guardian of the minor with the same rights that would have been enjoyed by the father had he been alive. The dower here is interesting because it consists of cash, fabric, and jewelry, not uncommon for this period when gifts (*shabka*) were becoming traditional.

1. The previously married adult woman (*ḥurma*) Zaynab, daughter of ʿAbd Allāh b. ʿAbd Allāh al-Zabīdiyya, married her betrothed Laʿdī al-Maghribī al-Nābilī. The dower (*ṣadāq*) was four gold maghribis, of which she admitted receiving one dinar and the rest delayed until death or divorce. She married herself and the mentioned husband accepted for himself a legal acceptance (*qabūl sharʿī*). He determined four silver *nisfs* as clothing allowance and she gave her legal acceptance to that. He took as condition upon himself (*ʿallaqa lahā ʿalayhi*) that if ever he took another wife or a concubine or moved her from where she lives at present, which is located in the Gura at the Suwayqi market, without her permission and she proves all this or part of it and she exempts him from one dinar of the rest of her dower, then she would be divorced one divorce with which she owned herself. With this I, the mentioned husband, permit my mentioned wife to live in the mentioned place as long as she remains married to me (*fī ʿiṣmatī*) a legal permission [...].[35]

2. In the presence of the honorable (*al-fāḍil*) Mayor (*ʿumda*) the Shaykh Muṣṭafā Rajab Murād, and Mr. Ibrāhīm Ḥusayn ʿAbdīn, and the Shaykh Saʿd ʿAlī Marfa and ʿAlī al-Qaṣabjī al-Miṣrī, *al-mukarram* (honorable) ʿAbd al-Wahīd son of *al-mukarram* Muṣṭafā ʿAbdīn married the minor virgin (*qāṣir bikr*) Salūma, daughter of the deceased ʿAbd Allāh Khalaf, in accordance with God's Book and the Sunna of

> His Prophet, the total dower being 2,000 piasters, 1,500 advanced, received by *al-mukarram* Muṣṭafā, son of the deceased Mahmūd ʿAbdīn, representing (*tawkīl*) [the bride's] mother, the woman Khadīja, daughter of the deceased Amīn al-Basrabī, whose *tawkīl* of her has been proven through the witness al-Ḥājj Ḥasan al-Ṭubjī al-Ṣabbāgh, Sulaymān b. Jinayna who knows the two of them. The delayed dower is 500 piastres [to be paid] at time of death or divorce. [The groom] took as condition upon himself (*sharaṭa lahā ʿalayhi*) as a central part of the contract (*fī ṣulb al-ʿaqd*) eighteen *dhirāʿ* (a measure about a meter) *banafsaj* (type of fabric) and two gold rings worth fifty piastres, which were also received by the mother's deputy. She was thus married by her mother according to the guardian's legal power of force (*wilāyat al-ijbār*), and the husband accepted for himself.[36]

As discussed above, another important condition widely included in marriage contracts has to do with a husband's travel away from home. This condition was particularly prevalent in contracts from cities such as Alexandria, where a large transit community of Maghribis (North Africans) lived, Isna, at a time of commercial boom during the eighteenth century, and Dumyat, an important center of trade during the Ottoman period. Such contracts show that it was common for marriages involving merchants to include a term allowing the wife uncontested divorce if the husband traveled for some specified period of time. In certain cases the term indicated that if he were to leave her "without any financial support" for a specific period of time, then she had the right to ask the qadi to divorce her. Given such marital agreements, when women came to court asking to be divorced, and could prove that the condition had not been met, no one could or did object to their requests.

Divorce records illustrate another aspect of the issue of traveling husbands. Wives expected to have their husbands with them and sued successfully in court to end the marriage when the husband had gone on a trip and stayed away for some time, depriving them of financial support, companionship, and a sexual partner. The following divorce cases illustrate various aspects of this situation. While in the first the woman claimed poverty, in the second this was a noble woman and her complaint was for lack of companionship. In both cases, the women were allowed to annul (*faskh*) their marriages by their own declaration.

> 1. [At the court] of the Maliki judge, it was proven to us, concerning al-Sharīf Muḥammad al-Miṣrī and his wife, the woman Amīna, daughter of [...], that the respectable al-Sharīf Muḥammad married the named Amīna for a known dower, consummated the marriage, and remained with her a little time, after which he traveled for one year and three months and did not leave her support or a lawful supporter

> [...] nor did he send her [support] during his absence, nor has she found someone to lend her support for herself during his absence. Before his departure he was a poor man, with no property, and she deserves having her marriage anulled (*faskh*) so she can marry another man who will protect/support her (*yasturhā*). [...] The named Amīna asked the judge [...] to enable her to annul (*faskh*) her marriage and her husband's *ʿiṣma* (protection, or marriage knot) [which the judge permitted after asking her to wait three days]. She then pronounced clearly, "I have dissolved (*fasakhtu*) my marriage from my husband's contract, al-Sharīf Muḥammad named above, and make legal dissolution of the marriage by one divorce."[37]

> 2. [At the court] of the honorable Muḥammad Efendī al-Bawlinī, the Maliki, on Monday, 22 Jumādā al-Awwal 1215, the woman Ṣalūḥa, daughter of the prince Muḥammad Agha, living in Damanhur [...] claimed that her husband, the prince Muṣṭafā, had gone missing for some time and there had been no news about him and his death could not be confirmed. She complained [...] of the emptiness of her bed and her need for marriage/sexual relations (*nikāḥ*). [...] The judge asked her for some time in order to get news of the husband. [...] She declared that she could not be patient and feared extramarital sex (*zinā*). [...] When [the judge] saw that divorce would be better, he ordered her to divorce herself and so ordered (*fa-amarahā fa-ṭallaqat nafsahā wa-ḥakama bi-dhālika*).[38]

The court played a role as conciliator in marital negotiations involving previously divorced couples. For example, a *raʾīs* (chief, captain, head craftsman) who was remarrying his wife agreed to raise the support he had been paying their suckling infant from one *fiḍḍa* per month to 45 *fiḍḍa* per month. The judge also allowed the wife to borrow the amount against her husband's credit if he did not pay her on time. The husband was also ordered to pay her the delayed dower of fifteen piastres from the first marriage, which he paid in court.[39] Some remarriage contracts included conditions to tie a husband's hands, the assumption being that the husband was at fault in the first divorce. Reconciliation also worked for married couples who were facing problems and came to court to establish new conditions for their marriage. A good example of this is a husband who came to court to make a declaration of commitments toward his existing wife, promising that if "he were to take another wife [...] or slave-girl, or left her for a period of ten days without financial support and legal supporter, and this was proven [...] and she was to free him of one-eighth of a dinar of her dowry, [...] she would be divorced one divorce by which she owned herself [...] and his wife [present with him in court] [...] accepted that for herself [...] and they reconciled on that basis."[40]

The reconciliation role of the court is also seen in cases involving family members. Examples are the marriage of a previously married woman with children who demanded that the husband accept the children in his home and assume the responsibility for supporting them;[41] and a husband's inclusion of general and specific conditions in his marriage contract such as when his mother-in-law could visit or his wife not leaving the home without his permission. When such conditions are broken, and the aggrieved party takes the matter to court, it is often to enforce the condition rather than end the marriage. The following two marriage contracts and one court litigation quoted below, involving living arrangements for family members, are good examples. The first contract involves the wife's mother; the second illustrates a living arrangement for the husband and the wife's son from a previous marriage; and the court litigation involves the support of a daughter from a previous marriage brought into the marriage by the wife. This litigation ended with the wife being asked by the court to bring in evidence of the conditions the husband had accepted at the time of the marriage.

> 1. [In front of] our lord (*sayyidnā*) the Shaykh Shams al-Dīn [...] al-Mālikī, reconciliation took place between *al-muʿallim* Abū l-Naṣr, son of *al-muʿallim* Nāṣir al-Dīn [...] and his wife Immat al-Ḥamān, daughter of al-Ḥājj Aḥmad [...] a legal reconciliation, knowing its meaning and legal consequences, that the last of what he owes his named wife in the form of previous *nafaqa* and clothing allowance up to this day is the amount of 48 new silver simani *niṣfs* and no more. The named husband also agreed that the mother of his named wife, the woman Badr, would live in her named daughter's house and that he would not ask her for support [reimbursement] as long as she lived with her in the port of Alexandria without causing trouble.[42]
>
> 2. Al-Ḥājj ʿUmar bin Muḥammad [...] married his fiancée Masʿūda, daughter of Muḥammad [...] against gold jewelry worth 12 gold sultani dinars, six dinars of which are currently due (*ḥāl*) and were received by her according to her statement, the rest becoming due from the husband at the time of death or divorce (*firāq*), according to the *madhhab* of whoever agrees with this from among the body of ulema (*al-sāda al-ʿulamāʾ*). [...] Her adult son from al-Raʾīs Muḥammad [...] gave her away in marriage in accordance with her wish and permission [...] after ascertaining that she is free to be married [...] following the end of her *ʿidda* from the Raʾīs Muḥammad [...] an *ʿidda* longer than the *ʿidda* of death which is four months and ten days. [...] The husband accepted for himself [...] and [accepted] as condition (*ʿallaqa*) that he would feed his wife's son from another man from what he eats, give [him] to drink from what he drinks,

> and allow him to sleep on his bed, and would not withhold from him any of his needed expenses [...] nor cause him any harm (*ḍarar*). [...] The husband also agreed to live where his wife lives and not to ask her or her son for any [reimbursement for support?] expenses as long as he lives there.[43]
>
> 3. Muḥammad Yūsuf [...] in Burj al-Silsila, claimed that his wife ʿAzīza, daughter of ʿAbd al-Ghaffār [...] has a daughter from another man whom he has supported for 12 years and he can no longer pay for her support. He asks that his wife give her [i.e., the daughter] to her son Ibrāhīm b. ʿAlī [...] or that she be responsible for her financial support. [...] She responded that he undertook the responsibility of [the daughter's] support when he married her. [...] He did not agree that he had done so and she was asked to bring evidence of her claim.[44]

Thus, in extensive divorce records we see that it was quite common for wives to sue successfully for divorce based on a husband's frequent travel away from home and because wives feared committing *zinā* (adultery) because of the husband's absence.[45] Qadis often permitted wives to borrow against their husbands' property to support themselves and their children or to receive their delayed dower.[46] With no showing of harm, wives could also initiate divorce by *khul*ʿ, and judges normally granted it to them. *Khul*ʿ is a form of no-fault divorce instigated by the wife in which she may reach an agreement with her husband to separate and come to court to make it official, or she could approach the qadi directlyn to compel this result. Because of the no-fault nature of *khul*ʿ, a wife is expected to give up her financial rights vis-à-vis her husband (dower, maintenance, etc.). In a *khul*ʿ court proceeding, the wife asks the qadi for *ibrā*ʾ (lit. release) by returning the financial status of the parties to that before the marriage; in some cases she could even be asked to compensate him financially. *Ibrā*ʾ, however, does not include maintenance due to the children, since that is not considered a wife's right to give up in return for being divorced.[47] In the modern period in Egypt, the availability of wife-initiated divorce had changed with legal reforms and, until the law was recently amended, both *khul*ʿ and *ibrā*ʾ were impossible for wives if their husband did not agree.[48]

## Modern Marriage Contracts

Modern marriage contracts are both similar to and different from pre-modern marriage contracts in some basic features. In the previous sections, by comparing pre-Islamic contracts to contracts after the advent of Islam, it was possible to see how custom (*ʿurf*) became transformed into Islamic traditions and stated in terms of Shariʿa law about marriage and gender relations. For example, while the Qur'an set out fundamental principles regarding who could marry whom and what was necessary to validate a marriage, it was custom that was largely responsible for its details, such as the expectations of the parties for setting up the household, the terms by which the couple could agree to live together, financial issues such as the transfer of money and property in the form of advanced or delayed dower and *nafaqa* (maintenance), and the bases for marriage dissolution. This custom was implemented through Shariʿa as it was developed by jurists (*fuqahāʾ*) and the courts of law.

The same process can be said to have happened as the early modern period broke away from the medieval. Marital traditions continued and changes in historical context were brought about by the development of Ottoman state hegemony. As early modern state institutions and structures appeared, the legal structure developed accordingly. As new laws were formulated, standardization of legal practices increased. Parallel to this growth was the growth of patriarchy, as evidenced by the scarcity, by the end of the sixteenth century (as the Ottoman state became more legalistic), of marital contracts containing conditions allowing wives to divorce future brides the husband may take. The development of the modern centralized state during the nineteenth century under imperialist control brought another major shift that had a dramatic effect on Egyptian women: the introduction of new legal codes borrowed from nineteenth-century Europe. The negative effect of these legal codes on women's rights in marriage negotiation and dissolution, in comparison to earlier eras, will become apparent in this section.

French and Egyptian marriage contracts before and after the nineteenth century illustrate similarities in recording methods and administrative attitude. Pre-modern court records of both countries included all types of transactions, one following the other on a first-come, first-served basis. In such a recording system, a marriage contract could be followed by a sales contract, a property dispute, and so on. But in both France and Egypt the shape of the archival record changed drastically during the nineteenth century with the application of a different method of organization and systematization according to the particular notary and nature of the transaction. Modern marriage contracts were placed together in separate records and classified under the name of the notary for France and the name of the *maʾdhūn* (a government-assigned official who transacts marriage and divorce) in Egypt. The job of the French notary and Egyptian *maʾdhūn* was to register marriages in the residential quarter to which they were assigned. The rules they applied were new rules and regulations set up by the state to achieve homogeneity and bureaucratic rationality.

Another important similarity between France and Egypt involved the semi-religious versus secular nature of the contract. Notarization of marriage existed in France since the fourteenth century and was required by law since the end of the sixteenth century. Contracts were registered in Egypt since the Pharaonic period and have been required by law since the sixteenth century. Notarization by the state did not mean that the contract had become completely civil. French marriage contracts continued to include statements such as *au nom de Dieu* (in God's name) or *celebré en face de notre mère l'Eglise* (celebrated in the presence of our mother Church) and Muslim marriage contracts contained the *bismillah* (in the name of God) or *Allāh waḥduhu lā sharik lahu* (God, the one, with no partner). The contracts themselves, however, were concerned with financial transactions and conditions of the marriage.

Pre-modern French marriages were celebrated in church first and then recorded in court. Quite often the magistrate went to the home of the bride to register the contract rather than the bridal party and its witnesses coming to him. This was particularly so with elite families. The same occurred with Egyptian marriage registrations: marriage was celebrated at home and then registered in court, and the qadi (judge) went to register the marriage in the homes of the elite.

The basic information included in modern and pre-modern Egyptian, French, Islamic, and Pharaonic marriage contracts was more or less the same. This information included the names of the bride and groom; their fathers' names; their guardians or deputies when present; names of witnesses to the marriage; the date and town where the marriage was transacted; the dower in detail; and whether the bride was a virgin or previously married. Sometimes they included the occupation of the husband and that of the bride and groom's fathers, including titles and addresses. French marriages and ancient Egyptian marriages also included the names of the mothers. The names of the witnesses to the marriage and of court witnesses are found at the bottom of the contract followed by their signatures or marks. While pre-modern Muslim contracts identified the qadi officiating and recording the contract, modern contracts were signed either by a notary or *ma'dhūn*. Pre-modern Muslim contracts also identified the *madhhab* of the qadi.

An implicit or explicit contractual exchange (vows in Christian contracts; *ījāb wa-qabūl*, lit. offer and acceptance, in Islamic ones), representing the contractual basis of the marriage, exists in all contracts surveyed. However, one significant difference exists between the French and Egyptian forms. In a typical French marriage, the bride addresses the groom with "I give my body to you as your true spouse," and the groom answers "and I receive it." This mention of "giving" the bride's "body" to the groom constitutes the most important difference between French and Islamic contracts. Neither Muslim marriage contracts nor those of ancient Egypt include any mention of the bride's body or the idea that marriage involved a woman's turning over of her "person/self" to her husband. This is confirmed by other facts. For example, in Muslim marriages, the dower was paid by the husband to the wife, while in French marriages a dowry (constituting the transfer of the wife's wealth to her husband) was conveyed, at least theoretically. Moreover, in ancient Egyptian marriage contracts, wives could lend money to their husbands or give them their wealth to invest, but the loan had to be guaranteed and returned, and the husband was accountable to the wife for her money that he invested. This means that Egyptian marriages since the pre-Islamic period recognized spouses as separate entities, whereas French law saw them as a couple or "family." We do not see the couple as one unit in Egyptian court records and the property of the wife remained her property and was neither conveyed to her husband nor became family property. Even though Islam frowned on divorce, it was recognized in Muslim marriage contracts, and permanency in marriage has not been part of Egyptian traditions since ancient times. The French experience is quite different as seen in the complete lack of divorce cases in French records, compared to their frequent occurrence in Egyptian archives.

When we turn to comparing pre-modern and modern Egyptian marriage contracts, we find again that the basic information they contain is similar. Beyond this, however, the differences between marriage contracts in the two periods are significant and many. The Ottoman marriage contract is like a blank sheet in which the basic marriage formula changes from place to place and marriage to marriage. In contrast, the modern contract is more of a standardized, "fill-in-the-blanks" official document applied throughout the country, and each specific marriage is given a serial number and Hijri and Gregorian dates. Birth certificates are required, to show that the bride and bridegroom have reached the legally prescribed minimum ages of sixteen and eighteen, respectively, and health certificates are presented at the time of marriage if the marriage is between foreigners.[49] On the marriage document is written, respectively, the spouses' occupations, nationalities, dates and places of birth, previous marriages, addresses at the time of marriage, personal identity card numbers with date and place of issue, and their mothers' names. A non-citizen must attach a photograph. Four copies of the marriage document are made: one is given to the husband, one to the wife's representatives (as was the case in pre-modern contracts), one is filed in the state archives, and the last remains with the *ma'dhūn*. Finally, the official marriage certificate notes the payment of required fees and fiscal stamps are attached to make it legal.

The detailed information included in modern marriage contracts reflects nation-state requirements natural to the modern period, such as use of the Gregorian calendar and the required use of identity cards. Diffusion of law worldwide gained momentum during the nineteenth century with advancements in transportation, communication, and the growth of commerce. Since the beginning of the century, Egypt had sent students to European academies (particularly French) to complete their higher education. On their return, they taught in Egyptian specialized schools (later named universities). At the same time European teachers were imported to teach in Egypt's schools and, following Egypt's military occupation by Britain in 1882, foreign advisors with executive powers were placed within all parts of the Egyptian administration. Furthermore, Egypt's court system was divided into four different jurisdictions: (1) mixed courts to handle legal disputes between Egyptians and foreigners; (2) national courts to deal with criminal, property, and commercial disputes; (3) Shariʿa courts to handle personal affairs of Muslims; and (4) *milla* courts to handle personal affairs of non-Muslim communities. European laws based on the Napoleonic Code were applied in the mixed and national courts,[50] religious laws of the various non-Muslim religious sects were applied in *milla* courts, and Islamic law was applied in Shariʿa courts. The division of the legal system did not stop the diffusion of each body of law and the philosophy underlying it from one court system to the other. Rather, national courts still had jurisdiction over the execution of decisions rendered by Shariʿa and milla courts, and Shariʿa courts had jurisdiction over disputes between members of different *millas* (non-Muslim) groups. The French legal system became the prototype for Egyptian courts, and French court decisions provided case precedents and guidance for Egyptian national court decisions. As for Shariʿa courts, legal precedents from Egyptian Ottoman Shariʿa courts did not constitute any form of precedent for the new Shariʿa courts even as to the personal status laws they applied. What had until then constituted Egyptian law for the new Shariʿa courts, accumulated over a long history and with remarkable cumulative consistency, was replaced by new codes which selectively chose from Hanafi legal doctrine,[51] supplemented by selections from Maliki doctrine when this was preferred by the state committees.

Egypt's modern personal status laws defined marriage as "a contract between a man and a woman by which she becomes lawful to him with the object of forming a family and producing children."[52] While the wish for legitimate children was central to marriage, the definition that marriage was for the "procreation of children" and "forming a family" was quite new for Egyptian legal and social discourses.

During the nineteenth century, Egypt witnessed the development of centralized nation-state structures, with new westernized codes and legal systems modeled after French and British systems and the introduction of institutions such as national legislatures, governmental bureaucracies imitating European ones, modern schools, and centralized transportation and banking. Significant to the present discussion, the new secular schools introduced a new philosophy of gender in its textbooks and classrooms.[53] In the new Victorian bourgeois environment promoted by the élites and middle classes in modern Egypt, the legal system developed to reflect traditions of gender existing in nineteenth-century Europe, laws and traditions that European women have since successfully fought against and thrown off. A code based on the Napoleonic Code was applied in Egyptian national courts, and, while it was not applied in Shariʿa courts, the patriarchal philosophy it brought to the new Egyptian legal system touched many areas of law, including family law (and consequently the marriage contract).

> The Code Napoléon [...] is especially based on the rights and authority of the husband as chief of the family, and on the respect which has to be paid to him by his wife and children. The husband is considered to be best able to manage the family fortunes, and in that respect and in his capacity as head of the family, the rights given to him sometimes override those of his wife and children.[54]

Scholars of the modern era sought justifications for the concept of superiority of the father in Islamic concepts such as *qiwāma* ("superiority"), and *ṭāʿa* (obedience), and these continue to be a major focus of conservative gender discourse today. Translated into law, this new philosophy narrowed a woman's right to divorce by requiring the acceptance of the husband unless she could prove that some form of harm had befallen her. Moreover, harm was not left up to the wife to claim and prove; rather a list was set up, which narrowed substantially the opportunities for divorce that women enjoyed under earlier practice. For example, to show harm, she had to produce evidence that she was either beaten and suffered bodily harm, such as a broken limb, or she could claim that her husband was impotent, which could be proven only after allowing him one year to cure himself. If she had prior knowledge of his impotence and did not sue for divorce, she had no right to ask the court for divorce on the ground of impotence; she could also be asked to undergo a physical exam to prove she was still a virgin.[55] The most important form of harm was lack of support, but proof of it was difficult and could drag on for years. Meanwhile, the husband retained full right to divorce his wife at will and without any control from the state. He also retained the right to marry as many wives (up to four) as he wished.

In other words, a new male state-patriarchy emerged in which the state lent its legal and coercive powers to maintain "the family" as the nucleus upon which the fabric of society was erected. "Keeping the family together" constituted the central discourse in allowing the father to reign over his children and his wife. In previous eras, marriage was conceptualized as an institution that sanctioned relations between a man and a woman and was a means of having legitimate children; the modern period, in contrast, viewed the purpose of marriage as the creation of a nuclear family, and state laws were guided toward keeping this family together. The roles of the husband and wife were seen as biologically determined by God.

Emphasizing biological difference was central to such arguments, and these arguments placed the substantive welfare of the family on the shoulders of the mother, with the father being the financial provider and protector.[56] Here we see the division of labor within the family: the woman was to be in the home raising children while the husband was out working. The legal system reflected this, such as in the courts judging a wife's obedience to her husband, rather than viewing her as an individual equal to him.

It is ironic that this new patriarchy emphasizing the *usra* or legal family, as it is referred to in Egyptian law, did not limit the husband's absolute rights to divorce or to take more wives—surely causes for disruption of an *usra*, financially and otherwise. Supporters of this inconsistency justify it by appealing to the rights given to males by the Qurʾan. However, other Qurʾanic injunctions, such as one enjoining having two members of their families attempt to arbitrate between a couple in conflict, were generally considered to apply not to *ṭalāq* by the husband but only to suits for divorce by the wife.

The new male authority is also exemplified through modern Egyptian guardianship laws. For example, "a mother has no right to guardianship (*wilāya*) over person or property according to the rule of law. But she could be selected as trustee (*waṣiyya*) over property by the father or the grandfather."[57] In contrast, in the pre-modern period, qadis (including Hanafi qadis) almost automatically gave guardianship to mothers over their fatherless children and their property when the mother sued for guardianship.[58] But, as applied in Egypt after the reforms, "guardianship over life and property" (*wilāyat al-nafs wa-l-māl*) could only belong to the mother if the male guardian (father, grandfather, brother, or uncle) delegated this authority to her. Even then, the male guardian held supreme authority over her actions. This is justified by reference to the formal Hanafi *madhhab*, but not the Hanafi *madhhab* as practiced in Egypt in pre-modern courts. A good example of this new state patriarchy is a 1974 court case in which a mother sued to extend her custody of her daughter until the latter married, a valid position under the Maliki *madhhab*. The Hanafi *madhhab*, on the other hand, mandates that a father's guardianship over girls begins at age twelve. In this case, the mother argued that the narrowing of Egypt's source of law on this issue exclusively to the Hanafi *madhhab* was unconstitutional since the Constitution never specified the Hanafi school as its source of law, but rather indicated that the Shariʿa was a "principal source" for Egypt's laws.[59] The judge rejected this argument and dismissed the case on the basis that the law-giver (*musharriʿ*) was the guardian of the state and therefore had the prerogative to choose the *madhhab* to apply and it was not up to the judge to question this selection.

Ultimately, placing Egyptian women under greater patriarchal authority has resulted in their peripheralization, and the limiting of their civil liberties and legal competence. Modern nation-states defined their power over territory and people by extending their jurisdiction over them and defining them as citizens or protégés. Women in particular experienced a new level of patriarchal control as laws of nationality were increasingly tightened. The reason for this is that as nation-states hammered out and homogenized citizenship laws, women were defined as holding whatever nationality their husbands held: "An indigenous woman who marries a Tunisian under French administration, automatically becomes a French subject."[60] The children from such a marriage would also follow the husband's nationality, creating a situation in which children of Egyptian mothers abandoned by their foreign fathers are today unable to find legal redress. Since Egyptian women are traditionally identified as "daughter of so and so" rather than "wife of so and so" in court and never legally take their husbands' names, one must assume that defining a woman through her husband was an imported idea.

Egyptian courts accepted the premise that a woman followed the nationality of her husband, but not where it involved spouses of different faiths. In an important 1909 case, Egypt's Court of Appeals refused to recognize the Russian citizenship of an Egyptian woman who had married a Russian in a Lutheran Church because she was a Muslim and therefore had to follow Islamic Shariʿa laws. In such cases, the court differentiated "political nationality" (*jinsiyya siyāsiyya*) and "sectarian nationality" (*jinsiyya ṭāʾifiyya*). The court explained that all Egyptians were joined by one political nationality, but their sectarian nationality varied according to the religious community.[61] This is another indication of how marriage became a strictly religious affair subservient to the findings of particular jurists selected by the state. Changes to gender relations brought upon by marriage and divorce thus became a matter for religious authority. The contractual nature of marriage in which the parties signatory to the agreement had control over the transaction was lost. Giving new personal status laws the sanction of holiness by giving them religious legitimacy placed them within a realm of the untouchable, making them very difficult to change. One could almost say that even though marriage and family fell largely in the realm of *muʿāmalāt* (worldly actions), they somehow gained a sanctity reserved to the realm of *ʿibādāt* (worship) and as God's laws the result was a difficulty to change them.

Limiting women's access to divorce under modern Egyptian law became one of the most serious consequences of the new personal status laws. This was realized in several ways, starting with the courts' non-recognition of contractual conditions in marriage contracts. When such conditional clauses were included in a contract, the court usually found the contract valid but the conditions invalid (*al-ʿaqd ṣaḥīḥ wa-l-sharṭ bāṭil*). By thus denying women the right to include conditions, the most important method by which they could control the nature of their marriages was closed off. A woman could no longer control her husbands' ability to take a second wife, define where she would live, stop him from traveling for long periods of time, ensure that he would treat her properly, or arrange that she could get out of the marriage if she wished. As replacement, the personal status laws of 1925 included the concept of *ʿiṣma*.[62] A woman's holding of the *ʿiṣma* is seen by *fuqahāʾ* as a husband's delegation to his wife of his right to divorce.

Since modern social discourse belittles a husband who allows his wife to hold the *ʿiṣma*, this sole remainder of the wife's control over the marriage is rarely resorted to except in marriages involving very wealthy, aristocratic, experienced women, or famous artists. Interestingly, when Egyptian women are asked about holding the *ʿiṣma*, they consider it an unacceptable practice and demeaning to men. When questioned further it becomes clear that most do not know that when a woman holds the *ʿiṣma* the man can still divorce his wife if he so wishes. The believed fiction is that she takes that right away from him, thereby denying his manhood.

Equally important to limiting women's access to divorce was the modern reinterpretation of *khulʿ* which historically had been a vital and widely-used method by which wives could get out of a marriage. Rather than recognizing the Islamic legal doctrine of *khulʿ* as a woman's right to divorce, modern laws made the granting of a *khulʿ* divorce contingent upon the husband's consent.

Another telling change in women's lives, again reflecting the new philosophy behind gender and family laws and the role of the state in the diffusion of law, is the establishment of new obedience laws. A new practice, unheard of in Egypt before the modernization of law, allowed husbands to incarcerate disobedient wives in a "house of obedience" (*bayt al-ṭāʿa*) as long as this house provided the minimum environment required for a woman of her class. Until the 1985 personal status amendments, the police actually dragged women away and forced them to live with their husbands in such houses. The *bayt al-ṭāʿa* was ostensibly based on the reciprocal relationship between the classical Islamic ideas of *ṭāʿa* and *nafaqa* (financial support). According to classical Shariʿa doctrine, a husband was expected to provide financial support for his wife while a wife had to be obedient to him, including not leaving the marital home without his permission if this is stipulated in the contract. But there is a serious difference between this traditional Islamic concept and the revised version legislated by the modern Egyptian state. In pre-modern courts, proof of disobedience (*nushūz*) meant that a husband had the right to withdraw financial support from his wife, but he could not force her to live with him or to "lock her up." The following early nineteenth-century case illustrates this.

> Ḥawāfī, son of the deceased Sulaymān al-Ḥawālī al-Dumyāṭī, came before us and informed us that he married a woman called Fāṭima, daughter of Nūr al-Dīn Abū Ḥassan in Dumyat and she remained with him for a time, then her parents came and took her from his

> house without his permission and returned to the named port. He followed them and asked that she return to his *ṭāʿa* and live with him in Dumyat. They refused so he asked the court to bring her [to court] and take her away from her parents so she could leave with him to Dumyat under his *ṭāʿa*. The judge agreed and sent a legal messenger (*qāṣid al-sharʿ al-sharīf*) and she came [to court] together with her parents and the judge informed them of what the husband said. She refused to travel with him to Dumyat or to go anywhere with him away from her family. [...] The judge then informed her that if she did not follow her husband and enter his *ṭāʿa* in Dumyat, she would be considered nāshiz and would lose the right to her *nafaqa* and clothing allowance due her from her husband and anything of the sort as long as she does not obey him. She responded the same as before so the judge declared her *nāshiz* with no *nafaqa* or clothing allowance from her husband as long as she was not obedient to him.[63]

In contrast, modern *ṭāʿa* law allowed husbands to force their wives to live with them against their will, sometimes even when the husband was a wife abuser. In a 1935 case, the judge refused an abused wife's appeal against a court order to place her under her husband's power:

> A husband has the right of sexual enjoyment and obedience by virtue of the contract and she has no right to hold back from delivering herself to him because of beating or abuse, and she does not have the right to refuse to live with him in a *bayt al-ṭāʿa* because he beats her and harms her as long as the house is appropriate and their neighbors are good, trustworthy people and are not biased toward the husband. If the husband beats and harms her, it is the job of the judge to reprimand him and stop him from abusing her.[64]

The connection between obedience and financial support has existed in Egyptian marriage contracts since ancient Egyptian times, but incarceration did not seem to be part of the equation until the modern period, with a new interpretation of the right to *ṭāʿa* and how it was to be executed. *Bayt al-ṭāʿa* is clearly a modern innovation and does not make an appearance in court records before the end of the nineteenth century. It is curious that despite this, *ṭāʿa* and *bayt al-ṭāʿa* continue to be understood as Islamic traditions following the Islamic Shariʿa. As for the concept of *ṭāʿa* itself, its meaning as "a wife's obedience to her husband" has actually changed little in meaning over history; it is in the legal interpretation of what is involved in *ṭāʿa* that there is significant difference. The *fuqahāʾ* past and present agree that a wife's *ṭāʿa* is required in return for her husband's financial support. For example, when a husband came to an Ottoman court to ask his wife to return to his *ṭāʿa*, she could refuse, as in the above case, or the judge could ask the wife for her requirements and he would order the husband to prepare a legal home for her.[65] A *ṭāʿa* case could end with the wife either refusing to go back and becoming *nāshiz* or accepting to be obedient and even to being confined in her home (*iḥtibās*), not leaving it without his permission. But here the similarities end and the differences are significant. Modern personal status laws give wives no choice in the matter, instead giving husbands an absolute right to their wives' *ṭāʿa*. Modern *ṭāʿa* laws require a wife to "surrender herself," a phrase that is itself very reminiscent of the French marriage language quoted above. Since the avenue to divorce was limited, due to the modern courts' refusal to recognize marital conditions in marriage contracts, and since *khulʿ* was only granted upon approval of the husband, getting out of a marriage became virtually impossible for women. Hence the significance of the 2000 *khulʿ* law, which returned the situation somewhat to what it had been before modern legal reform of the nineteenth century by allowing a wife to sue and receive a judicial divorce from the courts within three months, with or without the husband's agreement although following arbitration. Finally, it is very telling that this new state patriarchy in the form of modern *ṭāʿa* laws applies not only to Muslims but also to Copts[66] despite the fact that the Coptic community questioned incarceration earlier than the Muslim community did.[67] The basis for *ṭāʿa* among Copts was not the application of the Islamic Shariʿa, but from within Christian scriptures. Quoting Scripture, the Majlis al-Millī court of Damanhur committed a Coptic woman to her husband's *ṭāʿa* in 1953, stating that she should be "obedient to your man as Sarah was obedient to Abraham whom she called master." The court held:

> The obedience of a wife to her husband is a duty according to church law and according to the traditions of the Majlis al-Millī. [This is because obedience] is the cornerstone of the family, no matter what severity is involved in the interference by the executive authorities to assure execution by forcible compulsion (*al-quwwa al-jabriyya*). Without this the family would be under threat of tremendous dangers (*akhṭār jasīma*).[68]

NOTES

An earlier version of this paper was published in *HAWWA: Journal of Women of the Middle East and the Islamic World*. See Sonbol 2005.

[1] Maḥkamat al-Ṣāliḥiyya al-najmiyya, sijill 446:121–289 (964 AH/1557 CE).

[2] Cf. Alexandria, sijill 1:11–50 (957 AH/1550 CE), quoted in text at n. 43.

[3] This approach is problematic primarily because the word "family" or *usra* does not appear anywhere in the literature or legal records until the nineteenth century, while the word *ʿāʾila*, which does appear in the literature, does not make an appearance in the legal literature. That social units that can be referred to as family have always existed is indisputable, but their shape and inter-family and

intra-family relations are directly connected with the historical context in which they functioned. The nuclear family, *usra*, as a legally recognized unit with a male legal head is a modern construct.

[4] The following court case is an example of a wife suing her husband in court to enforce his financial obligations to her. It does not involve divorce.

> [At the court of] the honored Shafiʿi judge (*ḥākim sharʿī*), [...] the respectable Mr. Aḥmad al-Sayyid [...] legal representative of the woman Ṣafiyya, daughter of [...] sued her husband, the respectable ʿAlī ibn Ghānim [...] [claiming] that he owes her 7 riyals, the remainder of her advanced dower; 9 riyals, price of cotton; 1 riyal, price of cinnamon block; 6 riyals, the price of a quarter share of a shop that he took from her [...] and her clothing allowance for two years since he married her. He asked that the husband be asked about this and that he pay her what is owed. The defendant was asked and agreed that he was married to her since the date mentioned, that he clothed her with a (?) dress and three shirts and that he agreed to a dower of 8 riyals of which he paid 7 less 10 *niṣfs*, so he owed her 1 riyal and 10 *niṣfs*, and that he has already settled the price of the cotton with her. [...] The woman and her witness took the oath and asked the defendant to bring his evidence to court. He was not able to and asked that the woman give him her legal oath, which she did. [...] The named judge then ordered the man to pay her 7 riyals advanced dower and 10 *niṣfs* of silver to which he had confessed and to pay her two years clothing allowance, each year two seasons, each season one shirt, head cover, belt, underwear, and shoes.

Dār al-Wathāʾiq al-Qawmiyya: Dumyāṭ, sijill 9:180–3821(1215 AH/1800 CE).

[5] Rowlandson 1998, 210–211.

[6] In central Egypt; the closest town to it would be Minya, about 130 miles south of Cairo. The city no longer exists today.

[7] Marriage contract from Egypt's New Kingdom, repr. in Capel and Markoe 1996, 180.

[8] Idem.

[9] Cf. Qurʾan 30:21: "He created mates for you from yourselves that you may find rest in them, and He put between you companionship and mercy (*mawadda wa-raḥma*)." The definition of marriage as a contract allowing sexual intercourse (see Kecia Ali's chapter in this volume) and the stress that the scholars of *fiqh* place on issues of sexual rights in their long coverage and discussion of this subject gives a good idea about the production of *fiqh*. Since the Qurʾan clearly describes marriage as *mawadda wa-raḥma* and since marriage contracts do not focus on sexual relations, one must assume that the scholars' preoccupation with sex or sexual rights must have been due to questions brought to them for an opinion—they were usually muftis of their schools—or must have represented issues prevalent in the wider community at a time when legal principles were being laid down by a community establishing its institutions and laws. That marriage allows sexual intercourse (*yuḥallil al-buḍʿ*) is different than saying that this is what marriage was about. The question addressed by the scholars is important in determining how we are to understand their fatwas.

[10] Capel and Markoe 1996, 177.

[11] As an example:

Wāṣilī al-Qubrzlī, the tailor, came to the Majlis al-Sharʿ al-Sharīf to inform that his wife, Marūsa bint Dimitri al-Rūmī, does not listen to him and has gone out of his *ṭāʿa* [...] and asked that she be brought to court so as to talk to her about this. She came and the husband talked to her in the presence of her nephew [...] and the respectable Ḥusayn Agha Bāshā [...] and others present there. She refused to reconcile with her named husband and explained that he left her for three years without support (*nafaqa*). He offered the amount of eight thousand silver *nisf* as compensation but she refused, saying, "I do not accept it (*lā aqbaluhu*)," and showed disobedience (*nushūz*) and willfulness (*ʿisyān*). She was informed that she had no right to *nafaqa* and no clothing allowance was due her from her husband as long as she did not follow his wishes. She stood firm and the husband accepted her *nushūz*.

Dār al-Wathāʾiq al-Qawmiyya: Alexandria Mubāyaʿāt, sijill 120:281–908 (1230 AH/1814 CE).

[12] Egypt's Dār al-Wathāʾiq al-Qawmiyya and Dār al-Kutub have large collections of papyri that have yet to be studied. A major effort to restore them is underway. Egypt's social history will gain significantly once these records are studied especially due to historical specificities they will provide. The same can be said about textile collections.

[13] Both contracts are located at Dār al-Wathāʾiq al-Qawmiyya in Cairo, Egypt.

[14] Grohmann 1994, 1:73.

[15] Idem, 88–90. While child custody is worth an article of its own, it is worth pointing out that court records are replete with cases involving child custody of minors, guardianship of person and property, acting as guardian, financial support, and pay for suckling an infant child. It would be a mistake to take modern litigation regarding children, including the struggle by women to retain long-term custody over their children once they reach the age when they are to be handed over to their fathers, as central to the debates in pre-modern courts. The courts—then as now—were focused on what is best for the child. Child custody settlements were normally amicable and followed normal Shariʿa rules. When a divorced mother remarried, she expected to lose custody over her minor daughters to a female member of her family, usually her mother. If none existed, then the child went to a female member of the father's family, usually his mother. In a typical such case, the mother came to court and handed over her young child to her father who impressed on the court that his mother was willing to act as custodian (*ḥāḍina*): Bāb al-Shaʿriyya, 1564, 590:96–260. However, given the frequency with which mothers asked husbands to support their daughters and sons from previous marriages, and included this support as condition in the marriage contracts, we can conclude that, in fact, custody was a matter open to negotiation and that it was probably the norm for children to stay with the mother, even after a second marriage and even if the child was female, perhaps because the father was deceased or did not ask for custody for whatever reason.

[16] The bridegroom in this marriage contract is identified as a jurist (*faqīh*) and Qurʾan reciter (*qāriʾ*), the son and grandson of other *faqīh*s. Here, the guild-like nature of the clergy ulema, i.e., apprenticeship from father to son, is evident.

[17] Cairo, Museum of Islamic Art, doc. no. 14982, published in Suʿād Māhir 1978, 42–44.

[18] Manfalūṭ, 1808–1810 (cases 118, 119, 121).

[19] See Miṣr Iʿlāmāt, sijill 23:244–651 (1266 AH/1850 CE); Dishnā Ishhādāt, sijill 17:1–9, 3–15, 2–16, 3–25, 8–44 (1283 AH/1865 CE).

[20] Dishnā Ishhādāt, sijill 1:15–92 (1273 AH/1857 CE).

[21] Bāb al-ʿĀlī, sijill 106:342–1034 (1229 AH/1813 CE).

[22] Case of *ṭalāq muʿallaq*: here the husband takes an oath that he will divorce his wife a triple divorce if he has not paid a debt he owes within a specific time period.

> Muḥammad ʿAlī b. Muḥammad, known as Ibn al-Majnūn al-Mujayrī, gave legal witness that he guaranteed ʿAlī b. Ḥasan b. al-Ḥājj ʿAlī al-Qalishānī regarding what he owed al-Ḥājj Sulaymān b. Ḥasan [...] an amount of 310 new silver. [...] Al-Ḥājj ʿAlī took an oath that he would divorce by way of a triple divorce (*bi-l-ṭalāq al-thalātha*) his wife, the daughter of Muḥammad, who is in his *ʿiṣma* and marriage knot, that if by ten days of the coming month of Muḥarram he had not paid the amount due or had not made al-Ḥājj Sulaymān feel better, his wife Jazīya would be divorced three times.

Alexandria Wathāʾiq, sijill 1:481–1974 (958 AH/1551 CE).

[23] Al-Zāhid, sijill 657:309–1094 (982 AH/1574 CE).

[24] Maḥkamat Bāb al-Shaʿriyya, sijill 590:69–259 (972 AH/1564 CE).

[25] Alexandria Wathāʾiq, sijill 1:51–2227, 975 (958 AH/1551 CE).

[26] Dishnā Ishhādāt, sijill 1:1–9 (1273 AH/1857 CE).

[27] Miṣr al-Qadīma, sijill 103:95–221(1079 AH/1669 CE).

[28] Al-Ṣāliḥ, sijill 312:385–1866 (985–86 AH/1577–78 CE).

[29] Al-Bāb al-ʿĀlī, sijill 123:248–1291 (1056 AH/1646 CE).

[30] A typical contract would read: "[At the court of] the honored Ḥanafī, the respectable al-Shihābī Aḥmad ibn al-Muʿallim Muṣṭafā, known as Ibn al-Rasfawān married his betrothed, the woman Sharabiyya, the adult virgin, daughter of [...] for a dower of 25 dinars, 22 dinars paid in advance into the hands of her father, against 16 dinars compensation for a particular black mule known to her, and he accepted the compensation. [...] The remaining *ḥāl* mentioned [above] of 6 dinars and the delayed 3 dinars would be held for her over 12 years, with each year [her receiving] a quarter of a dinar. Her father married her to him accordingly." Dumyāṭ, Ishhādāt, sijill 40:32–83.

[31] Ishhādāt, sijill 1:24–38 (1273 AH/1857 CE).

[32] In front of a Hanafi judge, Alexandria, sijill 1:34–157.

[33] Maḥkama Jāmiʿ al-Ḥākim, 966[1559], 540:308–397.

[34] The term is unambiguous in court records as this 1550 Alexandria case shows: "Shihābī Aḥmad b. Muḥammad [...] asked to divorce his wife ʿAzīza [...] divorcing her by way of one divorce [...] so that she was divorced (*bānat*) from him and owned herself (*malakat nafsahā*). Thus she could not return to him except with a new contract with its own conditions (*bi-ʿaqd jadīd bi-shurūṭihi*)[...]" Alexandria, sijill 1:99–470 (957 AH/1550 CE).

[35] Maḥkama Jāmiʿ al-Ḥākim, sijill 540:200–898 (966–67 AH/1558–59 CE).

[36] Alexandria, Ishhādāt, sijill 1:6–40 (1273 AH/1857 CE).

[37] Alexandria, Ishhādāt, sijill 51:91–220 (1074 AH/1663 CE).

[38] Dumyāṭ, sijill 9:116–251 (1215 AH/1800 CE). This was not a unique case; wives often divorced themselves in court. Alexandria, sijill 51:146, 147–325 (1046 AH/1637 CE). Also, "I dissolved my marriage from my husband (*fasakhtu*

*nikāḥī*) and untied the marriage knot between him and me and became this way legally available (*ḥalālan*) to husbands." Ishhādāt, sijill 51:146, 147–352 (1073 AH/1663CE).

[39] Alexandria, sijill 95:285–408 (1182 AH/1769 CE).

[40] Maḥkamat Bāb al-Shaʿriyya, sijill 588:309–1266 (999 AH/1561 CE).

[41] See Abdal-Rehim 1996, who details such contracts.

[42] Wathāʾiq, sijill 1:408–1713 (957 AH/1551 CE).

[43] Wathāʾiq, sijill 1:184–829 (956 AH/1550 CE). Similar cases from the same volume are at pp. 184–829 and 183–824.

[44] Wathāʾiq, sijill 1:51–227 (956 AH/1550 CE).

[45] Isna, 30:11–43; Manfalūṭ, case 136.

[46] See Miṣr, Iʿlāmāt, 23:237–635; Manfalūṭ, sijill 5:26–122, 244–651; 5:38–136.

[47] Miṣr, Iʿlāmāt, sijill 23:162–456.

[48] Sijill 19:30–24 (1308 AH/1891 CE).

[49] ʿAqārī, sijill 22:10–3085 (1388 AH/1969 CE).

[50] Al-Jarīda al-Qaḍāʾiyya 1934 (publishing Egypt's National Appeal Courts decisions).

[51] According to a *firmān* dated 1273, the Hanafi *madhhab* was made the source of law in Egypt. Royal order (*irāda saniyya*) no. 28,1 states: "Item 4: Court litigation must be based on what is right and just in accordance to the holy *sharʿ* in regards to legal matters and the rights of believers. There must be scrutiny in establishing justice and passing judgments by applying the legitimate (*ṣaḥīḥa*) sayings of the great Imam (*al-imām al-aʿẓam*) Abū Ḥanīfa." Daʿāwī, sijill 1:17–31 (957 AH/1550 CE).

[52] Law No. 25 of 1929.

[53] See the excellent work by Mona Russell (2004) about the building of this new gendered education and the formation of Victorianism in Egypt through schools and text-books. Russell 2004.

[54] Butaye and de Leval 1918, 132.

[55] Majallat al-Qaḍāʾ al-Sharʿī 1926, 443–444; al-Fatāwā al-islāmiyya 1982, 2076.

[56] It should be noted that this connection between marriage and the creation of the nuclear family is found only in the personal status laws of states that were colonies of England and France. For example, the personal status laws of Algeria (a former French colony) define marriage as "a contract that takes place between a man and a woman according to the *sharʿ* [Islamic law]" and lists among its goals the formation of a family based on "affection, sympathy, cooperation, and morality of the couple and the protection of posterity [*ansāb*]." Law No. 84 (1984). Similar formulas define marriage in the laws of Syria, Iraq, and Jordan. In contrast, Kuwaiti law defines marriage as "a contract between a man and a woman who is lawfully permitted to him, the aim of which is cohabitation, chastity, and national strength." Law No. 51 (1984). Libya's laws define "marriage" as "a lawful pact which is based on a foundation of love, compassion, and tranquility which makes lawful the relationship between a man and a woman neither of whom is forbidden in marriage to the other." Law No. 10 (1984). Neither Kuwait nor Libya was under French or British colonial rule and their marriage definitions are closer to the traditional Islamic definition of marriage.

[57] *Al-Kitāb al-dhahabī* 1978, 1:234.
[58] See Sonbol 2006 for a discussion and court cases about the guardianship of women.
[59] Al-Bakrī 1991, 234.
[60] "La femme indigéne, qui épouse un tunisien administré français, devient *ipso facto* administrée française." Bulletin de legislation 1909 (Case XVI, 158, dated 10 March 1904), 191.
[61] *Al-Majmūʿa al-rasmiyya* 1938, 56–58 (Case 25, vol. 9, year 39).
[62] The Qurʾan refers to "the one in whose hands is the marriage tie (*ʿuqdat al-nikāḥ*)." Q 2:237.
[63] Alexandria, sijill 108:81–153 (1219 AH/1804 CE)
[64] Al-Jarīda al-Qaḍāʾiyya, sijill 1:12–13 (year 7) (1936 CE).
[65] Bāb al-Sharʿiyya, sijill 582:29–136 (955 AH/1548 CE).
[66] The laws were instituted by Law Number 25 for 1920 (amended in 1929, 1979, and 1985) for Muslims and Ordinances 140 through 151 of the Personal Status Laws for Coptic Orthodox Christians issued by the Majlis al-Millī in 1938 (reconfirmed by Court of Cassation in 1973).
[67] Maḥkamat Miṣr al-Jadīda al-Juzʾiyya 1956 (case 98).
[68] Majlis Millī 1953, 27–11 (case 15).

# *Five*

## QUESTIONS OF CONSENT: CONTRACTING A MARRIAGE IN OTTOMAN SYRIA AND PALESTINE

Judith E. Tucker

We have much information about the Islamic marriage contract in seventeenth- and eighteenth-century Ottoman Syria and Palestine. First, the registers of the Shariʿa (Islamic law) courts record the texts of many of these contracts, as well as litigation surrounding the rights and obligations they entailed, and thus give ample evidence of the contract's form and function.[1] Second, the Hanafi legal discourse of the day elaborates the doctrinal underpinnings of the contract; prominent legal thinkers (muftis) discussed and refined a range of issues related to the marriage contract in the fatwas (legal responsa) they issued, including its proper form, its necessary elements, the proper procedures for drawing up a contract, and the contexts within which the rights and obligations of husband and wife did or did not arise. In this paper, I look at just one such issue: that of female consent to the marriage contract. By exploring the ways in which the muftis and the courts handled this particular matter, I hope to raise a number of questions about the theory and practice of law vis-à-vis the marriage contract. What was the current legal understanding, as exemplified by the discussions of prominent local muftis, of the nature of female consent to a marriage contract? How was this understanding shaped by the Hanafi tradition? To what extent did this understanding inform court practice? What was the impact of such doctrinal discussions and court processes on the ways people actually approached the marriage contract?

In addressing the issue of female consent we enter, necessarily, socially contested territory. Historical context is critical here. In a society where the institution of the family under-girded many critical social, economic, and political relationships, we can expect the making of marriages to be a family concern: a marriage could reinforce or erode family bonds, convey or protect family property, and consolidate or dissipate family power and status. To require the active consent of a woman to a marriage contract could seriously impair a family's ability to arrange a critical marriage. To what extent did doctrinal discussions take cognizance of a family agenda in which the power to arrange strategic marriages was no doubt a jealously-guarded prerogative? Did legal discourse and legal practice resolve the inevitable tension between family control of marriage arrangements and a legal discourse that stressed the rights and obligations of an individual couple? Did the theory and practice of Islamic law governing marriage contracts transcend social pressures and uphold standards for a marriage contract that privileged individual right rather than family duty? The issue of female consent has much to tell us about the fluid relationship between Islamic law and society, with some clear relevance, I hope, to the problem of the marriage contract and female consent today.

## The Discourse on Consent

> Question: There is a virgin in her legal majority whose father married her to a man without her authorization (*idhn*) and she refused the marriage (and she was an adult at the time). If such is the case, is the marriage canceled by her refusal or not? And is her statement with oath that she refused the marriage (legally binding) or not?
>
> Answer: Yes, it is canceled by her refusal, and her statement with oath that she refused the marriage is (legally binding). Such is the situation, and God knows best.[2]

Khayr al-Dīn al-Ramlī, a renowned seventeenth-century Hanafi mufti from the Palestinian town of Ramla, delivered this fatwa, stating unequivocally that a woman in her legal majority (defined by the onset of menstruation at puberty) should not be required to enter a marital relationship against her wishes. Although her father stood as her natural guardian (*walī*) for the purposes of concluding a marriage contract, his power to act on her behalf in the marriage arrangements was clearly circumscribed by her right to refuse the marriage if she were in her majority.[3] She could not be required to argue that the marriage was inappropriate or defective—her personal opposition to the match was sufficient to render it void. Furthermore, her own statement that she had attained majority and had in a timely fashion refused the match was all the evidence a court would need to determine that the marriage was invalid. This is perhaps the clearest possible statement of the importance of a woman's consent to a marriage: her active refusal to consent results in immediate abrogation of the marriage contract. In issuing such an opinion, Khayr al-Dīn was following the lead of Hanafi jurisprudence which took the position that an adult woman could not be forced to marry against her own wishes and without her consent, and further, that her word as to her own refusal of the marriage must be accepted.[4] It should be noted that the Hanafi view that women have freedom in the contract of marriage just as in other contracts was not shared by other legal schools. Shafiʿi, Maliki, and Hanbali jurists all accept some level of restraint of a woman in the making of the marriage contract, although not in other contracts.[5]

Even in Hanafi legal thinking, not all cases of consent were so clear-cut. The first caveat concerned the girl still in her legal minority. All the fatwas issued by Syrian and Palestinian muftis of the seventeenth and eighteenth centuries assume that a minor girl's natural guardian—her father or, in his absence, her paternal grandfather—could arrange a marriage for her without her knowledge, much less her consent. The minor lacked legal competence, so she could neither accept nor refuse a marriage. A father could neatly sidestep the requirement of consent, then, by marrying off his daughter before she reached the age of puberty. Once married as a minor, a girl effectively lost her right of refusal. In the event that the guardianship of a girl, in the absence of her father or paternal grandfather, had devolved upon another individual who then married her off in her legal minority, however, the girl's right could be activated when she reached puberty through *khiyār al-bulūgh* (the option of puberty). For example, Ḥāmid al-ʿImādī, who held the official position of mufti in eighteenth-century Damascus, upheld a girl's right to refuse a marriage made by a guardian who was not her father or her grandfather when she came of age:

> Question: There is a woman who, as legal guardian, married her orphaned daughter to a suitable man with a fair *mahr* (dower), and the marriage was consummated. Then when she (the daughter) came of age, she chose *faskh* (judicial annulment) as soon as she reached maturity, and she declared that in court, and applied to the qadi [judge], and asked for an annulment following legal procedure. The qadi ruled on that and annulled the marriage. Is the annulment [valid] if such is the case?
>
> Answer: Since the plaintiff fulfilled the legal conditions, the above-mentioned marriage is cancelled by a legal annulment.[6]

This fatwa affirms that a girl who is married off in her minority by anyone other than her father or paternal grandfather can, indeed, refuse the marriage as soon as she reaches her majority.[7] The marriage she refuses may in fact have been a perfectly suitable one—with an appropriate groom and a good dower—and it may even have been consummated. Her own desire to leave the marriage is reason enough, however, to activate her right of refusal. To enforce her right, she must meet the legal requirement of requesting the annulment in a timely fashion as soon as she reaches her majority. The actual decree of annulment can only be made by a qadi, but if she is able to put her request before the judge in a period "immediately" after she reaches puberty, the judge should honor her request and annul the marriage regardless of the wishes of her husband or other family members.[8] Although this provision does not challenge the power of the father when it comes to arranging the marriages of minors, it does recognize that minor girls have an ultimate right of consent and seeks to remedy it at least in a partial fashion when the authority of the father over minor children is not at issue.

For the woman in her legal majority, as we have seen above, outright refusal of a marriage rendered it void, even if contracted by her father (or grandfather). The muftis had to consider, however, many of the legal refinements surrounding this right of consent. When and how should a woman signal her consent or refusal? What constitutes consent to a marriage? Did the right of consent or refusal signal a more active right to arrange one's own marriage? First, in order to consent to a marriage, a woman needed to know that a contract had indeed been made:

> Question: There is a man who pressed a claim against a woman that her father married him to her when she was a minor by way of his guardianship over her. She replied that she was in her legal majority at the time the marriage was contracted, and that she was not informed of the marriage. What is the ruling?
>
> Answer: Her word is accepted as proof of her majority at the time of the marriage if puberty is likely, [even] if the proof and hard evidence (*bayyina*) of puberty is lacking. And it is said in the *Tanwir*[9] and its commentary in the section on the *walī* that if her father married her off claiming the absence of puberty, and she said "I am of age," the marriage is not legally sound. And if she is an adolescent (*murāhiqa*), and the father and groom say no, she is a minor, then her statement is permitted as proof of her majority, and the adolescent can claim maturity, (although having) proof and hard evidence is preferable.[10]

In this case, a woman could claim that she had not been informed of marriage arrangements by her father at the time of the signing of the contract and therefore, as a result, the contract lacked the necessary element of her consent.[11] Now, a woman's right to refuse an arrangement was limited: she needed to signal her refusal as close to the time of the marriage as possible or else waive it; although there is no specified time limit, ordinarily she should refuse as soon as she is informed of the arrangement. In the above fatwa, a woman claims that she was not informed of her arranged marriage in a timely fashion, and her delayed refusal is the result of her ignorance of the entire proceeding. Not only is her testimony to her lack of awareness of the arrangement accepted, but the critical issue of whether she was physically mature and thus in her legal majority at the time of the writing of the contract (and thus enabling her right of refusal) is resolved solely by her retrospective claim to maturity. A woman's right to accept or refuse a marriage requires of course that she know that a marriage is being arranged; but the law also requires that she be fully informed about the prospective groom and the *mahr*. If the *walī* consults the bride before the marriage "but fails to mention [the name of] the groom and the [amount of the] *mahr* [. . .] the marriage is not legally sound."[12]

The muftis did not necessarily require, however, that consent be actively expressed. The virgin who keeps silent when informed of a marriage arrangement can be presumed to have consented, as long as she has been fully informed as to the particulars. A woman who is no longer a virgin, however, must express her consent in an active verbal manner because she is presumed to lack the reticence of a virgin concerning the matters of marriage. Overall, the thrust of these provisions seems clear: a woman's guardian should not make a mockery of the right of consent by withholding information from his charge who is, after all, a party to the contract.

The most active form of consent was contained in a woman's ability, as a party to the contract, to arrange her own marriage without the interference of her *walī*. In general, the Hanafi muftis of the time recognized a woman's right to marry herself off:

> Question: There is a free, legally competent virgin who married herself to her paternal uncle's son who was suitable for her. Is the marriage legally valid if her uncle did not approve it?
>
> Answer: Yes, her marriage is legally valid, and it is not conditional on the approval of her uncle. Such is the case and God knows best.[13]

Such marriage arrangements were perfectly permissible and binding as long as they met certain conditions:

> Question: There is a virgin of full legal age and maturity who wants to marry herself to a suitable man with a fair *mahr*. Can she do this? And her uncle and father do not have [the right of] veto?
>
> Answer: Yes.[14]

In the two preceding fatwas the right of a free woman in her majority (even if she is a virgin) to arrange her own marriage is confirmed even in the face of opposition from her natural guardian and other close paternal relatives. There were, however, some limitations placed on her choice of mate. Should she choose a man who did not meet the legal requirements of suitability (*kafā'a*)—his lineage, legal status, social class, and moral standards should all match or exceed those of her own background—her guardian could bring his objections to the judge and ask that the marriage be ruled defective. Similarly, the marriage contract she arranged should include a fair *mahr*, in the sense of a dower appropriate to her station in life.[15] Any marriage she contracted which lacked these two requirements might be subject to judicial annulment at the request of her *walī*. Still, a woman's basic right to make her own marriage arrangements, within certain parameters, was consistently supported by the muftis of the period. Her guardian could only raise obstacles by resorting to the court with claims about the absence of suitability of the groom and/or an inadequate *mahr*. The judge then had the responsibility to weigh the objections of the guardian against the woman's claim that this was a suitable marriage.

The Hanafi legal discourse of the time on a woman's right of consent in marriage arrangements, then, did recognize the privileged role of the family patriarch, the father or grandfather, in the making of a marriage contract. The guardian could agree to a marriage contract as proxy for his charge. If a girl were married off in her minority by her father or grandfather, she could not object to the marriage then or later. In the absence of the father or grandfather, other guardians had less leeway with arrangements for minors: marriages must meet the legal requirements of suitability and fair *mahr*; if not, a judge could take it upon himself to annul the marriage. Moreover, the bride could herself refuse such a marriage when she reached her legal majority even if the groom and *mahr* met legal standards and the marriage had been consummated. If a woman were in her legal majority when a contract was made, the power of the father/grandfather guardian was circumscribed: the contract was invalidated by her lack of consent to the marriage as long as (if she was a virgin) she made known her refusal by more than silence. And, according to what is perhaps the most critical doctrine in Hanafi legal discourse on the marriage contract in this period as far as women are concerned, a woman was also authorized to make a marriage contract without the permission or even approval of any relative, including her father or grandfather, as long as the contract united her with a suitable groom and provided a fair *mahr*. It is this last feature of Hanafi law—the recognition that women enjoyed an individual right to contract a marriage—that seems most at odds with our sense of the social realities of the time. To what extent did legal practice, as opposed to legal theory, honor female rights to accept, refuse, or even make a marriage contract that might run contrary to the wishes of the family and its patriarchs? The records of the Shariʿa courts help us understand the practices surrounding the marriage contract in this period.

## Consent in the Courts

Although muftis like Khayr al-Dīn al-Ramlī and Ḥāmid al-ʿImādī were respected legal authorities whose opinions carried significant weight in their respective communities, there is reason to believe that the Shariʿa doctrines on female consent reflected in their opinions were followed more in letter than in spirit in the legal practice of the courts. If the court records are any indication, the legal form and requirements of the marriage contract, including the insistence on female consent, appear to have been well known. We find many marriage contracts entered in the court registers in the eighteenth century: the records of the Jerusalem Shariʿa court records contain countless contracts, suggesting that most if not all marriages in that city were recorded in court. In Damascus and Nablus, however, marriage contracts are not so ubiquitous: we have a fairly steady number and seemingly representative set of contracts registered, but it is clear that not all the towns' marriages are accounted for.

These contracts adhere to a standard format that covers the legal bases, even when we are dealing with very different social classes. A contract that united the scions of elite families of the ruling group was fulsome indeed:

> In the name of God, the merciful, the compassionate.
>
> Praise be to God, the glorious creator; kind in what he brought forth. He who ordained marriage. Praise be upon our Lord Muḥammad, his kin, and his companions.
>
> This is what he—the pride of the grandees and the nobles, the possessor of munificence and gratitude, Muḥammad Āghā, son of the pride of the grandees and the nobles, the possessor of munificence and gratitude, the right honorable al-Ḥājj ʿAlī Jurbajī, son of the deceased prince of the honorable princes Yūsuf Bek—dowered her, his betrothed, the pride of the guarded women, the ornament of the venerable, the exalted veil, the inviolable temple, *al-sitt* (the lady) Fāṭima *khanīn khātūn*—the daughter of the prince of the honorable princes, grandest of the grandees, of the attributes of venerability and decorum, the purest and sweetest of people, the right honorable al-Ḥājj Ṣāliḥ Bāshā, governor of Gaza Hashin and Nablus, and al-Lajun, may God perpetuate his mercy and may his good deeds prevail, the virgin, the minor: a dower the value of which is 600 *zaltah*s of which she receives 400 *zaltah*s and the remainder of 200 *zaltah*s is owed by the groom until such time as separation by death or divorce.
>
> The pride of the scholars, the honorable ʿAbd al-Ghanī Efendi ʿAlī, son of the deceased *shaykh* Muḥyī l-Dīn, is the legal agent for the groom, and his honor, the aforementioned right honorable Bāshā is the guardian for the bride. The agency is witnessed by the pride of the scholars, our master *al-sayyid* Muḥammad Efendi al-Tamīmī, and the pride of the venerable preachers, our master *al-shaykh* ʿUmar al-Makkī the scribe. . . . 24 Dhū l-Qaʿda 1135.[16]

A contract for a more humble couple read rather differently:

> The groom, Ṣalāḥ Sharāra, son of Saʿad.

> The bride, the *ḥurma* (woman) Fāṭima, daughter of Nāṣir, who was previously married and has no legal impediments.
>
> The dower, 15 *ghurūsh adadiyya*, of which she will receive 10 *ghurūsh* now and the remaining 5 is deferred until separation by death or divorce. She was married by her agent, Muḥammad, son of Ṣalāḥ, whose agency was witnessed by Aḥmad, son of Ṣalāḥ Abī Hābīl, and Shishan Ṣāliḥ, son of ʿAqrūq, who have legal knowledge of her. The groom accepted the marriage contract for himself. End of Rajab 1138.[17]

Although the parties to these contracts stand at opposite ends of the social scale, the basic features of the contracts are the same. As with other recorded contracts of the time, they consist of: (1) clear identifications of the bride and the groom; (2) statements of their legal standing (major or minor); (3) precise descriptions of the dower, including its immediate and deferred portions; and (4), and most important for the present discussion, detailed attention to the relations of guardianship or agency that render the acceptance of the contract legally sound. In the first contract, that of a minor girl, the right of her father/guardian to marry her off is an unquestioned one which does not require any additional testimony or evidence. The groom, presumed to be in his legal majority, must accept the contract himself, which he does through an agent, whose agency in turn is attested to by two upstanding individuals. In the second contract, both the bride and the groom are in their legal majority and must accept the contract themselves, whether in person or through an agent. The groom in this case consented in person while the bride's consent was obtained through an agent, whose agency was once again witnessed by two men.

These contracts and, indeed, all others entered into the court record conform at least at a formal level to the requirement of female consent. Brides in their legal majority must either accept the contract in person, or have authorized an agent to accept it for them. This authorization in turn must have been witnessed by two trustworthy men, even if the agent is a very close relative such as a father or a brother. Most women whose contracts were registered in the Damascus, Jerusalem, and Nablus courts accepted the contract through an agent although a minority did agree to the marriage in person. But did adherence to this formal procedure signal true consent to a marriage? It is very difficult to discern. Most of the agents who spoke for brides were, not surprisingly, close relatives, commonly the woman's father or brother. And most of the witnesses to the delegation of this agency were themselves either male relatives or family associates whose independence of judgment could be questioned. If all the parties who spoke for and to a woman's consent had the same family agenda in mind, we may well wonder if a bride's views, and especially a bride's opposition, would ever get a hearing.

The suspicion that the muftis' advocacy of female consent did not always resonate with social practice, even in the context of the court system itself, is further confirmed by the way in which the court dealt with the few issues of consent that did reach the stage of litigation. One of these rare cases involved a Jerusalem woman who tried to dispute an unwanted marriage. In the late 1730s, a man came to court to claim her as his bride, saying that she had been given to him in marriage eight years previously when she was still a minor. The woman then claimed that she had never been married to this man, and refused to accede to his demand that she reside with him. The putative husband was able, however, to bring both her paternal and maternal uncles to court to testify that she had been properly married to him (presumably by her father or grandfather) when she was a minor. The judge then ruled that she must be immediately "delivered" to her rightful husband.[18] Whatever the original facts of the matter, this kind of case suggests that it could be very difficult for a woman to exercise her right of consent unless she had the support and backing of her family. This particular woman must have held out some hope that by coming to the court she could have the marriage declared false, but she was to be sorely disappointed. Although we do not find evidence of egregious violation of this right in the court records, neither do we find decisions that actively champion a woman's right to contest marriage arrangements that were made for her.

## Beyond the Rule of Law

If the courts appear to have been somewhat less than aggressive in enforcing a woman's right to consent to or refuse a marriage contract, even more questions arise once we move outside the orbit of legal institutions. In communities at least in principle under the rule of Islamic law, the muftis bemoan some irregular practices in marriage arrangements, practices that could effectively negate a woman's right of consent. Although most of the muftis' opinions concerning marital issues address routine questions about the details of the marriage contract, upon occasion they confronted flagrant violations of the law. Two social practices, both of which appear to belie the principle of female consent, were brought to their attention.

First was the practice of marriage by capture:

> Question: A man approached a woman, a virgin in her legal majority, who was married to someone else, abducted (*khaṭifa*) her in the month of Ramadan, and took her to a village near her own village. He brought her to the *shaykh* of the village who welcomed him and gave him hospitality and protection. There the man consummated the "marriage," saying "between us there are relations." Such is the way of the peasants. [...] What is the punishment for him and the

> man who abetted him? Should Muslim rulers halt these practices of the peasants [...] even by combat and execution?
>
> Answer: The punishment of the abductor and his accomplice for this grave crime is severe beating and long imprisonment, and even worse punishment until they show remorse. It is conceivable that the punishment be execution because of the severity of this act of disobedience to God. This practice—and one fears for the people of the region if it spreads and they do not halt it—will be punished by God. The one who commits this act, and those who remain silent about it, are like one who punches a hole in a ship, [an act] that will drown all the passengers. [...] It is the obligation of Muslim rulers to commit themselves to putting an end to this revolting practice [...] even if it means punishment by combat and execution.[19]

Such a marriage by capture eludes the laws governing marriage arrangements altogether. There is no proper contract, and thus the requirements of a suitable groom, a fair *mahr*, and a consenting bride are all put aside. We are left with an image of a woman's ultimate loss of choice, of a rape that robs her of all volition as well as the privileges that accrue from the marriage contract.

The term *khatf* (abduction) clearly connotes force, but how do we know that such a captured woman is an unwilling participant? Could abduction sometimes be used as a cover for elopement, a possibility suggested here by the fact that the woman had been legally contracted to someone else but was conveniently "abducted" before the marriage could be consummated? The fatwa's hypothetical tone, typical of the genre, lacks the concreteness and detail we need to answer this question. Nor do we have the kind of supporting anthropological evidence that could help us gauge the extent of this practice. The presence of this and other fatwas on the subject suggests, however, that the muftis thought marriage by capture was an issue in their community that needed to be denounced.[20]

A second practice that drew scrutiny was that of "exchanging" brides. Two families might agree to swap their daughters in marriage.

> Question: There were two men and each one married his minor charge to the other and they paid the *mahr*s [but] one of them did not deliver the full *mahr*. Should the other retain custody of his charge until the guardian [of the other girl] delivers it or not?
>
> Answer: The guardian who received the total *mahr* is obligated to hand over his charge, and the other is not so obligated, and [indeed] he is forbidden to hand her over. And if he has already surrendered her then he should take her back until [the *mahr*] is delivered. And God knows best.[21]

Here and elsewhere the marriage contract is a deal between two families or guardians who are exchanging brides in order to serve their own interests.[22] In many of these situations, it is insufficient or even non-payment of the *mahr* that is at issue; the exchange marriage was well known to the canonical doctrine and was denounced and invalidated on this ground. We may conclude that families sometimes made these arrangements precisely in order to minimize or avoid dower payments while at the same time they established strong reciprocal relationships. The disadvantages to the brides, at least in principle, were manifest: such arrangements could cheat them out of a dower, and their guardians' mutual interest in forging an exchange could foreclose any kind of real consent. Again, the practice is not completely transparent. We cannot be sure that such exchange marriages necessarily eliminated consent; perhaps the young women involved were more apt to be marrying relatives or close neighbors whom they were likely to know. Still, this kind of bartering of brides flew in the face of the muftis' doctrinal positions on female consent.

The extent of the practices of marriage by capture and the exchange of brides is difficult to pin down. The muftis tended, in their discussions, to locate such extralegal maneuvers in the countryside; it is out in the villages that such exchanges and abductions were likely to occur, not in their own urban backyards. Whether the right of female consent was more likely to be thwarted in rural areas is, however, an open question. The muftis themselves were generally town-dwellers from comfortable families whose views of peasant life cannot always be taken at face value. The phenomena of marriage by capture and exchange brides that they target, however, do suggest that at least some social practices of the time did not necessarily conform to the legal requirements of the marriage contract, including that of female consent.

## Conclusion

The Hanafi muftis who elaborated Islamic legal discourse in seventeenth- and eighteenth-century Syria and Palestine supported a woman's right to have a voice in her marriage arrangements. With the exception of the contracts marrying girls who had not reached their legal majority, a marriage contract made without a woman's informed consent was an invalid contract. And even for a marriage contracted during a girl's minority, she could reject it once she reached her majority if it was contracted by someone other than her father or grandfather. Furthermore, a woman in her legal majority could play a more active role by arranging her own marriage even against the wishes of her male relatives. The record of action in the Islamic courts suggests that women knew they had these rights and might, upon occasion, protest violations of these rights in front of the judge. This was not, however, a common occurrence, and the courts did not appear to play a central part in the championing of the woman's right of consent. In addition, there were social practices of the time—for example, marriage by capture and the exchange of brides—that eluded the rule of law.

What is the relevance of this or any study of the theory and practice of Islamic law in a past era? I think that the revisiting of Islamic legal history can help us contextualize the marriage contract in the present. We can argue that the Islamic legal tradition has, at least in part, a record of strong support for a woman's right to have a choice of marriage partner.[23] Then, as now, Muslim thinkers knew that this right threatened the power of the patriarch: marriage was and is embedded in a network of social and economic relations of paramount interest and concern to a woman's male relatives. In Hanafi legal doctrine, however, such considerations are irrelevant to the basic rights a woman enjoys as a party to a marriage contract: the right of consent and the right to a *mahr*, without which a contract is invalid. The muftis' uncompromising attitude on these issues, and their condemnation of any curtailment of these rights under social pressure, allow us to argue that the Islamic marriage contract can and should be an instrument for the empowerment of women. The muftis who elaborated Islamic legal doctrine were, of course, part of their communities and societies with interests and agendas of their own: we need to read their opinions as representative, in part, of the views and biases of the urban culture to which they belonged. Still, their criticisms of the practices of "other" communities can educate us about the ways in which the vested interests of patriarchy have occasioned partial and self-serving readings, or even a willful ignorance of, the requirements of marriage under Islamic law.

NOTES

[1] Not all marriage contracts were entered into the court registers; the practice of registration seems to have varied from place to place. These observations are based on personal surveys of the following court records: Maḥkama Nābulus (Nablus Islamic Court), sijills no. 4 (1134–1138 AH/1722–1726 CE and no. 5 (1139–1141 AH/1728–1729 CE); Maḥkamat al-Quds (Jerusalem Islamic Court), sijills no. 226 (1145–1146 AH/1732–1734 AD) and no. 230 (1151–5112 H/1738–1740 AD).

[2] Al-Ramlī 1856–1857, 21.

[3] On differences among legal schools on matters of guardianship in marriage and rules for consent, see Nasir 1986, 50–53. For some observations on court practices in nineteenth- and early twentieth-century Egypt in these matters, see Sonbol 1996a, 242–248.

[4] In giving precedence to a woman's statement that she had refused a marriage contract over a father's or husband's testimony that she had accepted a contract, the woman is being treated as a defendant whose position prevails over that of the plaintiff if the plaintiff is unable to meet certain standards of proof. See al-Marghīnānī 1957, 34–36.

[5] For their justification of such restraint, see El Alami 1991, 192–193.

[6] Al-ʿImādī 1881–1882, 1:32.

[7] In the case of granting the option of annulment to a girl whose marriage was arranged by her mother, al-ʿImādī follows the lead of Abū Ḥanīfa, founder of the Hanafi *madhhab*, and his disciple Muḥammad al-Shaybānī, but departs from the opinion of another key disciple, Abū Yūsuf, who did not think an appropriate marriage arranged by a legal guardian could be annulled by the bride upon coming of age. See al-Marghīnānī 1957, 37.

[8] Idem, 37.

[9] Most likely a reference to a seventeenth-century work of Hanafi *fiqh* and traditions.

[10] Al-ʿImādī 1881–1882, 1:28.

[11] We should note here that, again, al-ʿImādī follows the clear lead of Abū Ḥanīfa and Muḥammad al-Shaybānī in insisting that the bride retains her coming-of-age option to refuse a marriage until she is fully informed of the marriage. She does not, however, need to be informed of her legal rights in the matter at the time she is told of the existence of the contract. Al-Marghīnānī 1957, 37.

[12] Al-ʿImādī 1881–1882, 1:30.

[13] Al-Ramlī 1856–1857, 21.

[14] Al-ʿImādī 1881–1882, 1:31.

[15] According to Hanafi law, the "proper" dower is to be ascertained by studying what amount of dower was received by a woman's female relatives on the paternal side, and then taking "age, beauty, fortune, understanding, and virtue" into consideration in the individual case. See al-Marghīnānī 1957, 53.

[16] Maḥkama Nābulus, sijill no. 4:11.

[17] Maḥkama Nābulus, sijill no. 4:321.

[18] Mahkamat al-Quds, sijill no. 230:286.

[19] Al-Ramlī 1856–1857, 83.

[20] See also idem, 23.

[21] Idem, 29.

[22] See also idem, 30; al-ʿImādī 1881–1882, 1:18.

[23] The study of the history of legal doctrine and practice continues to be important. Some Hanafi legal thinkers have recently questioned the capacity of adult women to contract marriages independently. On the relevant case of Saima Waheed (1997), see Ali 1997, 156–174.

# *Six*

# THE ISLAMIC MARRIAGE CONTRACT IN AL-ANDALUS (10TH–16TH CENTURIES)

Amalia Zomeño

"The historian would be making [an] error of perspective if he did indeed confine himself to prescriptive statements, the terms of regulations and the formulae of legal documents, if he relied on what the words say and if he believed that they effectively governed people's behavior."[1]

## Introduction

In Islamic as well as in European societies the institution of marriage is governed not only by legal norms, but also by a set of social conventions expressed in rituals and ceremonies. An alliance between two families is not just a legally valid act, but also a socially relevant bond. A marriage contract can only result when legal norms and regulations have met, and perhaps struggled with, social and ritual conventions. Put another way, a marriage contract is a document that serves to define a social link in legal terms.

In al-Andalus in the Middle Ages, the process of reconciling legal and social spheres took place in a single face-to-face meeting between the clerks of the administration of justice, notaries, and witnesses, and the representatives of two families hoping to forge a new social alliance. It was in this meeting, which I will call here a "contracting session," that the legal knowledge of the notaries confronted and mediated the social and economic goals of the two parties.

In this essay, I will address the law and practice of marriage contracts in medieval al-Andalus, but in so doing I will heed G. Duby's warning quoted above—which caution should always be present in the mind of the historian—and not rely solely on doctrinal descriptions of the Islamic marriage contract. This paper will show that, while there was a high degree of agreement between social behavior and the strictures of Islamic law concerning marriage, that agreement was not perfect. The sources do not provide enough information to know whether agreement occurred because Islamic law shaped the parties' behavior or because the parties' knowledge of the law enabled them to give proper legal form to behavior possibly divergent from law. To discern an accurate picture of the practice of contracting a Muslim marriage in the tenth through sixteenth centuries on the Iberian Peninsula, I will utilize three sources of study: (1) the few actual Andalusi marriage documents that remain extant in the records, (2) formularies (*wathāʾiq* works) written to assist notaries in drafting marriage contracts, and (3) fatwa collections—collections of non-binding legal responsa by Islamic legal scholars—on marriage contract issues and legal problems. After surveying these source works, the format of this essay will then follow the basic format of the marriage contracts themselves, comparing, for each section, the recommendations given to notaries in the formularies with the actual documents available, analyzing the similarities and differences. I will then draw some conclusions regarding the nature of the Islamic law of marriage and its actual practice in medieval al-Andalus.

## The Andalusi Marriage Documents

The Arabs conquered the Iberian Peninsula in 711 CE, and their rule continued until the Christian reconquest of the Nasrid Kingdom by the Catholic Monarchs in 1492. To date, studies of the marriage practices in al-Andalus during these eight centuries of Muslim dominion have not been based on actual marriage documents, but on legal sources, especially compilations of scholars' opinions (fatwas), manuals for notaries (*wathāʾiq* works), and *ḥisba* manuals (intended for officers charged with insuring public morality),[2] although some studies using chronicles have contributed notably to the subject.[3] This is because the very few marriage documents that have survived date almost entirely from after the Christian reconquest and come from the Mudejars, the Muslim minority that continued as much as possible to practice its religion and to marry, as we shall see, in an Islamic way.[4]

Data for the period between the tenth and twelfth centuries are provided by three Andalusi *wathāʾiq* works: those of Muḥammad b. Aḥmad b. al-ʿAṭṭār (d. 399/1008),[5] Ibn Mughīth al-Ṭulayṭulī (d. 459/1067),[6] and ʿAlī b. Yaḥyā al-Jazīrī (d. 585/1189).[7] As far as I know, the earliest Muslim marriage document available to us dates from the end of the thirteenth century (1297 CE) from the conquered city of Valencia.[8]

By the thirteenth century the only part of the Iberian Peninsula that remained under Islamic rule was the Nasrid Kingdom of Granada (1231–1492). From this time we have two Granadan manuals for notaries, one by Abū l-Qāsim b. Salmūn (d. 767/1365)[9] and the other by Abū Isḥāq al-Gharnāṭī (d. 768/1366).[10] The documents are more abundant, five of them coming from the Granadan kingdom itself[11] and five others from the Mudejar communities of Aragón[12] and La Rioja.[13] Nine more come from the conquered Muslim communities of Calatayud (in Aragón) and Valencia,[14] which remained Muslim until the sixteenth century.[15] This brings the total number of surviving marriage documents from Granada, Valencia, Calatayud, and La Rioja to twenty. The earliest is dated 1297, the latest 1591. Only the four Granadan documents come from Muslims living under Islamic rule; the others belong to Muslims under Christian rulers, before their conversion to Christianity.

## *Wathāʾiq* Works: The Notaries' View

*Wathāʾiq* is the plural of *wathīqa*, the term used in al-Andalus to designate a "certified document." The *wathāʾiq* works are formularies, or manuals for notaries, showing them how legal documents should be written down. They provide model documents, in which the notary has only "to fill in the blanks," and give extensive recommendations on how to meet the demands of the parties involved while at the same time respecting the law. Typically, this kind of legal work suggests a basic model for every document, which is followed by several explanations and additional material that the notary may need in order to modify that model. Therefore, every model, or "form," is explained with reference to Islamic legal doctrine (*fiqh*), so that the notaries know why one formula should be used instead of another.[16]

The authors of the Andalusi *wathāʾiq* works were highly specialized jurists, as well as being highly skilled in Arabic, and most of the time they had a job in the administration of justice as notaries themselves or as counselors of the qadi. Their knowledge of Islamic jurisprudence is evident from their biographies, but also from the fact that in the explanations of the models they also incorporated legal material from previous legal works.[17] Ibn Salmūn in fourteenth-century Granada, for example, followed very closely—and quoted frequently—the formulary of Ibn Mughīth of Toledo, an eleventh-century author; many stipulations are very similar in both works and some formulas are exactly the same.[18] On the other hand, al-Jazīrī introduced a new model for the marriage contract, but was still heavily influenced by earlier Andalusi works. All of them based their models on Ibn al-ʿAṭṭār's compilation.[19] As some authors have pointed out, the marriage documents of Valencia in the sixteenth century follow very closely the formulae and directions suggested by Ibn Mughīth five centuries earlier.[20] The documents of Aragón, also from the sixteenth century, are clearly drawn up according to the directions of al-Jazīrī's handbook. The notaries of these Mudéjar communities also knew and used this work extensively. A question arises as to the extent to which changing marriage practices of Andalusi society are reflected in the *wathāʾiq* works. While formulae and wording remained the same over centuries, the authors of the formularies might have introduced some variations in their compilations of models. However, to my knowledge, there is no study that compares in detail the *wathāʾiq* works with the actual documents;[21] this article will try to make such a comparison as far as marriage contracts are concerned.

The first of the similarities between actual documents and the models of the formularies lies in their general structure. With few exceptions, they are organized according to the same pattern. In all the documents the specific components and the order in which they appear follow formulary models. This structure is as follows: (1) introductory formula followed by the names of the parties, (2) detailed description of the marriage payments, (3) conditions or stipulations (*shurūṭ*), (4) rights and duties of the parties, (5) guardianship (*wilāya*), (6) witness testimony, (7) signatures of witnesses and date. Thus, the structure of both the formularies and the actual marriage contracts remained the same for a long period of time—as long as the six centuries, in fact, that elapsed from the earliest *wathāʾiq* handbook I am using here until the last document I have found from Valencia in 1591. But, apart from structure, are there any differences in content or meaning? We shall discuss this below.

## Fatwa Compilations: The Muftis' View

The Andalusi fatwas supply another dimension to the picture provided by the documents and formularies.[22] The muftis at the time were critical of the notaries and their methods of drafting marriage contracts, since many of the legal problems about which the muftis were consulted had their origins in the contracts' imprecise phrasing and, sometimes, shaky legality. These juridical criticisms offer another view of the marriage contract in al-Andalus. In fact, as David Powers already pointed out, many fatwas explain and comment on the historical, social, and legal context, and also on the use, and misuse, of legal documents, including marriage contracts.[23]

Several fatwas from Granada, for example, answer the question of whether a marriage contract must be drawn up in order for a legal marriage to exist. These questions presented to the muftis reveal that much more important than the drawing up of a contract were the ceremonies that confirmed the social link created by marriage: the celebration of the wedding (*ʿurs*) and the exchange of gifts. The muftis accepted such practices as legally significant, since the publicity, the consent, and the agreement of a guardian for the bride were secured at the moment of such marriages.[24] The "social" conclusion of the marriage does not rely solely on the presence of a legal document notarized by professional witnesses.

Even when a notary was involved and the marriage contract formally drawn up, fatwas show that the documents do not always reflect actual practice.[25] A question posed to Ibn Lubb (d. 782/1381) in Granada, for example, mentions that although the custom of the notaries was to record the receipt of a certain marriage gift, this gift was never exchanged by the parties at that time, but rather somewhat later.[26]

The fatwa compilations, therefore, show that although many marriage documents were drawn up according to the models and to Islamic law, these documents did not always reflect the actual practice of the participants and their customary understanding of the legal implications of the marriage. In other words, the data provided by the Andalusi fatwas will help to explain the interpretation of the marriage documents by the parties as well as by the muftis at the time and their use in court when legal action arose from them.

## Beginning the Marriage Contract: The Initial Formula and the Names of the Parties

Andalusi marriage contracts usually began with certain formulaic sentences: the *basmala* ("in the name of God") and the *ḥamdala* ("praise be to God"), always followed by Qur'anic passages and sayings of the Prophet. These introductory formulae, the most standardized part of the contract, are recommended in all the *wathāʾiq* works, with the exception of the earliest one by Ibn al-ʿAṭṭār. Ibn Mughīth, for example, recommends beginning with the *basmala* followed by the *ḥamdala*, as is written in every Islamic document, and then thanking God by quoting the Qur'anic passage: "It is He who created from water a human being; then He made him kin by blood or marriage. Your Lord is All-Powerful."[27] He also suggests that notaries remind the parties, with a sentence inserted in the contract itself, of God's endorsement of marriage and His prohibition against fornication.[28] With certain variations in style and length, these handbook recommendations for invocations were followed by subsequent notaries. One of these documents, the marriage contract of the daughter of the sultan of Granada, has survived only in a Spanish translation made in 1553 by Juan Rodríguez, "scribe and translator of Arabic documents into Romance of Granada" (*escribano romanzador de las escrituras arábigas de Granada*).[29] In his translation he adds a note saying that, as a Christian, he refuses to translate the first part of the contract because, according to him, "it contains things that have nothing to do with the contract itself, being only mere praises to the one [God] Who should not be praised."[30]

After the invocations comes a second, shorter part of the formulaic introduction: a short sentence describing the kind of document about to be read. The simple formula was: "this is what so-and-so gave as *ṣadāq*" (*hādhā mā aṣdaqa fulān*),[31] or "this is a marriage document" (*hādhā kitāb nikāḥ*).[32] Immediately after this follow the names of both parties. According to the *wathāʾiq* works, only the personal names of the bride and groom and of their two fathers need be mentioned, leaving the notaries merely to substitute real names into the generic *fulān b. fulān* and *fulāna bint fulān*.[33] However, most of the notaries, perhaps at the request of the parties or hoping for a higher payment, tended to prefix the names with laudatory adjectives. In a document from Valencia dated 1568, for example, the names are written as follows: "This is what the young, respected and of high and noble origin Abū ʿUthmān Saʿd, son of the honorable, eminent, blessed and praiseworthy Aḥmad al-Jaqlīrī from the outskirts of ʿUrūba, gave as *ṣadāq* to his wife, the young, beautiful, noble, protected virgin, virtuous and praiseworthy Nazha."[34]

## The Marriage Payments

The marriage contract in al-Andalus is formally called *ʿaqd al-nikāḥ* or *kitāb al-nikāḥ*, but is most often called *kitāb al-ṣadāq, ʿaqd al-ṣadāq*, or simply *ṣadāq*.[35] This reflects the important role played by the husband's obligatory payment (*ṣadāq* or *mahr*).[36] In fact, under the Maliki school, prevalent in al-Andalus, this payment is one of the legal conditions required for the contract's validity,[37] the other two being the presence of the bride's guardian (*walī*) concluding the contract on her behalf, and two upright witnesses.[38]

According to the *wathāʾiq* works, the total amount of the *ṣadāq* must be registered first, including the currency in which it is to be paid. This stipulation of the total amount of the *ṣadāq* always ends with the sentence *naqdan wa-kāliʾan* ("one part in cash and another delayed"),[39] showing that the *ṣadāq* in al-Andalus was usually paid in two parts, prompt and deferred. The exact amount of the part of the *ṣadāq* requiring prompt payment (*naqd* in al-Andalus) should be stipulated immediately after this provision. All the *wathāʾiq* handbooks recommend the notary to register the *walī*'s receipt of the prompt payment on behalf of the bride from the hands of the husband for the purpose of providing her with a trousseau.[40] By explicitly noting the guardian's taking of possession of the prompt payment, as the *wathāʾiq* handbooks explain, "the husband will be exempted from further payment of this part."[41] Finally, the other part of the *ṣadāq*, the "deferred part" (*kāliʾ* in al-Andalus), should be included in this section of the marriage contract, specifying its exact amount and the exact delay for its payment.[42]

All the documents follow these guidelines concerning the documentation in the contract of the husband's obligatory marriage payment. All of the contracts mention that the prompt payment was already received by the guardian of the bride. The contracts also mention the deferred payment, usually asserting a payment period of two years. However, in addition to this obligatory *ṣadāq* payment, the documents show that the husband usually gave other gifts (sing. *hadiyya*) of varying importance to the bride. This additional gift means perhaps that the trousseau was not actually bought with the prompt payment of the *ṣadāq*, but provided by the husband as another contribution to the marriage. Many sixteenth-century Valencian documents include additional gifts such as rich clothes, quantities of linen and wool, expensive textiles, gold-embroidered silks, and jewelry, and thus this may have been a standard customary gift in the community.[43] The *hadiyya* also appears in some fourteenth-century fatwas from Granada, often legally assimilated to the *ṣadāq*.[44]

Since it was required under Maliki law that the *ṣadāq* be paid before consummation or the marriage would not be valid, the notaries were obliged to register in the contract that the prompt payment had been made and received. However, one Granadan fatwa issued by Ibn Lubb reveals that it was the custom of the notaries to register the receipt of the prompt payment even when the payment had in reality not been made.[45] The question posed to the mufti was made in general terms, without any reference to any specific problem, but it highlights the kind of legal problems that might emerge if the notaries do not reflect the payments according to reality. In fact, he was asked what one should do if the bride demands the prompt payment, which according to her was not paid, while the husband, pointing to what had been written in the contract, claimed he did. Of course, the question raises doubts about whether custom followed the legal requirement that the prompt payment be paid before consummation; perhaps it was paid later, or perhaps not at all. Perhaps the payment of the "prompt part" of the *ṣadāq* was the subject of an arrangement between the families who, independently of what was written or agreed to be written in the contract, chose a convenient moment and form for its payment. Essentially, the law and the contract did line up, but only for avoiding the invalidation of the marriage contract. What this fatwa clearly demonstrates is that, as historians, we should not always rely solely on the written documents.

The same occurred concerning the payment of the deferred part of the *ṣadāq*. In fact, as the fatwas explain, the deferral of part of the obligatory payment had its origin in custom, and Islamic law considered it licit.[46] Therefore, husbands were paying the obligatory *ṣadāq* in two parts, the deferred part being given several years after consummation. The jurists did not attempt to fix doctrinally any exact timing for the payment of the deferred portion; rather, the scholars considered the timing something to be fixed either by the parties' agreement or, if none, by custom, noting how the latter may change according to the place, time, and social status of the parties. The jurists did insist that, if a delayed payment is agreed upon by the parties, it should be registered in the marriage contract to avoid later legal problems.[47]

The documents of Granada show that when husbands died, the deferred amount due to their wives had to be extracted from the estate before the distribution among the heirs. This suggests that, whatever terms were agreed to by the parties, payment of the deferred portion was in practice often long delayed and paid only in the event of death (making it a sort of pension for the widow), or upon repudiation (*ṭalāq*) by the husband (making it analogous to alimony).[48]

The Andalusi formularies also make several recommendations regarding the explicit mention of other marriage payments in the contract. In general, these other donations were called *siyāqa* (nuptial gifts) and *niḥla* (presents), and usually refer to a transfer of property in the form of real estate (houses, arable land, or both). The *niḥla* was a donation made to the bride by her parents or to the groom by his,[49] to ensure the transfer of property to the next generation. The *siyāqa*, on the other hand, refers only to a payment made by the husband to the bride over and above the amount of the obligatory *ṣadāq*.[50] The additional recommendations provided in the *wathā'iq* works as guidelines for the inclusion of the *siyāqa* and the *niḥla* are simple: the notary should register in the contract the limits of the land (or the house), its physical situation in the village or city, whether all the property rights were fully transferred, and whether the marriage contract is conditional on the transfer of this property. The actual documents show that the detailed description of these additional payments constitutes the largest part of the contracts, making the marriage documents resemble inventories of the properties of both families. In fact, most of the questions reflected in the Andalusi fatwas regarding *siyāqa* and *niḥla* arise from inaccurate descriptions of the properties, their limits, and their values.[51]

The *siyāqa*, as the fatwas and documents show, often represented a very large part of the husband's property. As Hady Roger Idris has pointed out, the *siyāqa* might be as much as half of his estate.[52] However, questions related to the *siyāqa* in the Andalusi fatwas show that this property remained very frequently under the administration and control of the husband and his family. In fact, since some documents show that a *niḥla* received by the husband from his parents was transferred in part to the wife by *siyāqa* under the same marriage contract, the husband and wife often became co-owners of a property that had been transferred from the husband's family.[53] Lawsuits, as described in the fatwas, arose when the wife complained that she was not receiving the profits taken by her husband from her land.[54] Other questions show that when it came to divorce, a new arrangement between the families was necessary in order to avoid the husband's familial property falling into the hands of the wife's family.[55]

The *niḥla* was a very different kind of donation. Since it passed from one generation to the next, e.g., from father to daughter, it can clearly be considered a part of the inheritance. Many of the marriage contracts in which a *niḥla* appears concern orphans, who receive their inheritance shares only at the moment of their marriage, their property being kept in the hands of their guardians until that moment.[56]

On the other hand, the different sources illustrate problems brides faced in taking possession of the *niḥla*. According to the Maliki school, the *niḥla*, being made a condition of the marriage, was not considered a *hiba* (donation), but rather a contractual consideration for which the donor expects to receive a counter-consideration of comparable value (*hibat al-thawwāb*)—in this case the conclusion of the marriage. Unlike the *hiba*, the *niḥla* did not require the taking of possession in order to become legally binding.[57] The formularies give directions on this point, clearly specifying that taking possession is not required,[58] and the documents almost unanimously do not reflect a transfer of possession.[59] In addition, the fatwas show again that the father of the bride usually kept control of the immovable properties given to his daughter, as if they were a legacy and not a direct gift.[60]

The "contracting session" was therefore an opportunity for both families to demonstrate their economic status, and also to economically establish a new family unit. Ostentatious display clearly accounts for many of these donations. Several gifts, such as the trousseau, were shown in public during marriage celebrations, but others were only displayed by being formally recorded in the contract, although the real transfer of property was made, if at all, only after the marriage was fully established and considered permanent.[61]

## Stipulations in Marriage Contracts

After the description of the donations all the *wathāʾiq* works include instructions on how to write the conditions (*shurūṭ*) into the marriage contract.[62] For the marriage to be upheld, the conditions had to adhere to the general principles of the Maliki school.[63] The introductory wording of these stipulations is usually formulaic: "[The husband] promises voluntarily and willingly, in order to seek her friendship and trying to keep her happiness, not to..." (*wa-iltazama lahā ṭāʾiʿan mutabarriʿan istijlāban li-muddatihā wa-taqammunan li-masarratihā ʿalā...*)[64] and then follows the enumeration of certain stipulations. The *wathāʾiq* works always list the same conditions, namely:

1. The husband will not marry a second wife, or take a concubine, without the permission and consent of his first wife.[65]
2. The husband will not absent himself from his wife's side for more than six consecutive months, except to fulfill the obligation of the pilgrimage, in which case he is allowed three years and must make provision for his wife's maintenance (*nafaqa*) during his absence.[66]
3. The husband will not mistreat his wife, either physically or economically.[67]
4. The husband will not oblige his wife to move to a city other than the city where she lived before her marriage.[68]
5. The husband will not forbid his wife to visit her female relatives and male *maḥārim* (males in non-marriageable relation) or to receive visits from them.[69]

After listing these conditions, the formularies usually provide that the husband empowers his wife to free herself from the marriage link if he does one of these acts (*wa-in faʿala shayʾan min dhālika, fa-amruhā bi-yadihā*), that is, issue her own divorce and dissolve the marriage (*tamlīk*).[70]

Ibn Salmūn's *wathāʾiq* handbook constitutes a special case. His work is different from the others in that his first model for the marriage contract does not include any specific stipulations. The conditions, however, are fully explained later in his work, although not inside the main "form."[71] This perhaps explains why none of the fifteenth-century Granadan documents studied here enumerate any conditions, although we cannot safely conclude that the Granadan marriage contract never registered such clauses, since some fatwas of this period reflect problems related to them.[72]

Concerning these conditional clauses, the documents show only two variations: either they include no condition at all, or they list all of the "classical" conditions suggested in the handbooks, following their exact wording and guidelines. No Granadan document includes any condition at all. In Valencia the earliest document, dating from the thirteenth century, reflects all five conditions of the formularies,[73] but the five remaining Valencian documents are silent in this respect. In the four existing marriage contracts from La Rioja, two mention all the classical conditions[74] and the other two mention none. Similarly, one Aragonese document follows all the conditions[75] and two include none of them. Two other sixteenth-century Aragonese marriage documents do not even waste time copying the conditions from their formularies, but merely register that as far as the conditions are concerned, "the husband promises to fulfill all the stipulations included in al-Jazīrī's *wathāʾiq* work."[76]

The data provided by the Andalusi fatwas show that conditional clauses were often the cause of conflict between the contracting parties, who disputed their legality and interpretation. The fatwas also provide information on the existence of other conditions not mentioned in the formularies. A fatwa issued by Ibn Rushd (d. 520/1126) shows how the parties might differ in their understanding of the contract terms not only with each other, but with the judiciary. In addition to the general question of how the marriage contract should be framed when the woman has no marriage guardian and her marriage has had to be contracted by a judge, Ibn Rushd was asked about the nature of the stipulations in the contract and established what later came to be considered the official position of the Maliki school on the matter.[77] The questioner reports that the notaries usually specified, as we saw in the *wathāʾiq* works, that these conditions were voluntary promises (*bi-lafẓ al-ṭawʿ*) made by the husband seeking the happiness of his bride, although the custom of the people was to consider them as legally-binding stipulatory clauses (*shurūṭ*). Which one of these two interpretations, the questioner asks Ibn Rushd, should the judges follow?

Should they consider the conditions to be the husbands' legal obligation, as was customary? Or were they voluntary promises free of any legal consequences if the husband fails to fulfill them, as was written in the contracts? In the opinion of Ibn Rushd, even if the contract specifies that these clauses were voluntary promises, the judges should follow the custom and consider them as binding, but only when the custom is in fact thus. Ibn al-Ḥājj (d. 529/1135), whose opinions were gathered together with those of Ibn Rushd, held the opposite opinion: judges should base their judgments only on what was written in the contracts, and therefore the conditions constituted only informal promises. Ibn Rushd laid the blame on the notaries, who had not taken sufficient care to word the conditions precisely enough to make them enforceable.[78] The notaries, according to Ibn Rushd, did not properly register the clauses according to the law, and furthermore contradicted the actual custom of the people which considered them to be legally binding contractual conditions.

In fact, as described above, the formulae used in the marriage contracts, as suggested by the *wathāʾiq* handbooks and the works of Ibn Rushd, present the conditions as the result of the husband's kindness towards his wife, while they were created by the bride's family as a protection for her in cases of mistreatment, abandonment, even polygamy, or other kinds of marital power exercised by the husband, resulting, should the husband break one of the conditions, in a right to a *tamlīk* divorce.[79]

It is worth noting that the five "classical" conditions are not the only ones that appear in Andalusi fatwas. Other unique clauses are also referred to in fatwas sought by parties possibly wishing to defeat such clauses. For example, a fatwa from Fes in the fifteenth century discusses a clause by which a husband might promise to delay the consummation of the marriage for a year.[80] The necessity of this condition seems to have been especially relevant when the bride was still a minor (*ṣaghīra*), and when the couple planned to live in a new town, since, according to the jurists, the wife might need time to adjust to her new home. Another clause very frequently reflected in Andalusi as well as Maghribi fatwas was that by which the husband promises to pay the maintenance (*nafaqa*) of his wife's children from a previous marriage.[81] This clause may be especially useful to women who remarry after divorce or widowhood, in order to be able to support their children. Neither of these two clauses—the delay for a year of consummation and the providing of *nafaqa* for the wife's existing children—were included in the formularies, nor in the recorded marriage contracts I have found.[82]

Thus, specific stipulations in Andalusi marriage contracts seem generally to have followed one of two options: either all the classical formulary-based conditions were included, or none was. Yet in specific circumstances, such as a woman's second marriage or when the bride was a minor, some additional stipulations unique to her needs might have been added.

## Marital Life: Reciprocal Duties Between Husband and Wife

After the enumeration of conditions, the *wathāʾiq* works recommend the inclusion in the marriage contract of some reminder of the treatment the two parties are expected to give to and receive from each other. These statements are clearly of a standardized nature, including very formulaic wording with Qurʾanic quotations. They usually begin with a promise from the husband to treat his future wife kindly, making possible a harmonious life together.[83] A brief note follows reminding the wife of her reciprocal obligation to her husband, citing the Qurʾanic verse stating that men have a degree higher than women (*wa-li-l-rijāl ʿalayhinna daraja*).[84] In all the *wathāʾiq* handbooks these sentences end with the statement that the marriage is made according to the words of God (*wa-tazawwajahā bi-kalimāti Allāh*), and quoting the Qurʾanic passage "retain them in an honorable manner or release them in an honorable manner" (*imsāk bi-maʿrūf aw tasrīḥ bi-iḥsān*).[85] The actual documents repeat these Qurʾanic verses on married life in almost exactly the same way as they do the other recommendations of the *wathāʾiq* handbooks. The Qurʾanic passages are either quoted verbatim or paraphrased. In the handbooks of Ibn al-ʿAṭṭār and Ibn Mughīth these lines are followed by a brief mention of the social status of the bride, for example, specifying the husband's acknowledgement of his wife's possession of a servant while living in her father's house, and his promise to continue to provide her one while living in his.[86]

## The End of the Marriage Contract: Guardianship, Consent of the Bride, and the Witnesses

The last part of the marriage contract was usually dedicated to ensuring its validity. Two important conditions had to be fulfilled under Maliki law: the presence of the wife's guardian and the testimony of two qualified witnesses. In some cases a third requirement, the consent of the bride, also exists. The form of witnessing reflects these requirements, since the witnesses verify in their testimony that the applicable requirements are met, i.e., that the guardian is present and, if necessary, that the bride has given her consent.

The Maliki school requires that the woman herself does not conclude her own marriage, but must instead be represented by a male relative from her father's side, who conducts the marital negotiations on her behalf.[87] The bride's guardian was thus usually "present" in two parts of the marriage contract. First, he was included in the section recording his reception of the prompt portion of the *ṣadāq* from the husband in the name of his ward. Second, he is referenced at the end of the contract immediately before the testimony of the witnesses. This second explicit mention of the guardian was usually in a standard formula: "Her father, [so-and-so], marries her, she being a virgin under his legal tutelage and guardianship and being intact in her body, according to the power that God gave to him over her things by putting in his hands the right to contract her marriage."[88] After setting down this formula, witnesses were required to verify the agreement for both parties, using the formula: "As required by the groom (*nākiḥ*) and the guardian (*munkiḥ*), [the witnesses] verify with their testimony everything mentioned in this contract, basing their testimony on their knowledge of them both [the groom and guardian] and on what they heard from them, being in good health and right mind."[89] However, this formula was only used when the bride was a virgin under the guardianship of her father. According to the handbooks, modifications should be introduced when other situations exist—for example, when the bride was an orphaned virgin and a male relative other than her father was acting as her guardian. In fact, the latter situation is the most common in the actual documents.

According to the Maliki school there are two categories of guardians: one who possesses the right of constraint (*jabr*), and one who does not. The right of *jabr* is the capacity to conclude a marriage of a woman or of a minor male without his or her consent.[90] The documents show very different situations, but most of them involve a bride who is a virgin and an orphan, so that her marriage is concluded by her brother or, as in one of the documents, by her paternal uncle. For these cases, according to the law and as the formularies indicate, the bride must be asked for her consent. Therefore the documents register her consent in a very standardized way, with the words:

> She is an orphan and virgin under his guardianship and tutelage, and she is sound in body and mind, consulted about her consent, informed about the above-mentioned other party as a husband and about everything he has given as dower (*mahr*) in "prompt" and "deferred" parts, and informed that her consent will be implicitly understood by her silence and that it was necessary for the marriage that she give her consent.[91]

Immediately afterwards the witnesses testify, before signing the document, that the wife understood what her silence indicated and that she gave her consent.[92]

The formularies attach some importance to the correct wording of the description of the bride in this part of the marriage contract. She was typically described as a virgin (*bikr* or *ʿudhrā*)[93] and intact in regards to her body (*salīma fī jismihā*), so that if the husband found that she is not virgin (*thayyiba*) or with any defect not specified in the contract, he would have the right to return her to her father and annul the marriage.[94] The fatwa compilations present several questions related to this issue, and, according to the muftis, when problems arose the father was to blame for having willfully misrepresented his daughter in the contract.[95]

The witnesses provide legal proof of the parties' consent. The details of the offer (*ījāb*) and its acceptance (*qabūl*) must be clearly stated in their presence.[96] Witnesses also fulfilled the vital purpose of publicity. Since secret marriages (*nikāḥ al-sirr*) are forbidden by the Maliki school, witnesses are one way to provide the necessary publicity to the marriage.[97] It is for the same purpose that Ibn Salmūn recommends a marriage feast and a reception (*walīma*).[98] Although the publicity of the marriage could be achieved socially through ceremonies and feasts, witnesses were a legal means to assure its fulfillment. What the jurists called the formalities of the marriage (*ṣīghat al-nikāḥ*)[99] provided a middle ground between social and legal spheres. The questions reflected in the fatwas from Granada show that the celebration of a wedding party and the public exchange of gifts were the processes by which the new couple's union was socially confirmed.[100] The "contracting session" did not always take place at the same time as the celebration of the wedding. However, the witnesses were always present at that session, verifying that the legal requirements for the marriage had been fulfilled.

## Contract Negotiations

The meeting of notaries and the families for the process of drawing up a marriage contract—that is, the meeting between the legal and the social spheres—was surrounded in al-Andalus by a set of negotiations. These negotiations may have taken place before the session, but this remains obscure in the legal sources, since they occurred entirely in the social domain. Such negotiations typically covered the gifts to be exchanged as well as the place and conditions in which the married couple would live. Evidence shows that the wife usually kept a copy of the written contract during her marriage to use in case of legal action, especially when pursuing payment of the deferred part of her *ṣadāq*.[101]

## Conclusion

From this brief survey of marriage contracts in al-Andalus, three elements emerge as the matters of most concern to the participants and most crucial to the creation of the contracts:

1. The description of the property to be transferred between the parties, from which the notary must record, as the law demanded, that the prompt part of the *ṣadāq*, the first requirement for the legal validity of the marriage, had been given and received;

2. The inclusion of stipulations—not a subject of point-by-point negotiation, but something that tended to be agreed upon as a whole or not included at all. The stipulations' usefulness depended directly on their correct wording in the contract, often referred to by married couples contesting fulfillment of one of these conditions; and
3. The consent of the guardian and in some cases also of the bride, the correct fulfillment of the task of the guardian, and other conditions for the validity of the marriage. This information is recorded at the end of the contract, and its certification is one of the main functions of the witnesses.

The comparison between the actual documents and the *wathāʾiq* handbooks show that in practice Andalusi notaries followed their handbooks faithfully, copying the main formulae, wording, and structure, and introducing changes only according to the specific needs of the parties as revealed in three parts of the contract: the description of the main donations; the descriptions of the guardian and his ward and of the type of guardianship; and in the inclusion of the conditions. Two parts of the marriage contract are merely formulaic, imported from the formularies without change: the introductory lines and the description of the general duties and rights of the parties.

When fatwas were issued regarding a marriage contract question, the issue usually arose from the document's lack of precision, and, especially, from attempts by notaries to legalize a marriage contract without paying adequate attention to the real practices of the parties involved. This is especially clear with the payment of the *ṣadāq*, registered as received in the contract although not always truly given at the time it was recorded, or with the description of stipulations as "voluntary promises" while they were understood as mandatory conditions by the bride's family.

## NOTES

This paper was written thanks to a postdoctoral grant from the Ministerio de Educación y Cultura of Spain which funded my stay at Princeton University (1998–2000). I would like to thank Léon Buskens for his valuable comments on the first draft of this paper as well as for sharing with me his ideas on marriage contracts in modern Morocco. I would also like to thank Asifa Quraishi and Frank Vogel for their very valuable suggestions and ideas.

[1] Duby 1994, 4–5.

[2] See Carmona 1993, 53–66; Chalmeta 1995, 29–70. See also Zomeño 2000a.

[3] Guichard 1977.

[4] On the application of Islamic law in the Mudejar communities, see Wiegers 1991, 76–81; Echevarría Arsuaga 2000, 397–399.

[5] Ibn al-ʿAṭṭār 1983.

[6] Ibn Mughīth 1994. Ibn Mughīth's work was partially translated into Spanish in Vila 1931.

[7] Al-Jazīrī 1998.

[8] See Hoenerbach 1965, 116–124. Valencia was conquered by the King of Aragón in 1238.

[9] Ibn Farḥūn 1885: see margins for *Kitāb al-ʿIqd al-munaẓẓam li-l-ḥukkām fī-mā yajrī bayna aydihim min al-ʿuqūd wa-l-aḥkām*. The work of Ibn Salmūn was partially translated into Spanish by J. López Ortiz in López Ortiz 1927.

[10] Al-Gharnāṭī 1988.

[11] See Hoenerbach 1965, no. 3, 79–115; Seco de Lucena 1961, 8–9, 104–106; Gallego Burín and Sandoval 1968, doc. no. 58; Gómez Moreno 1944, 503–505 (also in Spanish translation without edition of the Arabic text).

[12] Hoenerbach 1965, 125–134.

[13] Hoenerbach 1965, 135–175.

[14] Some of these documents were found in the records of the Inquisition of Valencia (now in the Archivo Histórico Nacional de Madrid). They were in the hands of some relatives of the parties, being one of the proofs used by the Inquisition to persecute them as Moriscos. See Labarta 1980.

[15] The documents from Calatayud are edited and translated into German by Hoenerbach in Hoenerbach 1965, 176–193. Salvador Vila edited and studied one document from Valencia in the sixteenth century in Vila 1933. According to Vila, he received this document from the hands of A. González Palencia, who also found it in the Archivo Histórico Nacional, in Madrid. Four other documents from Valencia, found in the same archive, are edited and translated into Spanish by A. Labarta in Labarta 1983.

[16] On *wathāʾiq* or *shurūṭ* works, see López Ortiz 1926; Tyan 1945; Wakin 1972; Hallaq 1995.

[17] See Hallaq 1995.

[18] See López Ortiz 1927, 326–327.

[19] See Chalmeta 1995, 29.

[20] See Vila 1933, 186; Labarta 1983, 59.

[21] The only exception I know is Vila 1933; Vila is the author of the Spanish translation of the marriage chapters of Ibn Mughīth and editor of a marriage document of the sixteenth century. His comparison, however, includes only one document. More recently, the work by Shatzmiller studies both marriage contracts and Maliki texts, especially those concerned with women's property rights. See Shatzmiller 2007.

[22] I took most of the Andalusi fatwas which I discuss here from al-Mālaqī 1992; Ibn Rushd 1992; al-Wansharīsī 1981–1983.

[23] See Powers 1990, 231.

[24] See al-Wansharīsī 1981–1983, 3:28–30, 96.

[25] Powers 1990a.

[26] See al-Wansharīsī 1981–1983, 3:231–232.

[27] See Fakhry 1997, 25, 54; Ibn Mughīth 1994, nos. 4, 8; Vila 1933, 197; Labarta 1983, nos. 1, 62. A Granadan document, for example, quotes the Qurʾanic passage on the marriage with up to four wives (4:3). See also Seco de Lucena 1961, nos. 4, 8.

[28] Ibn Mughīth 1994, 20; Vila 1933, 197.

[29] See Gallego Burín and Gámir 1968, 268.

[30] Ibid.

[31] Ibn al-ʿAṭṭār 1983, 7; Ibn Mughīth 1994, 20; al-Jazīrī 1998, 12; Vila 1933, 197.

[32] On this part Ibn Salmūn recommends the notaries just follow the formulae used in the "old times." See Ibn Salmūn 1885, 4.

[33] See Ibn al-ʿAṭṭār 1983, 9; Ibn Mughīth 1994, 21; al-Jazīrī 1998, 12. The marriage contracts do not mention *zawj* but *zawja*, referring to the wife. This is more correct in Arabic, according to the *wathāʾiq* works.

[34] Vila 1933, 197. See also Seco de Lucena 1961, 104–105; Labarta 1983, 62.

[35] Ibn Salmūn explicitly mentions that in al-Andalus the Arabic terms for the payment by the husband and for the marriage contract itself are the same. See Ibn Salmūn 1885, 5. On the *ṣadāq* in fifteenth-century Granada, see Shatzmiller 2007, 19–40.

[36] On the transmission of property in the marriage in the Western Islamic countries during the Middle Ages, see Zomeño 2000a.

[37] The *nikāḥ al-tafwīḍ* by which the parties agree that the payment will not be written down in the contract, but they agree that an amount will be paid, is, however, valid. See al-Qayrawānī 1968, 180–181; Ibn Juzayy 1982, 207; Khalīl ibn Isḥāq 1919, 43, 48. See also Pesle 1936, 166.

[38] On the three conditions for the validity of the marriage in the Maliki school, see al-Qayrawānī 1968, 172; Ibn Juzayy 1982, 200; Khalīl ibn Isḥāq 1919, 3; Ibn ʿĀṣim 1882, nos. 172–173. See also Santillana 1926, 200.

[39] Ibn al-ʿAṭṭār 1983, 7; Ibn Mughīth 1994, 21; Ibn Salmūn 1885, 3; al-Jazīrī 1998, 12.

[40] The formularies mention that she is not entitled to take possession of the prompt payment since she is still under her father's guardianship (*idh hiya bikr fī ḥajrihi wa-wilāya naẓarihi*); see Ibn al-ʿAṭṭār 1983, 7; Ibn Mughīth 1994, 21; al-Jazīrī 1998, 13; Ibn Salmūn 1885, 3.

[41] Ibn al-ʿAṭṭār 1983, 7; Ibn Mughīth 1994, 21; al-Jazīrī 1998, 13; Ibn Salmūn 1885, 3.

[42] Ibn al-ʿAṭṭār 1983, 7; Ibn Mughīth 1994, 21; al-Jazīrī 1998, 13; Ibn Salmūn 1885, 3.

[43] See Labarta 1983, 62, 69, 79; Vila 1933, 199.

[44] On the assimilation of the *hadiyya* with the obligatory payment from the husband, see al-Wansharīsī 1981–1983, 3:43–46, 92, 129, 156–157.

[45] See al-Wansharīsī 1981–1983, 3:231–232.

[46] The Maghribi mufti al-Qābisī explains this legal history of the *kāliʾ* payments in al-Wansharīsī 1981–1983, 3:153. See also Zomeño 2000a, 223–233; Rapoport 2000, 1–16.

[47] Ibn ʿAbd al-Raʾūf 1955, 80; Khalīl ibn Isḥāq 1919, 43; Ibn ʿĀṣim 1882, no. 378.

[48] See Zomeño 2000a, 235–259; Shatzmiller 2007, 30–33. Note that delay in paying the *kāliʾ* does not in itself offend the contract, as long as it occurs with the wife's consent, since like any creditor she is free to excuse delay in payment of a debt.

[49] Ibn Mughīth 1994, 79–82; al-Jazīrī 1998, 29–30; Ibn Salmūn 1885, 10–12. Ibn al-ʿAṭṭār does not include any of these payments.

[50] Ibn Mughīth 1994, 37; al-Jazīrī 1998, 30–32; Ibn Salmūn 1885, 9–10. On these marriage payments, see Zomeño 2000.

[51] See al-Wansharīsī 1981–1983, 3:144, 145, 380–381, 388–390, 409–410, 411–412.

[52] See Idris 1970, 162. It is worth noting that at the same time in the Christian lands, only a tenth part of the properties of the husband would be transferred to the wife in a marriage as *arras*; see Beceiro and Córdoba de la Llave 1990.

[53] See Labarta 1983, nos. 2, 70; Vila, 1933, 199.

[54] Al-Wansharīsī 1981–1983, 3:192–193, 240–242, 410–411; 4:209–210, 220–221.

[55] See, e.g., al-Wansharīsī 1981–1983, 4:4, 5–6.

[56] See Seco de Lucena 1961, nos. 61, 105; Labarta 1983, 79–80. For some fatwas reflecting this same fact, see, for example, al-Wansharīsī 1981–1983, 3:147–148, 233.

[57] Linant de Bellefonds 1973, 311–411; idem, "Hiba," *EI*²; Schacht 1964.

[58] See Ibn Mughīth 1994, 80; Ibn Salmūn 1885, 11. Al-Jazīrī does not include the taking of possession in his modification of the *niḥla* payment, nor does he discuss it.

[59] The documents, in fact, reflect the acceptance by the groom of the properties given to him by his parents, but not the actual taking of possession by the bride of the property given to her by her parents.

[60] According to the Granadan mufti Ibn Manẓūr (d. 887/1482), since it was not legally required, the *niḥla* was not always effectively transferred. See al-Wansharīsī 1981–1983, 3:253–254.

[61] See Zomeño 2000a, 269; Shatzmiller 2007, 49–50.

[62] Ibn al-ʿAṭṭār 1983, 7–8; Ibn Mughīth 1994, 30; al-Jazīrī 1998, 14–17, 21–28; al-Gharnāṭī 1988, 20.

[63] Al-Qayrawānī 1968, 174–175; ʿAbd al-Raʾūf 1955, 81; Ibn Juzayy 1982, 223; Ibn ʿĀṣim 1882, no. 379; Pesle 1936, 33, Schacht 1964, 163; Chalmeta 1995, 53.

[64] See Ibn Mughīth 1994, 21. See also the same formula in Ibn al-ʿAṭṭār 1983, 7; al-Jazīrī 1998, 14.

[65] Ibn al-ʿAṭṭār 1983, 7; Ibn Mughīth 1994, 21; al-Jazīrī 1998, 14, 22; al-Gharnāṭī 1988, 17; Ibn Salmūn 1885, 16–17, 17–19. See also Ibn Juzayy 1982, 224; Carmona 1993, 63–65.

[66] Ibn al-ʿAṭṭār 1983, 8; Ibn Mughīth 1994, 21; al-Jazīrī 1998, 15, 22–25; al-Gharnāṭī 1988, 17; Ibn Salmūn 1885, 17, 19–23; Ibn Juzayy 1982, 224; Toledano 1981. See also Zomeño 2002.

[67] Ibn Mughīth 1994, 22; al-Jazīrī 1998, 15, 26; al-Gharnāṭī 1988, 17; Ibn Juzayy 1982, 225; Ibn Salmūn 1885, 17, 23–24. This clause is not included in Ibn al-ʿAṭṭār's *wathāʾiq*. Ibn al-ʿAṭṭār includes a model of the document that the wife should seek in this case: Ibn al-ʿAṭṭār 1983, 237–238. The same kind of document, extracted from Ibn al-Ḥājj's fatwas, could be found in Būtshīsh 1993, 180.

[68] Ibn al-ʿAṭṭār 1983, 8; Ibn Mughīth 1994, 21–22; al-Jazīrī 1998, 15–16, 25–26; al-Gharnāṭī 1988, 17; Ibn Juzayy 1982, 225; Ibn Salmūn 1885, 17, 24–25.

[69] Ibn al-ʿAṭṭār 1983, 8; Ibn Mughīth 1994, 22; al-Jazīrī 1998, 16, 27–28; al-Gharnāṭī 1988, 17; Ibn Salmūn 1885, 17, 26–27.

[70] Ibn al-ʿAṭṭār 1983, 7–8; al-Jazīrī 1998, 15; al-Gharnāṭī 1988, 17. On the *tamlīk*, see al-Qayrawānī 1968, 188; Ibn Juzayy 1982, 238.

[71] See Ibn Salmūn 1885, 15–27.

[72] See, e.g., al-Wansharīsī 1981–1983, 3:22–23, 134, 194, 200, 202, 230, 234.

[73] See Hoenerbach 1965, 118.

[74] See Hoenerbach 1965, 137, 169–170.

[75] See Hoenerbach 1965, 126–127.

[76] *Wa-ṭāʿa al-nākiḥ al-madhkūr li-zawjihi al-madhkūra jāmiʿ al-shurūṭ al-mutaḍammina fī ʿaqd al-Jazīrī*; see Hoenerbach 1965, 190. Or *wa-ṭāʿa al-nākiḥ li-jāmiʿ al-shurūṭ al-muʿtād al-musammāt fī Kitāb Ibni l-Qāsim al-Jazīrī*; see Hoenerbach 1965, 177.

[77] See Ibn Rushd 1992, 2:1037–1042. In al-Wansharīsī's version, see al-Wansharīsī 1981–1983, 3:113. See also Toledano 1981, 128–131.

[78] This opinion of Ibn Rushd, reflected in the *Miʿyār*, is quoted in two *wathāʾiq* works; see al-Gharnāṭī 1988, 18; Ibn Salmūn 1885, 16.

[79] On the procedure for the wife to seek divorce in these situations, see Zomeño 2002.

[80] See al-Wansharīsī 1981–1983, 3:6–10, 36–37.

[81] See idem, 3:19–20, 21–22, 24, 219, 400, 414.

[82] On the legal discussion of the validity of these two clauses, see Toledano 1981, 127.

[83] Ibn al-ʿAṭṭār 1983, 8; Ibn Mughīth 1994, 22; Ibn Salmūn 1885, 3. In al-Jazīrī (1998, 14), this part is included immediately before the mentioning of the conditions.

[84] Fakhry 1997, 4:28. See Ibn al-ʿAṭṭār 1983, 8; Ibn Mughīth 1994, 22; al-Jazīrī 1998, 14; Ibn Salmūn 1885, 3.

[85] Fakhry 1997, 2:229. See Ibn al-ʿAṭṭār 1983, 8; Ibn Mughīth 1994, 22; al-Jazīrī 1998, 13; Ibn Salmūn 1885, 3. Ibn Salmūn (1885, 7) explains that this formula, *bi-kalimāti Allāh*, means that a Muslim wife should not marry a non-Muslim, although others understand a much more immediate meaning, that the marriage is contracted according to the words (*kalimāt*) revealed in the Qurʾan.

[86] Ibn al-ʿAṭṭār 1983, 8; Ibn Mughīth 1994, 22. The difference between the two formularies is simply that Ibn Mughīth mentions explicitly that the husband is economically able to provide such a servant, while in Ibn al-ʿAṭṭār's work that fact remains implicit. Al-Jazīrī (1998, 28–29) includes this note in the end of his explanations on the stipulations.

[87] Al-Qayrawānī 1968, 174–175; ʿAbd al-Raʾūf 1955, 80; Santillana 1926, 202, 293–306; López Ortiz 1932, 56–57; Schacht 1964, 161. The Maliki sources, however, almost unanimously recommend consulting the bride. See Al-Qayrawānī 1968, 172–173; Ibn Juzayy 1982, 203; Ibn ʿĀṣim 1882, 361; Khalīl ibn Isḥāq 1919, 4–7; Ibn Mughīth 1994, 24; Ibn Salmūn 1885, 7.

[88] *Ankaḥahā iyyāhā abūhā fulān bikran fī ḥijrihi wa-wilāyat naẓarihi, salīma fī jismihā, bi-mā mallakahu Allāh taʿālā min amrihā wa-jaʿala bi-yadihi min ʿaqd nikāḥihā ʿalayhā*: Ibn Mughīth 1994, 22; See also an almost identical formula in Ibn al-ʿAṭṭār 1983, 9. See also al-Jazīrī 1998, 16; Ibn Salmūn 1885, 3, cf. 7.

[89] See Ibn Mughīth 1994, 22. Similar formulae are found in Ibn al-ʿAṭṭār 1983, 9; al-Jazīrī 1998, 16–17; Ibn Salmūn 1885, 3.

[90] See al-Qayrawānī 1968, 172–175, 180–181; Ibn Mughīth 1994, 24, 31; Ibn ʿĀṣim 1882, nos. 360, 364; Khalīl ibn Isḥāq 1919, 4–5.

[91] See, e.g., Hoenerbach 1965, 118.

[92] ʿAbd al-Raʾūf 1955, 80; al-Gharnāṭī 1988, 17; Khalīl ibn Isḥāq 1919, 7. See also Ibn al-ʿAṭṭār 1983, 12; al-Gharnāṭī 1988, 20.

[93] Al-Jazīrī (1998, 16) recommends to include both terms: *bikr* and *ʿudhrā*. On the social, as opposed to the legal, understanding of the terms *bikr* and *ʿudhrā*,

see al-Wansharīsī 1981–1983, 3:385. Cf. Toledano 1981, 54n3. On this formula, see also Shatzmiller 2007, 96.

[94] Ibn Salmūn 1885, 7–8.

[95] Al-Wansharīsī 1981–1983, 3:32–35 (repeated at 196), 130–131, 132, 133, 139, 166, 167, 191, 196–198.

[96] Ibn Juzayy 1982, 200; Khalīl ibn Isḥāq 1919, 3–4; Santillana 1926, 211–213.

[97] Ibn ʿĀṣim 1882, no. 376; Khalīl ibn Isḥāq 1919, 21; Santillana 1926, 221–222.

[98] Ibn Salmūn 1885, 3.

[99] Khalīl ibn Isḥāq 1919, 2; Ibn ʿĀṣim 1882, no. 335; Ibn Mughīth 1994, 31; López Ortiz 1932, 159; Carmona 1993, 54.

[100] See al-Wansharīsī 1981–1983, 3:96.

[101] That is why, according to Ibn Salmūn (1885, 8), the guardian should pay the paper and the salary of the notary.

# *Seven*

## INTERPRETING TEARS: A MARRIAGE CASE FROM IMAMIC YEMEN

Brinkley Messick

At her request, a young woman named Arwā appeared before a group of men and declared that she had reached her legal majority. The resulting document, prepared by one of the men, begins by stating that she first was legally identified by some individuals present, including two men and a woman who knew her by her voice. "She appeared behind a barrier wall (*ḥijāb*)," that is, outside the door to the room, "and bore witness to us [the document writer] and to the aforementioned [individuals named earlier] that physical maturity had occurred to her, and this by menstruation."[1] The fact of her legal majority established, Arwā then took further action on her own behalf in a legal struggle that by then had persisted for some months. It was March of 1958.

Fifteen years earlier, a contract purportedly had been written at the behest of two brothers named Muḥammad and Aḥmad, the sons of Nājī ʿAlī Muṣṭafā, from a highland village to the west of the provincial capital of Ibb, in Lower Yemen.[2] The brothers had agreed to marry their children—Muḥammad's daughter, Arwā, and Aḥmad's son, ʿAzīz—in what anthropologists technically call a parallel-cousin marriage. Both the son and the daughter were children, legal minors, and the contract was made on their behalf by their fathers. Years later, in litigation, one of the contending parties described this document as the "first contract." It was quoted in the court record as follows:

> A valid Shariʿa [Islamic law] contract was entered into by Muḥammad Nājī ʿAlī Muṣṭafā for his minor daughter, the free woman Arwā, with his brother's minor son, ʿAzīz, son of Aḥmad Nājī ʿAlī Muṣṭafā, and the contract was accepted for him [the minor son] by his father, the mentioned Aḥmad Nājī, [and this] according to the principles of the Book of God and the Sunna [prophetic traditions] of His Prophet, with a dower of those equivalent to her (*mahr mithlihā*), as a virgin. This was written on its date, July [no day specified], 1943. [Three named individuals] and others witnessed, and God is sufficient witness.

Some years passed and Arwā's father, Muḥammad, died, leaving her affairs and those of her minor brother in the hands of his brother, the children's paternal uncle, Aḥmad Nājī, who was made the legal administrator (*waṣī*) of the property they inherited from their deceased father. As Arwā and her cousin and husband-by-contract, ʿAzīz, were still minors, their marriage remained unconsummated.

Fourteen years passed before, finally, in 1957, Aḥmad Nājī (the uncle and father, respectively, of Arwā and ʿAzīz) began to take steps to complete the marriage purportedly contracted in 1943. As he later explained, he intended to "renew" the first contract, perhaps because the first contract, as will later appear, was liable to contest as to its authenticity. The death of his brother, however, necessitated an additional legal step. Under Zaydi law, in her first marriage as a virgin a woman must have a legal guardian, a *walī*, who enters into the marriage contract on her behalf. Typically, this guardian is the woman's father, or in his absence, her adult brother or other close male-line relative. As Arwā's paternal uncle, Aḥmad Nājī might have acted in this capacity himself, except for the fact that in this instance he already would be acting on the other side of the contract, representing his minor son. The additional legal step necessary would be to obtain from Arwā legal agency for someone to represent her in the marriage contract.

Aḥmad Nājī also wished to establish two other facts to fortify the "renewed" contract, and these would prove more complicated and contentious. One was that Arwā had reached the age of physical maturity (known legally as *bulūgh*). The second was that, as an adult, she had given her consent, her *riḍāʾ*, to the marriage. A several-part document establishing these various requirements was prepared in July 1957, and a copy of it was entered into the instrument register of the Ibb Province Shariʿa Court. It reads:

> There appeared before me the Head of the Village of [place name] with [name] and [name] and they together bore witness to the fact that the free woman Arwā, daughter of Muḥammad Nājī granted agency to and permitted her paternal uncle, Ḥājj Aḥmad Nājī, to marry her and to give her to his son ʿAzīz, the son of Aḥmad Nājī ʿAlī Muṣṭafā, for a dower of those equivalent to her among her paternal aunts, together with the complete silver. And they bore witness, together with others, that the aforementioned girl is legally mature.

The text continues, attending to the potential legal obstacle represented by the prior right of Arwā's brother, if mature, to represent her in the contract:

> And together with this there appeared the adolescent (*murāhiq*, i.e., not quite legally mature) brother of the mentioned girl, ʿAlī (son of) Muḥammad Nājī ʿAlī Muṣṭafā and, as a precaution against uncertainty as to his legal maturity, he granted legal agency to his paternal uncle

Aḥmad Nājī ʿAlī Muṣṭafā, following the permission from his sister, to give her to his son ʿAzīz, son of Aḥmad Nājī.

Arwā's uncle Aḥmad Nājī thus acquired the right by agency to represent her in the marriage contract. But, because he could not act simultaneously for both his niece and son in the same contract, a second agency was required. The document therefore continues:

And since the aforementioned son of Ḥājj Aḥmad is a minor, an adolescent, legally immature, and since the one who will accept the contract for him is his aforementioned father, a granting of agency occurred from him [the father, Aḥmad] to "the father" [an honorific] al-Sharafī [a nickname for Ḥusayn] the learned Ḥusayn b. Muḥammad al-Shāmī to enter into the contract of marriage with his son [on Arwā's behalf], and he [the father] would accept for his son on his behalf. Written on its date, 9 Dhū l-Qaʿda 1376 [1957].

Incorporating these previous steps, there follows the text of the marriage contract itself, which represented the "second contract" concerning these cousins:

Then there occurred the Shariʿa contract of marriage, from "the father" al-Sharafī [al-Shāmī], in accord with an agency granted to him by Aḥmad Nājī ʿAlī Muṣṭafā, in accord with an agency and permission to him from the free woman Arwā, daughter of Muḥammad Nājī and by her brother ʿAlī Muḥammad Nājī, to the son of Aḥmad Nājī, who is ʿAzīz, son of Aḥmad Nājī. The contract of marriage was accepted for him by his father Aḥmad Nājī ʿAlī Muṣṭafā, and this with the free woman Arwā, daughter of Muḥammad Nājī, with the presence of witnesses at the session who are [three named individuals] and others, and God is the best of witnesses. And this with a dower of those equivalent to her among her paternal aunts, and the stipulated silver, and [hope for] good conjugal relations, and God grants success, on its date, 9 Dhū l-Qaʿda 1376 [1957].

It was at this point that Arwā, her marriage now contractually "renewed" but still unconsummated, took matters into her own hands. She fled Aḥmad Nājī's (her paternal uncle's) household where she had been living, to the household of her maternal uncle (*khāl*), an individual named ʿAlī Muḥammad Qāsim.

If the post-revolutionary era in which I first lived in Yemen (1974–1976) provides any retrospective evidence, the strategy Arwā followed was a venerable one. The departure of the wife from the marital residence, typically to her father's house, is a characteristic step taken by women to attain some sort of redress or resolution to a marital problem. Departure by the wife engaged a mechanism of dispute resolution in which the woman's interests typically were represented by her father, or some other male-line relative. In difficult cases, the "return" of the wife could be the outcome of either a customary settlement[3] or the subject of a court ruling for "return of the wife" (*irjāʿ al-zawja*).[4] Arwā's situation was more complicated, however, since, as noted, her father had died, her brother was an adolescent, and she was living in the extended family household of her paternal uncle (her *ʿamm*). She therefore fled to the home of her maternal uncle. According to Anna Wurth,[5] who has studied Yemeni litigation in connection with marital conflicts in the 1990s, however, such recourse to the resources of the father or the extended family was only infrequently used by litigants now using the capital city courts. Most of these modern-day litigants were originally from distant locales in Lower Yemen and they now mainly lived in nuclear families.

In response to Arwā's flight, a court case was brought by her paternal uncle (*ʿamm*), Aḥmad Nājī, from whose house and from whose son she fled. In the Ibb Province Shariʿa Court, presided over by Judge Ismāʿīl ʿAbd al-Raḥmān al-Manṣūr, a claim was entered by Aḥmad Nājī, saying that the defendant, ʿAlī Muḥammad Qāsim and his accomplices "stole [*nahabū*] the wife of his son ʿAzīz." Aḥmad Nājī demanded that the judge enforce the "return of the wife of his son ʿAzīz to the residence of her husband." The two contract documents cited above were presented by Aḥmad Nājī as evidence and entered into the judgment record. The ensuing litigation ultimately led to Arwā's March 1958 appearance before a group of men to declare her legal majority (described above) in an attempt to claim control over her own marital affairs.

## "The Writer Writes"

Before turning to further discussion of this case, which I will examine in terms of its gendered evidence, disputants' motivations, legal arguments, and the judge's final ruling, I want to pause to examine how the practice of making a Muslim marriage contract is understood in a local, late nineteenth-century manual for notaries. In terms of distinct levels of legal writings, thus far I have mentioned the standard mechanisms for the application of law, namely, a contract and a court judgment. In what follows I also refer to several distinct dimensions of doctrinal legal texts: first, the notarial manual, an in-between legal genre, known as the *shurūṭ* (stipulations) literature, which encapsulates doctrine for the specific purpose of guiding contract writing; then, doctrine (*fiqh*) per se, including both the basic law book text (*matn*) and the commentary literature (*sharḥ*); and, finally, a further specialized level of practice-oriented doctrine, the rule-like "choices" (*ikhtiyārāt*) issued by reigning imams on specific points of law to guide judges in their Shariʿa court judgments. As the events of Arwā's case took place in the period before the Revolution of 1962, Shariʿa law in highland Yemen remained uncodified and unlegislated. These were the last decades of Shariʿa law application under an indigenous Islamic state.[6]

The brief chapter from the manual for notaries,[7] which I translate in full below, makes explicit a set of issues that a document writer ought to consider before actually writing a marriage contract. Many complex legal matters that are fully treated in the law books are mentioned here only in passing, with a pragmatic view to practice. These include: the waiting period (*ʿidda*) imposed upon a woman after the termination of her marriage; repudiation (*ṭalāq*) by the husband; dissolution (*faskh*) of marriage; the woman's marriage contract guardian (*walī*) and his guardianship (*wilāya*); the dower (*mahr*); the woman's consent (*riḍāʾ*); and, finally, such key features of the contract itself as the "offer" and "acceptance," derived from the sale contract model, and the bilateral consent (*tarāḍī*) of the contracting parties.

The part of the manual relevant for our purposes here reads as follows:

> It is required of whomever makes a contract for marriage, whether a judge or his deputy or an arbitrator (*muḥakkam*) from among the Muslims, that he knows the husband and his name and his descent (*nasab*), and the woman and her name and her descent. And if he does not know them, it is necessary that they are made known by two just witnesses. And it is necessary that he ascertains that she is free from any husband, or of a waiting period [after] any husband; whether she is a virgin or a non-virgin; whether her husband has died and she has completed her waiting period after him or has repudiated her and she has completed her waiting period after him; or whether her [marriage] has been dissolved [contractually] by a judge. And the repudiation or dissolution must be established for the notary (*al-ʿaqīd*, literally, "contractor") in Shariʿa terms or else he should not engage in the [new] contract, because the basic principle (*al-aṣl*) is the continuity of the marriage relation. And if the woman said, "I was married and he died, or he repudiated me, or my marriage was dissolved contractually," then evidence is necessary for this claim. And it is [also] necessary for the contractor to know the *walī* of the woman by his name and to verify the establishment of his *wilāya* by a Shariʿa method, not simply by the statement of the woman that "he is my *walī*." If it is found that the woman is legally eligible for marriage, and a [verbal] contract occurred between the *walī* and the husband, offering and accepting, and the woman having consented, as is required in Shariʿa terms, after ascertaining the above from the *walī*s and [in] the presence of two just witnesses, then the writer writes:[8]

> "There appeared So-and-so, son of So-and-so, *walī* of the free woman So-and-so, daughter of So-and-so, for himself," or, "by representation according to an agency document from So-and-so, and So-and-so, a daughter of So-and-so was married to So-and-so, son of So-and-so, by a contract that is legal and complete in its considered Shariʿa stipulations, with the presence of two just witnesses, So-and-so and So-and-so, with the mutual consent (*tarāḍī*), for a dower of (those) equivalent, whose amount is thus and so, surrendered by the husband," if he has surrendered it, or, if it remains the husband's financial obligation, he writes, "it remains (to be paid) as the financial obligation of the husband." And if her father has received this he would say, "Her father has received this for her benefit, by right of his Shariʿa *wilāya*." "[This] after the establishment of her status as a virgin of verified interdiction."
>
> He should write all that we have mentioned in three copies, two documents for the spouses, and a [third] document should remain with him to serve as a reference for him in case of need. Caution [is warranted] against negligence in mentioning the amount of the dower since disputes are many that are caused by greed, even if mention is made of the dower of those equivalent, due to the differences of the equivalent women among the relatives.[9]

In terms of its genre, this brief chapter on the marriage contract from the notarial manual is poised between the large and detailed literature of the chapters on "Marriage" and "Repudiation" in the Zaydi *fiqh*,[10] on the one hand, and the actual documents of local marriage agreements on the other. Largely implicit references invoke the pre-existing doctrinal corpus while its explicit designs attempt to properly constitute forthcoming written texts.

Shariʿa subjects must be either known or made known, their identities formally established, initially by means of full names, including, as mentioned in the manual, links of descent. This is a precondition for the principled intervention of the third-party writer, an individual whose authority and integrity are at stake when he prepares a written legal document following an oral transaction. If he does not know the prospective parties to a marriage contract, their identities may be verified by witnesses in an identification process that may be seen as a discrete opening step in the later witnessing of the contract itself. In preparing to write, the notary places a distinct emphasis on the woman's identity. This emphasis reflects the fourth of four conditions for a legal marriage set forth in Zaydi *fiqh*: after (1) a valid contract made by a legal *walī*, (2) the witnessing of two just witnesses, and (3) consent by the woman, then (4) "her identification" (*taʿyīnhā*) must occur.[11] Commentator al-ʿAnsī elaborates on this basic formulation by adding that it refers to:

> [T]he identification of the woman at the time of the contract and also the identification of the husband. "I accepted for one of my sons" [for example] is not sufficient. Identification of [the woman] can be obtained by a sign indicating her, such as if he [the *walī*] says, "I married you to this indicated individual [feminine], or the one [feminine] you know," even if she is absent. Or by a description such as "I married you to my oldest daughter, or youngest, or [my] white [daughter], or black," or such like among the designating descriptions for the woman, so that he [the other party, the husband, or his agent] will not confuse her with another. Or she can be identified by name, as Fāṭima or Zaynab, or such, or *laqab*, such as "I married you to my daughter, 'the Pious,'" or "the Pilgrim," or by a *kunya* for her, like Umm Kalthūm or Umm al-Faḍl, or such.[12]

In the notarial manuals, the critical issue prior to the writing of the document is the woman's current legal status and the potential for any impediment to her marriage (e.g., an existing marriage or required waiting period following a previous marriage). A woman's statement that she is married or divorced, or that a particular individual is her *walī*, must not be taken at face value but must be backed by formal evidence that satisfies the notary. As for the *walī*, he too must be known, both by name and by the legal terms, the *wilāya*, on the basis of which he acts in the woman's behalf, the typical case, again, being that the right pertains to a father with respect to his daughter. As the model contract notes and as we have seen in Arwā's case, the *walī* also may be represented in the contract by an agent whose agency should be verified by a document to this effect. In all such matters, it is the notarial writer's role and responsibility to demand accurate information before writing. His primary sources are his own knowledge and that of the two just witnesses. Potentially also, although it is not mentioned, he may refer to other documents, such as agency documents, divorce papers or court rulings.

In Arwā's case, it was at this key node of information-gathering by one of the contract-writing notaries prior to writing that a breakdown occurred. The overview provided in the manual chapter makes clear reference to the initial occurrence of the witnessed verbal contract between the *walī* and the husband, with the notary ideally attending. This spoken contract comes into existence with the use of the standard language of the "offer" and "acceptance," modeled on the general form of bilateral contracts in the *fiqh*. In the model document, however, this contractual language is not mentioned and the guiding rubric instead references the more fundamental issue of intent.[13] Thus the notarial writer states that the bilateral contract occurred "with the mutual consent" of the two parties, the *walī* and the husband.[14]

## Interpreting Tears

The third of four formal conditions of a marriage contract in Zaydi fiqh treatises, as mentioned above, is that the initial verbal marriage contract be predicated on the individual consent, or *riḍā*ʾ, of the woman. Since this is a unilateral form of consent, spoken statements may be taken as relatively secure evidence of inner intentions. But in the absence of explicit spoken words, difficult interpretive issues may be raised. The issue of tacit consent is gender-specific and represents a crucial substantive issue in such contracts, as will be demonstrated later with respect to the developments in Arwā's case.

In doctrinal terms, between the two major Yemeni schools of fiqh, the Shafiʿi and the Zaydi, we find a distinctive difference. In the view of the Shafiʿi *madhhab*, the subordinated indigenous school of Ibb and Lower Yemen, consent on the part of the betrothed woman is not always required.[15] Specifically, the Shafiʿis hold that in the case of a virgin, where the other marriage conditions are met, her father (or grandfather), acting as her *walī*, has the right to impose a marriage upon her. The conditions of this imposition (*ijbār*) include the absence of any manifest animosity (*ʿadāwa*) between the future couple, the existence of the appropriate social or moral equivalence (*kafāʾa*) in the spouse, and the woman's contentment with the dower.[16] In the case of a contract for a non-virgin, however, the Shafiʿi position is that it is illegal to make a marriage contract for her unless she has reached her majority and given her permission.

By contrast, the doctrine referenced implicitly in the notarial manual (and, as we shall see, explicitly in Arwā's case), is that of the official Zaydi school of the ruling imam, which, as noted, requires the consent of any free woman who is in her majority.[17] Generally, the woman's consent must be legally operative (*nāfidh*), and this is characterized by the twentieth-century commentator al-ʿAnsī as the case where, using his past tense examples, "she says 'I consented,' or 'I authorized,' or 'I gave permission,' or such like, which indicate that she has asserted her consent."[18] After this basic rule is set forth, the Zaydis also discuss the different circumstances of virgin and non-virgin women. The non-virgin is expected to make her consent known by an explicit statement. In place of a statement, only strong pieces of contextual evidence (*qarāʾin qawiyya*), such as, in the sample list provided by the commentator, "receipt of the dower or requesting it, active preparation for the husband and her going to the house of the husband, or her extending her hand to be hennaed,"[19] may be adequate to demonstrate her consent, and only then if such evidence is not undermined by indications of the woman's shyness towards, or fear of, her *walī*.

In the case of the virgin, however, while an explicit statement of consent is preferable, the jurists also anticipate instances of shyness, intimidation, and silence. Silence alone can constitute consent for a virgin woman, so long as she understands that she can refuse. Difficult interpretive circumstances may surround the actual ascertaining of such consent, however. Consent may be thought to occur "if the news of the marriage reaches her and to a witness to her condition no contextual evidence (*qarīna*) is apparent from which he understands her aversion to it, [and] instead, she was silent, or she laughed, or she fled from room to room in the house, or she cried to an extent not indicating sadness or dissatisfaction—since crying can be from happiness and it can be from distress."[20] But, the commentator continues, "if [the situation] is ambiguous, the reference is to the basic circumstance (*al-aṣl*), which is silence."[21]

Then, for the opposite situation, the doctrinal jurist offers some potential indicators of non-consent, typical nonverbal manifestations that constitute contextual evidence on the basis of which there is a probability that she opposes the marriage. Al-ʿAnsī's examples of such indications are her striking her face with her hand in despair, or "tearing at her breast, pleading woe, and fleeing from house to house, etc."[22] In these suggested legal readings of the nonverbal signs of the female inner state, fleeing "from room to room" indicates consent while the more extreme fleeing "from house to house" is taken as non-consent.

## Gendered Evidence

The details of Arwā's case illustrate not only the relationship of women to marriage contracts and litigation, but also the assumption of separate spaces and knowledge of men and women. At two points in the trial process Judge al-Manṣūr took steps to obtain crucial evidence about Arwā, evidence that could only be collected and evaluated by other women.[23] In some historical jurisdictions this has entailed reliance on women "experts." Near the beginning of the judgment record, immediately following the assertion by the claimant Aḥmad Nājī that Arwā had reached her legal majority, the text states, "there was an order from us," that is, from Judge al-Manṣūr, "to two just women [unnamed] to research and investigate the [matter of] the aforementioned having reached the age of mature discernment (*rushd*)." The concise findings are reported as follows: "The two just women stated that the aforementioned remains a minor at this time, not of full legal capacity, but [that] she is verging on physical maturity (*murāhiqa li l-bulūgh*)."[24] Defendant ʿAlī Muḥammad Qāsim seized on this finding and offered estimations of the ages of Arwā (not more than fourteen years) and of ʿAzīz (at this time not more than ten years); both, it is noted, had appeared in court. Then he pointedly observed that the purported "first" contract for their marriage was dated fourteen years and seven months ago.

The second instance of evidence privy only to women occurs near the end of the trial record regarding two documents Arwā is reported to have presented to the court. The first document (referenced at the beginning of this paper) records Arwā's appearance behind a barrier and the identification of her by her voice. This text comprises her formal announcement to the assembled document witnesses, including the writer, of her legal maturity (*bulūgh*) by reason of the abrupt onset of menstruation. The second document she presented directly supports the first. Here the final judgment record (the *ḥukm* document) reads: "[T]here was an inquiry (*istifhām*) of two just women from the house of his honor the Judge of the Province about what the aforementioned had reported concerning the occurrence of menstruation in her, and they testified to the occurrence to her of that, and that the aforementioned reached maturity by her period."

A very different type of evidence is provided about women from the perspective of male witnesses. Examples are the defense efforts to fix the children's ages so as to demonstrate the impossibility of the date of the "first" contract. Two pieces of testimony for the defendant concerned al-Ḥurra (the "free woman") Bilqīs, the mother of Arwā, and the free woman ʿĀʾisha, the mother of ʿAzīz and wife of the claimant Aḥmad Nājī. In the first testimony text we learn in passing from the specifying of Arwā's descent that her mother was also her father's patrilineal cousin, indicating that Arwā's parents were related in the same way as was envisioned for Arwā and ʿAzīz. The text reads in pertinent part:

> Aḥmad Ḥusayn Qāsim from the village of [X] bore witness to God that the free woman Bilqīs, daughter of ʿAzīz ʿAlī Muṣṭafā, mother of the free woman Arwā, daughter of the aforementioned Muḥammad Nājī, went to visit her maternal uncle ʿAlī Muḥammad Qāsim [the defendant] in the month of Jumādā II, the year 1362 [1943], and she was pregnant with the free woman Arwā, daughter of Muḥammad Nājī. And she stayed with him for two months and then she gave birth to the child she was carrying at the end of Shaʿbān 1362 [1943]. Then she stayed until the end of Ramaḍān when she returned to the house of her husband.

It also becomes clear from this that the defendant, ʿAlī Muḥammad Qāsim, is Arwā's maternal uncle only in the broader classificatory sense, since he actually stands in that specific relation to her mother. The first testimony thus provides some family history, both with respect to the purported marriage and to Arwā's fleeing to this same man's house some fourteen years later.

The next piece of testimony provides some background for the family of ʿAzīz, the prospective husband, revealing (again in passing) what may be the trace of still another patrilateral cousin marriage in the generation of ʿAzīz's maternal grandparents:

> Aḥmad ʿAbduh Qāsim from the village of [X] bore witness to God that Aḥmad Nājī repudiated his wife, the free woman ʿĀʾisha, daughter of Muḥammad Bayḥān, in the year 1368 [1948–49], and [that] the aforementioned [ʿĀʾisha] went to the house of her paternal uncle to be with her mother in the village of [X], and with her was her son ʿAzīz Nājī [sic], a nursing infant not more than two years of age.

It should be noted that there were counter-efforts on the part of the claimant to present evidence that the two children were living at the time of the contract, including one witness who said that on a date before the contract he was in attendance at ʿAzīz's circumcision (his *khitān*).

### Motivations

In the last process-recording segment in the judgment record, there is an entry of testimony which is relevant to understanding the parties' motivations in the conflict. The text reads:

> ʿAbd Allāh Nājī al-Muḥammad from the village of [X] bore witness to God that al-Ḥājj Aḥmad Nājī called to him from the window, since the house of the witness is next to the house of Aḥmad Nājī. He went in and found Sayyid Ḥusayn al-Shāmī and his son Aḥmad [who eventually wrote the "renewed" contract, countersigned by his father], and they ordered him to hear the agency grant by the free woman Arwā to her paternal uncle to contract for her with his son ʿAzīz. He said that he went out [of the room where the men were sitting] to go to her, and she was in a room next to the kitchen. He asked her about the agency by her, and she pleaded with him, by God and by the Shariʿa, to leave her alone and [she said] that she was not granting agency to anyone and that she was a minor. He returned to the room and informed them of this. And Aḥmad Nājī went out and in his hand there was a [...] stick and he beat her with this stick three [times], with the witness behind him watching. Then Aḥmad Nājī jumped on top of the aforementioned, stepping on her stomach with his foot, he [the witness] said, "until we saw her urine on her clothes and on the floor covering." Then the witness went with Aḥmad Nājī in to the room where Sayyid Ḥusayn and his son were. They said, "What did she say?" And the witness told them that she did not consent. And Sayyid Ḥusayn said, "If she does not consent, leave her alone, rushing is not good in this matter."

We know that, despite this, the "renewed" contract eventually was written. As this witness' testimony continues it reveals what may be the crux of the matter for the claimant Aḥmad Nājī, Arwā's paternal uncle:

> Aḥmad Nājī requested of Sayyid Aḥmad [al-Shāmī] that he write the contract document for the aforementioned [Arwā] with his son ʿAzīz, connecting her [to the family], because under his [Aḥmad Nājī's] control [as the appointed legal administrator, *waṣī*] was an inheritance pertaining to the free woman Arwā from her mother and from her father, and he feared that she would marry another man who would cause them trouble and 'Shariʿa' [that is, litigation].

This text indicates that Arwā's inheritance may have played a central role in the motivations of the several parties involved. Arwā's case is now seen not just as one of a forced marriage of a minor, but also one that turns on the fate of a woman's inherited wealth at the key juncture of her marriage, a significant issue in the context of a society based on patrilineal property relations.

For Arwā, the events described above may also have represented a turning point, the beating and the forced agency and contract of marriage turning her irrevocably against her uncle and causing her to flee his house. Her motivations, beyond whatever she may have felt towards her contracted-for cousin-husband, which is unknown, may be learned directly from her reported statements and also (but much less securely), through assertions made by the defendant, her maternal uncle ʿAlī Muḥammad Qāsim, and others. For example, basic information about Arwā appears in the first recorded responses by the defendant early in the litigation:

> ʿAlī Muḥammad Qāsim responded that the mentioned girl, the free woman Arwā, daughter of Muḥammad Nājī, was with him, and that her paternal uncle, Aḥmad Nājī, the claimant, wanted to marry her to his son ʿAzīz, and she is a minor. He contracted for her with his mentioned minor son, employing duress (*karhan*), and without her consent. [...] She fled to him [ʿAlī Muḥammad Qāsim] after her paternal uncle had inflicted injurious suffering upon her and beat her severely. [...]
>
> ʿAlī Muḥammad Qāsim stated that the aforementioned remains a minor until this time and that she does not consent to the contract, even if she did consent to the contract when she was beaten. When she arrived [at his household], ʿAlī Muḥammad Qāsim decided to have the aforementioned brought to him to know the truth. And he had her brought and she stated that she does not consent to the contract, and would never consent to it, and that her paternal uncle beat her severely as a result of her non-consent.

But what caused Arwā to be unwilling to accept the proposed marriage in the first place, before she was beaten? Leaving aside her feelings toward ʿAzīz, a possibility is raised in the course of the litigation. In the recorded response by the defendant immediately following the entry on the "first" contract, he describes Arwā as a girl, "whose father had died and [also] her mother, by poisoning, by he [that is, Aḥmad Nājī] who undertook the reckless falsification of this document [the "first" contract] [...]." This accusation, that the claimant Aḥmad Nājī had committed a double murder by poisoning (a fratricide and murder of his sister-in-law), is repeated later, but still without much development, when defendant ʿAlī Muḥammad Qāsim responds to the claimant's written statement. At this juncture, he states that Arwā, "does not want marriage with the aforementioned [ʿAzīz] because she is afraid of her paternal uncle Aḥmad Nājī for her life and her property, that he will extinguish her life (*rūḥ*) after having extinguished the lives of her father and mother by poison, as is known by the elite and the commoners [...], and the accounting will come on the Day of Accounting [Judgment Day]." For his refutation, claimant Aḥmad Nājī states in the written statement entered in the judgment record:

> As for what [the defendant] [...] says, that Muḥammad Nājī died by poisoning by his brother, this statement is a lie, and no consideration should be given [to] it. The aforementioned [the brother, Muḥammad] was sick and he was in jail on order of the Judge to Sayf al-Islām al-Ḥasan [the son of Imam Yaḥyā, governor of Ibb in the early 1940s], who jailed him. And when he became sick he was released from jail and he entrusted his will (*waṣiya*) to the responsibility (*dhimma*) of his brother Aḥmad Nājī. And if there had been any animosity between them, he would not have made the administration of his will his [brother's] responsibility.

In his ruling, Judge al-Manṣūr took no notice of either the murder accusation or the matter of the young woman's property.

According to the rationale attributed to Aḥmad Nājī, in his words as quoted by a witness to the "renewed" contract, his pursuit of the case may have been motivated by an attempt to keep patrilineal property within the extended family. On the other side, it is not clear the extent to which Arwā herself may have been "afraid," not only for her life but also for "her property," as the defendant, her maternal uncle, stated. We have no indications of the precise nature of the property Arwā inherited, but in late agrarian-age Yemen such wealth mainly involved immovables such as cultivated land or buildings.

Typically, an estate was allocated on paper (in shares) as a consequence of inheritance. This meant that the ownership of groups of adjoining terraces, and even single terraces, would be divided among the heirs. If a young heiress marries "in," that is, within the patriline, to an individual who is to her a male-line "cousin," her property will remain within the family in the following generation. But if she marries "out," to a man from another patriline, her property eventually will be passed to children who identify with this "stranger" family. What all this is thought to mean for family property-holding, as Aḥmad Nājī succinctly put it, is that this "stranger" line "would cause them trouble and Shariʿa [litigation]." A group of patrilineally-related property owners whose lands are concentrated in a place will, as a consequence of the transmission of property rights in the generation following an exogamous marriage, have to deal with "stranger" owners on adjoining terraces, or even, fractionally, within individual terraces. This outcome was thought to be undesirable, although this situation could also arise through a simple property sale. Against such transfers, however, "family" pressure could be applied to not sell to outsiders and there also was a formal legal mechanism of sale pre-emption (*shufʿa*), whereby certain sales of this type could be blocked and ownership recovered by an adjoining member of the family.

As this case and others demonstrate, however, "trouble and Shariʿa" are not necessarily avoided by marrying within the patrilineal group. Also, the passage of property to other patrilines through inheritance from "stranger grandmothers" was possible. Virtually all elite families, including those in the rural districts around Ibb, engaged in at least some strategic marriages with other families to create or cement alliances. Against such patterns of conflict within patrilines and of intermarriages between them, what sustains the patrilineal ideology of keeping control of patrimonial property through a preference for "in" marriages?

A potential explanation for the continuing vigor of such ideas, at least at mid-century in Yemen, lies in the convergence of "family" with "tribe," and specifically with the dictates of armed force in rural districts. Later in the case, the defendant comments that the claimant's case is supported by his underlings, "his subjects (*raʿiyyatihi*) who are under his domination (*sayṭara*)." Claimant Aḥmad Nājī appears in this court record, in short, as a man of property and the "retainers" mentioned presumably are the sharecropping tenants on his own land and on that of his deceased brother, whose estate he controls as administrator.

In Lower Yemen, a *shaykh*, or rural leader, was primarily an individual of great wealth, specifically wealth in cultivated land. In times of trouble, the property relations between *shaykh*-landlords and their tenants could translate, in the weak local version of the formidable tribes of Upper Yemen, into relations of armed support. Mobilizing his family networks, such an individual might call on an entire village, or villages, of sharecroppers to come to his support. If this sort of family-specific concentration of related holding is broken up into scattered properties and involves in-mixtures of individuals from other families, the local armed potential of the associated tenants similarly would be fractured and weakened. One of the important transformations of rural property-holding since the 1962 revolution, in fact, has been the dissolution of some of the old concentrated holdings, as former tenants broke tenancies that were in some cases generations-old, migrated to the Persian Gulf and elsewhere for wage employment, and returned to purchase land and otherwise assert their independence.

In Arwā's patrilineage, the property of her grandfather presumably had been divided between her father and her uncle (and other siblings, if any), and that which had passed to her father (leaving aside property sold or acquired) was divided between Arwā and her brother (one part to her and two parts to him). Since Bilqīs (Arwā's deceased mother) had herself married "in," Arwā and her brother could also have inherited patrilineal property (from their great-grandfather) through this channel as well. As has been noted, however, Arwā's immediate situation in resisting the proposed marriage was further complicated by the fact that Aḥmad Nājī also was the appointed legal administrator (*waṣī*) of her property during her minority. According to blunt assertions made by the defense, Aḥmad Nājī's motives were not to preserve the unified integrity of family property, but simply to grab it. In one of his early responses, for example, defendant ʿAlī Muḥammad Qāsim refers to "the irresponsibility and greed of Aḥmad Nājī in the coercion and consumption of the wealth of the minor daughter of his brother Muḥammad." This is reiterated by the defendant later in the case, where he says that Aḥmad Nājī attempted to "unlawfully appropriate (*istiḥlāl*) her wealth," and more specifically, that he "wanted the coerced marriage of the girl to unlawfully appropriate her wealth." No evidence is offered, however, of any irregularities, such as allegations of inappropriate sales or transfers.

On the side of the claimant, in witnesses' testimonies, there are traces of what may have been efforts by Aḥmad Nājī to financially induce or satisfy Arwā. Specifically, one of the witnesses to the agency from Arwā commented, on the basis of information provided by Arwā's grandmother and in the context of what is otherwise found to be false testimony, that Arwā's paternal uncle had promised her that he would provide for her. Another stated more concretely that the uncle had given two elaborate and valuable pieces of silver jewelry (known as *lawāzim*) to Arwā's grandmother for Arwā. Later in the case, however, in his lengthy written statement, Aḥmad Nājī states that when Arwā was taken by the defendant, she left his house with "all of what she took in the way of his jewelry, valued at four hundred riyals."

Was Arwā herself part of the claimant's patrimonial domain? One of Aḥmad Nājī's allegations against the defendant is that the latter had engaged in the "instruction" (*taʿlīm*) of the girl Arwā, that he "wanted the instruction and the turning of the woman against her husband." This trope of improperly influencing the minor girl necessitates little explication. We learn that the alleged influencing occurred early on, before Arwā fled to the home of the defendant: "There was from them," claimant Aḥmad Nājī states, "the instruction of the free woman Arwā, daughter of Muḥammad

Nājī, wife of ʿAzīz b. Aḥmad Nājī ʿAlī Muṣṭafā, and the causing of her departure from the house of her husband and from her paternal uncle." Aḥmad Nājī also refers to the defendant "and those with him as instructors (*muʿallimīn*)" and then glosses this as those individuals "covetous of the forbidden [women] of others."

Aḥmad Nājī also makes a legal point which concerns the position of the *ʿamm*, the father's brother, versus that of the *khāl*, the mother's brother. As noted earlier, those who have the right to be the woman's *walī*, or guardian, in marriage, are the male-line relatives (*ʿaṣaba*), in order of closeness of relationship. By contrast, the matrilineal uncle and others classed as *dhū l-arḥām* (uterine/female-line relatives) do not have the right to be the *walī*. "No *wilāya* to the relative who is not among the *ʿaṣaba*, such as the *khāl* [...] because they are among the *dhū l-arham*," states the law book.[25]

Such notions figure in Aḥmad Nājī's claim at the beginning as he demands that the judge enforce the return of the "stolen" wife, since the defendant is neither in the position (in relation to the girl) of close and non-marriageable relative (*maḥram*) with whom it is permissible for her to reside, nor that of possible *walī*. The marrying-off of a woman for whom one is the closest male-line relative is itself a right. As the law book says, "marriage is a right (*ḥaqq*) of the *walī*."[26] As for conjugal rights per se, that is, those rights established in Arwā as "wife," the key general term of individual property ownership (*milk*) has a specific and restricted application here. In one of the quoted pre-contractual passages prior to the second or "renewed" contract of marriage, the phrase translated above as "to marry her and to give her to his son ʿAzīz," actually employs a verb from the "m-l-k" root of "*milk*." Thus the permission Arwā is said to grant to her paternal uncle is to marry her "and give ownership in her to his son ʿAzīz" (*wa-yumliku bihā li-ibnihi ʿAzīz*). In this formulation she becomes a *milk* right of ʿAzīz in his status as her husband. This means, as specified in the law books, the *milk* of intercourse (*waṭʾ*), not that of the woman's substance (*raqaba*).[27] That is, it is a domain-specific type of use-right.

## Arguments

The legal crux of Arwā's case, the eventual basis for both the judge's ruling and the later finding of the Court of Appeals, is the law of marriage contract dissolution, or *faskh*. Dissolution of a marriage contract is one of three legal mechanisms (other than death) whereby a marriage can be terminated. The other two are the well-known *ṭalāq*, or "repudiation," an exclusive right of the husband; and *khulʿ*, a lesser-known type of agreement in which the wife compensates the husband and gives up her rights to such things as the postponed dower (*mahr*) and support (*nafaqa*) in order to gain her release from the marriage. *Faskh* is one of the specific areas of the law in which both of the twentieth-century ruling Zaydi imams, Imam Yaḥyā

(d. 1948) and his son Imam Aḥmad (d. 1962), issued guidelines for their appointed judges to follow. These guidelines are in the form of personal interpretive "choices," or *ikhtiyārāt* (also known as *ijtihādāt*), and represent a subset of their doctrinal positions on other aspects of marriage and the status of women. In his guidelines, Imam Aḥmad addressed: (1) the rules of repudiation, according to whether the husband is educated or not, and in terms of its illegal forms; (2) child custody; (3) the disobedient wife; and (4) marriage termination through *khulʿ*. Among the two imams' "choices" on *faskh*, the best-known concern the phenomenon of the absent husband. The hypothetical is an absent husband who has had no communication with the wife nor provided any support for her maintenance and that of his children, if any. (This hypothetical also assumes that he owns no local property that could be sold to support the wife.)

The two imams' "choices" on *faskh* based on the husband's lengthy absence provide an instance of simple legal change from father to son. Imam Yaḥyā's only *faskh* "choice" concerned the absent husband, however his son's "choices" comprised a set of possible conditions for marriage dissolutions, including the insanity of the husband, the husband's absolute poverty, the denial of intercourse to the wife, and, the doctrine argued for by the defense in Arwā's case, intense hatred, or what some American courts euphemistically refer to as "incompatibility." Among the appended materials to Imam Aḥmad's original set of thirteen numbered and rule-like "choices", originally issued in 1949, is a summary concerning a court case from 1951. Like another such case fragment (regarding dissolution due to the husband's insanity) which also appears in the appended materials, the case on dissolution due to hatred is related to three of Imam Aḥmad's thirteen regular *ikhtiyārāt*, which deal with marriage dissolution on other grounds (for example, the husband's absence, the husband's poverty, or the wife is denied her right to have intercourse). In the 1951 case, the analysis is complicated by the added issues of "timidity" (*nafūr*) on the part of the wife and the claim of the husband's impotency. An applicable rule, the "choice" or *ikhtiyār* itself is meant to be extracted from the following case summary:

> In a matter which occurred, the wife Laṭīfa, daughter of Muḥammad ʿAlī, and her opponent, her husband, Aḥmad Ismāʿīl Ḥasan, from ___, the court process is before me. The woman claimed, at first, that the marriage contractor for her was not her guardian (*walī*), and a judgment was given by the judge for dissolution of the marriage. Then, the appeal claim was entered and it was ruled on review that the contractor for her was from among her male-line relatives, [specifically] the paternal uncle's son, after testimony on descent and following a review-ruling by His Majesty, Our Master the Martyred Imam [Yaḥyā, who was assassinated in 1948], may God be pleased

with him. Then, in the interval, there became apparent in the woman extreme timidity. And there were numerous intermediacies between them to better the outcome, but the husband did not help. And the woman is young, and she claims that her husband was impotent, and she requested dissolution. I brought the situation to the attention of His Majesty [Imam Aḥmad], the Victorious for the Religion, and the answer (*jawāb*), from the palace, in the honored pen, may God support him, in what are his words:

"Blessings of God Almighty. If there are established to your satisfaction extreme timidity and hatred of the husband, then in the Shariʿa of Muḥammad bin ʿAbd Allāh [the Prophet], prayers of God for him, the clear solution is in the case of the wife of Thābit bin Qays. The woman must return that which she received as dower (*mahr*), and either repudiation by the husband or dissolution by the judge [shall be the final outcome]. Greetings to you. [Dated] 4 Ramaḍān 1371 [1951]."

On this is the signature with the words "Commander of the Faithful," God forgive him.

In this carefully reported text within a case summary, which exhibits the characteristic concision of such imamic discourse, the matter in question finds its "solution" in a kind of precedent, or textual *aṣl*, located in the early Islamic "case" of the wife of Thābit bin Qays.[28] In this exchange between the imam and the unknown judge, both the textual site of this early historical "case" and its factual details are left unstated. The task was to "find" the law so as to address an open problem posed by a pending judgment. Imams were originally meant to be qualified interpreters of the law (*mujtahid*), and in this authoritative interpretive act, the imam links present and past texts, and in the process renews his understanding of both. His gloss on the present case, that its distinctive features are "extreme timidity and hatred," becomes a gloss as well on the cited source case of the wife of Thābit bin Qays. Once articulated in this manner by the imam, his "choice" subsequently served as a rule to guide judgments in similar cases.

How does this specialized doctrinal category, the "choice" of a ruling Zaydi imam, actually figure in a particular case? Arwā's case illustrates how the specific source text for the "choice" on marriage contract dissolution on the basis of intense hatred can be (and was) referenced by a litigant, here the defendant, in support of her argument. Citations of "choices" occur in the judgment text in Arwā's case, but not in the tutored and highly implicit style of interchange by trained legal scholars, as seen above, and not located, as in many other court cases, in the judge's ruling. Rather, invocations of "choices" take the form here of pragmatic renderings by the parties in their pleadings during the litigation. With these discursive acts, the parties urge particular legal frames for the conflict. First, there is this passage from defendant ʿAlī Muḥammad Qāsim:

> [A]nd not concealed from the judge is that which is in the clear statement of the honored *ikhtiyār* of [Imam] Aḥmad, the Victorious, concerning the non-necessity [i.e. non-viability] of hatred in marriage. Rather, it is clear that [for] the married woman, if the judge verifies her hatred and her inability to be patient and to remain with her husband, due to hatred of being married, then it is required to make the husband repudiate [the wife] and, if he does not repudiate [her], then dissolution [is to be ordered] for her by the judge.

It seems clear from his use of the appropriate term "hatred" and the relatively close paraphrase of parts of the *ikhtiyār* in this oral pleading that the defendant had good legal counsel, including access to some version of the *ikhtiyār* itself. It also seems that in his reference to "the married woman" the defendant may concede the existence of the contract in order to then seek the application of the *ikhtiyār* on marital hatred. The defendant concludes:

> [T]he judge is a follower of the Shariʿa of God. God help us with [the claimant] Aḥmad Nājī who wants to unlawfully appropriate her by illegal means, which is not consented to by the Shariʿa, or Justice, or the honored *ikhtiyār*.

In contrast to this statement by the defendant, the claimant makes a different argument and cites a countervailing imamic *ikhtiyār*. The central evidentiary struggle in the case concerns the purported "first" and "second" (or "renewed") contracts of marriage, and it is this contractual basis, as opposed to the issue of "hatred," that the claimant would have the judge put into the foreground. To this end, Aḥmad Nājī explicitly references another *ikhtiyār* of Imam Aḥmad, the thirteenth of his free-standing original choices of 1949, which concerns the content (*jawhar*) of a judge's decision (*ḥukm*). This *ikhtiyār* requires the judge to ascertain the soundness of the substantive focus of the judgment. It states specifically that "diversions (*taʿlīlāt*) that are of no benefit except to widen the conflict, and the gulf between the disputants, and the give-and-take, and [serve to] alienate the [possibility] of resolution by a judgment of God, are not to be decided," that is, they are not to be taken into consideration by the judge in his ruling.[29] Evincing his own access to solid legal advice, the claimant appropriates some language from this imamic *ikhtiyār*, stating that the defendant

> spoke at great length in his response and he extended remarks to that which is irrelevant. As is comprised in the claim of the claimant,

> the conflict involves the contract, first and last, in each of two situations. The basic principle (*aṣl*) in the contracts of Muslims concerns the legality of the consensus-based Shariʿa principle (*qāʿida*), and it is obligatory for the judge, may God protect him, that he consider the content (*jawhar*) of the judgment (*ḥukm*), according to the *ikhtiyārāt*, without giving attention to other [issues brought up] in the give-and-take and thus like. He should interpret one matter (*qaḍiyya*), and that is that I have proven with witnesses the occurrence of the contract, and then the contract document.

In the end, the final outcome of the case bypassed both of these imamic "choice"-based legal arguments by the parties and instead engaged a further technical doctrinal dimension of contracts. As was seen in the vignette at the outset of this essay, a new material fact was established by Arwā as she appeared before a group of men to assert the advent of her legal majority due to the onset of her menstruation. This new fact created, in turn, a new legal situation of which Arwā immediately took advantage. Here, again, it is clear that she must have had good legal advice, this time concerning not imamic "choices" but the doctrine of the Zaydi school on the law of marriage.

A foreshadowing of the principle involved first appears in the judgment in the form of a counter-argument towards the end of claimant Aḥmad Nājī's long written statement. He refers to the existence of the "first" contract made for Arwā by her father, stating that such a contract, made for a minor daughter by her ideal *walī*, "is not like the contract [made for her] by other than he, which the woman can dissolve upon her legal majority (*bulūgh*)." He continues, "the contract of the father is, by principle, legally valid [and] not subject to the right of dissolution by her, as is textually stipulated in the legal school of the imam."

Returning to the document that resulted from Arwā's 1958 appearance (physically behind a barrier, but legally before the assembled men), we see that after her assertion of legal majority, there took place an important second part of what was a compound legal event: her dissolution of the contract of marriage. As stated in Arwā's written submission to the court:

> There was a request from the free woman Arwā, daughter of Muḥammad Nājī, to us [the document writer] and to those present with us, and they are [five named men], and this after her identification by those who know her voice [two of the above named men, and a named woman]: she appeared behind a barrier wall and bore witness, to us and to the aforementioned above, that physical maturity (*bulūgh*) had occurred to her, and this by menstruation (*ḥayḍ*), and that, as God Almighty knows best, the contract that was contracted for

> her by her paternal uncle Aḥmad Nājī with his minor son is extant, and [that] she has dissolved that [contract]. This the aforementioned [Arwā] uttered in the presence of the aforementioned witnesses on its date, 15 Shaʿbān 1377 (1958).

Reviewing these texts together, it becomes clear that both sides in the case evidently had read the law books and on this textual basis constructed their arguments and their legal acts. The claimant uncle, in arguing for the binding authority of the "first" contract, had been apprised of the passage (e.g. al-ʿAnsī 1993 [c. 1940] 2:36–37, citing the *matn* of *Kitāb al-Azhār*, the basic doctrinal text of the Zaydi school) which states that the right of choice (*khiyār*) pertaining to the minor at the point of her legal maturity, which allows her to dissolve the contracted marriage, pertains only to women not married by their fathers as their *walīs*.[30] Arwā, in placing emphasis on the "second" contract, was literally on the same page as her paternal uncle, as the above text illustrates. The law book goes on to state that, if the woman in question does not exercise her right to dissolve the contract in the same legal session in which she attests to reaching her legal maturity, she loses her right to do so. While Arwā recognized, in passing, the existence of the "second" contract arranged by her uncle, her acts, as reported in the resulting document, precisely satisfy the necessary technical requirement of the doctrine because they comprise, in the same session, both her bearing witness to her maturity and her *faskh* of this latter marriage contract.

### Ruling

The final ruling in Arwā's case is a conclusive marriage contract analysis by the judge. He holds that: (1) the first contract never existed, despite the recorded written instrument; (2) that the second contract existed, although it was based on false testimony and did not include the required consent; (3) that the dissolution of this second contact occurred; and (4) that as a consequence, and as confirmed by the judgment, Arwā is free to enter into another contract of marriage as she sees fit. This analysis is anchored in determinations of the justness (*ʿadāla*) of key witnesses, the necessary and sufficient basis for a ruling,[31] and on securely-witnessed instances of acknowledgment of fraud on the part of the earlier document writer (an interesting part of the case not a subject for present discussion) and of the advent of Arwā's legal maturity. The final judgment reads:

> That which is legally valid (*ṣaḥḥ*) for me [Judge al-Manṣūr] in this conflict is the existence of the contract from Aḥmad Nājī in the month of Dhū l-Qaʿda 1376 (1957), for the free woman Arwā, daughter of his brother Muḥammad Nājī, to his minor son ʿAzīz b. Aḥmad Nājī. Not legally established for me is that the contract occurred with her

consent, since the contractor [the notary], Sayyid Aḥmad b. Ḥusayn al-Shāmī, is just and trustworthy and he stated that she did not appear before him but that her consent and her permission to her paternal uncle for the contract and her legal majority were sworn to by [three named men], and they are known to me for their non-justness. This together with the fact that some of them were asked how they knew of the majority of the aforementioned [fem.] and they stated that this was from the word of her grandmother, the mother of Aḥmad Nājī. The contract took place but her maturity at the time of the contract was not certain. Whereas, on the date of Shaʿbān 1377 (1958), her maturity was certified with menstruation, and she made clear that she dissolved the marriage contract contracted for her by her paternal uncle with his son. This, and as for what Aḥmad Nājī claimed, that he had contracted for her confirming the [first] contract made for her by her father Muḥammad Nājī to the young man ʿAzīz b. Aḥmad Nājī in Rajab 1362 (1943), its [the "first" contract's] non-occurrence has been proven to me, according to what the writer of the contract document, the jurist Saraf al-Khāṭib stated, that there was fraud in it and that he discovered after writing it that the aforementioned girl and the aforementioned boy had not yet been born on that date, that is, in 1362 (1943), as is related in the document of *al-qāḍī*[32] ʿAbd Allāh al-Jamāʿī, authenticated with the script and signature of the District Officer of Jibla [a town near Ibb]. This is what I have found and [accordingly] I have ruled. There is no waiting period [for divorce] for the aforementioned [Arwā] since the dissolution took place before the consummation. Nothing forbids the aforementioned [Arwā] from marrying whomever she wants. Written on its date, 11 Muharram 1378 (July 1958). Ismāʿīl ʿAbd al-Raḥmān al-Manṣūr, Judge of Ibb Province.

## Conclusion

While Arwā was not the sort of young woman who would remain silent such that her tears necessitated legal interpretation, this 1958 Shariʿa judgment does preserve a poignant witnessed account of her crying. Attentiveness to human detail is characteristic of such Yemeni Shariʿa court records, as is richness of legal argument. As in other period cases, issues of intent, specifically here the prior consent of the young woman to the marriage, figure centrally in the final analysis. Central also are technical features of the marriage contract, notably including the specific rules of dissolution associated with a woman's legal majority. While some subtle legal matters are explicitly argued in this case, many others implicitly were in play, as can be demonstrated with reference to chapters of law book doctrine and to the specialized genre of the notarial manual. A distinctive feature of this

Yemeni material is the interpretive role of the Zaydi imam, a qualified jurist at the head of an Islamic state. For its key social backdrop, the case depends on the ties and tensions of kinship, and on the closely related property ties of this late agrarian era. Several women from Arwā's extended family appear as important supporting actors in the case, while others provide crucial female-specific knowledge that forms the basis for some of the key legal findings. Among the many males who figure in the case, there are both scoundrels of various types and motivations and others who would not countenance the abuse of a young woman's rights.

NOTES

[1] Unless otherwise indicated, all citations in this chapter are quotations from an unpublished judgment record of a Shariʿa case heard in the Ibb Province Court of Judge Ismāʿīl ʿAbd al-Raḥmān al-Manṣūr and decided by him on 11 Muḥarram 1378 (28 July 1958). Since the original judgment record I cite from takes the form of a rolled document, it is not possible to give page numbers. Document photocopy available in my records.

[2] I have changed only the personal names of the immediate parties to the case and I have concealed their place name.

[3] See Mundy 1995, 272, for the text of a "return" (*irjāʿ*) agreement.

[4] Cf. Würth 1995, 330.

[5] See Würth 1995.

[6] See Messick 1993.

[7] Al-Iryānī, ms. Jāmiʿ al-gharbiyya, Ṣanaʿāʾ, 64 fiqh, 79–80, Chapter 16, "Marriage."

[8] Here the document uses *fulān* (masc.) and *fulāna* (fem.), meaning "so-and-so" in lieu of names.

[9] Al-Iryānī n.d., 79–80, Chapter 16, "Marriage" (citation omitted).

[10] Al-ʿAnsī 1993, 2:3–117, 118–305.

[11] Idem, 2:22–36.

[12] Idem, 2:35.

[13] See Messick 2001.

[14] Al-Iryānī n.d., 79–80.

[15] Abū Shujāʿ 1894, 457; al-Muftī al-Ḥubayshī 1988, 347. The work by al-Muftī al-Ḥubayshī is a local nineteenth-century commentary on Ibn Raslān.

[16] Al-Muftī al-Ḥubayshī 1988, 347.

[17] Al-ʿAnsī 1993, 2:33; al-Shawkānī 1985, 2:271–272. Cf. al-Muṭahhar 1985, 1:101–102.

[18] Al-ʿAnsī 1993, 2:33.

[19] Idem, 2:33.

[20] Idem, 33–34.

[21] Idem.

[22] Idem.

[23] Cf. Messick 1993, 179–180.

[24] On the distinction between the two types of maturity, *rushd* and *bulūgh*, see Messick 1993, 78–79.

[25] Al-ʿAnsī 1993, 2:17.

[26] Idem, 2:22.
[27] Idem, 2:3.
[28] Al-Bukhārī 1974, 7:150–151.
[29] Imam Aḥmad, *Ikhtiyārāt*. Ms.
[30] This is known technically as *khiyār al-ṣaghīr*, the choice of the minor, and it has some conditions. For the post-Revolutionary legislation on this exercise of *faskh* at majority, see *al-Majalla* 1980, 34–36; for a discussion of cases, see Würth 1995.
[31] For a discussion of Zaydi evidence rules, see Messick 2002.
[32] In Yemen, *al-qāḍī* can mean judge (more often, however, the word used is *ḥākim*), but here it refers to a non-*sayyid* educated person.

# *Part Three*

## MODERN PRACTICE AND REFORM

# *Eight*

# LEGISLATIVE PROVISIONS AND JUDICIAL MECHANISMS FOR THE ENFORCEMENT AND TERMINATION OF THE ISLAMIC MARRIAGE CONTRACT IN MALAYSIA

Nik Noriani Nik Badli Shah

## Introduction

It is often stated that marriage under Islamic law is more in the nature of a civil contract than a sacrament. A Muslim marriage is essentially a contract between the parties, albeit a contract with significant religious, moral, and spiritual overtones. Although ideally a Muslim marriage should be for life (a saying of the Prophet[1] states that "of all lawful acts, the most detestable to Allah is divorce"),[2] Islamic law provides that when the marriage has irretrievably broken down, it should be terminated with kindness and not with rancor and ill-feeling between the parties, in accordance with the Qurʾanic injunction that "the parties should either hold together on equitable terms or separate with kindness."[3] Separation with kindness necessitates ensuring that the divorce is settled on fair and equitable terms. When the parties are unable to agree upon the terms of the divorce, judicial authorities must settle the legal issues that arise between them.

The conception of the Muslim marriage contract, as reflected in the classical Islamic laws governing divorce, is that of a contract that can be easily dissolved by the man, but that binds a woman to her husband in a bondage that she can never escape by her own will.[4] This view of the marriage contract is not in harmony with the Qurʾanic injunctions, such as the one that grants both spouses equal rights as to the appointment of arbiters in the event of a breach between them,[5] and with what is generally known about the marital life of the Prophet.[6] Under classical Islamic law, a husband who desires to terminate his marriage without the consent of his wife may do so with relative ease, while a wife who desires to terminate her marriage without the consent of her husband faces many difficulties. This law was mainly formulated in patriarchal societies during medieval and feudal times, which regarded divorce as the unilateral right of the husband. In this chapter, I will argue that there is a need to reinterpret the principles of Islamic law as contained in its original sources (the Qurʾan and authentic Sunna) so that the rules derived from them, and their codification through state legislation in Malaysia, reflect the Islamic spirit of justice and equity.

Thus far, efforts at codifying Islamic law in Malaysia have resulted in reaffirming the patriarchal vision of marriage and the role of wives. In Malaysia, where the personal law of Muslims is under the jurisdiction of each state,[7] many attempts have been made over the last twenty or thirty years to reform Islamic family law, and most importantly within that category, the rules regarding marriage and divorce. An attempt to streamline the administration of Muslim personal law and create uniform Islamic family law statutes was made during the move towards the codification of the Shariʿa (Islamic law) rules on marriage and divorce in the early 1980s, and the resulting Islamic Family Law (Federal Territories) Act of 1984 was to serve as a model to be followed by the respective state enactments.[8]

Unfortunately, signs of a conservative reaction surfaced in the early 1990s. This conservative reaction can be seen, for example, in the legislative and judicial recognition of the validity of the husband's pronouncement of *ṭalāq* (divorce by the husband's unilateral declaration) outside the court, on the one hand, and the re-emphasis on the issue of the wife's disobedience (*nushūz*) when she attempts to avail herself of divorce (*taʿlīq*) based on the husband's breach of a stipulation in the marriage contract, on the other hand.

This chapter reviews the use of the marriage contract in divorce law and practice in Malaysia. The first part discusses the state of Malaysian divorce law and practice when one spouse desires the termination of the marriage contract but the other party does not, with special focus on the disparity in treatment of divorces initiated by the husband as compared to those initiated by the wife. Specifically, it will illustrate the one-sidedness of the doctrine of *ṭalāq* as well as obstacles to wife-initiated divorce mechanisms such as *taʿlīq* (breach of marriage contract), *khulʿ* (compensatory restitution), and *faskh* (judicial dissolution). Key issues in these cases include the notion of the wife's disobedience and uneven burdens of proof upon wives seeking to establish grounds for divorce under the various non-*ṭalāq* means available to her. In these discussions, I will critique the law and practice from the perspective of women and the principles of the Qurʾan and Sunna, suggesting corrections to the law such as changing the understanding of *nushūz* from "disobedience of the wife" to "disruption of marital harmony by either spouse," and allowing a wider scope of breach of marriage contract stipulations as alternative, non-statutory, grounds for divorce. The final part of this essay looks at the financial consequences of divorce (especially upon women) and investigates improvements to the system from a modernist Islamic perspective including the option of setting terms for a financial settlement in the marriage contract.

### A. Malaysian Divorce Law and Application

The main types of divorce under Islamic law are *ṭalāq* (repudiation by the husband), *khulʿ* (redemption by the wife), *taʿlīq* (delegated repudiation by the wife upon the husband's breach of a stipulation agreed upon in the marriage contract), and *faskh* (judicial dissolution of marriage on one of the grounds provided under the law).[9] Each of these methods becomes complicated in practice when one spouse wants a divorce and the other does not.

In accordance with the injunction in the Qurʾan stating, "If you fear a breach between the twain, appoint (two) arbiters, one from his family and the other from hers,"[10] the Malaysian Islamic Family Law (Federal Territories) Act of 1984 provides for the appointment and duties of a conciliatory committee in cases where only one party desires a divorce or it appears to the court that there is a reasonable possibility of a reconciliation between the parties.[11] Where the conciliatory committee submits to the court a certificate that it is unable to effect a reconciliation and the husband refuses to pronounce one *ṭalāq* (declaration of divorce),[12] the court shall refer the case for arbitration by arbiters (*ḥakam*), one for each side.[13] If the arbiters are of the opinion that the parties should be divorced but do not hold authority from their principals to order a divorce, the court shall appoint other arbiters and shall confer on them the authority to order a divorce.[14] To avoid a situation where the parties have to undergo several overlapping processes of conciliation as provided under the current procedures, women's groups have proposed simplifying the procedures by granting to the court the power of immediately appointing the two arbiters to arbitrate between the husband and wife. The arbiters should also be given the authority at the outset to order a divorce if they are unable to effect reconciliation.[15]

#### 1. *Husband's Pronouncement of* Ṭalāq *Against the Will of the Wife*

It is well known that, according to the classical interpretation of Islamic law, the husband has the right to unilaterally dissolve the marriage contract through divorce by *ṭalāq*. Before the Islamic Family Law Act and state enactments came into force, it was common practice for Muslim husbands to pronounce the *ṭalāq* outside the court.[16] Modern statutory provisions have attempted to give a greater role to the courts in regulating this unilateral pronouncement of divorce and in granting orders for the termination of the marriage contract. Under the 1984 Islamic Family Law Act, a husband must file a divorce application with the court in accordance with the provisions of the act, and the court shall either permit the husband to pronounce *ṭalāq* or make an order for the dissolution of the marriage after due inquiry and investigation into the facts of the case. However, the act also allows the court to order the registration of a divorce pronounced by a husband outside of and without the permission of the court, if the court is satisfied that the *ṭalāq* is valid according to the rule of Islamic law (*ḥukm sharīʿa*).[17] Nevertheless, a man who pronounces *ṭalāq* outside the court has committed an offense under the statutory law and is liable to be punished with a fine not exceeding one thousand ringgit or imprisonment not exceeding six months or both.[18]

This reinstatement of the classical interpretation on *ṭalāq* reaffirms a shortcut for any husband wishing to terminate his marriage without obtaining the consent of his wife or undergoing conciliation proceedings. There have been a few cases, however, where the wife has disputed a pronouncement of *ṭalāq* made by the husband outside the court. For example, in the case of *Rojmah bte Abdul Kadir v. Mohsin bin Ahmad*,[19] the husband claimed that he had divorced his wife in his house by pronouncing three *ṭalāq*s in her presence, and subsequently made an application for divorce under the Islamic Family Law Act. At the court hearing, the wife denied that the husband had pronounced the divorce at home on the date specified. The husband admitted that he could be mistaken about the date but said that he did pronounce the divorce. The learned judge of the Syariah (Shariʿa) Court did not ask the husband to produce witnesses and ruled in his favor. The Syariah Appeal Board allowed the wife's appeal, and the case was ordered to be retried before another judge. In its judgment, the board expressed its regret that the serious matter of divorce had not been treated with care and circumspection by the lower court. The board pointed out that divorce, although allowed in Islam, is said to be the most hated of permitted things in the eyes of Allah, and therefore great care must be taken in dealing with an application for divorce to ensure that the requirements laid down in the Qurʾan and Prophetic tradition and in the Islamic Family Law Act are complied with. In a case where the pronouncement of divorce is disputed, all the evidence available should have been called for and considered. Unconsidered questions included: whether the wife was in her menstrual period or not (the practice of the Prophet disapproves of the pronouncement of *ṭalāq* during the wife's menstrual period),[20] whether she was pregnant, whether the parties had children, why the husband decided to end the marriage, whether the dower had been paid to the wife, and the question of compensation for the divorced wife (*matāʿ*) and of matrimonial property. As there were many defects and omissions in the trial, the Appeal Board ordered that the case be retried before another judge, who should hear the witnesses produced, record all the evidence and arguments offered, and decide whether the husband had pronounced the divorce as stated. The learned judge should also make orders regarding the custody and maintenance of the children, the place of residence, the payment of compensation, and the division of the matrimonial property.

Another example of a wife's disputation of her husband's alleged pronouncement of *ṭalāq* is a case from the State of Selangor, *Zainab binti Mahmood v. Abd Latif bin Jusoh.*[21] In this case, the Syariah Court had also allowed the husband's application for the registration of the divorce by one *ṭalāq*, but the Syariah Appeal Board, in allowing the wife's appeal against the registration, held that although *ṭalāq* is the right of the husband, it is not to be exercised simply as the husband pleases, because "of all lawful acts, the most detestable to Allah is divorce." Moreover, the Board found errors of law and also of fact: the husband/respondent claimed to have pronounced the divorce on the wife/appellant on 10 July 1988, but in his application to contract a polygamous marriage on 13 September 1988, he had stated that the appellant was his existing wife and that she had consented to his new marriage, and he had also continued to pay maintenance to the appellant until December 1989. Because the wife/appellant did not consent to the claimed divorce, a conciliatory committee was appointed so that the divorce could be conducted upon equitable terms (*maʿrūf*) in accordance with the Shariʿa rules. These cases, however, are rather exceptional, as it is difficult for a wife to oppose her husband's desire for divorce since *ṭalāq* is recognized as the husband's right. It can also be seen that the Board in *Rojmah v. Mohsin* was more concerned with the question of ancillary relief for the wife, and the Board in *Zainab v. Abd. Latif* was also concerned with the manner of conducting the divorce, rather than with the question of preventing the divorce.

### 2. *Wife-Initiated* Taʿlīq *Divorce Without the Consent of the Husband and the Issue of* Nushūz

There is no shortcut (i.e., unilateral *ṭalāq* option) for a wife who desires to obtain a divorce without the consent of her husband. But she can undertake the longer process of applying for a divorce by *taʿlīq*. *Taʿlīq* is applied when the marriage contract includes a stipulation entitling the wife to a divorce upon the husband's breach of its provisions. However, in practice, *taʿlīq* divorces are hard to obtain in Malaysia because when the wife presents her breach of contract claim in court, the defense is often to raise the issue of "disobedience" (*nushūz*), and the courts often require proof that the wife is not *nushūz* as a condition to dissolution on grounds of *taʿlīq*.

*Nushūz* is generally regarded as a wife's disobedience against her husband, although nowhere in the Qurʾan does it say that a wife must obey her husband,[22] and moreover the term *nushūz* in the Qurʾan is used for both the wife[23] and the husband.[24] The Islamic Family Law Act, however, limits its references to *nushūz* to instances of a disruption of marital harmony by the wife and not those by either spouse. According to the act, *nushūz* exists when the wife "unreasonably refuses to obey the lawful wishes or commands of her husband, that is to say, inter alia, (a) when she withholds her association from her husband; (b) when she leaves her husband's home against his will; or (c) when she refuses to move with him to another home or place, without any valid reason according to Islamic legal rulings."[25] The effect of a finding of *nushūz* is that the wife is not entitled to marital maintenance until she "repents and obeys the lawful wishes and commands of her husband, [and thus] she ceases to be *nushūz*."[26]

As stated above, the issue of the wife's *nushūz* has become problematic in cases where she applies for a divorce on the ground that the husband has breached a contractual stipulation, such as not providing for her maintenance. For instance, in the case of *Aisny v. Haji Fahro Rozi*,[27] the trial court held that although the form of *taʿlīq* used (the standard *taʿlīq* used in the state of Selangor) did not touch on the question of obedience, it did mention maintenance as an obligation of the husband and therefore it was necessary for the wife to show that she was not *nushūz* when applying for *taʿlīq* based on the husband's failure to provide maintenance for her. The claimed evidence of *nushūz* in this case was: (1) the wife moving out of the matrimonial home; and (2) the wife caveating four pieces of land registered in the husband's name. Another issue was the question of some stocks and shares in the wife's name. The court held that the wife was not *nushūz* because circumstances showed that the husband had acquiesced in her decision to move out of the matrimonial home, and that the wife was justified in caveating the lands because they were properties jointly acquired during the marriage. However, the trial court dismissed the wife's application for divorce on the ground that she could have obtained sufficient maintenance through the stocks and shares in her possession. In other words, the trial court assumed that the shares registered in the wife's name actually belonged to the husband and were the provision for her maintenance. On appeal, the Syariah Board of Appeal reversed this last ruling, holding that because there was no evidence that the shares belonged to the husband it would be wrong to expect the wife to maintain herself out of her own property.

The trial court in *Aisny v. Haji Fahro Rozi* had placed an unduly heavy burden upon the wife, and even after deciding that she was not *nushūz*, had apparently required additional proof that the shares registered in her name were her own property and not the property of her husband. A contrasting approach is illustrated in the Syariah Board of Appeal judgment in the case of *Fakhariah v. Johari*.[28] In that case, the Board of Appeal held that the issue of *nushūz* was irrelevant and need not arise when the *taʿlīq* agreement clearly and unconditionally stated that every time the husband failed to give sufficient maintenance to the wife for a period of four months or more, then she could make a complaint to the Syariah judge. If this was found to be true, then a divorce would be effected. Alternatively, even if a wife's right to maintenance is conditional upon her obedience, the board stated that a husband contesting a wife's claim of non-maintenance must first apply for a court order declaring his wife to be *nushūz*, and then to take additional active steps to settle the matter if he was serious in wishing his wife to return to him.[29] Unfortunately, the whole issue of the wife not being *nushūz* as a pre-condition for her entitlement to obtain relief from the court was given a new emphasis in the 1994 amendments to the Islamic Family Law Act, which disentitle a divorced wife from receiving *ʿidda* (post-divorce waiting period) maintenance if she is *nushūz*.[30]

(a) Standardization of *Taʿlīq* Provisions and the Possibility of Recognizing Optional Stipulations

In Malaysia, spouses usually include in their marriage contracts the stipulations that are enumerated in the standard-form *taʿlīq* attached to the marriage certificate.[31] For example, one stipulation that is often included states that the husband must not fail to pay maintenance for a period of three months or more, or cause harm to the wife. The standardization of the terms in *taʿlīq* stipulations, however, greatly limits the parties' freedom to stipulate their own contractual arrangements, and in particular, weakens the bargaining position of women. There have recently been suggestions from various women's groups that additional or optional stipulations should also be expressly allowed in the *taʿlīq* agreements, that the statutory law should make it clear that individual couples may put in other stipulations agreed upon between them (as many people may not be aware of this option for individual agreements), and that these should also be recognized in state legislation and upheld by the courts.[32] These additional contractual terms, they argue, should be written according to the choices and arrangements agreed upon by individual couples, especially now that prescribed statutory stipulations are also available as grounds for a divorce by *faskh* (court-ordered divorce), ever since the Islamic Family Law Act adopted the more liberal Maliki school's grounds for *faskh*.[33] Previously, the grounds available for a court-ordered divorce were confined to the restrictive grounds of the dominant Shafiʿi school which limited them to incapacity to perform marital obligations and inability to pay maintenance. They did not include, significantly, a husband's wilful refusal to pay maintenance, or ill-treatment of the wife. Breach of a marriage contract stipulation was already included as a ground for divorce prior to the Islamic Family Law Act, but it has always been recognized under *taʿlīq*, and not under *faskh*. I do not propose to go into the details of the technical procedural requirements, but it is important for a wife to know whether she is applying for *taʿlīq* or *faskh* divorce, as there are different applications forms to be filled, and if she has filled in the wrong application form, her case may be dismissed on a technicality.

In view of this overlapping of grounds, the present statutory grounds for the *taʿlīq* remedy (i.e., failure to pay maintenance or harm to wife) would appear to be almost redundant because these are also grounds for court-ordered divorce. But some point out that the issue of whether a marriage is terminated through *taʿlīq* or through *faskh* is still relevant to the financial consequences of the divorce, because a woman who obtains a divorce through *taʿlīq* need not lose her right to compensation from the husband, whereas there is no provision for compensation under a *faskh* divorce. Nevertheless, with the freedom to add new non-statutory *taʿlīq* provisions in a marriage contract, women would gain greater bargaining power in their attempts to secure just and equitable terms in the marriage contract.

Women's groups in Malaysia have proposed that among the optional terms that should be legally recognized in a marriage contract is a stipulation controlling polygamy, that is, one which restricts a husband's freedom to take another wife. Although conditions in individual marriage contracts entitling the wife to a divorce in the case of the husband taking another wife are recognized as valid in various other Muslim countries,[34] this condition has not been expressly recognized in Malaysia, either by statutory legislation or through judicial decision. The difficulty in obtaining recognition for such a stipulation in the marriage contract is due to the fact that Muslims in Malaysia are predominantly followers of the Shafiʿi school of law, which has classically held such a condition to be inconsistent with the precepts of marriage and therefore invalid.[35] The Hanbali school, on the other hand, is reported to be the most liberal regarding the freedom to make stipulations in contracts of marriage.[36] Since *siyāsa sharʿiyya* (understood as meaning the government has a choice in selecting any legal rule in accordance with Islamic law) is now applied in Malaysia to allow adoption of the rule of any recognized jurisprudential school on particular issues—as already exemplified by the statutory recognition of the Maliki school's grounds for dissolution of marriage through *faskh*—there is no reason why the Hanbali law on the freedom to stipulate a condition against the husband taking another wife should not be recognized in Malaysian legal reforms. Moreover, polygamy is restricted, and is certainly not incumbent or even recommended in Islam, and it is difficult to see how a promise by the husband not to take another wife during the marriage could be regarded as a stipulation contrary to the prescribed effects of that marriage contract. On this reading, Malaysian women's groups have argued that a wife who desires the termination of her marriage contract upon a husband's breach of a monogamy clause should be entitled to relief.[37]

### 3. *Termination of Marriage Contract Through* Khulʿ, *the Role of the Court and of the Arbiter*

A wife who has no legal ground for complaint against the husband may apply for a divorce by *khulʿ* (literally, "renunciation"), which in classical Islamic law was a divorce by which the wife obtains her husband's consent to divorce by some sort of compensation (e.g., return of the dower).[38] In Malaysia, there is still some controversy as to whether the husband's consent is necessary for a *khulʿ* divorce. The 1984 Islamic Family Law Act does not expressly cover the point but appears to provide a process whereby *khulʿ* may occur without the consent of the husband, but only after the parties have gone through an elaborate and lengthy procedure involving the court, a conciliatory committee, and two rounds of arbitration with two sets of arbiters.

The process of appointing arbiters to resolve issues in *khulʿ* divorces was applied by some of the Shariʿa courts in Malaysia even prior to the codification of the Islamic family law statutes in the 1980s. For instance, in the 1979 Kelantan case of *Talib v. Sepiah*,[39] the wife had applied for a divorce from her husband. As the husband refused to agree to a divorce even through *khulʿ*, the court ordered both parties to appoint their respective arbiters. The arbiters were unable to resolve the matter because the husband's arbitrator did not agree to a divorce. The court then appointed another arbitrator for the husband and conferred upon him the authority to effect a divorce. The husband appealed to the Appeal Board but his appeal was dismissed and the court's decision affirmed.

4. *Judicial Dissolution of Marriage*

A final method available to a wife seeking a divorce against the consent of her husband is to apply for a judicial dissolution of a marriage (*faskh*) upon a court finding of sufficient grounds. This method has been used from time to time in Malaysia, but it has not proven an easy road. For example, in a case in Negeri Sembilan, *Rosilah v. Abdul Rahman*,[40] the wife had applied for *faskh* and made various allegations against the husband including that he had neglected to provide maintenance and that he was involved in black magic. The husband denied the allegations, claiming that the wife's assertions were due to the fact that she was suffering from mental illness, producing a medical report from a consultant psychiatrist in support of this theory. The court appointed a conciliatory committee. The committee stated that reconciliation could not possibly be achieved since the wife was determined to separate. It recommended that the case be settled through ordinary *ṭalāq* or through *khulʿ*.[41]

The court rejected the wife's *faskh* application as well as the committee's recommendation, holding that none of the wife's allegations had been proven and that the husband still loved the wife and was concerned that she should receive treatment for her illness. On appeal by the wife, the Syariah Appeal Board held that since efforts to reconcile the parties had not succeeded, the best way out was to accept the conciliatory committee's recommendation for application to be made for a divorce either by *ṭalāq* or *khulʿ*. This case illustrates that although *faskh* might be considered a viable alternative to the other methods of wife-initiated divorce, as it turns out, women in Malaysia have often found *faskh* divorces more difficult to obtain than *khulʿ*.[42]

## B. Financial Consequences of Divorce

Issues of maintenance and financial compensation to the wife vary according to the type of divorce. For instance, under the Shafiʿi school of law the payment of compensation is incumbent in the case of every innocent divorced woman who is repudiated (*ṭalāq*) by her husband, except a woman whose dower has been stipulated and who is divorced before consummation of the marriage. The clearest authority for this right to financial compensation for divorced women is a verse in the Qurʾan that states: "For divorced women, maintenance/financial provision (*maṭāʿ*) should be provided on a reasonable scale, this is a duty on the righteous."[43]

One mandatory form of maintenance for a wife following *ṭalāq* is financial support during *ʿidda*, the required waiting period of three to four months before a divorce becomes final. The Qurʾan emphasizes that the scale for *ʿidda* maintenance should be the same as that of the maintenance during the marriage.[44] Confusion between *ʿidda* maintenance and *maṭāʿ* has led some to believe that a divorced woman's financial claim upon her former husband is limited to her three-month *ʿidda* maintenance. Yet the Qurʾan makes a clear distinction between *ʿidda* maintenance (*nafaqa ʿidda*) and post-*ṭalāq* financial compensation (*maṭāʿ*), with the latter being recognized as a right separate and distinct from *ʿidda* maintenance. The Qurʾanic injunction for the provision of "*maṭāʿ* [...] on a reasonable scale"[45] makes no mention of the *ʿidda* period or any specific limit for *maṭāʿ*.

The Islamic Family Law Act[46] therefore provides for the payment of compensation (*maṭāʿ*) in addition to the woman's right to *ʿidda* maintenance. However, in cases of divorce initiated by the wife when she has no legal complaint against the husband (*khulʿ*) the payment of compensation (often a reimbursement or returning of the dower, or *mahr*) is due from the wife to the husband.[47] It is also possible for the couple to decide upon the financial consequences of divorce in their marriage contract. In a case decided many years ago, *Sakamah v. Tasmin*,[48] the husband registered a piece of land in the name of the wife in trust for him on the express stipulation in the marriage contract that if she requests a divorce she would re-transfer the land to him or pay him the value thereof. It was held by the court that "the agreement was a perfectly proper one [...] and this divorce itself was in a recognized form, i.e., the Khulu [*khulʿ*] divorce."[49] A more recent case exemplifies the specification in the marriage contract of the amount of financial compensation due to the wife in the event of divorce. In *Hamzah v. Fatimah Zaharah*,[50] the husband, upon marrying the wife, had agreed to pay her RM 5000 if he divorced her. When he eventually did so, she claimed the money, and the court held in her favor: she had fulfilled her term of the obligation by marrying him and the husband was then obliged to fulfill his term of the contract as "there is no law in the Muslim religion that prohibits a wife or would-be wife from entering into a contract with her husband."[51] The above cases, *Sakamah v. Tasmin* and *Hamzah v. Fatimah Zaharah*, were decided in the civil courts prior to the conferral of exclusive jurisdiction to the Shariʿa courts over matters relating to the personal law of Muslims. Nevertheless, there is no reason to suppose that the outcomes would have been different had they been decided in the Shariʿa courts, making reference to the standard Islamic contract law rule that stipulations in contracts that either restate, or support and reinforce, the effects of the contract prescribed by Islamic law are indeed lawful.[52]

The Shariʿa courts in Malaysia may also take into account Malay customary practices that do not conflict with the principles of Islamic law. Malay customary practices are usually taken into account with regard to the financial settlement on matrimonial property. It seems that the courts in *Sakamah v. Tasmin* understood the agreement as defining the amount of compensation payable to the husband if the wife were to ask for a *khulʿ* divorce, and the agreement in *Hamzah v. Fatimah Zaharah* as defining the amount of compensation payable to the wife if the husband were to divorce (*ṭalāq*) the wife.[53]

The right of a wife divorced by *ṭalāq* to receive compensation is generally recognized under Islamic family law in Malaysia. If the wife is *nushūz* (in Malay, *isteri nushūz*, meaning literally "*nushūz* wife"), this does not disentitle her to compensation if she is divorced. In *Piah v. Che Lah*,[54] the wife's claim for *ʿidda* maintenance was dismissed as she was found to be *nushūz* at the time of the divorce, having left the matrimonial home without the husband's permission. However, her claim for compensation was allowed. The Chief Qadi (judge) said essentially that compensation is to be paid by a husband who divorces his wife, and it is payable in all cases of divorce except if the wife obtains a *faskh* divorce because of the husband's inability to consummate the marriage, or if his whereabouts are unknown, or if the husband obtains a *faskh* divorce because of some defect of the wife. With regard to the amount of compensation, the husband in *Piah v. Che Lah* had a low income, but he was not completely without means, as he had received a gratuity of RM 2645.45 upon his retirement and was receiving a monthly pension of RM 100. The court decided that the sum of RM 500 was reasonable.

The Appeal Committee has ruled out some lower courts' practice of assessing compensation awards with reference to the duration of the marriage. In *Rokiah v. Mohamed Idris*,[55] the learned Chief Qadi had assessed the compensation at a daily rate of RM 1 multiplied by the 35 years, 3 months and 5 days of the marriage, totaling RM 12,695. The husband's appeal was allowed on the issue of quantum, the amount of compensation. The assessment of compensation based on the length of the marriage is the practice adopted by the Syariah Court of Singapore, but the Kuala

Lumpur Syariah Appeal Committee held that it could find no juristic basis for it and that it seemed to run counter to the essence of compensation, or *maṭā'*, which is meant to salve the feelings of the wife on being divorced. The Appeal Committee examined the awards of compensation in a number of cases in Malaysian states and decided that in view of the trend of the decisions the award of RM 12,695 in that case was excessive and reduced it to RM 6,500. The Appeal Committee also referred to *Piah v. Che Lah*, mentioned above, and agreed that "recalcitrance" (*nushūz*) on the part of the wife does not deny her the right to obtain compensation if she is divorced.

It may be said that the awards of *maṭā'* by the Syariah courts in Malaysia are usually not very substantial.[56] However, it should not be forgotten that an underlying rationale for the relatively low compensation awards is related to the existence of the concept of matrimonial property (*harta sepencarian*). For instance, in *Rokiah v. Mohamed Idris*,[57] the Syariah Board of Appeal, while allowing the husband's appeal as to the excessive amount of compensation, at the same time allowed the wife's appeal as to her right to matrimonial property. The Syariah Appeal Board awarded the wife one-third of the value of the properties acquired by the husband during the marriage. The lower court had rejected the wife's claim to matrimonial property on the ground that she had made no financial contribution towards the acquisition of the properties. The Board, in rejecting this idea, held that the wife's indirect contribution by looking after the household and family must also be considered. The Board referred to the classical view relating to the Islamic marriage contract, under which it is understood that it is not compulsory for a wife to serve her husband in cooking, washing clothes, and the like, as the intention of the contract of marriage is for them to enjoy each other's company. Therefore, the Board held that where the wife in fact helps the husband in looking after the house and the family and in keeping him company in his life, profession or business, and he is able thereby to acquire property by his efforts, the wife has contributed indirectly to the acquisition of the property.

The case of *Rokiah v. Mohamed Idris* is a triumph for Muslim women in Malaysia because, although it allows the husband's appeal to reduce the amount of compensation, more importantly it allows the wife's appeal on the whole issue of matrimonial property. The second part of the judgment of the Syariah Appeal Board refers to the concept of matrimonial property, and in it the Board appears to confirm that the Malay customary law on matrimonial property—that is, giving the wife a share in the properties acquired by the husband during the marriage, even though the wife had made no financial contribution towards the acquisition of those properties—is in accordance with, and supported by, the principles of Islamic law.[58]

In earlier cases, where a wife who had made no financial or direct contribution was awarded a share of matrimonial property, reference was made merely to Malay customary law and not to the larger principles of Islamic law. This may account for the refusal of the trial judge in *Rokiah v. Mohamed Idris* to award the wife a share of the matrimonial property; with the increasing trend towards "Islamization" in Malaysia, the judge may have become reluctant to base his judgment merely on Malay customary law.

In a more recent case, *Noraini Mokhtar v. Abd Halim Samat*,[59] the Kelantan Syariah Appeal Court granted the wife half of the property that was registered in the joint names of the parties, and also half of the property acquired during the marriage that was registered in the husband's name only. Both parties had made equal financial contributions towards the property registered in their joint names. Regarding the property registered in the husband's name, the Appeal Court referred to Qur'an 2:228: "And wives shall have rights similar to those over them, according to what is equitable (*maʿrūf*), and men (husbands) have a degree over them." The Appeal Court says that the "degree over them" is related to the issue of financial maintenance: wives have rights in relation to their duties and husbands have rights in relation to their duties. It is generally the husband's duty to acquire property for the household, and it should be categorized as jointly owned property, as long as there is nothing to indicate otherwise, for example if it is his property through gift or inheritance.

## Conclusion

It might be observed that Islamic law acknowledges that it would be impractical as well as undesirable to insist upon the continuation of a marriage when one of the parties to the marriage contact is determined to end it. The fact that Islam permits divorce, even if it is the most detestable of all lawful things, illustrates that it is not in favor of forcing a man and woman to continue together in a hateful union. However, there should be adequate legislative provisions and mechanisms to ensure that the termination of the marriage contract is carried out in a fair and just manner to both parties, as well as to the children of the marriage.

At present, in spite of the statutory controls over divorce, the husband who desires to terminate his marriage without the consent of the wife is still in a more advantageous position as compared to the wife who desires to terminate her marriage without the consent of the husband. Moreover, although the law grants certain financial rights to divorced women, such as the right to compensation and matrimonial property, women's groups have pointed out that the many obstacles that exist in the way of women-initiated divorce (including *taʿlīq* and *faskh*), usually due to the burdensomely high standards of proof required, have often led many wives to renounce their financial claims in order to obtain their husbands' consent to the divorce, and thus to facilitate divorce proceedings.[60] This is chiefly due to the classical interpretation of Islamic law that was mainly formulated under the influence of a patriarchal society that regarded divorce as the unilateral right of the husband. I have argued here that there is a need for the principles of Islamic law as contained in its original sources (the Qurʾan and authentic Sunna) to be re-subjected to interpretation through *ijtihād* in order to equalize the justice afforded to men and women in divorce resolutions done in the name of Islam.

A challenge to this *ijtihād* is the fact that although Malaysia had embarked on a program for the reformulation of Islamic family law in the 1970s and 1980s, signs of a conservative reaction unfortunately surfaced in the early 1990s. This conservative reaction can be seen, on the one hand, in the increased recognition of the validity of the husband's pronouncement of *ṭalāq* outside the court, and, on the other hand, the re-emphasis on the issue of the wife's *nushūz* when she attempts to avail herself of the husband's breach of a stipulation in the marriage contract (the *taʿlīq* provision). In order to do away with the notion of *nushūz* as "disobedience of the wife to the husband" and to recognize it as "disruption of marital harmony by either spouse," there needs to be a general re-understanding of the basic premise that the Islamic marriage contract is a contract of partnership between the two parties. A marriage contract should not be viewed as a contract of submission of the female to the male, nor should it be viewed as a contract of dominance of the husband over the wife.

The modernist views described in this essay rest on secure Qurʾanic foundations and seek to ensure rights and gender equality in Muslim societies. But many Muslims and court officials often challenge such egalitarian interpretations, branding them as either too radical or as modern innovations veering away from the traditions of early or formative Islam.[61] The traditionalists' position on women's rights rests heavily on the notion that there is no gender equality in Islam, while the assertions of the modernists and contemporary Muslim women scholars are based on a thoughtful, principled, and context-sensitive reexamination of actual texts.[62] For modern reforms to be successful and effective in practice, the reformists need to raise the awareness of the Muslim community that the reforms are not due to the influence of secularization, but are based upon sources and principles from within the Islamic framework.

## NOTES

[1] Peace be upon him.

[2] E.g., in a well-known *ḥadīth* narrated by Ibn ʿUmar in "kitāb al-ṭalāq" in *Sunan Abī Dāwūd* (transl. 1984).

[3] Qurʾan 2:229. Qurʾanic translations are taken from the translation by Abdullah Yusuf Ali.

[4] Hamadeh 1996, 334, 335.

[5] Qurʾan 4:35.

[6] For instance, the Prophet's behavior with his wives was "a mixture of courtesy, softness and affection which appeared surprising in the harsh society of that day." Bakhtiar 1996a, 8.

[7] The Malaysian federal constitution provides that, except with respect to the federal territories, the personal and family law of persons professing the religion of Islam is under the legislative jurisdiction of each state. Item 1 of List II (the state list) in the 9th Schedule to the Federal Constitution.

[8] Although Muslims in Malaysia are predominantly followers of the Shafiʿi school (*madhhab*) of Islamic law, in the 1970s and early 1980s Malaysia embarked upon a remarkable program of reformation of Islamic family laws under the doctrine of *siyāsa sharʿiyya*. This program held that in order to serve the best interests of the community, the state in the codification of its laws may choose from among the opinions of different schools of law and select the most pragmatically suitable option. The 1984 Act defined *ḥukūm sharīʿa* as Islamic law according to any recognized *madhhab*; however this definition was amended in 2005 to mean Islamic law according to the Shafiʿi *madhhab*, or according to either the Maliki, Hanbali or Hanafi *madhhab*, thus re-asserting the pre-eminence of the Shafiʿi school, as well as restricting its recognition to the rulings of the Sunni schools of law.

[9] Provided for in the Islamic Family Law (Federal Territories) Act, 1984, §§ 47 (*ṭalāq*), 49 (*khulʿ*), 50 (*taʿlīq*) 52 (*faskh*).

[10] Qurʾan 4:35.

[11] Islamic Family Law (Federal Territories Act), 1984, §§ 47(5)–15.

[12] Pronouncement of a single *ṭalāq* results in a revocable divorce, while pronouncement of a triple *ṭalāq* results in an irrevocable divorce where the parties cannot remarry each other unless the woman has married another husband and her subsequent marriage is also dissolved. Qurʾan 2:229–230 states: "A divorce is only permissible twice [...] if a husband divorces his wife (with the third *ṭalāq*) he cannot after that remarry her until she has married another husband and he has divorced her."

[13] Islamic Family Law Act, § 48.

[14] Section 48(5) provides that the arbiters shall endeavor to obtain from their respective principals full authority, and in cases where the arbiters are unable to reconcile the parties but lack the authority to order a divorce, then only would the court appoint other arbiters under § 48(6) and confer on them authority to order a divorce.

[15] SIS, NCWO, and AWL 1997.

[16] Ibrahim 2000, 249.

[17] Islamic Family Law Act, § 55A.

[18] In practice, the husband in such cases is usually ordered to pay a fine.

[19] 3 M.L.J. xxx. (1991).

[20] The practice of the Prophet disapproves of the pronouncement of *ṭalāq* during the wife's menstrual period. Sahih Muslim (transl 1976), n. 1933 to *ḥadīth* 3491–93.

[21] 8 JH 297, (1991).

[22] Wadud-Muhsin 1992, 77.

[23] Qurʾan 4:34.

[24] Qurʾan 4:128.

[25] Islamic Family Law Act Section 59(2).

[26] Id. Section 59(2).

[27] 2 M.L.J. xxvi (1990).

[28] 1 M.L.J. lxxvii (1993).

[29] This was expressed as an alternative view in *Fakhariah v. Johari*. The view that *nushūz* was a relevant issue but that it was for the husband to first prove *nushūz* and that if he had not done so, then he should not raise the allegation of *nushūz* after the wife applies for a divorce, was also discussed by the trial court in *Salemewegam v. Mohd Anuar* (1983) 5 J.H. 109.

[30] Islamic Family Law Act § 65(1).

[31] The entry in the Marriage Register of the prescribed *taʿlīq* is provided for in section 22 of the Islamic Family Law Act.

[32] SIS, NCWO, and AWL 1997.

[33] Islamic Family Law Act § 52.

[34] Nasir [2]1990. Also in Moroccan Family Code (Moudawana) of 2004, Art. 41 which provides that polygamy is forbidden when the wife stipulates in the marriage contract that her husband will not take another wife.

[35] Al-Nawawī 1977, 308.

[36] Hamid 1976, 30, 31.

[37] E.g., SIS and AWL 1996.

[38] *Khulʿ* is also known in Malay as *cerai tebus talaq* (divorce by redemption).

[39] 1 J.H. (1) 84 (1979).

[40] 8 J.H. 249 (1991).

[41] The statutory provision on *ṭalāq* provides that a wife may also initiate an application for divorce by *ṭalāq*, and if the court is satisfied that the marriage has irretrievably broken down, the court shall advise the husband to consent to the divorce.

[42] This case of *Rosilah v. A. Rahman* is not really a typical case; I cite it to make a point regarding the lower court's rejection of the recommendation by the conciliatory committee (i.e., that while the wife's allegations were unproven, the couple should be divorced through *ṭalāq* or *khulʿ*, because reconciliation was impossible since the wife was determined upon separation) rather than as an illustration on *faskh* cases in general. However, it is generally true that if the wife's allegations do not fulfill the court's usually rather high standard of proof, it is difficult for the wife to obtain either a *taʿlīq* or *faskh* divorce. In cases where physical cruelty is proven, however, the Syariah Appeal Board will hold that this battery (even if not habitual) is sufficient to establish grounds for divorce, as it did, for example, in *Hairun v. Omar* (1990) 8 J.H. 289. The trial court had dismissed the wife's application for *faskh* as it interpreted the words "habitually assaults" in the statutory provision on *faskh* to mean "frequently." The board allowed the wife's appeal as it held that "habitually assaults" does not mean physical assaults, as there is a difference between "assault" and "battery," and that the question of "habitual" is only relevant in cases of mental cruelty.

[43] Qur'an 2:241.

[44] Qur'an 65:6 ("Let the women live [in *ʿidda*] in the same style as you live, according to your means: Annoy them not, so as to restrict them").

[45] Qur'an 2:241.

[46] Islamic Family Law Act § 56.

[47] For both *maṭāʿ* and *khulʿ* compensation, where the parties are unable to agree, the amount of reasonable compensation shall be determined by the court.

[48] M.L.J. Rep. 38 (1938).

[49] Idem.

[50] 1 M.L.J. 361 (1982).

[51] Idem. The "contract" in *Hamzah v. Fatimah* is meant in the sense of "stipulation" in the marriage contract.

[52] Hamid 1976, 22.

[53] The concept of deferred dower (*mas kahwin hutang*) is not well known nor well received among Malay Muslims, perhaps due to popular misunderstanding about the idea of deferred dower. It is often regarded with contempt and ridicule among many Malays, as it is thought to imply that the bridegroom does not have enough money to get married since he can not afford to pay the dower to the bride at the time of marriage. The "dower" in Malay marriages is usually divided into a nominal sum (called *mas kahwin*) of RM 80 stated in the standard form, and *wang hantaran*, which usually ranges between RM 2,000 to RM 10,000 depending on the circumstances of the parties. According to custom, both the *mas kahwin* and *wang hantaran* are ceremoniously presented on the wedding day. It is therefore embarrassing for both the bride and bridegroom to declare that the dower is "deferred." On the other hand, the concept of post-divorce *maṭāʿ* is better known, better established, and more acceptable among Malay Muslims; this may be due to the influence of Malay custom or a cultural phenomenon. It was remarked that "A more embarrassing phenomenon is the word *mut'ah* [...] in Malay this means consolatory gift given to a woman on divorce; but in Arabic unfortunately it means temporary marriage and survives today in the language only with the worst possible connotation." Ibrahim 1975, Editor's Note.

[54] 3 J.H. 220 (1983).

[55] 3 M.L.J. ix (1989).

[56] The trend of cases show that where the husband's income was below RM 500 per month, the *maṭāʿ* awarded was between RM 30 to RM 500; where the husband's income was between RM 500 to RM 1,500 per month, the *maṭāʿ* awarded was between RM 500 to RM 1,500; and where the husband's income exceeded RM 1,500 per month, the *maṭāʿ* awarded was RM 2,000 and above.

[57] 3 M.L.J. ix (1989).

[58] The first case which explicitly links matrimonial property to the principles of law in Islamic jurisprudence is the case of *Mansjur v. Kamariah* [1988] 3 M.L.J. xliv, where the Syariah Appeal Board declared that the principles on *mushāʿ* (mixed properties), and the Hanafi ruling on *sharikat al-abdān* (partnership) may be extended and applied to claims for matrimonial property. In this case, the Appeal Board confirmed the lower court's award of half the value of the property to the wife. Perhaps the difference between *Mansjur v. Kamariah* and *Rokiah v. Mohamed Idris* is that in the former the wife had made a direct contribution by actively assisting the husband in clearing and cultivating the property in question, i.e., the piece of land in a land development scheme acquired by the husband during their marriage. In the latter case, the wife's contribution was said to be indirect—in the form of looking after the home and the family. The Islamic Family Law Act, in section 58, also provides for the division of matrimonial property.

[59] 1 C.L.J. (Sya) 21 (2005).

[60] SIS, NCWO, and AWL 1997.

[61] Othman 1996, 25.

[62] Idem, 28, 31.

# Nine

## MARRIAGE CONTRACTS AND WOMEN'S RIGHTS IN SAUDI ARABIA: *MAHR, SHURŪṬ*, AND KNOWLEDGE DISTRIBUTION

Lisa Wynn

This essay examines the marriage contract as a social institution among the urban middle and upper classes in Jeddah, Saudi Arabia, specifically asking how it works to protect women's rights in Saudi Arabia.[1] I will argue that knowledge about the rights a woman may gain from the marriage contract is legitimating changes in women's roles in society, and ensuring their economic independence through the role of the *mahr* and through increasing control over their own property.

Marriages in Saudi Arabia are based on a contract whose terms are to be negotiated ahead of time, between two people and their families. Unlike the optional western prenuptial agreement, the marriage contract is a required element of an Islamic marriage. In Saudi Arabia, the marriage contract is seen as an Islamic legal institution that ensures certain rights for women for the duration of the marriage. Saudis assume that men will have the final word in the post-marriage living arrangements unless the woman and her family have specified otherwise before the marriage takes place. Women who want to ensure for themselves a non-"traditional" marriage—to work outside of the home, for example, or not to be responsible for certain household chores that are considered her duties—write these goals as conditional clauses in the marriage contract. Men, on the other hand, do not have to legally protect their rights within marriage, since they are considered to be the final authority in the home.

My approach is informed by anthropological studies of law which argue that legal systems can only be understood as they are embedded in society and relate to a much wider realm of social action and meaning.[2] In the Saudi case, what is more interesting than the formal juridical tenets of law is the way that the law is implemented and negotiated between actors, and the way this is changing with time. For example, Saudis are increasingly insistent that women enjoy the right to work after marriage and to manage their own income independently of their husband and household, and marriage contracts are used to secure these rights. Further, Saudi women are convinced that they possess certain inalienable rights under Islamic law. Yet, in practice, the rights a woman is able to claim depend largely on whether her claims have the support of her male relatives. Since it is considered shameful to take a case to a judge to be settled, disagreements over a woman's rights after marriage are usually settled within the family by the woman's male relatives, who negotiate with her husband on her behalf. The marriage contract itself is drawn up by the woman's male relatives, not by the woman herself, with the result that she is able to obtain only those conditions her relatives are willing to negotiate for her. Thus, the abstract rights of a married woman cannot be understood outside of a whole social context of kinship, class, the relationship between the woman and her male relatives, and the relationship between the wife's and the husband's extended families.

Annelies Moors has shown in her study of women and inheritance in Palestine that one cannot explain actual inheritance practices with reference to legal codes.[3] Her fieldwork showed that, despite the fact that Shariʿa law guarantees for wives and daughters a fixed share of the deceased's property, women often defer their rights to inheritance, which in turn increases their brothers' sense of honor toward them and binds them to their female siblings in relationships of obligation for future maintenance. And as Ziba Mir-Hosseini has argued in her analysis of Islamic marriage and divorce laws in post-revolutionary Iran, "It is misleading to take Islamic family law at face value and evaluate women's position[s] according to what the law entitles them to. The law and what it entails can only be understood through its application; in other words, the law cannot be isolated from the wider context within which it is meaningful."[4]

There is a trend among Muslim feminists and reformers to look at the legal aspects of Shariʿa law that empower women and protect their rights.[5] Muslim activists have lobbied for Islamic education and introduction of Shariʿa law as a way to counteract, transform or terminate certain cultural practices that disadvantage and devalue women socially (such as the dowry practice in India and Pakistan). Yet at the same time, universalizing discourses that focus on formal religious codes run the risk of obscuring the very real cultural variations that persist in the face of a transnationally shared religion. Edward Said[6] and others have pointed out the problematic features of any approach that reduces the Middle East, its history, culture, and politics, to Islam. A perspective that takes into account cultural variations and how they interact with formal, legalized religious tenets is necessary to work against this universalizing tendency.

Any legal system lays down general principles and laws which, when applied to concrete and particular situations, leave vast scope for filling in blanks with customs and social norms. Shariʿa law is a shared, transnational ideology which bounds and dictates certain realms of social and cultural action, but it leaves others open to a wide range of distinct cultural norms and individual decisions and actions. Islamic law, to paraphrase Lawrence Rosen, establishes the parameters of the permissible; within this framework, a great variety of individually unique and culturally specific relationships can be bargained out.[7]

In Saudi Arabia, debates over women's rights always take as their basic reference point the rights given to women in Islamic law. Thus, when, for example, a Saudi woman wants to work as a doctor or a teacher, despite traditional expectations that a woman's work is in the home, she does so by pointing out that women in the time of the Prophet Muḥammad worked outside of the home, and that Islamic law permits her to reserve the right to work as a stipulation of her marriage contract. While this naturally limits the lexicon of the demands that she can make to those which can be justified by Shariʿa law and the sayings and life of the Prophet Muḥammad, it nevertheless makes her case a very strong one, since Islamic law is recognized as the ultimate authority in Saudi Arabia. Islam "lends legitimacy, security and cultural authenticity to arguments for all positions."[8]

Structurally, this essay is divided into three parts. In the first two parts I examine two categories of cultural and individual specifics that are written into the Islamic wedding contract in Saudi Arabia: first the *mahr*, or dower, which is paid to the bride by the groom (or his family), and then the *shurūṭ*, or optional conditional clauses, which are written into the contract, usually by the woman (or her family). In the third part I examine the distribution of knowledge about the contract and the role of the *mahr* and *shurūṭ*. I argue that any interpretation of the marriage contract as a tool for enlarging women's rights in marriage has to be seen within the context of her relationship to her own family, since it is not the bride who most often negotiates the terms of the marriage but rather her parents.

The data in this essay are based on a series of interviews with Jeddah women conducted in 1994 and 1995. In 1994 I interviewed thirty-two women, covering a wide range of topics pertaining to women's changing role in society; in 1995 I interviewed a more limited number of these women, plus two male Saudi lawyers, specifically on the topic of marriage contracts. I am indebted to the rich work of anthropologist Soraya Altorki, whose study of three generations of elite Saudi women has helped put my own much more limited data in a broader historical context.[9] I also owe a great deal to Homa Hoodfar, whose broad base of comparative knowledge about marriage contracts among different economic classes in Iran and Egypt has helped me to identify and highlight what is specific to the Saudi case.[10]

## The *Mahr* and Division of Financial Responsibilities

Saudi women are a significant part of the workforce in Saudi Arabia, working in fields such as medicine, teaching, banking, and business. If they work for the government, which is the employer of a great number of Saudi women, mostly in medicine and teaching,[11] their salaries are legally fixed at rates guaranteed to be equal to those of men working in equivalent positions. Thus, in families where the woman is working outside of the home, her salary is a significant sum of money. And yet even in what sociologists would describe as a "two-income household," the woman is not expected to contribute her salary to the household, for this is considered the man's responsibility. Individual arrangements may lead to a more flexible division of financial responsibilities in the home,[12] but the people I interviewed all said that, in theory at least, the wife is not expected to contribute her salary or personal wealth for shared household expenses, no matter how wealthy she is, and that this logic is grounded in religious principles. Religious principles aside, most Saudi men consider it shameful to take money from their wives or daughters for something that is properly a man's responsibility. As one man told me when I suggested that his wife's income could contribute to household expenses, "That is women's money. Women's money is for women's things. I could never use it for the household. *'Ayb* (shame)." This attitude towards women's money seems to have persisted through several generations and despite great changes in women's access to money in the form of salaried incomes.

Indeed, in many arenas, money is closely tied to cultural notions of masculinity and male honor. The people I interviewed stressed that it is the husband (and his family) who is expected to cover the financial expenses of setting up and maintaining a house. This starts from the very beginning of married life, when the husband is responsible for paying for at least one, if not both, of the two wedding parties (the *milka* and the *dokhla*). The expenses for these can be huge, since, for the middle and upper classes, it involves renting two spaces for the wedding (separate spaces for the male and the female guests), providing musical entertainment, lavishly catering the whole affair, hiring a photographer to document the event, and purchasing two costly jewelry sets he gives to the bride (the *shabka*). He also pays the *mahr*, a substantial sum of money or property that must be paid to the bride at the time that the two are married. He is further responsible for providing the couple's apartment or house, and they cannot be married until he has completely furnished it and it is ready for them to live in.

The Saudis I interviewed stressed the husband's complete and sole financial responsibility in providing the house and furnishings. Yet Soraya Altorki, an anthropologist who studied a group of elite families in Jeddah, puts this in historical perspective by noting that this is a more recent development, and that in the past the woman brought to her conjugal house "a dowry which includes the complete furniture of two bedrooms, a salon, a living room, and a kitchen, as well as personal clothes to last her for at least a year."[13] This dowry was usually paid for out of the *mahr* (dower) she received or which was paid to her father or surrogate. Yet, according to Altorki, in the early 1980s an innovation was becoming acceptable whereby the groom paid a minimal *mahr* but furnished his own house. Later, the *mahr* among the elite families reached figures ranging from SR 100,000 to SR 200,000, which was usually put directly in a bank account for the bride and not used for her trousseau; the apartment and furniture for the new bride and groom could be paid for by the families of either the bride or the groom, depending on their relative wealth.[14]

This change is significant, since it leaves a large sum of cash, as well as the traditional gift of gold and jewels given to the bride, in the woman's hands, and it is not spent on furnishings for the apartment. Obviously, all these changes are class-specific. My Saudi informants, most of whom were from a less elite background than Altorki's informants, said that the wife may provide items for the kitchen, and if there is a henna party (*laylat al-ḥinnāʾ*) before the *dokhla*, the wife's family will pay for this. However, they insisted that the vast majority of the expenses fall to the groom and his family to provide. This was the general line expressed about ideal arrangements, which may stand in contrast to actual negotiations between the bride's and groom's family to ease the financial burden placed on the men. I have only a limited number of cases (only two) where my informants supplied actual figures and precise division of financial responsibilities for a marriage they were describing, both among middle-class families.[15] In both these cases, the groom supplied the apartment and its furnishings, in addition to paying a *mahr* to the bride which she disposed of as she wished. In both cases, the whole sum of the *mahr* was less than SR 50,000 and was spent at the time of the wedding for clothing and, in one case, to fly in some foreign relatives of the bride's mother's family, a choice made solely by the bride. In one case, the mother of the bride (who was related to the groom through marriage and strongly favored the match) helped him to furnish the house, even making curtains herself, yet she would not let the final marriage celebration take place until the apartment was completely furnished and ready to live in, since that was an indisputable prerequisite for married life, and, at least in the ideal, the groom's responsibility (despite her actual assistance to the groom).

This ideal (historically recent as it may be) stands in contrast with the norm and practice in other Muslim countries in the region, such as Egypt, where the husband provides the apartment or house and the wife's family is typically responsible for furnishing it. In such cases, the division of financial expenses between the husband and wife is written into the wedding contract, since, in the case of divorce, the woman keeps all the furniture she has contributed to the household. This may be used as a way of justifying her continued residence in the home after divorce, particularly if the couple have children.[16]

By contrast, in Saudi Arabia, upon divorce the woman is unequivocally expected to return to her father's or a brother's household and she leaves her husband's house and its furnishings behind. This is part of the reason why most people consider it the groom's responsibility to provide the house and its contents, since ultimately it is his property and will revert to him in case of divorce. The cost and size of the wedding party is verbally negotiated and not usually written into the wedding contract. The quality and size of the apartment and its furnishings is verbally negotiated, or may be left to the discretion of the groom and his family subject to the bride's family's approval, and this may or may not be written into the contract.

Thus the main financial issue to be written into the wedding contract is the amount of the *mahr* that the groom provides to the bride. As far as I know, in Saudi Arabia there is no tradition of a deferred dower stated in the contract to be paid in case of divorce or the husband's death, as is seen in other parts of the Arab world.[17] All the people I interviewed indicated that the *mahr* must be paid in full by the time of the second wedding ceremony.[18] All of my informants, whether speaking in general or specific terms, said that this *mahr* is the bride's personal wealth to dispose of when and as she sees fit. Many of the unmarried women I interviewed said that they would use it to buy clothing and personal luxury items, while the older married women said that the best thing to do with it is to put most of it into savings, perhaps reflecting what they thought would be the wisest thing for their daughters to do with the money.

The generational gap in opinions about how the *mahr* should be spent is significant, and will be discussed later in this essay. What is important to emphasize here is that it is the bride's right to do what she likes with the *mahr*. The same holds true for the woman's salary. It is entirely hers to dispose of as she wishes, and while that might include partial subsidization of household expenses, in general this is considered a deviation from the norm, and shameful to the husband. More often, her income goes to her own personal savings, and towards providing luxury items for herself or her children. The ideology against the use of women's money toward shared household expenses was also voluntarily offered by some of the women interviewed as an explanation for why women under Shariʿa law inherit only half of what their male relative counterparts inherit: since women must be provided for by the male relative with whom they reside, since they are never required to use their own wealth for household responsibilities, and since women's money is theoretically only used towards personal "luxury" items, they do not need the same amount of inheritance money as do men.[19]

In the case of divorce, the woman returns to live with her family (either her parents or perhaps a brother or even a sister's family, depending on family circumstances). If they divorce prior to the final wedding party, the *dokhla*, and she is still a virgin, then she generally returns the money and jewelry that the groom has already given her, but keeps any other small gifts (such as smaller jewelry items, perfume, trinkets, etc.) which he has given her during the interim courtship period. If they divorce at any time after the *dokhla*, then she retains all of the *mahr* and the jewelry.[20]

Socially speaking, the substantial *mahr* paid by the groom before marriage, along with the other marriage expenses that he must finance, serves to manifest his social standing and his (or his father's) financial ability and willingness to support a new household. The *mahr* is also a key element in the wedding contract that protects the woman in the marriage. Saudi women argue emphatically that it is not a market exchange in which her value is determined by the amount of the *mahr*, but rather a gift from her husband. The women I interviewed stated that, functionally, it is a means of ensuring that a bride starts her married life as an economically independent being, whether she works outside of the home or not, and in spite of the fact that her husband is expected to provide for all family and household expenses. Since the money goes to her alone, it gives her a basis of financial independence from both her family and her husband.

Besides this, Saudis argue, the *mahr* protects her against divorce, since the huge sum invested by the husband into the marriage gives him an economic incentive not to use divorce as an easy solution to marital problems. According to Shariʿa as interpreted in Saudi Arabia, the man can divorce his wife by merely stating the fact, whereas the woman who seeks a divorce must take the case before a judge to argue that her husband has not fulfilled his marital duties. But the husband knows that if he divorces her, he forfeits to her all the money that he has given to her and invested in the wedding parties.

The case of one woman is illustrative. Nejwa was contracted in marriage to a cousin while still in high school, but because her mother insisted that she finish college before getting bogged down in the responsibilities of married life, the couple postponed the commencement of married life for more than four years, until after graduation. The family was a very conservative one: Nejwa and her future husband were barely allowed to speak to each other, and not to see each other at all, despite their having already signed the wedding contract. The contract specified the *mahr*, but it had not yet been paid. The groom got tired of waiting and one night he was complaining to his friends, who convinced him to divorce Nejwa and free himself from the tedious waiting period. The next day he immediately regretted his actions. Yet a judge in the town had heard from one of the witnesses present about his act and personally summoned him to the court and required him to draw up a new contract, specifying a new *mahr* (although the sum did not change from the first contract). The judge noted that he had thus expended one of the three divorces he was allotted, and verbally warned him that in the future he must take divorce much more seriously.

Ziba Mir-Hosseini and Annelies Moors have both argued that, in post-revolutionary Iran and in Palestine, respectively, the *mahr* is a key element to consider when examining women's access to divorce.[21] The Saudi women to whom I spoke emphasized that the *mahr* and the husband's economic investment in the marriage prevent him from using divorce as a manipulative tool during marital arguments. Yet they also used it to justify the relative difficulty that women have in obtaining a divorce, since if she could divorce as easily as her husband, it would be all too easy for her to end the marriage and escape with all the money that he had invested in it.

In the past, women's access to private sources of wealth, such as the *mahr* or money they inherited from deceased relatives, was limited since, although her right to inherit was religiously guaranteed, in practice the segregation of the sexes usually meant that she turned over the de facto management of this wealth to a male relative; often, she was not aware of the precise amount of her wealth, since requesting specifics was an implicit challenge to the honesty of her relatives and thus shameful.[22] But in the past two decades, many Saudi banks have opened women's branches that are staffed solely by women who help other women to invest their money. This ensures that principles of sex segregation in Saudi Arabia will not prevent women of even the most conservative families from exercising their Islamic right to manage and dispose of their personal wealth as they choose.

Anthropologists have long debated the cultural, social, political, and economic meaning of marriage payments (broken down into the subcategories of groomwealth or dowry, and bridewealth or dower/*mahr*) in different societies.[23] Throughout the Middle East and elsewhere in the Muslim world, there is great variation in the social meaning of marriage payments. Even in Saudi Arabia, the amount of the *mahr* and the bride's access to it varies, particularly between urban and rural areas. Despite this variation, women in Jeddah marshal scriptural citations and episodes from the life of the Prophet Muḥammad to justify their interpretations of how *mahr* should be used and distributed.[24] Thus, while unifying religious principles cannot explain the social meaning of *mahr* in urban Saudi Arabia, they can be used to legitimize it as well as to mobilize support for change to traditions, as Altorki shows when she describes how educated women are increasingly using religious arguments to insist on the management of their own money.[25]

## Conditional Clauses in the Marriage Contract

In the absence of economic necessity for two incomes, how do (at least some) Saudi women ensure their right to work or study outside of the house? The other major category of terms written into the marriage contract, besides the *mahr*, is that of conditional clauses (*shurūṭ*) that set out certain expectations and standards for married life. Most commonly these clauses specify that the woman will continue her education after she is married, unhindered by her domestic responsibilities, or that she will be allowed to work outside of the home. All of the women I interviewed suggested these two things as the most important and common conditions for a contemporary Saudi woman to include in her marriage contract. Most saw this as a kind of insurance of the woman's freedom, whether or not she had definite plans for working or for pursuing a university degree.

The women I interviewed also said that the bride might specify that she does not want to live with her husband's family, but rather in a nuclear household, out of the reach of a potentially domineering mother-in-law. This confirms Altorki's observation that there is a general trend away from viripatrilocal to neolocal residence, which "reflects a desire of wives in the younger generation to assert their autonomy vis-a-vis their husband's mothers."[26] Another condition that some women specify is that they will live in a certain city, so as to ensure that her husband's work will not require her to move and be uprooted from her own family and friends which constitute her personal female and kin support network. Some suggested as a possible condition that she have a personal driver, so as to give her freedom of mobility otherwise denied her by the Saudi law against women driving.

While these are the most common kinds of conditions, the conditions can be as specific as the bride's own interests and the groom's resources permit. Safa, for example, told me that she was going to stipulate in her marriage contract that her husband must provide a darkroom in their house or apartment, since she had a personal passion for photography. However, conditions that include something that is considered prohibited (*ḥarām*) (such as, for example, a work situation that requires the woman to be alone with men, or unveiled); or that prohibit something that is considered allowed (*ḥalāl*) under Islam, are invalid. As an example of the latter, all the women I interviewed said that a woman could not stipulate that her husband not be allowed to take additional wives, since that was his God-given right in Islam (as it is interpreted in Saudi Arabia) and she did not have the right to deprive him of it. She could, however, write in a clause that, should he marry another woman, she would be granted a divorce if she wanted one, or that he would have to pay her a certain amount of money, or that she would be given a separate house to live in with her children. Although the women I interviewed said that these were possible conditions, they also considered them unlikely ones, and none had written or foresaw writing such a clause into her own contract. There seemed to be a sense that such demands were shameful; one woman commented that it was only "Egyptian film stars" who would write such a condition into her marriage contract, but normal women did not have the right—or the gall—to make such demands on their husbands, particularly since it is his Islamic right to have up to four wives.

In theory, both the bride and groom may write conditions into the contract; in practice, it is usually only the bride who writes these conditional clauses. The reason for this dichotomy may have to do with Shariʿa laws on divorce in Saudi Arabia. Since the woman is required to appeal to a judge for a divorce, and has to persuade him with a reasonable explanation as to why a divorce is required, the conditions written into the marriage contract provide the grounds for determining whether or not the husband has fulfilled his duties as a husband. For the man, no such case needs to be made for him to divorce his wife.

These conditions of the marriage contract are used to negotiate married life both before and after the wedding. The legal contract is a continual reference point for defining roles and responsibilities, and may be referred to especially in cases of disputes to legitimate or disqualify one party's demands. The following is an interesting example of how one woman used the contract to negotiate the terms of her marriage and her domestic responsibilities. Rana's family had stipulated in her marriage contract that she should be allowed to finish her college education after getting married. While still in college, she had a child, and her domestic responsibilities began to overwhelm her studies, yet her husband refused to hire a maid to help take care of the house and their child, since, as he argued, that was her responsibility. Rana appealed to her father, who then intervened. He informed her husband that, since finishing her education was one of the conditions of the wedding contract, it was his legal responsibility to find a way to make sure that she was able to do that, and that meant hiring household help. Faced with this united father-daughter front, Rana's husband acquiesced and hired a maid. It should be noted that, for Saudis, the government-provided college education is not only completely free, but students, both male and female, are even given a significant stipend to help with living expenses. Thus her husband was making no financial outlay for her education itself, and the only expense came with the hiring of outside labor, which could be paid for out of this student stipend. Evidently the husband was less concerned about the financial cost of his wife finishing college than with holding his wife to what he saw as her domestic responsibilities within the home.

Rana used the contract as a way of sidestepping her "traditional" cultural household duties: cooking, cleaning, and raising children. She and her father managed to do this not by redistributing household duties between husband and wife, but by appealing to his sense of responsibility as the main provider, the one responsible for all household expenses. A third person was brought in from outside to do the hardest and most time-consuming labor. Rana still retained the role of household manager, directing the maid's work and doing what was considered to be the most definitive, critical, and artful parts of the food preparation and childrearing. It is thus a solution that depended on his wealth and, more generally, the availability of cheap labor in Saudi Arabia. It does not challenge the general principles of the gendered distribution of labor within the marriage, and note how very class-specific it is.[27] Yet it did in this case prove to be a solution enabling Rana to stay in school.

What is especially interesting about this case is the way post-marriage domestic arrangements were negotiated with reference to the wedding contract. Also critical is the role of the extended family—in this case, Rana's father's intervention and his clout as an older authority figure—when she herself was unable to persuade her husband. It indicates the enduring importance of the extended family in mediating married life, in spite of the trend towards nuclear residences. This case shows how the woman's kinship network provides her a strength vis-à-vis her husband that the legal document alone could not give her.

What I want to point out here is the flexibility that these conditional clauses provide and the way the marriage contract allows for a very personal and historically specific demarcation of the woman's rights and her expectations for married life. She is not limited only to a narrow, canonical, or "traditional" definition of what constitutes a proper marriage under Islam. To demand a divorce, she does not have to argue that he has failed to perform his sexual duties as a husband, nor must she prove some extreme condition of physical abuse or neglect. The conditional clauses give her (or him) the opportunity to personally, legally, and religiously delineate expectations for married life that, within certain boundaries, are as individually specific as the bride and/or groom desire. Moreover, the marriage contract, unlike the western prenuptial agreement to which it is often compared, is not optional, but rather constitutes the legal union itself.

## Knowledge Distribution and Writing the Marriage Contract

Yet the fact that the Muslim marriage contract is mandatory does not necessarily mean that it will include conditions dedicated to protecting women's rights. We need to further look at who it is that negotiates the conditional clauses, and whether the young, inexperienced bride is fully informed of her legal entitlements in Islamic law.

First, we need to look at which parties negotiate this contract. In Saudi Arabia, it is not the bride who is acting at this point, except on the sidelines. It is her family, and especially her father, who takes the primary public negotiating role with the family of the groom when he comes to propose. Yet it is usually the bride's mother who plays a critical role in determining what the young woman has written into the contract, in conjunction with or through her husband, the girl's father. And, I would argue, it is the mother who is most aware of how important this marriage contract is, and the *mahr* and *shurūṭ* that are written into it. The young women whom I asked about the *mahr*, for example, mostly envisioned spending it on clothes and other similar commodities. In contrast, their mothers more often suggested that a girl would be wise to put it in savings, although they emphasized that it is the girl's money to do with as she wishes, that it belongs solely to her, and that it could not be spent by her family or husband. They always pointed out that such was guaranteed to women under Shariʿa law, and often they made negative comparisons with the dowry system in India (where the bride pays the husband) to show how in Saudi Arabia, Islam protected women's rights against other, potentially oppressive cultural systems.

As far as the conditional clauses (*shurūṭ*) of the wedding contract are concerned, most of the young women whom I spoke to (all teenagers, at or approaching the age of marriage) did not have more than a vague idea about the wedding contract and what sorts of things could be written into it, although they did have their own ideas about what they expected after marriage in terms of school and work. The first paper I wrote on the subject celebrated the liberating and rights-safeguarding role of the marriage contract.[28] When I was rethinking the topic for this essay, I started to think a little more skeptically about this. I had interviewed thirty-two Saudi women on a wide range of questions relating to the changing role of women in Saudi society, which included questions about marriage and the wedding contract. As I reviewed my materials, I was struck by how few of the young, unmarried women really knew much about the whole process and about what they would put into their contract. At the time, I had virtually ignored this, considering the interviews with these young women to be uninformative on that topic. Instead I had focused on what the older, married women had said to me and used these as my primary sources. It was only later that it struck me that my neglect of these interviews was a serious methodological error, and that these absences and gaps in knowledge were key pieces of information. They point to significant differentials in the knowledge base of different generations. They indicate just how dependent these young women are upon their families when it comes to the "rights" they can demand through their marriage contract. Their options are restricted, first of all, by the lack of knowledge about what their options are, in terms of the process of writing the contract. Second, the fact that it is not the young women themselves but their families who negotiate and write the contract with the groom and his family suggests that their personal demands are limited to what they can convince their families to request for them.

In fact, all the interviewees who talked about the contract's *shurūṭ* spoke of these as being demanded by the bride's mother.[29] For example, let me return to the case of Nejwa, a young woman who had only been married for about two years at the time I interviewed her (now a mother of four who is working on her Ph.D.). When she was still in high school, her parents proposed to her that she marry a cousin with whom she had interacted when she was younger, but whom she had not seen since she had reached puberty and started veiling. She agreed, and was technically married with the wedding contract signed before she started college. But her mother insisted that the marriage contract include the condition that the couple not celebrate the final marriage ceremony, the *dokhla*, until after she graduated, four years later. I knew that Nejwa considered her college education very important. Yet she emphasized that it was her mother who insisted that she stay in school and not marry until she had graduated. She never spoke of it as her own demand vis-à-vis her husband.

## Conclusions

Even as Saudi society is moving more and more towards a model of romantic love as the basis for a marriage,[30] the extended family continues to play an important functional role in mediating women's demands in married life, especially in the early years of the marriage. In the case of Nejwa, for example, recall that her husband became exasperated during the long period of waiting for her to finish the college degree. It was thus perhaps useful for Nejwa to portray this as her mother's demand, rather than her own, lest it produce lingering resentments over the amount of time she made her husband wait before starting their married life together. In the case of Rana, what she was unable to achieve on her own was obtained through the intervention of her father, whose authority vis-à-vis her husband was much greater than her own. There is strength in numbers, age, and authority. And when relations between the couple risk becoming antagonistic because of conflicting desires or expectations, the intervention of an older authority figure can defuse the tensions of a one-on-one conflict, and can provide an external "scapegoat" of sorts to preserve marital harmony.

This should caution us about attributing to the marriage contract too great a part in empowering Saudi women. In theory, it is an opportunity for women to make demands about married life that are backed by the force of law. And in practice, it is being used to ensure for women greater mobility out of the house and out of their own and their husbands' kinship networks, as it secures the right for women to study and work within a wider society of unrelated Saudi women, even at the expense of their traditional responsibilities in the household. However, this cannot be understood outside of the context of the woman's embeddedness within her own family. First of all, in the Saudi families I researched, it is not the woman who does the negotiating with her future husband, but rather her father and mother, so whatever she demands is mediated by what they think is appropriate for her, or what she can persuade them to request for her, or what she can insist upon vis-à-vis her own family (which is one step removed from what she can insist upon vis-à-vis her husband). Second, many women being married for the first time are quite young and may not have the experience and knowledge base to know what they can or ought to demand. As a result, the rights and privileges that are legally secured for women through the *mahr* and the *shurūṭ* written into the marriage contract cannot be understood independently of the woman's kin relationships, norms of gender interaction within her own family, the social class of her and her husband, and a host of other social factors that mediate between law and its implementation.

## NOTES

[1] There are two reasons for this explicit gender bias. First of all, the fieldwork situation largely limited my interactions to the female realm, because of the strict segregation of men and women in Saudi Arabia. Women were my colleagues and friends, and it was inappropriate for me to interact much with the men of their families. Thus my informants are mostly women, with the exception of two male lawyers with whom I conducted very limited and formal interviews, and one man with whom, through kinship ties, I was able to have more extensive conversations. The second reason for this gender bias is because in Saudi Arabia the wedding contract is itself seen as a tool for guarding women's rights in marriage. All female informants who spoke about the marriage contract emphasized that this was the role of the *mahr* (dower) and the *shurūṭ* (conditional clauses) that are written into the contract.

[2] Rosen 1984, 1989; Geertz 1983, 167–234.

[3] See Annelies Moors 1995, 1996.

[4] Mir-Hosseini 1993a, 59.

[5] Ezzat 1994; Al-Munajjed 1997, 27–28; Yamani 1996; Afshar 1996.

[6] Said 1978.

[7] Rosen 1989, 79.

[8] MacLeod 1991, 76; see also Pharaon 2004.

[9] See generally Altorki 1986.

[10] See generally Hoodfar 1991, 1997.

[11] Al-Munajjed 1997, 95; Yamani 2000.

[12] See Al-Munajjed 1997, 88–91.

[13] Altorki 1986, 64.

[14] Idem at 139.

[15] The information is considered sensitive, so only the people to whom I was closest were willing to share such private details with me.

[16] Hoodfar 1997.

[17] See, e.g., Moors 1995.

[18] One person spoke of a situation in which the full *mahr* had not been paid at the time of the wedding, and when the groom later wanted to divorce, he could not do so until he had produced the full sum promised at the time of the wedding. Although structurally this is like the deferred dower (*mu'akhkhar*), it was not actually written into the contract as one. This was the only case that I heard of like this.

[19] See Al-Munajjed 1997, 21.

[20] None of the women I interviewed spoke of the tradition of *khulʿ*, whereby a woman can obtain a divorce, even if the man refuses to divorce her, by returning all property given to her at the time of marriage. I do not know if this tradition is practiced in Saudi Arabia.

[21] Mir-Hosseini 1993a; Moors 1996.

[22] Altorki 1986, 24.

[23] See Comaroff 1980 for a review of different anthropological theories.

[24] Al-Munajjed 1997, 22.

[25] But this kind of religious argument goes both ways; see Wynn 1994 for an example of how similar religious arguments are used by Saudi commentators to reinforce traditional female roles in the family.

[26] Altorki 1986, 33.

[27] Most of the women I interviewed avoided household chores and other domestic responsibilities by hiring household help, and not by redistributing some of the chores and child-raising responsibilities to their husbands. However, there has recently been a great deal of public concern over the role of maids and other domestic labor in the Saudi family. See, e.g., al-Anṣārī 1990; Badr 1985. It is generally argued that foreign maids and nannies who help raise the children are a source of cultural, linguistic, and religious corruption. Newspaper articles and editorials frequently call for the woman to return to her proper role raising the children to avert the influence of these foreigners in the home.

[28] See generally Wynn 1996.

[29] This might be a bias explained by the fact that fieldwork conditions limited me to interviewing mostly women, and thus I have little insight into how a father might conceptualize the process.

[30] See, e.g., Wynn 1997.

# *Ten*

## A WOMAN'S RIGHT TO TERMINATE THE MARRIAGE CONTRACT: THE CASE OF IRAN

Ziba Mir-Hosseini

### The Problem

The Islamic marriage contract reflects a patriarchal emphasis in society, and the disparity between men's and women's rights in the contract is sustained largely through the rules regulating its dissolution. Muslim jurists define marriage (*nikāḥ*) as a bilateral act (*ʿaqd*) in which a woman plays an active role: she is a party to the contract's formation in that she (or her guardian, *walī*) either offers or accepts the marriage. On the other hand, when it comes to the termination of a marriage contract, a woman's will is subordinated to that of her husband, who is given the right of *ṭalāq* (repudiation). As defined by jurists, *ṭalāq* is a unilateral act (*īqāʿ*), which acquires legal effect through the declaration of only the husband. A woman cannot be released from marriage without her husband's consent, although she can secure her release through offering him inducements by means of *khulʿ*, which is often referred to as "divorce by mutual consent." If she fails to secure his consent, then her only recourse is the intervention of the court and the power of the judge either to compel the husband to pronounce *ṭalāq* or to pronounce it on his behalf. Known in classical law as *faskh* (rescission), *tafrīq* (separation), or *taṭlīq* (compulsory issue of divorce), this outlet became the basis on which women can obtain a court divorce in the contemporary Muslim world. The facility with which women can obtain such a divorce, and the grounds on which they can do so, vary in different schools of Islamic law and in different Muslim countries.[1]

Men's exclusive right to *ṭalāq* presents women with a real problem when the marriage is under strain or breaks down, and is an important target in feminist critiques of women's rights in Islam. It is a sword of Damocles in men's hands, which tilts the balance of power in marital relations in favor of the husband and ensures that women are kept in a state of limbo and disempowerment. Among the ways Muslim jurists proposed to redress this inequality—apart from the expansion of the grounds upon which a woman could obtain a court divorce—has been the insertion of a stipulation in the marriage contract by which the husband gives the wife the delegated right to divorce herself on his behalf. Known as *ṭalāq al-tafwīḍ*, this option is regarded by reformers and supporters of women's rights as the most effective way to protect women. In the absence of legislation, it is argued, a delegated divorce stipulation is the only option in Islamic law to put women on par with men in terms of access to unilateral divorce.[2] This option has been dealt with extensively in the literature,[3] and I have no intention of discussing it at length here, except to point out that *ṭalāq al-tafwīḍ* fails not only to address the inequality inherent in the notion of *ṭalāq* but also to protect those women who most need protection: those whose husbands abuse their right to *ṭalāq*. This is so because it is premised on the notion that termination of marriage is a right that belongs to the man, who can use it in whatever way he chooses, including delegating it to his wife. So all depends on the good will of the man.

In practice it is neither common nor easy for a woman to acquire the delegated right to divorce. She (or her agent) must negotiate this at the time of marriage, when the parties are less likely to think of, and make provisions for, its breakdown, and indeed it is often seen as a bad omen even to mention the word *ṭalāq*, or to have a divorced person present during the *ʿaqd* ceremony, let alone to negotiate such a right for the bride. If she tries to negotiate the right subsequently, for example in the course of a marital dispute, it is unlikely that she will be able to secure the necessary good will of the man.

Insertion of a stipulation is, thus, at best a half-solution, and at worst no solution at all. It can be effective only if it is compulsory, that is, if it is automatically inserted in every marriage contract, and then only if it is unconditional. To my knowledge no Muslim state has done this, and none is likely to do so. Iran is one of the few countries where the insertion of a delegated divorce stipulation in marriage is required by law, but, as we shall see, it is neither unconditional nor has it put women on a par with men in terms of access to divorce.

The issue of divorce must be tackled from a different angle. The question that must be asked is: Can the unequal construction of men's and women's rights to termination of the marriage contract be addressed within the parameters of Islamic law? If so, how, and under what conditions? These are the questions that I explore in this essay. I do so with reference to Iran, where the marriage contract has served as a medium for negotiating the gender inequalities inherent in classical Islamic law and where the issue of women's rights has been at the heart of jurisprudential debates in religious seminaries. The case of Iran indicates the potential of Islamic legal doctrine (*fiqh*) to redress the gender inequalities inherent in the marriage contract when the political will to do so is created. Women's massive participation in the popular revolution that led to the establishment of an Islamic Republic in 1979, and in Iranian political life since then, not only subverted notions of gender roles and relations constructed in traditional Islamic jurisprudence but made women a political force in Iran that no longer can be ignored. With the Shariʿa as the law of the land, its custodians had no choice but to recognize the realities of contemporary life, including women's changed position in society, their expectations in marriage, and their increasing demand for equal rights with men. These realities led to questioning the jurisprudential constructions of gender rights in marriage and society, of which the notion of *ṭalāq* is one.[4]

In this chapter, I begin with an outline of salient features of the marriage contract in classical Shiʿi law, with a view to identifying the assumptions behind the rules regulating its formation and dissolution. I then present and contextualize two juristic arguments that represent a radical break from these underlying assumptions. I came across these arguments in 1995 during fieldwork on gender discourses among the religious scholars in Qom, the site of learning and religious power in Iran.[5] Both of them are now in the public domain (published in two women's magazines), as part of a lively debate about women's rights in Islam that took a new turn and intensity with the creation of the Islamic Republic in 1979.

## Marriage as Contract: Formation and Termination

In line with other schools of Islamic law, in Shiʿi law marriage is a contract imbued with religious ideals and values. It is one of the very few acts that cross the boundary between *ʿibādāt* (ritual/spiritual acts) and *muʿāmalāt* (social/private acts).[6] In spirit, marriage belongs to *ʿibādāt*, in that Muslim jurists define it as a religious duty ordained by God. In form, it comes under the category of *muʿāmalāt*, in that Muslim jurists define it as a civil contract between a man and a woman such that any sexual contact outside this contract constitutes the crime of *zinā* (fornication), and is subject to punishment. In its legal structure, marriage is a contract of exchange with defined terms and uniform effects and is patterned after the contract of sale (*bayʿ*), which has served as model for other contracts. Imbued with a strong patriarchal ethos, the essential components of the marriage contract are: the offer (*ījāb*) by the woman or her guardian, the acceptance (*qabūl*) by the man, and the payment of dower (*mahr*), a sum of money or any valuable that the husband pays or undertakes to pay to the bride before or after consummation, according to their mutual agreement.[7]

With the contract, a woman comes under her husband's *ʿiṣma* (authority, dominion, and protection), entailing a set of defined rights and obligations for each party: some with moral sanction and others with legal force. Those with legal force revolve around the twin themes of sexual access and compensation, embodied in concepts of *tamkīn* (submission) and *nafaqa* (maintenance). *Tamkīn* (unhampered sexual access) is a man's right and thus a woman's duty, whereas *nafaqa* (shelter, food, and clothing) is a woman's right and a man's duty. A woman becomes entitled to *nafaqa* only after consummation of the marriage, and she loses her claim if she is in a state of *nushūz* (disobedience).[8] The contract establishes neither a shared matrimonial regime nor identical rights and obligations between spouses: the husband is the sole provider and owner of the matrimonial resources and the wife is possessor of the *mahr* and her own wealth. The only shared space is that involving the procreation of children, and even here a woman is not expected to suckle her child unless it is impossible to feed it otherwise.

In line with the logic of the contract, a man can enter into more than one marriage at a time (up to four permanent ones in all schools, and in Shiʿi law also as many temporary marriages (*mutʿa*)[9] as he desires, or can afford), and he can terminate each contract at will: no specific grounds are needed, nor is the wife's consent or presence required. Under classical Shiʿi law, to be released from her marriage a woman can either buy her husband's consent by means of *khulʿ* or *mubārāt* (Ar. *mubāraʾa*, the so-called divorce by mutual consent) or resort to the option of *faskh* (annulment or rescission). In *khulʿ*, separation is claimed by the wife because of her extreme dislike (*ikrāh*) of her husband, and there is no ceiling to the amount of compensation that she may be asked to pay. In *mubārāt* the dislike is mutual and the amount of compensation should not exceed the value of the *mahr* itself. In *faskh*, marriage is dissolved as a result of the absence or presence of a condition in one of the parties.[10]

Like *ṭalāq*, *faskh* is a unilateral act and comes under the category of unilateral acts in Shiʿi law, but it is different from others in its legal structure and effects. First, it does not follow the formalities of *ṭalāq*: the pronouncement of a certain formula, the presence of witnesses, the woman being in the state of menstrual purity. Second, the wife is not entitled to any portion of her *mahr* if annulment occurs before consummation of the marriage; she is entitled to half of her *mahr* only if the annulment is due to her husband's inability to perform sexual relations. Third, although a woman needs to observe the same waiting period as in *ṭalāq*, the husband has no right to resume marital relations within this period. Fourth, *faskh*, regardless of how many times it happens between the couple, does not create a temporary or permanent bar between them, whereas the third *ṭalāq* creates a temporary bar to future marriage of the two and the ninth *ṭalāq* creates a permanent prohibition. Finally, both parties have a more or less equal right to seek the annulment of their marriage.[11]

A woman can resort to the option of *faskh* in two situations: the existence of a condition in the husband that makes the continuation of marriage untenable for her, or the absence of a condition in the husband that he claimed to possess at the time of marriage. As to the first, the husband's insanity or sexual defect (impotency, or absence of penis or testicles), either at the time of marriage or subsequently, constitutes the only grounds that enable a woman to terminate the marriage. As to the second situation, there is more flexibility and it varies with the kind of agreements that the parties have made at the time of marriage or stipulated in the contract.[12]

To exercise her right to *faskh*, a woman does not need to secure the consent of her husband or the intervention of the judge, although in the case of her husband's impotency she is required by the judge to wait for a year in case it is a temporary affliction.[13]

With this background, we can now return to the central question of this essay: Can there be an equal construction of the notion of divorce in Islamic law, in the sense that a woman's wishes are taken into account in terminating the contract in the same way as when the marriage is contracted?

## Rethinking Women's Right to Termination: The Argument of Ayatollah Saneʿi

In September 1995, I posed the above question to Ayatollah Yusef Saneʿi in a meeting arranged by the editor of *Payām-e Zan*, a women's journal run by male clerics and published by the Qom seminaries.[14] Saneʿi is a high-ranking cleric who played a major role in transforming the legal system in the early years of the Iranian Revolution. He was the State Prosecutor-General and is a former member of both the Guardian Council and the Supreme Judicial Council, the two highest legal bodies in the Islamic Republic. He returned to Qom in 1984, and since then has devoted himself to religious scholarship and teaching. He is a prominent cleric with a reputation for progressive opinions on women's issues and family matters, exemplified for instance by his advocacy of family planning and of raising the legal age of puberty for girls from nine to thirteen.

Ayatollah Saneʿi's response to my question was an emphatic "yes." He then produced the following correspondence in which Ayatollah Khomeini expressed a similar view:

> In the name of God the Merciful
> To the Leader of the Islamic Revolution of Iran
> His Excellency Ayatollah al-ʿUzma Imam Khomeini
>
> After greetings and respect, certain issues get disputed in the Guardian Council and eventually your honored opinion is to be followed; among these are some articles of the Civil Code, one of which pertains to divorce: if the continuation of marriage causes the wife hardship (*ʿusr va ḥaraj*), she can demand divorce (*ṭalāq*) by recourse to the religious judge (*ḥākim-i sharʿ*) who, after ascertaining the matter, will compel the husband to divorce, and if he refuses, the judge himself will conduct the divorce.
>
> Some of the jurists (*fuqahāʾ*) in the Guardian Council reject this [that the judge can conduct a divorce] and argue that hardship (*ḥaraj*) is caused by the need to abide by the contract of marriage; even if the hardship argument is valid here, it can only remove the need to

abide by the contract and create for women the right of annulment (*faskh*). Given that instances in which annulment can take place are limited by consensus [of jurists], and [hardship] is not among them, therefore *faskh* is strongly ruled out.

Other jurists hold that the argument for hardship here is not confined to the requirement [to abide by the terms] of the contract, but the root of hardship is that *ṭalāq* is exclusively in the hands of the husband, and according to the harm argument we remove this exclusive control and through recourse to the religious judge and with proof of hardship, out of precaution, the husband is compelled to [pronounce] *ṭalāq* or the judge himself effects it. Please state your esteemed opinion on these matters.

In the Name of God

Caution demands that first, the husband be persuaded, or even compelled, to [pronounce] *ṭalāq*; if he does not, [then] with the permission of the judge, *ṭalāq* is effected; [but] there is a simpler way, [and] if I had the courage [I would have said it].

Ruhullah al-Musavi al-Khomeini

The above document, in effect a fatwa (legal opinion), is to be found in *Ṣaḥīfeh Nūr* (The Book of Light), which contains Ayatollah Khomeini's rulings and utterances. It is dated 1982, when pre-revolutionary divorce laws were being amended to eliminate any discrepancies with Shariʿa. The question was posed by Ayatollah Saneʿi to settle a dispute between himself and other members of the Guardian Council, the body whose task is to ensure that laws passed by the parliament are in line with Shariʿa. The dispute was over the court's power to issue a divorce without a man's consent. Before any further discussion of the document and what Ayatollah Khomeini meant by "there is a simpler way," we need to put it into its context, which is that of the dismantling of the Family Protection Law and the resulting need to expand the grounds upon which a woman can obtain a divorce.[15]

The Family Protection Law (FPL), enacted in 1967 and regarded as one of the most progressive laws in the Muslim world, not only removed the husband's extra-judicial right to *ṭalāq* but also placed women on more or less equal footing with men in terms of grounds for divorce.[16] The FPL achieved this by means of procedural devices, thus avoiding an open confrontation with the Shiʿi *fiqh* notion of divorce, which had been codified as part of the Iranian Civil Code (*qānūn-i madanī*) and grafted onto a new judicial system in the early twentieth century.[17] These procedural devices made it an offense to register a divorce without a court certificate, subject to a penalty of imprisonment for six months to a year for all parties involved, including the registrar. This innovation had the effect of bringing all divorces into the courts, which in effect amounted to the abolition of a man's right to *ṭalāq*. New courts were set up with their own procedural rules, empowered to deal with all types of marital disputes, and presided over by civil judges, some of them women. In the absence of the spouses' mutual consent to divorce, the court would, upon the establishment of certain grounds, issue a certificate referred to as "impossibility of reconciliation," which then enabled the party seeking the divorce to register it without the other party's consent. New marriage contracts were issued in which these grounds were inserted as stipulations, thus providing further legitimacy for the specific conditions upon which a divorce certificate could be obtained from the court.

As noted, under classical Shiʿi law, in the absence of her husband's consent, the only grounds upon which a woman could seek the termination of her marriage were her husband's impotency or insanity. These had already been expanded in the 1930s, however, when *fiqh* rules of marriage and divorce were partially reformed and codified to include the husband's refusal or inability to provide for his wife, his refusal to perform his marital (sexual) duties, his maltreatment of her, and his affliction with a disease that could endanger her life (Civil Code, Articles 1129 and 1130). This was done by using the legal device of *talfīq*, that is, adopting provisions from other schools of Islamic law. To broaden these grounds further, the FPL resorted to another legal device: the insertion of stipulations into the marriage contract granting the wife the delegated right of *ṭalāq* after recourse to the court, where she must establish one of the listed conditions. Prior to 1967, it had been up to the woman, and in effect her family, to negotiate such a right. This seldom happened and, when it did occur was confined to the property-holding middle and upper classes. The FPL made these stipulations an integral part of every marriage contract.

To secure the approval of the clerical establishment, the draft of the FPL was discussed with high-ranking clerics, including Ayatollah Hakim, a leading Shiʿi jurist resident in Najaf. Yet the militant clerics saw the reforms introduced by the FPL as an interference with Shariʿa and a violation of sacred Islamic laws. In 1967, Ayatollah Khomeini commented:

> The "Family Law," which has as its purpose the destruction of the Muslim family unit, is contrary to the ordinances of Islam. Those who have imposed [this law] and those who have voted [for it] are criminals from the stand-point of both Shariʿa and the law. The divorce of women divorced by court order is invalid; they are still married women, and if they marry again, they become adulteresses. Likewise, anyone who knowingly marries a woman so divorced becomes an adulterer, deserving the penalty laid down by the Shariʿa. The issue of such unions will be illegitimate, unable to inherit, and subject to all other regulations concerning illegitimate offspring.[18]

In February 1979, soon after the victory of the Revolution, Ayatollah Khomeini's office declared that the FPL was non-Islamic, and announced its suspension and the reinstitution of the Shari'a provisions for divorce as embodied in the articles of the Civil Code.[19] Six months later, the FPL courts were abolished and replaced by Special Civil Courts, which were presided over by a *ḥākim-i shar'* (judge trained in *fiqh*).[20] Established by an act with the same name, the new courts are in effect Shari'a courts. "Special" here denotes their freedom from the laws of evidence and procedure contained in the Civil Procedure Code, investing them with the same degree of discretionary powers as the pre-revolutionary FPL courts. Yet some of the reforms introduced under the FPL were retained, though in an ad hoc way and under a different legal logic. Men's unilateral (but not extra-judicial) right to divorce was restored: a divorce could be registered only when the two parties reached a mutual agreement. The only cases that had to appear in court were those where one party, either the husband or the wife, objected to the divorce or its terms.[21] Men were not required to provide grounds, while women could obtain a divorce only upon the establishment of grounds, which were basically the same as those available to them under the FPL. At the same time, measures were taken to compensate and protect women in the face of divorce as well as to expand their access to it. This was done, once again, by the insertion of new sets of stipulations into the marriage contract and by empowering the new courts to issue (or withhold) a divorce requested by a woman. This time, however, as *fiqh* rules could no longer be circumvented, new arguments for these measures had to be found within *fiqh*.

Since 1982, new standard marriage contracts have been issued carrying two stipulations that marriage registrars are required to read aloud to couples. The first, intended to deter men from using the *ṭalāq* option, entitles the wife to claim half the wealth that her husband has acquired during marriage, provided that the divorce is neither initiated by her nor caused by any fault of hers, the court deciding whether or not fault lies with the wife. The second stipulation, aimed at enlarging women's access to divorce, gives the wife the delegated right to divorce herself after going to court and establishing one of the conditions inserted in her marriage contract. This in effect enables women to obtain a judicial divorce on more or less the same bases as before the Revolution; the only difference is that, in conformity with the *fiqh* mandate on divorce, now the basis for these rights is the husband's agreement to them in the marriage contract. Interestingly, however, whether the husband actually agreed to these terms or not has no effect in practice, since the presence or absence of his signature under each clause is ignored and full power to grant the divorce lies with the judge.[22]

The next problem that had to be addressed was how to deal with cases where the marriage took place before 1982 and the contract did not contain the second stipulation. This was solved by amending certain articles of the Civil Code. Article 1130 was amended to empower the judge to issue (or withhold) a divorce requested by a woman if he believes that the continuation of marriage will entail *ʿusr va ḥaraj* (hardship and suffering). This is a general *fiqh* principle which allows a rule to be lifted when adherence to it creates hardship. In the sphere of marriage, its implication is that, for a woman, remaining married is a rule as long as her husband desires it; to be released from a marriage she needs to prove that its continuation is causing her harm. The divorce stipulation inserted in marriage contracts in 1982, which provides women with specific grounds upon which they can obtain a court divorce, can be seen as an attempt to identify and list circumstances that can render marital life intolerable to the wife. In other words, these amendments are modern Shiʿi jurists' attempts to define the broad and vague concept of "hardship" in marriage.

**Rethinking the Legal Form: Ayatollah Saneʿi's Argument**

It was in this context that Ayatollah Khomeini's intervention was sought, as the high-ranking jurists could not agree on the question of when a judge should exercise discretion to grant a divorce against the husband's will or of what entails "hardship" for women in marriage. In his letter, Ayatollah Saneʿi sets out the two juristic positions on effecting a divorce without the husband's consent, and asks for Ayatollah Khomeini's opinion. Khomeini is obviously in favor of the second position, that is, giving the court a free hand in issuing a divorce requested by a woman on the grounds of "hardship." He then adds "there is a simpler way, if I had the courage."

This simpler way that even Ayatollah Khomeini had not dared to utter was, Ayatollah Saneʿi argued, that if a woman asks for a divorce but her husband refuses to give his consent, such a refusal is on its own the proof of her "hardship" in marriage. In such a case, either the wife can divorce herself—because, according to the *fiqh* principle of alleviating "hardship," the husband loses the right to object to her desire for divorce—or, according to another general *fiqh* principle of "no harm" (*lā-ḍarar*), she can demand that the marriage be dissolved through the option of *faskh*.

I asked Ayatollah Saneʿi about the legal form that this type of separation would take. I reproduce our exchange:

> Saneʿi: The form hasn't yet been defined in our laws; as I said before, our laws are incomplete. This is what Imam [Khomeini] says; whenever marital life becomes difficult for a woman and we see that she can't continue her marriage, she can annul (*faskh*) the contract.
>
> Mir-Hosseini: Does she need the permission of a religious judge?

> Saneʿi: Permission is merely a precaution, so that *ṭalāq* [is pronounced] instead of *faskh*. However, the significance of the whole argument is that there is no need, and a woman can separate. She goes to the court as a matter of formality, to have the separation registered, not to establish grounds for such a separation, according to *sharʿ* [divine law] as we understand it. Islam does not say that a woman must stay and put up with her marriage if it is causing her harm—never! When the Imam was asked about the situation of the wives of those who disappeared during the imposed war [with Iraq, 1980–1988], he wrote that these women can take a representative [for the husband] and divorce themselves.[23]

As elaborated by Ayatollah Saneʿi, this view indicates a radical break from the assumptions underlying dissolution of marriage, and thus opens the way for addressing the inequalities inherent in the notion of *ṭalāq*. It takes into account a woman's wishes, and leaves it to her, not to the court or the judge, to decide whether the continuation of marriage causes her harm and hardship. This takes the notion of marriage as a contract of equal partners to its logical conclusion, that is, the consent of the two parties is required, not only in the formation of the marriage contract but also for its continuation. A woman's right to dissolve the contract through *faskh* puts her in more or less the same position as the man in terminating the marriage through *ṭalāq*. This is a far cry from the stance that Ayatollah Khomeini took in 1967 over the pre-revolutionary regime's reforms of the divorce laws.[24]

## Rethinking Divorce Theories: The Arguments of Hujjat al-Islam Saʿidzadeh

What remains implicit in Ayatollah Saneʿi's arguments is made explicit in a paper by Hujjat al-Islam Muhsin Saʿidzadeh, entitled "The Foundation of the Equality Perspective in Modern *Fiqh*: The Case of Divorce," which deals with underlying *fiqh* assumptions and theories regarding marriage and its dissolution.[25] Saʿidzadeh is a young cleric, one of a new generation that has come of age intellectually in the Islamic Republic and has been influenced by ideas outside the traditional centers of Islamic learning in Iran. He is the most vocal clerical proponent of gender equality. In his writings on various aspects of women's rights in Islamic law, which have appeared in women's journals in Iran since 1992, he has tried to reconcile *fiqh* theories with current social realities.

His arguments stem from three points. First, divorce cannot be considered separately from *fiqh* theories and assumptions regarding marriage. Based on terms employed in the Qurʾan and the sayings of the Prophet, his "equality perspective" reaches the conclusion that marriage rests on the principle of "unilateral protection." Second, according to the consensus of the jurists, marriage is a customary affair and was a pre-Islamic tradition. Islam accepted this tradition and did not create it. Unilateral protection was appropriate for that era, and since it was chosen by the people themselves, the new religion did not address the core theory on which divorce rested, but merely restricted men's excessive power. To do so, it limited the number of wives a man could have and the number of times he could divorce the same woman. In other words, the Qurʾan did not reform marriage and divorce as institutions (as they are the product of custom) but merely placed certain conditions on men, since the marriage contract places women under their protection. But Islam's silence, not criticizing an existing situation or institution, does not necessarily mean that it ordains that situation or institution forever and disapproves of its modification.

The third and last of Saʿidzadeh's underlying points is this: In deducing the terms of divine law, the first task of a jurist is to identify the subject of the ruling (*mawḍūʿ al-ḥukm*), just as a physician must make a correct diagnosis before finding a cure. The subject of marriage is the social and civil aspect of relations between the sexes. In other words, men and women are the subject of marriage and divorce, since both need each other and are parties to the contract. The error of previous jurists lies in their failure to correctly identify the subject of the rules of marriage and divorce. They have confused the cause (*ʿilla*) of marriage (here, unilateral protection) with the subject of the ruling (here, civil relationship between men and women). Instead, says Saʿidzadeh, "unilateral protection" must be regarded as a social theory, reflecting the state of affairs of the society in which the Qurʾan was revealed, not the subject matter of a divine ruling.

Having set the framework of his argument with these three points, Saʿidzadeh then elaborates on marriage practices at the time of the Qurʾanic revelation. In the pre-Islamic era, he argues, only men were given social rights and responsibilities, and as a result the subject of marriage was understood to be men. With the marriage contract, women of the time came under the protection of the tribe (generally) and the husband (specifically), exactly like camels and sheep. Men could remove the protection at any time and release the women, since a woman was not a party to the contract but rather its subject. Unilateral protection was the basis of family links, and parts of this culture are still evident in the written sources and the idioms used. For example, "*ṭalāq*" in Arabic means "release," to "untether" from the tie of protection. It is used to refer to either a camel that is untethered, no longer under the control of a drover, and free to graze where it wants, or a sheep that has left the herd and no longer has the protection of a shepherd. In that culture, the separation of a sheep from the herd was analogous to that of a woman from her kin-group and tribe: the shepherd's care was like the control and protection provided by the husband.

Islam accepts the principle of protection, Saʿidzadeh contends, but leaves its form to be defined by the people of each era. This is so because the form of protection, its framework, and the manner of its application are relative, changeable, and subject to the demands of time and place. In every time and place people can alter the form of this theory; since alteration in form (not nature) is permitted, the by-products—i.e., legal consequences—of this alteration are also permitted. The form that this principle took in early Islamic society was only one instance. Says Saʿidzadeh:

> We cannot assume that only this instance among many other instances of protection is sanctioned by a religion which is based on revelation and absolute reason! Our explanation and analysis, therefore, is that since that instance was accepted by the people of that era and was useful for them, it was left as it was. But people of this era want a different form. Islam does not concern itself with the form but with the principle.
>
> The Qurʾan did not reform marriage and divorce as institutions—as they are products of custom—but merely placed conditions on the man (the party who takes a woman and releases her). In other words, we are dealing precisely with the form [of protection] not the principle. So while retaining the principle, as it is the cause (*ʿilla*), we can now change its form and solve the problem of *ṭalāq*, as people of this era demand a new form and women no longer accept the old form.[26]

The essential issue that jurists must now address, according to Saʿidzadeh, is the unilaterality or bilaterality of the protection. He continues:

> In the present era, protection can take any one of the following forms, as accepted by people: (1) government protection of the family, (2) men's protection of the family (generally) and of women (specifically), (3) women's protection of the family, and (4) spouses' shared protection of the family. Acceptance of each of these forms will affect divorce in a different way. If we accept the first form, divorce will become governmental and will come under the control of the judge in charge, exactly like any other social contract, such as establishing and dissolving a company; the [distinct] form of judicial divorce stems from this. If we accept the third form, then divorce will be in the hands of women, exactly opposite to the second form, the one presently accepted by Muslim societies. If we accept the fourth form (which seems the most suitable for people of this era), then both men and women can divorce, and their rights in divorce become equal.[27]

In anticipation of, and to preempt, potential criticism, Saʿidzadeh concludes his paper with a caveat:

> In response to those who say that the rulings (*aḥkām*) of religion are eternal and immutable, and that therefore the above deduction cannot be accepted, I must say: (1) eternity and immutability pertain to principles (*uṣūl*) and rulings, not details and forms (*ashkāl*)! We too consider the rulings of Islam to be eternal and immutable, but distinguish principles from forms; (2) as for "discerning the cause,"[28] the accepted views of the Shiʿa have it that if the *mujtahid* [independent interpreter] jurist knows or discerns what the cause of a ruling is, or what were the reasons that influenced the creation of the ruling, then he can give a fatwa on the basis of his understanding. In other words, Shiʿi *fiqh* views admit that once the cause of a ruling becomes clear to the jurist, by means of either rational or narrated proofs, he can act in accordance with his opinion. *Fiqh* views in recent years are more inclined than their predecessors towards the validity and proof of this view.[29]

Saʿidzadeh's radical ideas and outspokenness have made him one of the victims of the struggle between modernists and traditionalists, which took a new turn after the unexpected victory of the "moderates" in the election of Mohammad Khatami as president in the spring of 1997. In June 1998, after the publication of an article in the now-closed liberal daily newspaper *Jāmeʿeh*, in which he compared religious traditionalists in Iran with the Taliban in Afghanistan, Saʿidzadeh was arrested and detained without trial. He was released five months later, but "unfrocked", that is, he lost his clerical position and is "forbidden-pen"—his writings cannot be published.

## Conclusion

The answer to the question with which I began this essay is "yes, there can be an equal construction of divorce in Islamic law, but not through the traditionally-recognized mechanism of a contract stipulation delegating the husband's rights to the wife." Rather, the two arguments I have discussed are examples of the ways in which termination of marriage can be legally defined at the outset to accommodate social realities and contemporary women's aspirations for gender equality. These ideas are found in the comments of Ayatollah Saneʿi and Hujjat al-Islam Saʿidzadeh. What I find most significant about these two views is that neither is predicated on the notion of insertion of stipulations in the marriage contract, which, in my view, sidesteps the problem. Both jurists go back to fundamentals and ask new questions. In my view, no radical change can be argued and sustained unless the whole notion of the gender relations informing the Islamic marriage contract is re-examined. This, in time, can open the way for radical and positive changes in Islamic law.

Whether this will ever happen, whether the new juristic arguments will ever be translated into legal rulings, depends on the balance of power between traditionalists and modernists in each Muslim country, and on women's ability to organize and participate in the political process. But it is important to remember two things. First, *fiqh* is reactive in the sense that it reacts to social realities, to the situation on the ground, and that it has both the potential and the legal mechanisms to deal with women's demands for equality in law. This is best seen in Ayatollah Khomeini's own radical shift in position *vis-à-vis* reforms of divorce laws in pre- and post-revolutionary Iran. This is potent proof of the extent to which political realities and expediencies can shape the views of custodians of the Shariʿa. Yet what happened to Hujjat al-Islam Saʿidzadeh is another potent proof of the difficulties involved and the price that has to be paid for dissent from conventional views. His main offense was to expose to the public debates and arguments that traditionally belonged in the seminaries.

Finally, it is important to remember that *fiqh* is still the monopoly of male scholars, who not only continue to define the scope of women's rights in Islam but whose accredited knowledge of women and their rights comes from texts all written by men, all constructed with juristic logic, reflecting the realities of another age and a different set of interests. This monopoly needs to be broken, and it can be done only through women's participation in the production of knowledge.[30]

NOTES

This chapter is based on research conducted in Iran in 1995 and 1997, funded by the Nuffield Foundation and the British Institute of Persian Studies. I am grateful to both organizations for their generous help. The original draft was presented at the Islamic Marriage Contract conference at Harvard Law School, Islamic Legal Studies Program, January 29–31, 1999. I am grateful to Ann Elizabeth Mayer and Richard Tapper for reading and commenting on an early revision. The present chapter does not take account of publications since 2000, or of my own changed perspective, on both of which see Mir-Hosseini, "When a Woman's Hurt Becomes an Injury: 'Hardship' as Grounds for Divorce in Iran," in *Hawwa: Journal of Women of the Middle East and the Islamic World* 5:1 (2007), 111–126.

[1] Among the classical schools, the Maliki is the most liberal and grants woman the widest grounds upon which she can initiate divorce proceedings. Among modern states where Islamic law forms the basis of family law (not considering Turkey, where Islamic law is not the source of family law since Kamal Atatürk's reforms), in Tunisia women enjoy the easiest access to divorce in law. See Nasir [2]1990, 125–142. For reforms in divorce laws, see Anderson 1976; Mahmood 1972; El Alami and Hinchcliffe 1996.

[2] For a concise guide, see Carroll and Kapoor 1996.

[3] See, e.g., Carroll 1996.

[4] Although women active in Islamist politics did not—unlike their secular counterparts—openly challenge the gender discourse of the Revolution, by the late 1980s there were clear signs of dissent, as increasing numbers of women voiced objections to the discriminations that were placed on them in the name of the Shariʿa. See Mir-Hosseini 1996; Mir-Hosseini 1996a.

[5] See Mir-Hosseini 1998 and 1999a.

[6] There are, of course, differences among the schools of Islamic law, but they share the same inner logic and patriarchal bias. See, for instance, Esposito 1982.

[7] For a concise discussion of the terms of the marriage contract and their adoption by legal codes in Arab countries, see El Alami 1992; and El Alami and Hinchcliffe 1996.

[8] *Nushūz* literally means "rebellion" and it implies the abandonment of marital duties. Despite the fact that it is acknowledged that such abandonment can take place on the part of both spouses, in *fiqh* sources the term *nāshiza* (rebellious) is used only in the feminine form and in relation to maintenance rights.

[9] For this form of marriage, see Haeri 1989.

[10] See Ḥillī 1985, 751–883; and Dāmād 1986, 341–443.

[11] See Katouzian 1989, 277–279.

[12] The essence is that after marriage the wife discovers the absence of a specified attribute (*ṣifa*) without which she would not have agreed to enter the contract.

[13] For a discussion of *faskh* in Shiʿi law and its translation in contemporary Iranian family codes, see Mehrpour 2000, 112–123.

[14] For background to this journal, see Mir-Hosseini 1999a, chaps. 3 to 5.

[15] For pre- and post-revolutionary family laws in Iran, see Mir-Hosseini 1999, 192–196.

[16] Bagley 1971; Hinchcliffe 1968.

[17] Enacted between 1927 and 1935, those articles of the Civil Code that relate to marriage and divorce are in effect a simplification and codification of dominant opinion in Shiʿi *fiqh*; for a brief account of Iranian family law, see Mir-Hosseini 1999.

[18] Algar 1985, 411.

[19] Communiqué of February 26, 1979, see Tabari and Yeganeh 1982, 232.

[20] For these courts, see Mir-Hosseini 1993.

[21] This was the case between 1979 and 1992, when the divorce laws were amended once again, requiring all divorces to appear in court. See Mir-Hosseini 1999.

[22] For the new grounds and their difference from FPL, and for court procedure in the 1980s, see Mir-Hosseini 1993, 54–83; and Mir-Hosseini 1998.

[23] For a fuller account of Ayatollah Saneʿi's views, see Mir-Hosseini 1999a, 147–168.

[24] For changes in Khomeini's judicial rulings relating to women's rights, see Mir-Hosseini 2000.

[25] Published in *Payām-e Ḥajar* (journal of the Islamic Women's Institute headed by Azam Taleqani) Farvardin-Ordibehest 1377 (April–May 1998), 51–53. For the text of the article in English and a discussion of Saʿidzadeh's views, see Mir-Hosseini 1999a, chap. 8.

[26] Mir-Hosseini 1999a, 270.

[27] Idem.

[28] *Tanqīḥ al-manāṭ*. Technically the phrase means "connecting the new case to the original case by eliminating the discrepancy between them." See Kamali 1991, 213. Literally, *tanqīḥ* means purifying, *manāṭ* means cause; it implies that a ruling (*ḥukm*) may have more than one cause, and the jurist has to identify the proper one.

[29] Mir-Hosseini 1999a, 271.

[30] Although there are now a number of female scholars, they focus their energies mainly on the field of Qur'anic interpretation (*tafsīr*) rather than law (*fiqh*). For instance, see Hassan 1987 and 1996; Mernissi 1991; Wadud-Mohsin 1999.

# *Eleven*

## THE ISLAMIC MARRIAGE CONTRACT IN EGYPT

Mona Zulficar

### Introduction

Unlike the situation under the Roman Empire and in pre-Islamic Arabia, the relationship of marriage in Egypt was always essentially a contractual relationship based on the free will and mutual consent of its parties and reciprocity of their rights and obligations.[1] Marriage in pre-Islamic Arabia took a variety of forms, including polyandrous, temporary, and polygynous marriage, slave-marriage, and marriage by inheritance (where the wife would be inherited by her deceased husband's next of kin without a new dower and the children conceived during that second union would carry the deceased husband's name). All those forms were regulated by custom. Similarly under the Roman Empire marriage took several forms, all based on ownership and supremacy by the husband. In ancient Egypt, however, marriage always had a contractual nature, being based on the mutual consent of both parties.

With the advent of Islam, the marriage relationship in Egypt became even more explicitly contractual. Still regulated by a voluntary civil contract rather than a religious one, concluded by the free will and mutual consent of its parties and often including substantive terms for the continuation of the contract, marriage under Islam also gave rise to reciprocal rights and obligations governed by Islamic principles and legal doctrine. For example, termination of the marriage contract could be effected by the husband unilaterally or by the wife through a court judgment. However, if the marriage contract provided that the wife retained her right to divorce unilaterally, this condition would be valid and upheld, thus underscoring the contractual nature of the marriage relationship. This formulation of the legal basis of marriage as a civil, voluntary, and contractual relationship that is legally binding on the parties represented a fundamental change and reconceptualization of the institution of marriage.

Analysts may argue that the marriage institution legitimized by Islam has created a hierarchical structure that discriminates against women and paves the ground for male control and women's seclusion. Its patriarchal, patrilineal, and polygynous features seem to have a negative impact on the position of women.[2] On the other hand, feminists engaged in Islamic religious discourse may argue that Qur'anic texts, including explicit texts related to marriage, provide a strong basis for equality between the sexes in general, as well as equality and reciprocity within the marriage institution in particular.[3] For example, the Qur'an states: "Wives have rights corresponding to those which husbands have, in equitable reciprocity."[4] Further, Islamic legal provisions of equal rights and obligations with respect to religious duties, crime and punishment, economic and financial independence, to contract, and to own and dispose of property challenge the assumption that patriarchal control is inherent in the original sacred book. Moreover, discriminatory practices such as polygamy may be interpreted as a condoned exception which may be restricted or regulated by law. Similarly, the husband's unilateral right of divorce is condemned by the Prophet as most abhorrent to God, and Islamic law allows it to be balanced by a similar right retained by the wife in the marriage contract in addition to the wife's right to unilaterally terminate her marriage by repudiation (*khul*ʿ). Finally, strong legal arguments could be offered based on the legitimate need for religious reform to reinterpret and reconcile Qur'anic verses relating to women. Such reform would promote a new interpretation which takes into account the historical context and social dynamics prevailing in pre-Islamic Arabia in the seventh century.

Hence, it may be argued that the Islamic marriage institution has either a positive or negative impact on the position of women in a society at a given time, depending on the socio-economic conditions and the prevailing cultural patterns which affect the role of women, the impact of religion, or the cultural approach to interpretation of the religious texts. However, the contractual nature of the Islamic marriage contract remains at all times a neutral legal framework which may be used to restore the balance between the rights and obligations of the husband and the wife under any legal system. The contract may also be abused to further strengthen its features of patriarchal and male control. Yet the contractual nature of the marriage relationship in Islam affords at least the opportunity of flexibility to the woman to incorporate a variety of conditions into her marriage contract, such as restricting the husband's right to polygamy, assuring herself a unilateral right to divorce, or other substantive or financial conditions to give her security, so long as these do not run contrary to public policy.[5]

This essay addresses the experience of the Islamic marriage contract in Egypt. After a summary of Islamic legal doctrine and Egyptian statutory law on marriage and divorce, I will address the "New Marriage Contract" movement in Egypt, as a response by the women's movement to the discriminatory impact of these laws on women, and a proactive tool for women's empowerment drawing upon their own heritage and religion. Appendices following this essay offer the reader a look at the various revisions of the New Marriage Contract as it progressed through the various political and social pressures it encountered.

## I. The Contractual Nature of the Marriage Institution in Egypt

With the Islamic marriage contract, the nature of marriage in pre-Islamic Arabia evolved from its pre-Islamic form to become a doctrine of mutual consent. Roman law witnessed a similar evolution, as marriage moved from several forms, all based on a relationship of ownership and supremacy by the husband, to, in the later period of the Roman Empire under Justinian's Code (533 CE), a form based on mutual consent.[6] However, in ancient Egypt, the marriage contract was always based on mutual consent. No woman could be forced to marry against her will. The offer and acceptance between the husband and wife reflected the contractual nature of the marriage relationship. Thus, the husband would typically say that he gives his bride so much as dower (*mahr*) and that if he ever stopped loving her and married another woman, he would pay her an additional amount as compensation. The husband also assigned all his property and income at the present time and in the future to his wife at the time of concluding the contract. The wife would reply that she accepted the offer and the dower and has thereby become his wife. However, if she ever stopped loving him or loved another man, she would repay the dower and assign to him all her property.[7] Divorce was possible, although it was difficult, and the wife was entitled to divorce her husband if that condition formed part of the marriage contract. The wife retained her financial autonomy and property after marriage and the husband and wife had the option to own property in common, if they so wished.

Hence, while the Islamic marriage contract constituted a fundamental reformulation of the conceptual framework of marriage in pre-Islamic Arabia and represented a more advanced formula than that prevailing under Roman law at that time, in Egypt the Islamic marriage contract came as a natural development of the fundamental contractual features that already governed the marriage contract in ancient Egypt. The new framework also brought Islamic religious sanction for the contractual nature of marriage as well as additional features useful to parties engaging in marital contract negotiations.

One element introduced by Islamic law was the validation of individualized optional stipulations in the contract. Court archives in Egypt demonstrate that marriage contracts were concluded according to the principles of Shariʿa during the Ottoman period, and that these contracts included additional substantive conditions (i.e., in addition to the minimum legally required data on the parties: their age, status, residence, the amount of the dower, and witnesses).

It was common for marriage contracts in towns and cities to include conditions restricting the husband's right to take a second wife and providing for the wife's right to compensation, divorce, or both in case of breach of this undertaking or mistreatment. Contracts included the husband's commitment to support his wife's children from a previous marriage and not to be absent or depart from his wife for longer than an agreed period of time.[8] In case of breach by the husband, the wife could seek and obtain a divorce (*taṭlīq*, judicial divorce) from the Shariʿa judge without forfeiting any of her financial rights and might also be entitled to damages if it were so provided in the marriage contract. (If there were no fault by the husband, the wife could still pursue judicial divorce, but allocation of the *mahr* would depend upon the judge's assessment of blame on each spouse.) If the wife, on the other hand, wanted a divorce without having to prove fault by the husband, she had the option of *khulʿ*, divorce agreed by mutual consent of both spouses. In the case of disagreement, she could automatically obtain a divorce through *khulʿ* by a court judgment, but usually at the price of her financial rights to deferred dower, alimony, and sometimes also by payment of additional compensation to the husband for any damages he suffered. The latter would necessarily be within the limits of the advanced *mahr* she received upon conclusion of the marriage contract, which is usually a nominal symbolic amount.

It should be noted that the substantive conditions included in marriage contracts during the Ottoman period varied depending on the socio-economic patterns, the geographical location (the north or south), and the rural or urban dimensions of the case. These factors, as well as the differing rules of the schools of Islamic law (*madhhab*) chosen in the marriage contract, contributed to variations between actual marriage contracts. Nevertheless, the inclusion of conditions as a general practice was recognized as part of the cultural heritage, due to its continuous and consistent application: "Whether the bride came from a prosperous family or one of modest means, the inclusion of conditions in the marriage contracts was a commonplace thing."[9]

However, this approach and use of the marriage contract to safeguard women's interests and restore the balance to this contractual relationship started to change in Egypt after the issuance of the first Personal Status Law in 1920[10] and its amendment in 1929.[11] These laws represented an advanced and progressive step reflecting the overall liberal political and social climate generated by the 1919 Egyptian revolution against British colonialism. These laws were based on the most liberal opinions of the Islamic legal schools on each relevant issue and were not restricted to the prevalent and officially recognized Hanafi school. In 1931, Law 87 on the organization of Shariʿa courts was issued and, as a result, the marriage contract became a standard "fill-in-the-blanks" form listing only the minimum legal required information (name, date, age, title, etc.). With this law, the Egyptian legislature expressed its view that there was no further need for substantive conditions in the marriage contract, since these were already covered by the law. This was not completely true, as the laws passed in 1920 and 1929 placed no restrictions on polygamy, for example, and did not codify *khulʿ*. Registration regulations passed in 1931 made one exception: to permit the insertion of the wife's right to divorce herself in the marriage contract. This condition continued to be added to the marriage contracts concluded particularly by wealthy families.

In time, however, the marriage contract has lost its contractual features and has become more like a registration certificate. The only issue of negotiation is the dower. This often includes a symbolic amount in advance, as families agree on sharing the costs of procuring and furnishing the conjugal home, pursuant to traditions where the husband provides the apartment and appliances and the wife provides all other furnishings. A much higher deferred dower is considered to preempt divorce on the part of the husband by making it financially difficult.[12] This deferred dower practice is a reaction to the present state laws that do not restrict divorce by men in any way.

Because the 1931 standard marriage contract could no longer be used as an instrument of restoring gender balance in marriage nor of protection of the wife's rights, this need had to be satisfied elsewhere. Cultural practices eventually devised a new separate list (*qayma*) of the wife's furnishings and belongings. This list has become a recognized tradition observed by the vast majority of lower- and middle-class families in Egypt. It usually includes inflated prices and is signed by the husband in the form of a trust receipt. This trust receipt is kept by the wife's family, and if the husband mistreats their daughter, or fails to fulfill his obligations, or divorces her for no cause against her will, he is required to deliver all the items on the list or pay their inflated prices, otherwise he will be accused of breach of trust (a criminal misdemeanor).

It should be noted that the decline in using the marriage contract as a contract of agreement and the disappearance of conditions protecting the wife's interest starting in 1931 are not in themselves signals of a deteriorating overall position of women. In fact, this same period witnessed modernization and progressive advancement of women's status in all political, economic, and social spheres as a result of their expanded access to education and employment. This is reflected in the laws enacted and policies implemented during this period in Egypt. The three constitutions that have so far been adopted by Egypt (in 1923, 1956, and 1971) also testify to this fact. The 1956 Constitution confirmed for the first time equal political rights and hence full equality between men and women before the law. Article 40 of the present Constitution of 1971 reaffirms the principle of equality before the law and equal opportunity of all citizens without any discrimination based on sex, race, language, religion or creed. Article 11 of the 1971 Constitution confirms that "the State guarantees the reconciliation of women's duties towards her family and her work in society, and her equality with man in the political, social, cultural, and economic fields, without prejudice to the principles of Shariʿa."[13]

The apparent contradiction between the advancement in the overall position of women and the decline in the use of the marriage contract to assert their rights can be explained by the fact that the pace of advancement made in laws governing women's private and family lives did not match the pace of advancement made in the fields of education, employment, and (to a much lesser extent) politics, as well as the laws governing women's lives as citizens. This is because modern secular codes govern employment, education, property, economic activities, politics, crime, and punishment, but laws based on the principles of Shariʿa govern personal status laws. The dichotomy is illustrated by one scholar's statement that "nothing exemplifies more the contradictions of modern state patriarchy than the fact that Muslim women can aspire to becoming the heads of governments, yet they face other insurmountable difficulties in divorcing their husbands."[14]

It should be noted that the vast majority of the laws in Egypt provide women with equal opportunities, free of discrimination, in compliance with the Egyptian constitution. However, Egyptian personal status and family laws discriminate against women in contradiction with the constitution. The reference to "principles of Shariʿa" in Article 11 of the constitution is intended to reconcile this conflict. The personal status laws have attempted to find a basis for discrimination against women in tradition, customs or religion and have particularly exploited religion unfairly to justify that discrimination. The 1981 amendment of the 1971 Constitution that makes the principles of Shariʿa a fundamental source of legislation is an attempt to legitimize this exploitation. Egypt's reservations to Article 2 (political measures to be undertaken to eliminate discrimination) and Article 16 (marriage and family law) of the Convention for the Elimination of All Forms of Discrimination against Women (CEDAW) barring any "prejudice to the principles of the Shariʿa" provide further proof of this dichotomy and confirm the unfair attempt to exploit religion to reconcile the conflict.

Moreover, attention should be given to the meaning of the phrase "principles of Shariʿa," which is used to qualify any commitment by the state, under the principles of CEDAW, to ensure equality under family laws. There is no agreed definition in the constitution or in Egyptian law on the meaning of this term. However, the explanatory memorandum issued in connection with the 1981 amendment of the 1971 Constitution defined the term as "the general principles of Shariʿa consistently agreed upon by Islamic jurisprudence (*fiqh*)." Reference to jurisprudence underlines the evolving and dynamic nature of the principles of Shariʿa, which in turn opens the door to redefining and reinterpreting religious texts in the light of modern developments.[15] To sum up, the use of the marriage contract to provide conditions that protect women's rights and restore equilibrium to the marital relationship contractually, rather than by application of law, is not necessarily indicative of the advancement of women's overall status.

Similarly, the decline in such practice is not synonymous with deterioration in the position of women. However, the use of such an instrument of social change that is deeply rooted in their own cultural and religious heritage is a reflection of the dichotomy in which Muslim women live in modern life and a demonstration of a legitimate and clever mechanism historically used by women to resolve contradictions between their public and private lives, and to challenge patriarchal control, religious misinterpretations, and discriminatory family laws.

## II. The New Marriage Contract: An Attempt to Bring the Islamic Marriage Contract Back to Life

The idea of the "New Marriage Contract," as it is known in Egypt, was first introduced in 1985 during the preparatory stages of a consciousness-raising and legal literacy campaign, which resulted in a booklet called "The Legal Rights of Egyptian Women in Theory and Practice."[16] The booklet was addressed "to the men and women of Egypt, with the aim of helping every Egyptian woman striving to achieve a better life for herself and her family to acquire a better understanding of her rights and obligations under Egyptian law, and of reminding her that she is not alone."[17]

The campaign attempted to use law and legal awareness as an instrument of social change. Its aim was to bridge two types of gaps between legislation and social reality. The first gap was between secular, modern, and progressive laws and the culture and traditions that impeded their implementation. Examples of such laws are those relating to political rights, education, and employment which are not sufficiently exercised by women or are not properly implemented. The second gap existed in cases where women's needs for development and empowerment surpassed or contradicted the outdated personal status laws, which resisted change and exploited religion to legitimize discrimination against women. In response, the campaign sought both to build awareness of legal rights and to challenge the restrictive traditions and cultural heritage in an attempt to redefine such heritage. The campaign and the booklet were launched by a group of seven Egyptian women. We called ourselves "The Communication Group for the Enhancement of the Status of Women in Egypt," but became known as the "Group of Seven." The Group of Seven included prominent professional women and NGO leaders, such as Aziza Hussein, an internationally recognized NGO leader in Egypt and the Arab world, and Mervat Tallawi, then-Egyptian Ambassador to Austria and formerly Minister of Social Affairs and first Secretary-General of the National Council for Women, which was established in 2000. I served as the group's lawyer and draftswoman.

The New Marriage Contract was annexed to the booklet.[18] It was drafted on the basis of a field survey and discussed in several workshops.

The primary strategy was to use the draft contract as a tool for consciousness-raising, increasing awareness that the marriage contract is a civil contract and that it is allowed under the principles of Shariʿa to include specific conditions in the contract reflecting the mutual agreement of the parties. At another level it was an attempt to bridge the gap between the rights of women under Shariʿa principles and the personal status codes. The latter did not recognize certain of those rights, such as the *khulʿ* or the *ʿiṣma* (*ṭalāq tafwīḍ*), which is the right to reserve in a contract of marriage a woman's right to divorce herself without having to resort to the court, or the woman's right to restrict her husband's right to take a second wife. Though legitimate under Shariʿa principles, these rights remained unknown, hidden to the public, unrecognized by the then-current laws and regulations, and culturally perceived as taboo.

The New Marriage Contract incorporated all these controversial conditions in a model contract and, in checklist format, provided the option to agree or disagree to each condition by simply selecting or deleting them. This was intended to facilitate the process of overcoming social pressure and the standard patriarchal strategy used to discourage the assertion of women's rights in marriage contracts, namely, projecting shame on the couple: on the groom for accepting such conditions, and on the bride for failing to maintain confidence in the "gallant manhood" of the groom. In contrast, the standard form of the marriage contract attached to the 1931 Minister of Justice regulations governing the registrars of marriage contracts was merely a certificate identifying such things as the parties, their age, their status, and the witnesses. In 1992, the Egyptian Ministry of Justice decided to reconsider this old standard form in the context of drafting a new law of procedure in personal status matters. The Ministry of Justice recognized the negative role played by the standard form of the marriage contract from a procedural perspective. At the same time, a member of Parliament presented a draft law to make a medical examination before marriage a legal requirement.

The Ministry of Justice prepared its new draft standard form of the marriage contract to achieve two basic objectives, both relating to matters of form rather than content. First, it focused on accurate identification of the status and age of the parties. This involved using photographs in order to avoid improper abusive practices noted particularly with respect to forged delivery of divorce notices. It also suggested restricting the use of medical certificates as an admissible method of determining the age of the parties, particularly the bride, in order to combat early marriages below the minimum age of marriage (sixteen for women and eighteen for men). Finally, the draft required precise information on the profession, work or employment of the parties, and on the place of concluding the contract.

The second focus of the Ministry of Justice was to make a medical examination certificate a condition precedent to registration of the contract, requiring the registrar to show the certificates to the parties, at which time they had the freedom to conclude or decline the marriage. The Grand Mufti (a state official charged with issuing religious-legal opinions) approved the draft, but objected to concluding the marriage in the event one of the parties suffered a serious illness that permitted separation. In such a case, he asserted in a written (unpublished) opinion to the Ministry of Justice, it is the registrar's duty to refrain from concluding the marriage contract, as maintaining and protecting the health of the parties and that of the future generation was a valid objective sought by Shariʿa principles. The Ministry of Justice amended its draft accordingly and promised that a list of such serious illnesses would be determined by a decision of the Minister of Justice in consultation with the Minister of Health. Here it is important to note that, while these changes were useful and advantageous to some women, they did not in any way change the pre-existing practices which discouraged parties from including substantive conditions in the marriage contract.

In preparation for the International United Nations Conference on Population and Development and the corresponding Non-Governmental Organization (NGO) Forum, which convened in Cairo in September 1994, more than four hundred Egyptian NGOs agreed by consensus on a platform document containing their recommendations. The document was the product of a democratic consultation process involving NGOs from almost all the governorates of Egypt, through six committees, including the Gender Equality Committee. This committee, which I chaired, adopted the New Marriage Contract and called for the amendment of the Marriage Registrars Regulations to permit the inclusion of substantive conditions in marriage contracts, as well as the amendment of the 1931 standard form marriage contract to explicitly provide the option to include substantive conditions.

A survey conducted in 1994 showed that the majority of men and women were not aware that including substantive conditions in the marriage contract, such as prohibiting the husband from taking a second wife or granting the woman the right to divorce herself, was legitimate under Shariʿa principles. They were also not cognizant of their legal rights and obligations under the law. The majority did not understand the significance of the word *ʿiṣma*, signifying the woman's delegated right to unilateral divorce (*ṭalāq tafwīḍ*) without which there is only the husband's *ṭalāq* right, and that authorizing the woman to retain this right in the marriage contract does not prevent the husband from exercising the same right.[19]

An analysis of divorce cases in Egypt at the time demonstrated that divorce for prejudice (*ḍarar*) was very difficult for women to obtain because of the strict rules of evidence applied under the Hanafi school of law. A divorce case filed by a woman would take between five to seven years on average, and she may not even be able to obtain a divorce at the end of that period. Many agreed that legislative change was needed. Meanwhile, however, the New Marriage Contract provided an immediate solution without having to wait for legislation to be passed: wives would simply retain the delegated right to extra-judicial divorce in their marriage contract, thus avoiding lengthy divorce litigation. When arguments in favor of the New Marriage Contract were submitted to the National Women's Commission, it adopted the concept and prepared a new draft of the contract employing a series of questions and answers to be administered and completed by the registrar.[20] This form was criticized by the Egyptian women's movement because it was perceived to question rights already guaranteed to women by the constitution, such as the rights to education and employment. This draft was therefore dropped. However, the first National Women's Conference in June 1994 did put the general issue of new forms of marriage and divorce contracts at the top of its recommendations that year.

A third draft marriage contract[21] was adopted by the National Women's Commission in 1995. It represented a merger between the NGO concept of substantive conditions and the matters of form proposed by the Ministry of Justice in its draft. The new draft included a blank page, where the parties could fill in their agreed-upon conditions, followed by a footnote listing suggestions as to conditions that may be incorporated by the parties, sending the clear message that such conditions are legitimate under the principles of Shariʿa. This third draft was approved by the Grand Mufti (presently the Sheikh al-Azhar)[22] in 1994 prior to its adoption by the National Women's Commission. However, it was subject to aggressive attacks, particularly by the then Shaikh al-Azhar Jādd al-Ḥaqq, who declared that this issue should be closed. Significantly, the Shaikh al-Azhar did not object to the New Marriage Contract on any religious or legal basis, but declared that it would discourage marriage between young people and cause social problems.

The struggle continued and the campaign for the New Marriage Contract developed into a campaign for a new law on procedures in personal status matters. This campaign was supported by the annual National Women's Conferences, held by the National Women's Commission and presided over by Mrs. Suzanne Mubarak. This law was eventually passed as Law No. 1 of 2000 on Certain Issues and Procedures in Personal Status Matters. The new law approves *khulʿ*, which gives the wife a unilateral right to terminate her marriage contract in exchange for a waiver of her financial rights to deferred dower (*mahr*) and financial maintenance under the law. The new law also provides for a unified mechanism whereby the same court would consider all the relevant cases filed as a result of a divorce case, and provides for the formation of a special fund to be managed by Nasser Social Bank for the immediate execution of court judgments on maintenance (*nafaqa*) of the wife and children, while reserving the bank's right of recourse against the defaulting husband. Additionally, the new law facilitates divorce procedures for women and recognizes for the first time a woman's right to retain the right to divorce herself written into the marriage contract. Finally, the new law provides for a family insurance system and stipulates that new standard forms of marriage and divorce contracts and other documents, as well as new marriage registration regulations, have to be issued by the Minister of Justice. As a result, the Minister of Justice issued Decree 1727 of 2000 on August 16 of that year amending the Marriage Registrars Regulations, and at the same time issued a new form of the Marriage Contract.[23] This new form has satisfied the concerns on matters of form previously expressed by the Ministry of Justice, which, moreover, has positively responded to the fifteen-year struggle of the women's movement and allowed substantive conditions to be included in the marriage contract. In 2004, Law No. 10 on Family Courts was issued to establish the first specialized family courts in Egypt applying alternative dispute resolution mechanisms. Moreover, Law No. 11 on Family Insurance was issued establishing a fund to finance execution of court judgements on financial maintenance (*nafaqa*). These laws represent further positive results for the women's movement in Egypt which started with the progress achieved by Law No. 1 of 2000.

## III. The New Marriage Contract: An Instrument of Social Change

In the historical context, the New Marriage Contract is not novel. Court archives in Egypt show that Islamic marriage contracts, including conditions to protect women's interests and rights and restrict the husband's authority over his wife have been a common practice all over Egypt even before 1517 in the Ottoman period. However, the New Marriage Contract, first introduced in 1985 and evolved through two more drafts until it became the official standard form in 2000, was novel in many ways in the context of the existing cultural, political, and social environment of 1985. This can be illustrated in several ways.

First, the New Marriage Contract represented a proactive strategy last used by the women's movement in the 1920s when Egyptian women took off their veils and demonstrated in the streets in support of the 1919 revolution against British colonialism. The women's movement had become accustomed to a defensive approach in reaction to the vigorous attacks of the conservative religious extremist movement, which had accelerated in the 1980s and 1990s. Moreover, the women's movement suffered a severe setback in 1985 when the Supreme Constitutional Court declared the 1979 amendments[24] to the Personal Status Law of 1920 and 1929 unconstitutional (after fifty years of resistance to change). Although the court's judgment ruled that the amendments were unconstitutional for reasons related to form and not substance, it was a serious indication of the threat represented by the religious extremist movement and its new tendency to employ ordinary legal and judicial methods as means to advance its policies.

As a reaction to this threat, the women's movement in Egypt mobilized to attempt to pass a new law as a substitute for the one that was repealed. However, the substituting law, issued on July 4, 1985,[25] made a major concession, under pressure of the religious extremists, who were represented by five parliamentarians allied with the liberal New Wafd Party. The concession was to give up a right granted by the repealed law giving the first wife an automatic right of divorce, without having to prove harm, upon request to the court within one year after discovering that her husband took a second wife against her will. The new law as presently in force requires the first wife to prove material or moral prejudice in order to obtain divorce for prejudice (*ḍarar*) in such a case. The lesson learned from this experience was that the women's movement had to move forward and make progress or else face inevitable setbacks. Hence, the New Marriage Contract appeared to be an appropriate strategy to claim women's rights under the principles of Shariʿa unrecognized by the current laws and prevailing culture. This strategy challenged the patriarchal, social, cultural, and religious dogma in an attempt to claim new ground.

The movement for the New Marriage Contract adopted a strategy of engagement in the religious discourse based on women's reading of their rights under the principles of Shariʿa. For the first time in the Egyptian women's movement, we reclaimed our right to redefine our cultural heritage as Muslim women under the principles of Shariʿa. It was evident that we could not rely on the modern constitutional grant of equality before the law, as this did not equally apply under family laws, which claimed to be based on the principles of Shariʿa. We could not afford to shy away from the challenge and continue using a strategy based solely on constitutional and human rights. We had to prove that the standard religious discourse could also be used by women to defend their cause. The religious extremist groups consistently place women's issues at the forefront of their published agenda to implement Shariʿa principles or "codify" Shariʿa and assert their cultural identity. They therefore accuse any secular feminist opposition of being anti-Islamic, an agent of either the "non-religious" Eastern bloc or the "corrupt" Western bloc. It was therefore essential for the women's movement to diversify its approach and adopt a credible strategy that could reach out and win the support of simple, ordinary, religious men and women. The New Marriage Contract, an Islamic concept deeply rooted in indigenous culture, represented a new vision of cultural and social realities of women in their everyday lives which reconciled issues common to both the religious discourse and the secular feminist discourse.

Ibn Ḥanbal (eponym of the Hanbali school of Islamic law) and Ibn Taymiyya (a famous fourteenth-century Hanbali jurist) approved the inclusion of substantive conditions in the marriage contract, provided such conditions did not violate the imperative rules of Islam. The other three major schools of Islamic law did not prohibit the inclusion of conditions in the marriage contract, but required that such conditions should be compatible with the object of the contract, a test they interpreted much more restrictively than the Hanbalis. Under Egyptian law, the personal status laws are not based on the teachings of a single legal school. Although the Hanafi school is predominant, the legislator has often adopted the opinions or solutions of one or several schools on any one issue, as deemed in the best interest of society. (For example, divorce for prejudice is based on the Maliki school of thought while proof of prejudice to obtain divorce is based on the Hanafi school of thought).[26] Hence, it would be legitimate and consistent with common Egyptian legislative practice to adopt the Hanbali theory on stipulations in marriage contracts.[27] With the issue of Law 1 of 2000, these arguments were adopted by the Drafting Committee formed by the Minister of Justice,[28] which included the author of this chapter, and a new form of the marriage contract allowing the inclusion of substantive conditions was issued as the new standard form.

The New Marriage Contract, in all its phases (including the current form), was drafted in a manner that respected the human right of informed choice by women and men, in that it did not impose any conditions. All the conditions were suggested merely as options to be freely selected by the parties to the contract. The only mandatory condition in the standard form supported by both the women's movement and the Ministry of Justice was the medical examination. This, however, became optional under the current new form issued in August 2000. In this, the Egyptian women's movement for the marriage contract demonstrated that its engagement in the religious discourse was not inconsistent with the mainstream human rights and secular feminist movements.

## IV. Enforcement and Termination of the Marriage Contract

### A. *Legal Effects of the Marriage Contract*

However, even after the recent legislative changes, the New Marriage Contract—which is based on the Islamic marriage contract—could be instrumental in avoiding litigation altogether, enhancing amicable settlement, and using litigation efficiently to enforce the terms of the contract or terminate it for breach without the need to prove prejudice. The Islamic marriage contract may have many beneficial legal effects. The first is a deterrent effect: under the principles of Shariʿa, the conditions of a contract are legally binding and must be respected, except for conditions that violate imperative rules of law. The conditions of the marriage contract are the most worthy of conditions to uphold and observe, according to a confirmed saying of the Prophet.[29] Also, under Egyptian law, substantive conditions may be included in the marriage contract, provided such conditions are compatible with the object of the contract. Examples of conditions that would be invalid include those permitting prohibited acts such as temporary marriage or polyandry, or prohibiting fundamentally legitimate acts, such as barring sexual intercourse.

If the marriage contract contains a condition that is prohibited or infringes on the rights of third parties, such a condition is invalid, but the contract itself remains valid. On the other hand, if the marriage contract imposes an obligation on one party for the benefit of the other, which is not legally prohibited, does not infringe upon third parties' rights, and does not restrict the obligor's freedom in carrying out lawful actions, such a condition is valid. If, however, the condition does restrict the obligor's rights with respect to otherwise lawful actions, the condition is still valid but not enforceable through strict performance (i.e., enforceable against the obligor by force); however, breach entitles the other party to terminate the marriage.

To apply these rules, a condition in a marriage contract that obliges the husband to pay a monthly allowance to his wife is valid, legally binding, and enforceable against the husband. On the other hand, a condition prohibiting the husband from taking a second wife is valid but not enforceable against the husband. However, the latter entitles the first wife to terminate the marriage contract for breach of contract in addition to compensation for damages suffered. It is this legally binding nature of contractual obligations under the principles of Shariʿa in general and with respect to obligations under the marriage contract in particular that gives the conditions in the marriage contract a deterrent force. Thus, respect for the contract terms may encourage parties to uphold their obligations or amicably settle their disputes through negotiation rather than in court.

Another effect of formal acceptance of the Islamic marriage contract is to create a means of specific performance to enforce certain financial expectations included within it. Valid conditions in a marriage contract may be enforced against the obligor, by the force of law. Hence, if the parties to the contract agree on payments to be made by either the husband or the wife during marriage or upon divorce, such payments are enforceable. In addition, failure by the husband to make payments of financial maintenance or deferred dower constitutes a criminal offense punishable by imprisonment under Egyptian law. Similarly, if, for example, agreements on ownership of property with respect to the conjugal home or the right to use leased property in case of divorce are included in the marriage contract, such agreements would be enforced by the court.

It should be noted that enforcement of agreed contractual conditions through the court involves accelerated procedures and avoids the burden of proof of the existence of the obligation or of prejudice. Hence, if all the household furnishings are agreed to belong to the wife in the contract, a court order obliging the husband to deliver all such belongings to the wife upon divorce would be easy to obtain and enforce. Needless to say, such an agreement in the contract would avoid lengthy and repetitive litigation over the question of ownership. Such an agreement would also replace the custom of making a husband sign a trust receipt which could then be used to charge him with a misdemeanor for breach of trust in the case of a dispute over the wife's belongings upon divorce.

Another positive effect of the marriage contract is the option to compensate failed contractual expectations. That is, in the event that a valid term or condition in the marriage contract is unenforceable for any reason, the obligor can terminate the entire contract for breach, or claim compensation, or both. Hence, if the contract provides for the wife's right to continue to use the leased conjugal home in case of divorce and the lease on the property expires before the divorce, the wife may claim compensation in lieu of enforcement. Similarly, if the husband undertook in the marriage contract not to marry a second wife and then breached this stipulation, the wife can, in addition to termination of the contract, claim compensation for damages suffered as a result of the husband's breach. In such a case, prejudice is assumed and does not require any further proof. However, the amount of compensation would be assessed by the court, unless it is determined in the contract.

Finally, several unique aspects of the New Marriage Contract revolve around the question of termination. First, the New Marriage Contract provides the wife with two options for termination by divorce: (a) the right to retain the right to divorce (*ʿiṣma*), and (2) termination for breach. With respect to the wife's *ʿiṣma* right, she has an option to retain a right of divorce in her marriage contract equal to her husband's. Although jurists construe such a condition as a delegation of authority by the husband, they unanimously recognize it as irrevocable, treating it like a contractual term. The Shariʿa Courts in Egypt from the 1930s to the 1950s repeatedly passed judgments confirming the validity and enforceability of this condition. For example, in one 1931 case the Shariʿa Court stated:

> As stipulated under Shariʿa principles, women do not have a [unilateral] right of divorce except if this is a condition [in the marriage contract]. If he marries her on condition that she hold the matter of her divorce in her hands, such contract and such condition are valid. This [right] has become known among the people who use it intentionally. An example is the event of marriage on 17 May 1930, No. 30 in Tanta, where he married her provided she held the right of *ʿiṣma*, giving her the right to divorce herself whenever she wants. As there is no doubt that both parties understood this condition

> and intended to agree on it, and as the wife has divorced herself by virtue of the certificate dated 14 October 1931 by the Tanta Shariʿa Court, she is deemed to have exercised her right under Shariʿa and under the Law.[30]

The judgment was appealed by the husband and confirmed by the Court of Appeals.

Another decision that emphasizes the importance of the wording of the contract provision giving the wife the right of divorce is a 1937 judgment of the Tanta Shariʿa Court.[31] This judgment deemed the wife's exercise of her right to divorce herself three times (thus making the divorce irrevocable) to be invalid because the wording of the relevant provision in the marriage contract did not explicitly give her the right to divorce herself more than once. Hence, such a divorce would be revocable under the law.[32]

The wife's retention of *ʿiṣma* is allowed and exercised in Egypt today and is immediately enforceable before the registrar without recourse to the court. However, prevailing patriarchal culture and tradition discourage the inclusion of such a term in the contract, as it is socially perceived as sign of mistrust in the husband and his family. This is one of the reasons for the women's movement's recommendation to include the right of *ʿiṣma* as a standard condition in the first draft form of the New Marriage Contract in Egypt, to be deleted if it is not agreed to, rather than as something to be added. This would help to facilitate the negotiation process for the wife and her family.

The second type of wife-initiated termination provided for in the New Marriage Contract is termination for breach of a contractual condition by the husband. Under the present law, a divorce-seeking wife who has not retained the right to unilateral divorce in her marriage contract has to prove to a court fault on the part of her husband. She must also prove that such fault has caused her prejudice (*ḍarar*) of a type that would, in comparison to her peers, make the continuation of marriage impossible or impracticable. Reference to her peers is intended to incorporate by reference an objective test related to social class, level of education, and employment of the wife, which takes the diversity of custom and definition of prejudice among the various societal classes into account. In other words, it is an objective test that takes a subjective assessment into consideration.[33]

Analysis of court judgments demonstrate that proving fault and prejudice is very difficult. Cases finding such prejudice show that extreme levels of injury are required: for example, a husband's accusation of the wife and her family of theft,[34] or physical assault by the husband against the wife.[35] But testimony about overhearing marital disputes (without witnessing them in person) or "seeing the effect of battering on the wife's face without witnessing such battering or verbal abuse by the husband" is "incomplete and unacceptable as proof of prejudice."[36] These cases and others demonstrate that obtaining a divorce for prejudice through the court is largely ineffective because it is difficult to prove, costly, and time-consuming. On the other hand, if the marriage contract includes a provision that has been breached, then it is unnecessary to prove prejudice. It should be noted, however, that Law 1 of 2000, which is a procedural law applicable to all citizens, be they Muslim or Christian, has adopted the civil rules of evidence provided for under the Law on Evidence and made the Law on Procedures the basic reference applicable to any matter where Law 1 of 2000 is silent. This is a qualitative sign of progress because it has eliminated the application of Shariʿa law to matters of procedure in family disputes. This change is expected to make proof of *ḍarar* more possible for women seeking divorce for prejudice.

B. *Enforcement and Termination of the New Marriage Contract*

The current incarnation of the New Marriage Contract[37] forms part of the Marriage Registrars Regulations. These regulations provide for several optional conditions that the parties are free to incorporate (or not) in the blank page left in the marriage contract for this purpose. Skeptics opposing the marriage contract campaign have questioned the advantages of including such conditions for the purposes of enforcement and termination. The following is an analysis of the potential beneficial impact of including such conditions on the present status of family disputes in Egyptian courts.

Ownership of the Assets of the Conjugal Home

The conjugal home's contents, including furniture and other movable assets, customarily belong to the wife. Because the previous standard form of the marriage contract (passed by decree of the Minister of Justice in 1931) did not allow the incorporation of this fact into the model contract, culture devised the *qayma*, the trust receipt described above.[38] But the *qayma* is an unhealthy solution to an unhealthy imbalance in the marital relationship. It does not address the underlying cause of the imbalance. The husband has unrestricted powers of divorce under the law, so instead of regulating their use in order to avoid abuse, the *qayma* gives the wife or her family a weapon by which she may use the law strategically to restore the balance of power by threatening the husband with criminal proceedings, in case of need. This solution promotes litigation and encourages animosity and divorce rather than promoting amicable settlement. In the absence of a written contract or *qayma*, both the husband and the wife may file petitions claiming ownership of the contents of the conjugal home. Either party would have to present invoices or other documentary evidence of ownership of all or part of such contents in order to prevail in court.

In many cases it becomes very difficult to prove ownership of assets after many years of marriage. The stronger party is then induced to take possession of the assets using physical force, resulting in complaints of misdemeanors of theft or misappropriation. If there is a *qayma*, whether it is true or fictitious, it usually takes the form of a trust receipt. This form usually encourages the wife to file a misdemeanor complaint against the husband for misappropriation or breach of trust, which in turn encourages the husband to file a counter-complaint against the wife accusing her, for example, of theft of funds or movables belonging to the husband from the conjugal home. These claims are likely to occur in addition to the civil cases filed by each of the parties claiming ownership of the assets, compensation, or both.

By way of contrast, if the marriage contract (which is an official legal document registered with the Ministry of Justice) included a provision determining the ownership of the assets and contents of the conjugal home, in case of divorce, any relevant dispute would be resolved as follows. If the marriage contract provided that ownership vests with the wife, she could, if she wished to leave the conjugal home and take possession of her assets, report to the police and obtain their support to enforce her right to take possession of the assets, in reliance upon the provisions of her marriage contract. If the husband filed an action before the court to challenge her rights, his case would be rejected immediately based on the explicit provisions of the marriage contract. Alternatively, if the marriage contract provided that the contents of the conjugal home belong to the husband, he would follow the same procedures as above, if he were obliged to leave the home. If the wife had to leave, it would suffice, to eliminate any risk of abusive litigation, to report to the police that she has left the conjugal home and ask them to verify and register in their report that she has left its contents in it. Hence, a written agreement in the marriage contract on the ownership of the contents and movable assets of the conjugal home would eliminate a large amount of criminal litigation and possibly civil claims, replace the unhealthy tradition of the *qayma*, and possibly even promote amicable settlement between the husband and the wife, whether through conciliation or amicable termination.

### The Conjugal Home

According to the present law,[39] if the conjugal home belongs to the husband by ownership or lease rights, a divorced wife must leave the home if she does not have custody of the children. If she does have custody, the husband has to leave the conjugal home or provide an alternative residence for her and the children in her custody until the custody period expires.[40] In practice, according to custom, leases or title deeds of conjugal homes are written in the name of the husband, even if he has undertaken to give his wife such home or if she or her family has paid for it, in whole or in part. In case of divorce, an abusive husband obviously finds himself in a powerful position, even when the wife has custody of their children, because he can set up his former wife in an alternative residence that is usually not appropriate or of lower standard than the original home, as a sign of vengeance or punishment to the wife for obtaining a divorce, or in order to keep the better home for his future marriage. This normally results in at least two court cases over the suitability of the alternative home or the wife's right to use the original home. But an agreement in the marriage contract on this matter would enable the public prosecutor to pass a quick decision in favor of the party entitled to use of the conjugal home pursuant to the marriage contract. Court action by the other party would then be futile.

### Agreement to Payments to the Wife in Case of Divorce Against Her Will

According to the law, a wife is entitled to her deferred dower (*mahr*), financial maintenance for at least one year (*nafaqa*), and alimony for at least two years, as compensation depending on the number of years of marriage and circumstances of the divorce. Assessing the amount based on the husband's income, obtaining a judgment, and enforcing such a judgment against an abusive husband may take up to two years. Moreover, cases exist where unemployed wives are divorced after twenty to thirty years of marriage and find themselves without a home or financial support two or three years after divorce (when maintenance ends) notwithstanding such a long marriage. But if the marriage contract included conditions requiring the husband to make a flat payment or a monthly payment to the wife after divorce, the obligation would be enforceable. The court would normally issue a payment order upon request by the wife and would have no discretion as to the amount payable pursuant to the contract. This would eliminate at least litigation by the wife claiming maintenance, alimony or compensation, in which the amount due is usually underestimated and enforcement faces obstacles and suffers delays. Such conditions in the marriage contract would entitle the wife to obtain payment orders which would be easily enforceable against the husband in case of a divorce. Arguments have been made by the women's movement that the amount of compensation agreed in the marriage contract should be subject to an index or any similar mechanism, to allow adjustment for inflation in case of divorce of long-married women.

### The Wife's Right to Work, Continue Education or Travel Outside of Egypt

The present personal status rules contradict the constitution by making the wife's exercise of her constitutional right to work, continue her education or travel out of Egypt subject to the husband's consent. This requirement is based on the law as amended in 1985,[41] which confirms that the husband has an obligation to financially maintain his wife, beginning at the date of a valid marriage contract, provided she delivers or is deemed to have delivered herself to him, meaning she has agreed to consummate the marriage.[42] This law, which is based on the principles of Shariʿa, uses the economic power of "financial maintenance" to give the husband certain superior rights of control. His obligation to provide financial maintenance has thus been interpreted to mean an obligation on the part of the wife to be obedient to his wishes. The law, however, recognizes that the only penalty for disobedience by the wife is suspension or lapse of her right to financial maintenance.

The law provides that the wife does not need permission if she leaves the home for reasons authorized by Shariʿa, permitted by custom or for work, unless she abuses her right to work and the husband requests that she not do so. But court precedents show that the wife's right to work is not subject to the husband's permission if such was stipulated in the marriage contract, if the husband knew before marriage of his wife's work and did not object, if the wife worked after marriage and he did not object, or finally if she had to work because of financial need.[43] The stipulation in the New Marriage Contract regarding a woman's right to work was subject to fierce debate among members of the women's movement in Egypt. Some refused to include it in the proposed options, as it raised doubt about individual constitutional rights (to work, education, and travel) which should not be questioned. They argued that the mere suggestion that such matters were subject to a contractual agreement violated the constitution and the human rights of women. Others responded that there was no doubt that women's rights to work, continue education, and travel are constitutional human rights; however, there is a need to face the reality of the personal status laws, custom, and traditions under which a wife requires her husband's consent in order to work, without risking loss of her rights to financial maintenance.

The latter trend also argued that there was a need to challenge the existing patriarchal culture and to change the personal status laws. Assertion of a wife's rights in the marriage contract constitutes one strategy to induce such changes. Thus, if wives asserted their constitutional rights under the marriage contract, these rights would be upheld by the court in case of dispute. Agreement in the marriage contract on the wife's right to continue higher education, for example, which may involve cost or travel to foreign research institutes, would eliminate future disputes or abusive denial of such rights by the husband. Similarly, recording in the marriage contract that the wife works would eliminate the need for at least two court cases—one by the wife claiming financial maintenance and the other by the husband claiming that she is abusing her right to work against the best interests of the family and that, therefore, she is *nāshiz* (disobedient) and does not deserve financial maintenance. A third case would then have to be filed by the wife in case the husband objected to her right to travel for work or otherwise. The court is likely to reject the husband's claim and grant her a favorable judgment if she proves that her husband had previously consented to her right to travel and that travel was required as part of her employment obligations. If the marriage contract included confirmation of these rights, the courts would have no discretion and would have to uphold the wife's request and reject any challenge by the husband. If the husband denied his wife any of these rights and filed an "action for obedience" against her, or divorced her abusively for exercising any of those rights, the action for obedience would be rejected and the court would automatically deem the divorce abusive for breach of contract. The court in both cases would confirm the wife's legitimate right to financial maintenance and deferred dower as well as alimony in the case of divorce. Moreover, the wife would be entitled to terminate the contract and obtain a judgment of divorce for prejudice, without losing her financial rights or giving up such rights, based on the husband's breach of contract, without having to prove prejudice or that such prejudice made the continuation of marriage impossible, as compared to the situations of her peers. It should be noted that Law 1 of 2000 on Certain Issues and Procedures in Personal Status Matters gives the competent judge exclusive jurisdiction to issue *ex parte* orders preventing the husband, the wife or their children from travel, confirming that the judge could only issue such an order for good cause and thus take that power away from husbands. This provision was included in response to several cases of abuse, which involved women occupying senior governmental positions who were unable to travel because their husbands withheld their permission. Moreover, in 2001 the Supreme Constitutional Court issued a judgment declaring the provisions of a decree by the Minister of the Interior requiring the husband's permission as a condition for issue or renewal of the wife's passport to be unconstitutional. As a result, a husband cannot at present unilaterally stop his wife from traveling by withdrawing his permission to the government to issue her a passport. However, a husband or indeed a wife may apply for an *ex parte* court order to stop the other party from traveling for good cause.

### Agreement Not to Take a Second Wife

According to the personal status law as amended in 1985,[44] a wife may request a divorce if her husband takes a second wife, if she suffers material or moral prejudice as a result of the second marriage, of a nature such as makes the continuation of marriage impracticable among her social peers, even if she has not stipulated in her marriage contract that the husband should not take a second wife.[45] Hence, an action for divorce initiated by the wife in such a case must be supported by evidence that the second marriage has, in fact, caused her material or moral prejudice. Such prejudice is no longer assumed, as was the case under the 1979 Law (which was ruled unconstitutional in 1985).[46] On the other hand, if the marriage contract included a condition that the husband would not take a second wife, prejudice would be assumed without any need for evidence. The court would in such a case be bound to grant the wife divorce for prejudice based on the husband's breach of contract and would confirm all the wife's financial rights under the contract, including compensation for damages suffered.

### The Wife's Right of Divorce (*ʿiṣma*)

A wife's right to delegated divorce (*ʿiṣma*) is a legitimate right under the principles of Shariʿa, and its inclusion in the marriage contract gives the wife the right to divorce herself before the marriage registrar, without recourse to the court. Moreover, it does not prejudice the husband's right to divorce, contrary to popular belief. The legal effect of this condition is to confirm equal rights of termination for both the husband and the wife. This is a natural reflection of the contractual nature of the marriage contract. If a contract is concluded based on mutual consent, it is natural to require termination by mutual consent or provide for a unilateral right of termination by either party. In addition, including this condition in the marriage contract would save the wife lengthy, costly, and strenuous procedures before the court—which could continue for as long as seven or eight years without success—or alternatively would save her the loss of her financial rights to deferred dower and financial maintenance as in the case of *khulʿ*.

## Conclusion

In conclusion, the issuance of the new standard form marriage contract by the Egyptian Minister of Justice in 2000, in response to a long struggle by women activists, recognized a much needed Islamic law-based solution to the inequities present in existing Egyptian family law. The primary mechanism for women's empowerment under this recent Islamic Marriage Contract model is the enforceability of stipulations in the contract (a practice brought in by Islamic law, improving on the already existing ancient Egyptian practice of marriage contracts). The above conditions, which are proposed to be included by young men and women in their marriage contracts, are all legitimate rights of women under the principles of Shariʿa which are denied or restricted by the Egyptian personal status laws or by culture and tradition.

To make the New Marriage Contract enforceable, these conditions would be upheld by the courts through either strict performance or as an acceptable basis for compensation or for termination of the marriage contract for breach. These conditions are provided as options to be either included or not included in the marriage contract, as mutually and freely agreed by the husband and the wife. Specifying these options in the Marriage Registrars Regulations and obliging the Marriage Registrar to inform the couple of the options enables the couple to make their decision based on informed choice, rather than on popular misinterpretations of religion. Moreover, each agreed condition in a marriage contract would result in a decrease in the amount of divorce litigation in Egypt, in addition to promoting amicable settlement of disputes between the parties and increasing the chances of conciliation. Finally, including these conditions as standardized options approved by a decree of the Minister of Justice based on an opinion by the Grand Mufti sends a clear message that these conditions are legitimate and comply with the principles of Shariʿa. This, in addition to awareness-raising campaigns by NGOs and through the media, would encourage the application of these conditions and challenge the existing patriarchal culture and its popular misinterpretation and exploitation of religion to justify discrimination against women.

NOTES

1 Dr. F. Naguib, from a lecture entitled "The Marriage Contract in Egypt" given to the Judges Club, Cairo, June 1994.

2 Ahmed 1992, 45, 62, 63.

3 Idem.

4 Qurʾan 2:229.

5 Provisions that would be contrary to public policy include, for example, temporary marriage (in Sunni law) or polyandry.

6 Fahmy 1946.

7 Durant 1962, 265.

8 Abdal-Rehim 1996.

9 Hourani 1992, 119–121.

10 Egyptian Law No. 25 of 1920.

11 Idem.

12 This is contrary to the practice during the Ottoman period when experienced women required a larger amount of advanced dower because the deferred dower was often subject to dispute. Abdal-Rehim 1996.

13 Constitution of 1971, Art. 11 (Egypt).

14 Amira El Azhary Sonbol, paper given at the Marriage Contract in Islam workshop at Harvard Law School, May 30 and 31, 1997. On file with the author.

15 Zulficar 1995.

16 Zulficar et al. 1992.

17 Idem.

[18] See Appendices for text of various drafts of the New Marriage Contract.

[19] National NGO Committee "Egyptian NGO Platform Document for the ICPD" 1994, 35–36.

[20] See Appendix 2 for text of this draft of the contract.

[21] See Appendix 3.

[22] Al-Azhar is one of the most historical and respected centers of Islamic learning in the world.

[23] See Appendix 3.

[24] Egyptian Law 44 of 1979, amending certain provisions of Law 25 of 1920.

[25] Egyptian Law 100 of 1985, amending certain provisions of Law 25 of 1920.

[26] Kamāl 1993, 94.

[27] The Hanbali school was, in fact, common in Egypt during and before the Ottoman period and was applied in that country until the 1930s.

[28] A committee is formed by a decision of the Minister of Justice for the purpose of drafting each law.

[29] Raḍwān 1993, 51.

[30] *Majallat Muḥāmā al-Sharʿiyya*, year 34, 1932, pages 370–371 (citation omitted).

[31] *Majallat Muḥāmā al-Sharʿiyya*, year 7, pages 81–83.

[32] Law 25 of 1929, Art. 5. This article considers any divorce as revocable except the third divorce, divorce before consummation of the marriage, divorce in consideration of a waiver of the husband's financial obligations—which is a type of *khulʿ*, or divorce for a defect in the husband, for mistreatment and desertion, for taking a second wife, or for absence or imprisonment of the husband. In the case of an irrevocable divorce, except for the third divorce, a new contract of marriage and a new dower are required in order for the couple to resume married life. A revocable divorce allows unilateral revalidation of the original marriage contract by the husband within the waiting period.

[33] "The Supreme Court has consistently decided that the criterion for assessment of prejudice under Article (6) of Law 25 for 1929 is a subjective criterion and not material. However, the assessment whether such prejudice makes continuation of marriage between the husband and wife impossible is a substantive matter left to the discretion of the substantive court and its assessment differs depending on the [social] environment of the married couple, their culture and social milieu. As the judgment appealed [by the husband] has concluded that continuation of marriage between the parties is not possible, to the extent that the husband has accused the wife and her family of theft and several court cases have been filed, then the contested judgment [giving her divorce for prejudice] is valid." Supreme Court Judgment of Nov. 1, 1978 at 1674; Supreme Court Judgment of Mar. 29, 1967 at 697, Technical Office Compilation.

[34] Supreme Court Judgment of Nov. 1, 1978 at 1674; Supreme Court Judgment of Mar. 29, 1967 at 697, Technical Office Compilation.

[35] Supreme Court Judgment of Nov. 9, 1977 at 1644, Technical Office Compilation (case involving husband breaking wife's necklace, dirtying her clothes, and inducing people in the street to encircle her).

[36] Supreme Court Judgment of June 11, 1991, Appeal No. 36 for 59J.

[37] See Appendix 3.

[38] See supra p. 235.

[39] Law 25 of 1920, as amended by Law 100 of 1985.

[40] The mother has custody of her minor children until they reach the age of fifteen, or until marriage for her minor daughters, as determined by the judge.

[41] Law 25 of 1920, Art. 1.

[42] Financial maintenance is not due to the wife if she gives up her religion, refuses to consummate the marriage or leaves the conjugal home without her husband's permission, which includes implicitly travel out of Egypt.

[43] Kamāl 1993, 10.

[44] Law 20 of 1925, Art 11, added by Law 100 of 1985.

[45] For example, in one case the Supreme Court held that:

> The conclusion of the appealed judgment based on the testimony of witnesses, that the Plaintiff's (husband's) taking a second wife and living with his second wife in the conjugal home of the Defendant (the first wife) constitutes persistence by the husband in causing her material and moral damage, is valid.

Supreme Court, Case No. 129 for Year 59J of 5/3/1991.

[46] See supra p. 241.

# APPENDIX 1

## 1st Draft of the New Marriage Contract

## Certification of Marriage Contract

On the ______ day of ______, at _____ o'clock,

In the presence and by the hand of ______________, Registrar of ____________ district which lies within the jurisdiction of the Personal Status Court of ____ ______, at the house situated at _______________, the following Marriage/ Reinstatement Contract was issued:

First: (1) Name of Husband:

Occupation:
Nationality:
Date of Birth:
Domicile:
ID No., date and place of issue:
Name of husband's mother:
Name of his other wife or wives at date of Contract, if any, and their domicile(s):
Place in which husband's family is registered in the Civil Registry:
Town or Village:
District:
No.:
Civil Registry:

Has Married/Reinstated:

(2) Name of Wife:

Occupation:
Nationality:
Date of Birth:
Place of Birth:
ID No., date and place of issue:
Name of wife's mother:
Name of former husband and date of divorce, if any:
Place of registration of wife's family in the Civil Registry:
Town or Village:
District:
No.:
Civil Registry:

In legal matrimony according to Shariʿa Law and Sunni scriptures, with legal consent and acceptance between the husband and the wife or the Attorney she has appointed and empowered before us and in our presence to conclude this Contract and receive the dowry on her behalf, after identifying them by legal means of identification and ascertaining that no legal impediments to the marriage exist in either party and ascertaining also that:

(a) The Husband:

Receives a salary, pension or income amounting to L.E. _______ per month and is capable of earning money and providing for his wife and their offspring.

Has/Does not have property in excess of L.E. 500.

Is married/not married to another woman and, in case he is married, she has been/will be notified of this marriage by me in accordance with law.

(b) The Wife:

Has/Does not have a pension or salary from the government or from her place of employment.

Is a minor having/not having property in excess of L.E. 500.

(c) The spouses are of marriageable age as shown above.
(d) The spouses have undergone the special medical examinations and have submitted results which confirm that they are free of any disease preventing their marriage.

Second:

The parties have agreed on *ṣadāq* as follows:

| | |
|---|---|
| Immediately due: | Received by: |
| Deferred amount thereof: | Until legally due: |

Third:

The parties agree as follows:

1. To treat one another in a kind and humane manner, to cohabit and cooperate in work and in caring for the affairs of the family, the home and the raising of the children.
2. The husband shall be bound alone/jointly with the wife to provide a suitable independent/joint conjugal home, and the wife shall be bound alone/jointly with the husband to provide the necessary furniture.
3. The husband shall not marry another woman without the wife's knowledge and consent; otherwise the wife shall be permitted to divorce herself without need to prove damage.

4. The wife shall be entitled to exercise her right to education and to work outside the home.
5. Either party may work outside Egypt for a period of up to three years in which case the other party shall be bound to accompany the departing spouse abroad, without prejudice to the interest of the children, if any, and subject to availability of adequate educational facilities in the new place of residence.
6. The wife shall have the right to divorce herself, especially if the husband takes another wife without her knowledge and consent, if he mistreats her or their children, if she declares that cohabitation between them has become impracticable or if he deserts her for a period of not less than eight months.
7. The husband shall be bound to provide for his wife and family at a standard conforming to the standard of living of the families of the spouses at the time of their marriage.
8. The wife—especially the working wife—shall be bound to contribute to the living expenses of the family, without prejudice to the husband's obligation to provide for his family.
9. In the event that he divorces his wife against her will after a marriage that has lasted more than fifteen years, the husband shall be bound to waive his right to the conjugal home in favor of the wife and their offspring, if any, even after the expiry of the wife's legal custody period of their children.
10. In the event that she divorces herself against the husband's will, the wife shall be bound to waive her right to the deferred dowry and the alimony, including "muṭʿa" alimony.

Fourth:

This Contract has been witnessed by:

Name:
ID No.:
Nationality:
Date and Place of Birth:

Standing as surety for the husband is ____________________ whose suretyship was accepted by ____________________ at the time of the signing hereof and this Contract is made in one original and three copies, one delivered to the husband, one to the wife or her attorney, and the third to the Civil Registry.

Date:

Duties in the amount of:
Remitted on:

The following have affixed their signatures hereto before us:

The witnesses:
The husband:
The wife:
Attorney for the wife:
The Registrar:

N.B. In case the parties do not wish to include any of the conditions set forth in "Third" above, such condition shall be crossed out, signed and stamped with the Seal of State.

# APPENDIX 2

## 2nd Draft of the New Marriage Contract
Developed by National Women's Commission and Ministry of Justice
(including medical examination and photos)

Questions posed to each of the Husband and Wife who replied as follows:

1. Do you agree that your wife should continue her postgraduate studies?

| Agree | Disagree |
|---|---|

2. Do you agree that your wife takes future employment?

| Agree | Disagree |
|---|---|

3. Do you agree that your wife may change her job to any other job that is compatible with her qualifications?

| Agree | Disagree |
|---|---|

4. Do you agree that your wife may travel for a legitimate cause outside Egypt with the children or without the children?

| Agree | Disagree |
|---|---|

5. Do you agree not to take a second wife and that if you do take a second wife, your first wife may divorce herself?

| Agree | Disagree |
|---|---|

6. Do you agree, in case you divorce your wife, for reasons not due to her fault, to compensate your wife in addition to her legal rights? If yes, will the compensation be a lump sum or a monthly payment? Please indicate amount and term.

| Agree | Disagree |
|---|---|

7. What have you agreed upon in relation to the marital home in case of divorce, without prejudice to and in addition to the rights prescribed by law?
8. What have you agreed upon in relation to the furniture and moveables in the marital home, in case of divorce?
9. Do you agree that your wife may divorce herself if she waives all her financial rights?

| Agree | Disagree |
|---|---|

I have advised each party of the other party responses.

Additional Conditions:

By the Husband:

| Agreed to by the Wife | Disagreed to by the Wife |
| --- | --- |

By the Wife:

| Agreed to by the Husband | Disagreed to by the Husband |
| --- | --- |

# APPENDIX 3

## 3rd Draft of the New Marriage Contract
Joint NGO/Ministry of Justice Draft
(approved by the Grand Mufti, presently the Grand Imam Shaykh al-Azhar)
(provides for medical examination and photos)

As stipulated by Shariʿa, the following matters can be the subject of a binding agreement upon marriage. The prospective wife and husband may freely agree upon any, some or all of these matters.

1. Agreement on the ownership of the marital home's furniture and to whom it should devolve in case of divorce.
2. Agreement on who should keep the conjugal home in case of divorce, without prejudice to the current law on maternal custody.
3. A specific amount of compensation to be given in monthly installments or cash to a wife who is divorced against her will, in addition to her other legal rights.
4. The right of the wife to obtain employment and education or to continue education, as well as her right to travel abroad for a legitimate cause.
5. Agreement that the husband may not take a second wife.
6. Agreement on the wife's right to divorce herself. (This does not deprive the husband of his right to divorce her.)
7. Agreement that the wife may give up all her financial rights in exchange for an irrevocable divorce, in case such divorce is due to no fault by the husband.

In addition to agreement on the above provisions, it is legal for both parties to agree on any other matter provided that such agreement does not make illegitimate matters legitimate or vice versa.

The parties agree as follows:

______________________

______________________

______________________

# APPENDIX 4

## Form of Marriage Contract

After verification by the undersigned, Marriage Registrar of ____________ reporting to ____________ Court and examination of the ID of the husband________ _______, born in _______ governorate, _______ city, on __/__/____, and

By examination of the ID/birth certificate or medical certificate showing age by the Ministry of Health Inspector of _________ or Medical doctor of the Health Group of _____________, that the wife was born in _____________ governorate, __________ city, on __/__/____.

Both parties or their representatives have expressed their wish to notarize their marriage contract. After advising them of the legal and Shariʿa prohibitions to such marriage, both have confirmed that they are free of such prohibitions and confirmed that they are free of any diseases that permit divorce (*tafrīq*).

On this ________ day of _________ (H) and _________ (C), at _________ in the presence of the undersigned ____________ the Registrar of _________ reporting to _______________Court for Personal Status at [the place of conclusion of the contract] located at _______________.

This marriage contract has been concluded between

A. The husband ___________ concluding the contract by himself or through his representative, who is ______________.

Nationality of the husband ________ Religion _______ Date of Birth __/__/___
Place of Birth __________ Profession __________ Place of Residence __________
_________ Place of Work ___________________ ID No. __________________
Date of Issue ________________ by Civil Registrar ________________ National Registration No. ________________
Name of Mother ________________
Address for Notices _____________________________________________
Address of conjugal home ____________________________________________.

After he confirmed that he has no other wife or that he has the following wives:

1. address:
2. address:
3. address:

B. The wife _______________ (name and legal representative, if any) and status _____________ (first marriage or otherwise).

Nationality ___________ Religion ____________ Date of Birth ____________ Place of Birth ________________________ Profession _______________ Place of Residence ______________ Place of Work ____________ ID No. ____________ Date of Issue ______________ by Civil Registrar _______________ National Registration No. _______________ Name of Mother _______________ Address of Notices ____________________________________________

for a dower (*mahr*) of ([1]) of which _____________ is in advance and _____________ is deferred until it falls due according to Shariʿa, a legitimate marriage according to the Book of Allah and his Prophet on the basis of the legitimate consent by the husband/his representative and the wife/her representative.

Special Conditions

Both parties have agreed upon the following([2]) _______________
____________________________________________________________________
____________________________________________________________________
____________________________________________________________________
____________________________________________________________________
____________________________________________________________________

Number of Insurance Policy ___________________________________________

All the foregoing has been witnessed by
1. __________________ Nationality ___________ Religion ______________ Date of Birth ___________ Place of Birth ____________ Work ____________ Place of Residence _______________ Proof of Identity by _______________ Issued from _______________ Date of Issue _______________ National Registration No. _______________

2. _______________ Nationality _______________ Religion ______________ Date of Birth ___________ Place of Birth ___________ Work ______________ Place of Residence _______________ Proof of Identity by _______________ Issued from _______________Date of Issue _______________ National Registration No. _______________

Drawn in one original and three counterparts one for the husband/his representative, the second for the wife/her representative, and the third for the Civil Status Registrar Office. The original shall be kept in the Registrar.
Receipt No. _______________ dated _______________

The Husband/his representative The Wife/her representative Witnesses
1.
2.

The Marriage Registrar The Court Seal

Notes:

Article (33) 5 of the Marriage Registrars Regulations amended by Decree No. 1727/2002 reads as follows:

"The Marriage Registrar shall, before notarization of the [marriage] contract:

1.
2.
3.
4.
5. Advise the couple or their representatives of the special conditions, which may be agreed upon in the marriage contract, including for example:

    (a) agreement on which party owns the conjugal home's movables;
    (b) agreement on which party would have the sole right to benefit by the conjugal home in case of divorce or death;
    (c) agreement that the husband shall not take a second wife without the written approval of his wife;
    (d) agreement to allocate a lump sum amount or a regularly paid amount by the husband to the wife if he divorces her against her will;
    (e) agreement to delegate to the wife the right to divorce herself.

All such conditions shall be in addition to the rights determined by law and Shariʿa and without prejudice to third party rights."

# APPENDIX 5

## SELECTIONS FROM EGYPTIAN PERSONAL STATUS LAWS

A. Law Number 25 of 1929, as Amended by Law Number 100 of 1985 Concerned with Certain Matters of Personal Status

[Where significant, changes made by Law No. 100 of 1985 ("1985 Law") from the original Law No. 25 of 1929 ("Former Law") are marked: (i) where additions are made this is noted; (ii) where deletions occur, the eliminated material from the Former Law is included, italicized between square brackets.

[Also, for comparative purposes, material from Law No. 44 of 1979 (here referred to as the "1979 Law") is given italicized between square brackets. The 1979 Law, known as the "Jihan Sadat Law," was invalidated by decision of the Supreme Constitutional Court in 1985, on the ground that, in promulgating the Law by Presidential decree, President Sadat had failed to observe constitutionally mandated procedure. Except for the differences noted, the 1979 Law and the 1985 Law are virtually identical.]

I. Divorce (*ṭalāq*)

Section 1. *Ṭalāq* [pronounced] by one intoxicated or under duress has no effect.

Section 2.

Section 3. *Ṭalāq* accompanied by a number, explicitly or by a gesture, has effect only as a single [divorce].

Section 4.

Section 5. Every *ṭalāq* may be revoked, except one which completes the three, *ṭalāq* before consummation, *ṭalāq* in return for property, and *ṭalāq* which this Law... provides is final (*ṭalāq*).

Section 5 (bis) [added by 1985 Law] It is obligatory upon the divorcing husband that he record an attestation (*ishhād*) of his *ṭalāq* before the registrar with jurisdiction, within thirty days of occurrence of the *ṭalāq*.

The wife shall be considered to know of the *ṭalāq* if she is present at its recordation. If she does not attend, the registrar must inform her personally before a notary of the occurrence of the *ṭalāq*. The registrar must deliver a copy of the attestation of the *ṭalāq* to the divorced wife or one delegated by her, in accordance with procedures to be issued by decision of the Minister of Justice.

The consequences of the *ṭalāq* shall be in effect from the date of its occurrence, unless the husband conceals it from the wife, whereupon its consequences for inheritance and other property rights shall take effect only from the date of her learning of it.

[*1979 Law, Section 5 (bis):*

*The divorcing husband must at once record an attestation of his divorce before the registrar with jurisdiction.*

*The consequences of the ṭalāq with respect to the wife shall take effect only from the date of her knowledge of it.*

*The wife shall be considered to know of the ṭalāq if she is present at its recordation. If she is not present, the divorcing husband must inform her of the occurrence of the ṭalāq before a notary in person or at the place of her residence to the location of which the divorcing husband shall lead. . . .*]

II. Discord between the Spouses, and Declaration of *Ṭalāq* for Harm (*ḍarar*)

Section 6. If the wife claims that the husband has caused her harm (*ḍarar*), such that continuation of the conjugal community between spouses of their like (*amthālihim*) is impossible, she may request from the judge judicial divorce (*tafrīq*). In that event the judge shall declare against him her divorce (*ṭalāq*) by a single final *ṭalāq*, if *ḍarar* is proved and he is unable to reach reconciliation between them. If [the judge] refused the request, and she repeats the complaint, and *ḍarar* is not proved, the judge shall appoint two arbitrators, and give judgment in the manner set forth in sections 7, 8, 9, 10 and 11.

Section 7. It is required of the two arbitrators that they be persons [Former Law: men] of good character (*ʿadl*) from the families of the spouses if possible, and if not, then from others who have knowledge of their situation and have capacity to achieve reconciliation between them.

[Sections 8–11 of the Former Law were entirely replaced in the 1985 Law. The former provisions are as follows:

Section 8. The two arbitrators must apprise themselves of the causes of the discord, and exert themselves toward reconciliation. If [reconciliation] is possible by a specific method, they may decide upon [that method].

Section 9. If the two arbitrators are unable to achieve reconciliation, and the fault is the husband's, or of them both, or it is unknown [which is at fault], then the [arbitrators] shall decide upon judicial divorce (*tafrīq*) by a single, final divorce.

Section 10. If the two arbitrators differ, the judge shall order them to study the matter again, and if the difference continues between them, others shall be appointed.

Section 11. The two arbitrators must submit to the judge what they decide upon, and the judge must give judgment in accordance with that.]

Section 8 [entirely new in 1985 Law but amended by Law 1 of 2000 to provide for a maximum of two months for reconciliation procedures by arbitrators].

a) [A time limit of six months is fixed for the arbitrators to achieve reconciliation]
b) [The court may allow an additional period of up to three months]

Section 9 [entirely new in 1985 Law]. The conduct of the work of the arbitrators shall be unaffected by the failure of one of the spouses to attend a session of arbitration, if he was notified.

The two arbitrators must inform themselves of the causes of the dispute between the parties and exert their effort to reconcile them in any manner possible.

Section 10 [entirely new in 1985 Law]. If the two arbitrators cannot achieve reconciliation,

a) If all the fault is on the part of the husband, the arbitrators shall suggest judicial *taṭlīq* by a final *taṭlīq*, without thereby affecting any right of the wife deriving from the marriage or the *taṭlīq*.
b) If all the fault is on the part of the wife, they shall suggest judicial *taṭlīq* against an appropriate compensation which they will estimate, to which the wife shall be obligated.
c) If the fault is shared they shall suggest judicial *taṭlīq* without a compensation, or with a compensation appropriate to the degree of fault.
d) If the case is unknown, and it is unknown which of them is at fault, the arbitrators shall suggest a judicial *taṭlīq* without compensation.

Section 11 [entirely new in 1985 Law]. The arbitrators must submit their report to the court stating the causes upon which it is based. If they do not agree, it shall reappoint them, with another [arbitrator]...If they differ or do not submit their report within the time specified, the court shall undertake evidentiary [proceedings]. If the court is unable to achieve agreement between the two spouses, and it becomes clear to it that marital life between them is impossible, and the wife insists on *taṭlīq*, the court shall give judgment declaring *taṭlīq* between them by a single final *taṭlīq*. [The judgment shall include] termination of all of the property rights of the wife, or of some of them, and also an obligation on her to pay the appropriate compensation, if there is a need for any such measures.

Section 11 (bis) [added by 1985 Law] It is incumbent on the husband that he acknowledge in the document of marriage his marital status. If he is married, then he must clarify in the acknowledgement the name of the wife or wives to whom he is married, and the places of their residence. The registrar must inform them of the new marriage by a registered letter entailing knowledge of receipt.

It is permitted to the wife whose husband has married another wife that she request divorce (*taṭlīq*) from him, if she suffers harm (*ḍarar*), whether material or moral, which makes it impossible to maintain the conjugal community between two of their like (*amthālihim*), even if she had not imposed in the contract a condition that he not marry another wife.

[*1979 Law, Section 6 (bis):*

*...It is considered an act harmful to the wife the joining of her husband with another wife without her consent, even if she had not provided against a second marriage as a condition in the contract of her marriage.....*

If the judge is unable to reconcile them, he shall declare *taṭlīq* by a final *taṭlīq*. The right of the wife to request divorce (*taṭlīq*) for this reason shall fail on passage of one year from the date of her knowledge of the marriage with another, unless she had consented to this explicitly or implicitly. Her right to request divorce shall revive every time he marries another.

*The right of the wife to request judicial divorce (*tafrīq*) shall fail with the passage of one year [the rest substantially the same]*

If the new wife did not know that he was married to another, and then it appears that he is married, she also has the right to request divorce (*taṭlīq*).]

Section 11 (ter) [added by 1985 Law] If the wife refuses to obey the husband without right, the *nafaqa* of the wife is suspended from the date of refusal.

She shall be considered refusing without right if she does not return to the marital home after the invitation of the husband to her to return, by notice before a notary in her presence or in the presence of one who is delegated by her. He must declare in this notice the place of residence.

The wife has the right to object to this before the Court of First Instance within thirty days of the date of this notice. She must declare in the objection document the legal grounds on which she relies in her refusal to obey him, and if she fails to do so, judgment shall be given denying her objection.

The suspension of the *nafaqa* shall obtain from the date of termination of period of objection, if she does not present it within the period.

The court on considering the objection, or upon the request of one of the spouses, shall intervene to end the dispute between them by a compromise which continues the marriage and proper marital relations. If it is clear to [the court] that the difference is deep-rooted, and the wife requests declaration of *ṭalāq*, then the court shall undertake the arbitration procedures set forth in sections 7 through 11 of this Law.

V. Support (*nafaqa*) and the waiting period (*ʿidda*)

Section 17. No claim shall be heard for *nafaqa* during an *ʿidda* for a period exceeding one year from the date of the *ṭalāq*.

Likewise, there shall not be heard a contested claim for inheritance by reason of marriage of a divorced wife whose husband died more than one year before the date of the *ṭalāq*.

...

Section 18 (bis) [added by 1985 Law]. The wife with whom a valid marriage has been consummated, who is divorced by her husband by *ṭalāq* without her consent or without a cause arising from her, is entitled, above the *nafaqa* for her *ʿidda*, to a *mutʿa* payment in the amount of two years' *nafaqa* at least, [the latter fixed] with regard to the situation of the divorcing husband as to whether he is well-off or poor, the conditions of the *ṭalāq*, and the period of the marriage. The divorcing husband may be allowed to pay the *mutʿa* in installments.

Section 18 (ter) [added by 1985 Law] [Provides for father's obligation to pay child support]

Section 18 (quater) [added by 1985 Law] The divorcing husband must provide for his minor children from his divorced wife and for their female custodian an appropriate independent residence. If he does not do this during the period of the *ʿidda*, they shall continue to occupy the rented marital residence, without [the presence of] the divorcing husband, for the period of the custody.

If the marital residence is not rented, the divorcing husband has the right to live there independently if he obtains for them an independent appropriate residence after the end of the period of the *ʿidda*.

The judge shall give the female custodian the choice between independent residence in the marital residence and the fixing for her of a rent for an appropriate residence for the children in her custody and herself.

...

[*The divorced wife who has custody has the right after her divorce to remain independently with her children in the rented marital residence, as long as the divorcing husband has not provided another appropriate residence. When the custody is ended, or the divorced wife remarries, then the divorcing husband has the right to occupy without the divorced wife the same residence, if he has the legal right to resume use of it.*]

...

VII. Age of Custody

Section 20. [Former Law: The judge may permit women's custody of the male child after seven years [of age], up to nine [years of age], and of the female child after nine years [of age] until eleven years [of age], if it is clear that the interests of [the child] require this.]

The right of women's custody shall terminate for the male child on his attaining the age of ten years, and for the female child her attaining the age of twelve years. The judge may, after these ages, maintain under female custody the male child until the age of fifteen and the female child until she is married, but without the custody wage, if it is clear that the interests of [the child] require this.

...

IX. General Provisions

Section 23 (bis) [added by 1985 Law] The divorcing husband shall be punished with imprisonment for a period not exceeding six months, or a fine not exceeding two hundred pounds, or both, if he violates any of the provisions of Section 5 (bis) of this Law.

The husband shall be punished with the same punishment if he gives to the registrar false declarations of his marital status or of the places of residence of his wife or wives or divorced wife in violation of that provided in Section 11 (bis).

B. Law No. 25 of 1920, as Amended by Law No. 100 of 1985 Concerned with Support (*nafaqa*) and Certain Matters of Personal Status

[Again, deleted material from the original law, here Law Number 25 of 1920 ("Former Law"), is marked in italics between square brackets.]

Section 1. [Former Law: The support (*nafaqa*) of the wife who submits herself to her husband, even if only constructively, is considered a debt owing by him from the time of the husband's refusal to pay it despite its being obligatory, without [this obligation] being dependent upon judicial action or agreement between the two [parties]. The obligation to pay it is cancelled only by payment or release.]

The support (*nafaqa*) of the wife is obligatory on the husband from the date of the valid contract if she submits herself to him, even if only constructively, and even if she is well-to-do or differs with him in religion.

Illness of the wife does not bar her right to *nafaqa*.

The *nafaqa* includes food, clothing, housing, costs of cure, and other items required by the Shariʿa.

The *nafaqa* is not owed to the wife if she apostatizes, or refuses of her will to submit herself without right, or is forced to this for a reason not attributable to the husband, or she leaves [the home] without the consent of her husband.

It shall not be considered a cause for the termination [of the obligation to pay the] *nafaqa* of the wife her leaving the marital home, without the permission of her husband, in cases which are permitted to her by the ruling of the Shariʿa, in accordance with that on which there appears a text or prevails a custom, or which is required by a necessity, or her leaving for lawful work, as long as it does not appear that her exercise of this lawful right is vitiated by abuse of the right, or contradicts the interests of the family and the husband requests her to cease it.

C. Law No. 1 Year 2000[3] on Issuance of the Law Organizing Certain Issues and Procedures in Personal Status Matters

First Section. The attached law applies to adjudicative procedures in matters of personal status and *waqf* and applies to those matters on which there is no specific text in the rules of the Code of Civil and Commercial Procedure, the rules of the Code of Evidence in Civil and Commercial Matters, and the rules of the Civil Code in matters of administration and liquidation of estates.

...

Fourth Section. The Regulation Organizing the Shariʿa Courts issued by decree law no 87 year 1931 is repealed.... [Numerous other procedural laws are repealed also.]

* * * *

## LAW ORGANIZING CERTAIN ISSUES AND PROCEDURES IN PERSONAL STATUS MATTERS

* * * *

### Third Chapter
### Complaint and Trial

First Section
In Matters of Guardianship of the Person

Sec. 16....

Sec. 17....

Sec. 18. As to claims for guardianship of the person, the court must propose settlement (*ṣulḥ*) to the litigants. One who fails to attend the settlement conference despite his knowledge of it and without acceptable excuse shall be considered to reject the settlement.

As to claims of *ṭalāq* and *taṭlīq* (court-declared *ṭalāq*), no judgment shall be issued in either unless the court exerts effort to attempt settlement between the spouses and is unable to attain it. If the spouses have a child, the court shall offer settlement twice at least over a period of no less than thirty days and no more than sixty days.

Sec. 19. In claims for *taṭlīq* (court-declared *ṭalāq*) for which the law requires appointing two arbitrators, the court must charge each of the two spouses to name an arbitrator from his family—insofar as possible—in the next following session at most. If either of them fails to appoint his arbitrator or neglects to attend this session, the court shall appoint the arbitrator for him.

The two arbitrators are obliged to appear before the court at the next session for it to appoint them to decide whatever they may arrive at together. If they differ or one of them fails to attend, the court shall hear their statements or the statement of whichever of them is present after the swearing of the oath.

The court has the right to adopt whatever the two arbitrators arrive at, the statements of either of them, or anything else recorded in the papers of the case.

Sec. 20. The two spouses may reach agreement between them on *khulʿ*. If they do not reach agreement upon it, and the wife brings her complaint seeking (*khulʿ*), releasing herself and seeking *khulʿ* from her husband by surrendering all her Shariʿa financial rights, and returning to him her advanced dower that he gave to her, the court shall give judgment against the husband for her *taṭlīq*.

The court shall not give judgment of *taṭlīq* for *khulʿ* except after attempting settlement between the spouses and appointing two arbitrators to pursue efforts at settlement between the spouses during a period not to exceed three months in the manner explained in paragraph two of Sec. 18 and the first and second paragraphs of sec. 19 of this law, and after the wife has declared clearly that she hates life with her husband, that there is no way to continue married life between them, and that she fears that she will not uphold the limits of God because of this hatred.

The consideration for *khulʿ* shall not include surrender of the custody (*ḥaḍāna*) of small children, their maintenance (*nafaqa*), or any other right that they have.

*Khulʿ* results in every case in a final *taṭlīq*.

The judgment in every case shall not be subject to appeal in any manner.

Sec. 21. In the event of its denial no proof of *ṭalāq* shall be considered unless an attestation (*ishhād*) is made and the *ṭalāq* is registered. If an attestation is made and the event is to be recorded, the marriage registrar shall make clear to the two spouses the weightiness of *ṭalāq* and invite them to choose an arbitrator from his family and an arbitrator from her family to reach reconciliation between them. If the two spouses together insist on the immediate occurrence of the *ṭalāq*, if they declare together that *ṭalāq* has already occurred, or if the husband declares that he has performed the *ṭalāq*, then the *ṭalāq* must be registered after the attestation.

All the preceding rules apply to the case where the wife requests *ṭalāq* of herself if she had reserved this right to herself in the marriage contract.

...No proof of *ṭalāq* shall be considered with respect to either of the spouses unless he, or someone delegated by him, was present during the proceedings to register it or from the date of its announcement in an official document.

Sec. 22. Without prejudice to the right of the wife to prove her husband's retraction of his divorce of her by all means of proof, there shall not be accepted in the event of denial the claim of the spouse that he retracted the divorce, as long as he did not announce this retraction in an official document before the expiration of sixty days (for a woman who is menstruating) or ninety days (for a woman whose *ʿidda* is determined by months) from the date of the registration of the divorce. This is as long as she is not pregnant and she does not admit that her *ʿidda* had not expired before she became aware of the retraction.

NOTES

[1] (*Ṣadāq*) should be written in figures and letters.

[2] Any agreed upon conditions may be included provided such conditions do not prohibit (*ḥalāl*) and do not permit (*ḥarām*) (i.e., do not violate public policy).

[3] *Official Gazette of Egypt*, No. 4 (bis) of 29 January 2000.

# *Twelve*

## ADVOCACY FOR REFORM IN ISLAMIC FAMILY LAW: THE EXPERIENCE OF SISTERS IN ISLAM

Zainah Anwar

### Introduction

Muslim women in Southeast Asian countries, in particular countries like Malaysia and Indonesia, have traditionally enjoyed many more freedoms and rights than their sisters in the Middle East and South Asia. In Malay society, as in other Southeast Asian systems, cultural traditions or customs known as *adat* define and affirm women's roles and their public contribution or participation, often in positive, non-hierarchical ways.[1] Thus Malay-Muslim society has evolved in this part of the world in ways that recognize women's role in the public space and women's right to be treated as independent individuals. Women have always owned and inherited property in Malaysia. Women work outside the home, whether as farmers in an agrarian society, factory workers, teachers, lawyers, doctors, engineers or chief executives in today's industrializing and modernizing society. Seclusion, or purdah, is not part of Malay culture. Women are not expected to veil when outside their home, and men and women mix freely in the public space, whether at work, weddings or other public functions. Women have never needed the written permission of their husbands or male guardians to obtain a passport or travel abroad. There has never been a tradition of segregated women's rooms or quarters in a Malay household. Women today enjoy equal access to education. Almost seventy percent of students in the public universities are women because girls are outperforming boys in their studies, a trend reflected in many other societies in both the west and east. Forty-eight percent of Malaysian women are in the workforce.

The advances women have made in Malaysia and the recognition of women's right to public life led to a remarkable program of codification of a uniform Islamic Family Law in the early 1980s, resulting in legislation that was among the most enlightened in the Muslim world at that time.[2] It granted women many rights and protections from injustice. The new law introduced five strict conditions that a husband must fulfill before permission can be granted for him to engage in polygamy: He has to prove that the intended polygamous marriage is "just and necessary," that he has the financial means to support all his wives and dependents, that he would be able to accord equal treatment to all his wives, that the proposed marriage would not cause harm to any existing wife in respect of her religion, life, body, mind, morals or property, and that there would be no reduction in the standard of living of the existing wife and dependents.[3] Polygamy can only take place with the permission of the court.

The law also provided that divorce must be pronounced only in court. Extensive grounds for divorce were extended to women. A woman is entitled to a *taʿlīq* (promise) divorce if her husband breaks the statutory marriage contract by failing to maintain her for more than four months, or by abusing her or by deserting her for over a year. Further, she is entitled to apply for a *faskh* (annulment, or court-ordered termination of marriage) divorce on twelve different grounds. This includes the ground of cruelty, defined as the husband habitually assaulting the wife or making her life miserable by cruelty of conduct, or if he has more than one wife and he fails to treat her equitably in accordance with Islamic law.[4] Even though Malaysian Muslims follow the Shafiʿi school of law, the legal drafters used the juristic principle of public interest (*maṣlaḥa*) to include the more extensive grounds for divorce found in the Maliki school.

Finally, the wife is also entitled to a division of the matrimonial property (*harta sepencarian*), whether she has financially contributed to its acquisition or not. Recognizing the principle of custom (*ʿurf*), the drafters adopted an *adat* practice that the labor and time a person puts in that enables that person's spouse to acquire assets or to enhance their value, in this case the woman playing the role of mother and wife, are taken into consideration when dividing the assets.

However, over the years, there has been a growing concern that the reassertion of conservative Islam and traditional patriarchal beliefs justified in the name of religion have been chiselling away at the rights already gained. This has led to amendments to the Islamic Family Law that are regressive and detrimental to women and that undermine women's ability to access those rights previously granted to them under the law. Like many other Muslim countries, Malaysia is caught in the throes of worldwide Islamic revivalism. Like many other countries, too, it is the rights and status of Muslim women that have become the first casualty in the battle to prove a group's Islamic credentials. Since the 1980s, the Islam traditionally practiced in Malaysia has evolved to adopt more Arabic inflections of the religion, reflecting the culture of gender and family relations of a more patriarchal and tribal Middle Eastern society.[5] Over the past several years, women in Malaysia have seen a steady erosion of their freedom and rights in the areas of law and access to justice in the Shariʿa system, social rights in the family, dress, public participation, and socialization between the sexes. Today, Malaysians see increasing segregation of men and women in public spaces. Women come under tremendous pressure to conform to a new definition of what constitutes a good Muslim woman, in terms of her role as wife and mother, and in terms of dress, conduct, and behavior at home and in public.

At both the social and political levels, the Islamic agenda in Malaysia is being dominated by the discourse of the Islamist groups, which demand the establishment of an Islamic state and implementation of Islamic laws. Their dominant influence can be seen in several new laws, policies, and amendments to existing Islamic laws, introduced in the 1990s, which increasingly reflect a trend towards repression of women's rights and the fundamental liberties of citizens living in a democratic country. In all these instances, women's groups such as Sisters in Islam[6] have led the way in protesting against these efforts to reverse the status women have enjoyed in Malaysia as well as attempts to deny Muslim women the same legal rights and protections granted to their non-Muslim sisters, as the Malaysian government responds to demands to amend or repeal discriminatory civil laws with reforms that benefit only non-Muslims.

## Amendments to Islamic Family Law Detrimental to the Rights of Muslim Women

Since the early 1990s, several states in Malaysia had adopted amendments to the Islamic Family Law, to the disadvantage of women. First, amendments allowed a polygamous marriage contracted without permission of a court to be registered, upon payment of a fine or jail sentence. This led to a proliferation of illegal polygamous marriages contracted in southern Thailand or by illegal marriage syndicates operating in Malaysia. In some states the number of polygamous marriages contracted without court permission is more than three times the number of officially sanctioned ones.[7] With the new loophole in the law, these marriages can now be registered, upon the payment of a minimum fine for breaking the law. This minimal fine does not act as a deterrent. No man has been imprisoned for breaking this law.

Second, the amendments deleted the fifth condition for polygamy, which required that there be no drop in the standard of living for the existing wife and dependents. This change makes it easier for a man to get permission to take a second wife, thereby endorsing polygamous marriages that financially harm the first wife and children. It seems this amendment was made because some religious scholars argued that this condition makes it impossible for men to be granted permission for polygamy, the standard of living of the first wife and children being inevitably affected by the existence of a second family.

Third, the amendments permitted registration of divorces pronounced outside of court. This amendment enables a court to approve divorces pronounced by a man without the court's previous permission if it is satisfied that the *ṭalāq* (repudiation) is valid. The result is similar to the amendment allowing registration of illegal polygamous marriages, thus undoing earlier salutary reforms that depended on judicial intervention. The purpose of the original law reform was to avoid some of the evils of the common practice of unilateral declarations of divorce by irresponsible husbands. If, in order to be registered, a divorce must be announced in court, then the court can require that all ancillary claims be settled before the divorce can be registered. This amendment is a serious setback, because divorce is now often granted to men without any ancillary claims being settled. Research shows that, as a result of this amendment, the number of men who unilaterally divorce their wives outside court is almost triple the number of those who applied for divorce through the court system.[8] More cruelly, there are cases where women find out that they are divorced merely through a bureaucratic letter from the Shariʿa court informing them of their husbands' unilateral act.

Other amendments eliminated a woman's right to maintenance if she committed *nushūz*[9] (disobedience, or was *nāshiz*); the right to accommodation if she committed *fāḥisha*[10] (open lewdness); and the right to seek maintenance in part from the father for an illegitimate child.[11] The amendment to terminate maintenance for a wife's being disobedient has led to widespread abuse by husbands who want to evade their responsibility to support their wives. In many divorce cases, the husband has failed to maintain his wife for years during the marriage; as part of the divorce settlement, the wife would generally submit an application for arrears in maintenance. It is common now, however, for a wife who initiates divorce to receive a letter from the husband's lawyer accusing her of *nushūz*, which she then has to disprove in court. In a number of cases studied, the court seldom asked the husband to prove his allegation of *nushūz* while the woman's evidence disproving his claim was disregarded.[12]

All these amendments taken together reflect the increasingly conservative turn that Islam in Malaysia has taken, especially with regard to the rights of women. Where is the justice in all these amendments that violate the spirit of reform and justice for women that informed the original Islamic Family Law introduced in the early 1980s? Even further discriminatory amendments were made to the Islamic Family Law between 2003 and 2005. These changes include: (1) the "just and necessary" condition in polygamy was amended to "just *or* necessary"; (2) the *faskh* grounds for divorce were extended to include men; (3) gender-neutral language is employed to enable either party to a polygamous marriage to make a claim for a division of the matrimonial assets at the time of the second or subsequent marriage, thus enabling a husband who takes a second wife to claim for a division of his wife's assets; and (4) a husband may obtain a caveat on his wife's property in order to make a legal claim for a division of her matrimonial assets.

These amendments led to public outrage and a revolt among the women senators in Parliament. This led the Malaysian cabinet in 2006 to order a further review of the amendments to deal with the complaints of injustice by Muslim women. As of May, 2007, the new amendments are drafted but are yet to be submitted to Parliament for adoption.

In Malaysia, Sisters in Islam (SIS) has played a leading role in pushing the boundaries of women's rights in Islam within the context of a fast-changing Malaysia. On the one hand, Malaysia is a country that is quickly modernizing and industrializing. It is multi-ethnic and multi-religious and relatively democratic. Its federal constitution respects fundamental liberties, outlaws discrimination on the basis of gender, and upholds the equality of persons before the law. On the other hand, Malaysia is caught up in the throes of Islamic revivalism and demands for women to play a more conservative role as obedient wife and selfless mother. Through its reading of the Qur'an, as well as through consultations and studies with Islamic scholars inside and outside the country, SIS has developed a framework and a methodology through which it argues for justice and equality for Muslim women in contentious areas such as polygamy, equal rights, dress and modesty, domestic violence, freedom of expression, and other fundamental liberties.

## SIS Advocacy Work

As part of the effort to influence law and policy making, SIS has submitted several memoranda and letters to the Malaysian government. These documents cover such issues as the appointment of women to judgeships in Shariʿa courts, the right of Muslim women to equal guardianship, reform of the laws on polygamy specifically, reform of the Islamic Family Law as a whole, the administration of justice in the Shariʿa system, and reform of the Shariʿa criminal laws. In two memoranda addressing the reforms of the Islamic Family Law as a whole, SIS expressed its concerns about provisions in the law that discriminate against women in substance or in implementation or violate women's fundamental liberties, and further offered a justification for why these provisions should be amended, including specific proposed textual changes.

Among the reforms in the Islamic Family Law sought by Sisters in Islam and other women's groups in Malaysia are: (1) to amend the standardized *taʿlīq* agreement (marriage contract) to provide for the right of a wife to obtain a divorce if her husband takes another wife; (2) to create a new provision allowing courts to order maintenance of a first wife and children, as well as to award to the first wife her share of the property jointly acquired by her and her husband prior to his second marriage;[13] (3) to provide that divorce can only be registered after a lapse of three months from the date of divorce if the Chief Registrar is satisfied that an interim order has been made for the custody and maintenance of dependent children, the maintenance and accommodation of the divorced wife, and the payment of *mut'a* (compensation) to her; (4) to make it mandatory for courts to order default judgments for dissolution of a marriage when the husband repeatedly fails to appear in court;[14] (5) to redefine *nushūz* as a disruption of marital harmony by either husband or wife and to make it an offense for the husband as well as the wife to commit and to define the husband's *nushūz* (as it is defined in the Shari'a) as "failure to provide the wife with adequate maintenance, clothing, place of abode, and her entitlements according to Shari'a"; and (6) to repeal the section of the law that states that a wife loses her right to maintenance upon her adjudication as having committed *nushūz*.

As can be expected, any movement for reform takes years. It seems easier to stop new laws from being submitted to Parliament than to amend or repeal an existing law, especially when it is made in the name of religion. The problem is compounded because in the area of religious laws, there is little consultation with stakeholders because of a common belief that only the ulema have the knowledge and the right to promulgate these laws. Yet in other areas of law reform, the government has been open to public consultation. For example, in the drafting of the Domestic Violence Act, the Child Act, and the Law Reform (Marriages and Divorce) Act that regulate the personal status of non-Muslims, extensive consultations were held with civil society groups. In the latter case, a Parliamentary Select Committee was established to travel around the country to hear submissions from the public. In the end a new personal status code that recognized equality in marriage and divorce between non-Muslim men and women was promulgated.

It was only due to the public outrage over the recent further discriminatory amendments to the Islamic Family Law that consultations were held with women's groups to review those amendments. While reform of the legal framework is important in order to set standards for the establishment of rights and remedies for women, even the best of laws designed to protect women will remain ineffective if prejudicial social attitudes prevent women from getting access to their legal rights.

In spite of the many enlightened provisions of Malaysia's Islamic Family Law, women complain endlessly of gender bias in the law's implementation. Therefore, pushing for legal reform alone without any accompanying change in attitudes and values of those who implement the law is not enough to ensure that they will be implemented in the substance and spirit in which they were originally formulated. Rights granted in law often remain on paper only because of prejudices and weaknesses in implementation and in the Shari'a court system itself. The chief problems of implementation are as follows.

First, many Shariʿa rulings display gender bias. For example, a man can divorce his wife instantaneously with just the pronouncement of *ṭalāq* (divorce by repudiation of the wife, performed by saying the word *ṭalāq* aloud three times), but a woman initiating divorce has to face procedural obstacles and delays in court before she can obtain one. This is especially so if the husband challenges the divorce. Even in cases where the woman possesses sufficient evidence to qualify her for divorce under the many conditions provided in law, once a husband challenges her petition, long delays set in. When women initiate divorce, the Shariʿa courts seem to be concerned with maintaining the marriage, against the will of the woman, the best interests of the children, the rule of law, and the principles of justice. But when a man initiates a divorce, there seems to be little interest in saving the marriage. The man's wish is usually granted in just one hearing because his ability to divorce his wife at will is considered a right in Islam.

Second, no time limit has been set for each step of the process a woman has to undergo in her application for divorce. As a result, the husband's failure to attend counseling sessions, to be present at court hearings or to attend arbitration proceedings can delay the divorce by several years. Even though the law provides that the arbiter appointed by the court can pronounce divorce on behalf of the husband if the parties fail to effect reconciliation, the courts are reluctant to use this provision, usually claiming that they do not want to take responsibility for the dissolution of a marriage.

Third, there is no uniform federal Shariʿa system in Malaysia, one which administers a single uniform Islamic family law for the whole country. Since religion is a state matter, model laws drafted at the federal level must be adopted by each state's Legislative Assembly. Laws are amended at this level, leading to varying and conflicting provisions between the different states. The local nature of the family laws enables men to forum-shop in order to take advantage of the most convenient law for personal gain. Thus, for example, in the case of Aishah Abdul Rauf v. Wan Mohd Yusof Wan Othman,[15] the defendant was able to circumvent the decision of the Selangor Shariʿah Appeal Committee (which rejected his application to marry another woman) by simply crossing the border to the State of Terengganu in order to marry. Not only does the Selangor decision have no force in another state, Terengganu's polygamy laws do not require the husband to obtain the permission of his first wife, and the applicant does not have to fulfill any specific conditions before legal permission is granted. The outcome is left entirely to the discretion of the judge. Similarly, a man who has been ordered to pay maintenance to his wife and children can easily evade payment should he move to another jurisdiction. The Shariʿa court of one state has no jurisdiction to enforce an order given by the court of another state. Instead, the aggrieved woman must begin a new application process to obtain an enforcement order from the state in which the children's father resides.

These issues represent serious and urgent problems besetting the administration of justice in the Shariʿa system in Malaysia. The situation has reached a point where women are no longer confident that they can obtain justice through the legal system and where many men feel that they can blithely ignore Shariʿa court summonses and break the law with impunity because they know that the Shariʿa court will ultimately protect their interests. Prompted by this grave situation, in 1999, SIS conducted a study of the experience of single mothers in the Shariʿa courts and identified the common problems they faced, many of which are enumerated above.

But this patchwork approach to reform the most discriminatory provisions of the Islamic Family Law has brought little success. Indeed, further discriminatory amendments were made, including some through the crafty use of gender-neutral language to extend rights traditionally enjoyed by women to men, but with no reciprocal extension of rights traditionally enjoyed by men to women.

In 2006, Sisters in Islam began to to refocus its energies, shifting from a patchwork approach to law reform to working on a comprehensive reform of the Islamic Family Law within a general framework of justice and equality. Spurred by the success of the women's movement in Morocco and the comprehensive reform of the Moudawana, the Personal Status Code, which recognizes the equality of men and women within marriage, as well as the success of other women's groups in family law reform in traditional societies such as Turkey and Fiji, many Muslim women's groups are beginning to draft new model Muslim Family Laws. An international initiative to bring together women's groups working on family law reform in Muslim contexts is also in the planning stages. It intends to generate a more informed international public debate on women's rights in Islam, increase public awareness on the necessity for reform, and share scholarship and advocacy strategies to push for the successful reform of Muslim Family Laws in many countries, including Malaysia.

The obstacles to reform remain monumental, of course. While there is growing acknowledgment among some top political and religious leaders in Malaysia of the validity of the complaints forwarded by women's groups and the necessity for reform, the system as a whole remains largely resistant to change. Because the laws in question are under state jurisdiction rather than federal, it is more difficult for women's groups to organize and advocate effectively in Malaysia, as they have to deal with fourteen separate state jurisdictions. Moreover, while the federal government is relatively sensitive to women's issues and believes in a progressive Islam that recognizes women's rights, state authorities tend to be far more conservative.

Sisters in Islam also recognizes that, while law reform is important, enlightened provisions that uphold women's rights and formally acknowledge gender equality are not enough, as the Malaysian experience has shown. Traditional attitudes and values that regard women as inferior to men influence women's access to justice. It is important that women's groups continue to work for law reform to ensure formal equality, but they must also focus on raising public consciousness on women's rights and initiate gender-sensitivity training to change widespread gender bias in the implementation of the law. In the past four years, SIS has embarked on a gender, Islam, and women's rights training program targeted at people such as journalists, lawyers, young leaders, and service group providers to build a core constituency of women and men with the courage to speak out on rights in Islam.

Law reform must also be accompanied by mobilization of public opinion to build a constituency that will support the demand for change to a level where the government can no longer afford to ignore it. Through advocacy strategies such as writing letters to the editor and press statements, holding press briefings, lobbying key decision-makers, and alliance building, SIS has created a public space that enables citizens to engage in a more informed and critical debate on these contentious issues and to demand that their voices be heard in the process of making policy in the name of Islam. It is this raised public consciousness and the support of the media in highlighting the diversity of voices in the debate on Islamic matters that are critical in stalling the efforts of the conservative and political Islamists to monopolize and impose their dominant understanding of Islam in the lawmaking process.

This is a long-term struggle, but women's groups have to work tirelessly to make their voices heard and, together with the press, maintain constant pressure on the government to respond to and recognize the right of Muslim women to be treated as human beings of equal worth and dignity, to end the use of religion to discriminate against women, and to enable them to enjoy the rights already granted to them under Malaysian law.

NOTES

1 See Othman 1997.

2 Islamic Family Law (Federal Territory) Act, 1984.

3 Idem.

4 Idem.

5 For an understanding of the radicalization of the Islamic movement in Malaysia in the 1970s and 1980s through the influence of Middle Eastern and Pakistani Islamic groups, see Anwar 1987.

6 Sisters in Islam is a research and advocacy group founded in 1987 that works on women's rights within an Islamic framework. Its objectives are to end injustice and discrimination against women, to promote a framework for women's rights

in Islam that takes into consideration the realities and experiences of women, and to create public awareness and reform laws and policies on issues of equality, justice, freedom, dignity and democracy in Islam. Sisters in Islam Home Page, http://sistersinislam.org.my (last visited April 17, 2007).

[7] For example, statistics from the Shariʿa courts in Selangor showed that in 1995, the courts granted permission for polygamy in only 82 cases. However, 350 cases of illegal polygamous marriages were recorded. By September 1996, this number had increased to 410.

[8] See Mohamad 1996.

[9] A wife is said to be *nāshiz* if she unreasonably refuses to obey the lawful wishes or commands of her husband, for example, when she withholds her association with her husband, when she leaves her husband's home against his will, or when she refuses to move with him to another home or place. Islamic Family Law (Federal Territories) Act, 1984, 59(2).

[10] Islamic Family Law (Federal Territories) Act, 1984, 71(2).

[11] The Islamic Family Law (Federal Territories) Act, 1984, 80, was amended to remove the right to make a claim against the father to maintain his illegitimate child.

[12] See Mohamad 1996.

[13] This order should be made automatically by the court without the need for an aggrieved wife to make a specific application. SIS strongly feels that it is unjust for a wife who has struggled together with her husband to uplift their standard of living to be subsequently deprived of enjoying the just fruits of her labor and be forced to sacrifice when her husband marries another woman. The interests of the aggrieved wife and children must be protected. A division of property and assets could at least mitigate some injustice, from a financial point of view.

[14] Many women have had to endure inordinate and unjust delays—often lasting several years—in their applications for divorce. SIS proposed that in the event that the husband is absent for a maximum of three occasions within a maximum time frame of six months, the court should proceed to record the pronouncement of one *ṭalāq*.

[15] Malayan Law Journal, [1990] 3 MLJ lx.

# *Thirteen*

## IMPROVING THE STATUS OF WOMEN THROUGH REFORMS IN MARRIAGE CONTRACT LAW: THE EXPERIENCE OF THE NIZARI ISMAILI COMMUNITY

Ali S. Asani

### Introduction

The patriarchal nature of Islamic religious institutions is frequently cited as a major factor contributing to the inferior status accorded to women in many Muslim societies. All over the Islamic world the authority to interpret scriptural texts traditionally has been exercised by religious scholars, the *ʿulamāʾ*, a loosely constituted group whose membership is, by tradition, largely comprised of males. Consequently, this class of scholars has promoted interpretations of the Shariʿa that are frequently patriarchal and detrimental to the position of women in many Muslim societies. In the process, as the scholar-activist Riffat Hassan points out, the *ʿulamāʾ* have arrogated to themselves the task of defining the ontological, theological, sociological, and eschatological status of Muslim women.[1]

Islamic marriage law, as traditionally formulated by the *ʿulamāʾ*, has been particularly problematic for the inequities it imposes on women. It has, therefore, been singled out as an area of reform by those wishing to improve the status of women in Muslim societies. This essay addresses the marriage contract in the context of an Islamic religious institution that, at least in its contemporary history, does not fit the traditional anti-feminist patriarchal mold: the Imamate of the Nizari Ismaili community. It discusses the manner in which the Ismaili imam (the hereditary spiritual leader of a minority Shiʿi community) has used the full weight of his religious authority to ameliorate the status of Ismaili women. Since the marriage contract is often a symbolic focal point for gender relations, changes instituted by the Imamate in Ismaili marriage contract law, beginning in the first decades of the twentieth century, have been an integral part of the larger project of redefining the role of women in the Nizari Ismaili community. In the process of this reform, as we shall see below, the significance of the institution of marriage for women was reinterpreted and its legal and social frameworks were radically changed. A major focus of the paper will be the primary architect of this reformation, Sultan Muḥammad Shāh Āgā Khān III (1877–1957), the forty-eighth Nizari Ismaili Imam, under whose seventy-two-year leadership the most dramatic changes in Ismaili marriage contract law were instituted.

**Ismaili Doctrine and Reform Efforts**

Among Shiʿi Muslims, the Nizari Ismailis are the only group that currently claims to have a living imam, commonly called *Ḥāżir Imām* (present Imam) or *Imām-i Ẓamān* (Imam of the time). According to their belief, the imam, by virtue of his direct descent from the Prophet Muḥammad's daughter Fāṭima (d. 633) and son-in-law ʿAlī (d. 661), is endowed with special knowledge (*ʿilm*) to interpret the Qurʾan and provide authoritative guidance on all matters, religious and otherwise. Moreover, the imam possesses knowledge of the inner or esoteric (*bāṭin*) aspects of the divine revelation. It is their belief in the infallible guidance and authority of the living imam that sets Nizari Ismailis apart from the majority of Muslims, both Shiʿi and Sunni. In the eighteenth century, the imams of the Nizari Ismailis were given the hereditary title "Aga Khan" by the Qajar Shah of Iran; it is by this title that they are popularly known today. At present, the Nizari Ismailis believe that Shah Karīm al-Ḥusaynī, Aga Khan IV, is the forty-ninth imam in direct succession from the first Imam ʿAlī. The Nizari Ismailis number between eight and ten million, living in over twenty-five different countries in South and Central Asia, sub-Saharan Africa, Europe, and the Americas.

Since the late nineteenth century, the Ismaili imams have employed the authority of their religious office to embark on an ambitious program of reform within the Nizari Ismaili community. The impetus for reform stemmed from the need to respond to the growing impact of modernization and nationalism on the community and the need to define its identity within the context of the larger Muslim community (*umma*). The reforms involved changes not only in interpretations of faith and religious practice, but also in health, education, social welfare, and economic aspects of the community's life.

As mentioned above, improving the status of Ismaili women was a passion of Aga Khan III whose work has been continued after his death in 1957 by his grandson, the current Aga Khan IV. That this was not entirely a male-driven reform program is apparent from the active involvement of several women from the Aga Khan family in guiding and implementing change. Since Aga Khan III succeeded to the leadership of the Ismaili community at a very young age, after his father's untimely demise in 1885, his mother, Lady ʿAlī Shāh, was one of the most significant influences in his life. A granddaughter of the Iranian Qajar ruler Fatḥ ʿAlī Shāh, Lady ʿAlī Shāh played an important role in guiding community affairs during her son's youth.[2] In later life, Aga Khan III's wife, Umm Ḥabība, was also engaged in various social causes within the community. The current Aga Khan's daughter, Princess Zahra, is similarly involved in guiding policies related to education, health and social welfare, particularly as they affect Ismaili women and youth, at the Aga Khan's headquarters in Aiglemont, France. In 1997, she convened the first-ever international conference of Ismaili women in Toronto, Canada, focusing on the economic empowerment of Ismaili women.

An example of Aga Khan III's interest in improving the status of women is his declaration in 1926 that Ismaili women are free and independent. "Your Imam has brought you total freedom," he said in a speech to his women followers.[3] He further declared, "I do not want Ismaili women dependent on anyone—their parents, husbands, or anyone except God."[4] Critical of interpretations of Islam that do not recognize the rights and dignity of women, he wrote:

> I have not the least doubt that the whole spirit and teaching of my ancestor the Holy Prophet encouraged the evolution of all legitimate freedom and legitimate equality between men and women. The responsibility before God for prayers, for action, and for moral decisions is the same for men and women. I firmly believe that in encouraging education amongst my religious followers, and in trying as far as possible to give them equality—women with men—I have carried out the spirit of the holy message of my ancestor [Prophet Muḥammad].[5]

He was also critical of forms of veiling and gender segregation such as purdah (veiling and/or physical seclusion) and *zenāna* (confinement of women to the home) prevalent in some Muslim societies, causing many women to be totally secluded and marginalized from public life. Thus, he urged:

> There is absolutely nothing in Islam, or the Koran, or the examples of the first two centuries [of Islamic history], to justify this terrible and cancerous growth that has for nearly a thousand years eaten into the very vitals of Islamic society. [...] [This custom] means the permanent imprisonment and enslavement of half the nation. How can we expect progress from the children of mothers who have never shared, or even seen, the free social intercourse of modern mankind? This terrible cancer that has grown since the 3rd and 4th century [sic] of the Hijra must either be cut out, or the body of Moslem society will be poisoned to death by the permenant [sic] waste of all women of the nation.[6]

Accordingly, Aga Khan III strongly discouraged this type of segregation of women in the Ismaili community, encouraging them to participate fully in all activities. In a speech to the Muslim women of Pakistan he urged them to fight for their right to pray in mosques:

> The women here, to my horror, are forbidden to take part in the religious life of the country. In practically every Muslim country the women are allowed to go to mosques for Friday prayers. [...] [P]erhaps the greatest blot in Pakistan is the neglect of Friday prayers by Muslims generally but above all not giving women occasions for participating in these most important prayers. If you are forbidden even prayer[,] what can you expect? The first thing to agitate for is to get your right for your prayers [...]. On that foundation of religious equality, you can then build social, economic, patriotic and political equality, with men.[7]

Aga Khan III was also a strong supporter of the right of women to vote in the electoral process and to hold elected office; he argued that the inclusion of women would ensure that socially unjust laws would not be enacted. As early as 1918, he demanded the extension of the political franchise to women at a time when more radical Sunni ulema were not prepared to allow Muslim women out of the home. Other Muslim leaders argued that Islam did not sanction such a franchise to women.[8]

Aga Khan III's passionate views on the status of women led him to introduce a comprehensive reform program for women within the Ismaili community which included, among its most significant components, better education and economic opportunities. In a 1925 address to the Ismaili community, he declared: "All the knowledge that is available in the world—all of it—must remain open for girls to learn and acquire. Girls should be provided with such education that they can run their own lives."[9] Addressing the girls in the audience, he said: "If your father does not allow you to learn then you should say to him: 'We want education.'"[10] A few decades later he advised Ismaili parents that if they had two children, a boy and a girl, and could afford to educate only one, they should educate the girl, not only because it would make her a better mother but also because it would empower her economically.[11] According to him, women should be educated not merely to provide educated and intelligent wives and daughters, sisters and mothers, but they should be educated for their own happiness and welfare.[12]

## Marriage Law Reforms

Aga Khan III used his authority as imam to revise and add to the personal law sections of the constitutions that governed the Ismaili community, especially those concerning marriage rites and laws. The constitutions were revised repeatedly to keep pace with the many changes that the community was experiencing over the course of the twentieth century. The intent of these reforms, which were implemented in a gradual series of steps, was to affirm the status of women as equal partners in marriage and also provide as much protection as possible to women who were economically dependent on their husbands. For instance, the rights of women in polygamous marriages with potentially irresponsible husbands were protected by several laws. In the 1905 Ismaili constitution, for example, polygamy was allowed with the provision of maintenance for the first wife;[13] a few decades later, it was permitted only for specified reasons and under prescribed safeguards;[14] and by 1962, in the constitution promulgated by Aga Khan III's grandson and successor, Karim Aga Khan IV, polygamy was strictly prohibited. Marriage could be solemnized between two Ismailis only if "neither party has a spouse living at the time of the marriage."[15]

To ensure that young girls had the opportunity to receive an education, they were protected from being married off too early. Child marriage was outlawed, and anyone guilty of such a crime, or of giving a bride for monetary considerations, was to be punished.[16] Restrictions were gradually placed on the minimum age young girls (and boys) could marry: the 1925 constitution stated that no girl could be married before she was fourteen;[17] and by 1962 the minimum age was raised to sixteen with the stipulation that if the bride had not attained the age of twenty-one at the time of the marriage she had to obtain the consent of her parents, or guardians, or, failing that, the consent of the Ismaili Council.[18] As the Aga Khan's policy of encouraging women's education brought changes in their status, marriages performed in proxy by parents or guardians of the bride were discontinued. Rules relating to the conduct of the marriage ceremony in the 1946 constitution explicitly stated that the "bride shall take her seat open-faced next to the bridegroom."[19] It was also mandated that the bride was to sign the marriage contract of her own free will and that "parents can no longer arrange betrothals and weddings against their daughters' wishes."[20]

In the case of divorce, the autocratic and "virtually unfettered right" of a husband to repudiate his wife, which is widespread in many Muslim communities, was denied.[21] A husband intending to divorce his wife had to justify his reasons before the local Ismaili Council which, as the institutional representative of the imam, had the right to grant or deny a divorce. Divorce petitions, while permissible, could only be granted after the council had ascertained that the marriage had genuinely broken down. A woman was given substantial equality in this regard for she, too, could apply for a divorce. Among the several grounds upon which a woman could file for divorce were: (1) neglect or failure of the husband to provide maintenance for a period of one year, or (2) the husband had become and was still impotent subsequent to the marriage.[22] Marriage disputes were to be arbitrated by specially-appointed tribunals, whose membership had to include at least one woman.[23] If the tribunal deemed it fit to grant the couple a divorce, there were numerous clauses ensuring that the ex-husband would provide amply for his divorced wife and children. Finally, through authority and persuasion, Aga Khan III tried to counteract the social stigma against divorcees; in one directive (*firmān*) to the community he noted that "it is against the principle of Islam not to get married to a divorced woman."[24] He made similar pronouncements encouraging the remarriage of widows.[25]

Beyond the changes instituted in the rights of women in marriage, Aga Khan III's reform program, with its goal of economically empowering women, aimed at preventing women from entering marriages simply out of economic necessity:

> I am trying to guide our young women's lives into entirely new channels. I want to see them able to earn their living in trades and professions, so that they are not economically dependent on marriage, nor a burden on their fathers and brothers. [...]
>
> The next step is to achieve a new system of economic independence so that they [women] can marry whomsoever they like and whenever they like. Hitherto a girl had to marry early to ensure her existence, transforming matrimony into some form of permanent lunch-card. [...] [W]omen equipped with means of earning a livelihood need fear nothing.[26]

The Imam conceived of free choice in marriage as the "holiest of blessings" and if a marriage failed due to irreconcilable differences, "a healthy, wholesome, unashamed divorce is the only solution."[27]

Aga Khan III's program of improving the status of Ismaili women has been continued by his successor to the imamate, Aga Khan IV, although the strategy and style of the grandson differs from that of his grandfather. Under Aga Khan IV the focus has been on empowering women through programs of educational and social development for the entire community rather than the explicit articulation of women's rights through legal and religious ordinances. The consequences of the policies of both imams have been dramatic. Ismaili women now participate in the public sphere, in both religious and social contexts, in ways that are impossible for most non-Ismaili Muslim women. In the religious sphere, during congregational prayers in most *jamāʿāt khāna*s (houses of congregation) around the world, Ismaili men and women pray side by side in the same hall without any physical barriers or partitions to separate them. It has also become common for Ismaili women to lead a mixed congregation of both men and women in prayer and officiate during religious ceremonies, something that is highly unusual in most Muslim communities. Further, educational and professional accomplishments of Ismaili women have led to their playing prominent roles both within and outside the community. It is becoming increasingly common to see women in leadership positions in Ismaili institutions at both local and national levels.[28]

All of this is not to suggest that the policies of Aga Khans III and IV were completely successful in their objectives and that discrimination against women in the Ismaili community has been eliminated. At a recent international Ismaili Women's Forum in Toronto, Princess Zahra, Aga Khan IV's daughter, pointed out that although Ismaili women have on the whole attained a status that is relatively better than that of their non-Ismaili Muslim peers, forms of discrimination and barriers to societal change continue to persist.[29] This suggests that the reforms initiated by the imams have not been entirely successful in attaining their goals and that there have been certain constraints in their effectiveness. What are some of these limitations?

Although the imams themselves have been progressive and forward-looking in their vision, they have had to be pragmatic. Some of their reforms have been difficult to realize fully when segments of the community have chosen to ignore their guidance and not abide by the regulations in the personal law sections of Ismaili constitutions. For instance, although regulations governing Ismailis in many parts of the world enjoin members of the community to limit expenditures on engagement and wedding ceremonies, countervailing pressures stemming from societal and cultural norms for lavish celebrations have been so powerful that significant curtailment of expenses has been difficult to achieve, especially among middle and upper income families. Conservative attitudes towards the rights of women stemming from deeply embedded social and patriarchal prejudices have been difficult to eradicate, notwithstanding the imams' directions permitting women free choice in marriage. This is particularly true in cases where traditional extended patriarchal family structures prevail. In reality, local customs concerning the role and status of women continue to exert an important influence on family and community life. Consequently, a discrepancy still exists between the rights officially accorded to Ismaili women and actual practice.

Furthermore, among more conservative members of the community, the reforms instituted by the imams were criticized as being based on western values rather than Islamic ones.[30] In one particularly vitriolic attack on the imam's policy concerning women, an individual condemned the "vices of Hollywood" filtering into the community.[31] Aga Khan III responded by insisting that his guidance was based on the teachings of the Qur'an interpreted in the modern context:

> This gentleman has talked about the vices of Hollywood coming among the young ladies of the *Jamat* [community]. I hate the vices of Hollywood. But what about the worst vice of the slavery of women in *purdah, burqah* [veiling] and *zenana* [confinement of women to the house] where women are reduced to the moral insignificance of vegetables and physical wrecks, of diseases such as tuberculosis, etc.

> God does not consider anybody moral who is out in a cage or box and locked. The only morality is those who resist temptation of evil and with honour carry their head high, having seen the attraction of the bad and chosen the good. [...] While the words of the Koran remain the same, every generation, every century, every period must have a new and different interpretation of the past, otherwise Islam will die and will not survive the competition of some healthy less rigid competitors. [...] [T]hinkers even in Pakistan realize that the rigidity of formal Islamic customs and religious ceremonies kills.[32]

To prevent a small minority community from being splintered into further factions and schisms fueled by a conservative backlash, the imams have also had to implement their vision gradually over a period of time, being careful to take a long-range view of their innovations so as "to minimize the shock of sudden and sweeping changes."[33] Many practices such as polygamy, child marriage, and excessive expenditures on weddings were slowly curtailed in phases before being outlawed altogether.[34] The imams also needed support for their reforms from community leaders of various councils, tribunals, and boards responsible for administering programs at local, national, and international levels. Since these leaders, who generally serve in a voluntary capacity in community institutions, are directly responsible for the implementation of reforms, their ability and professional capacity to correctly interpret the imams' guidance are crucial. However, until recently, the institutional leadership has been effectively dominated by men with the bare minimum of female representation as mandated by the constitution. Often, a sole "lady member" in charge of the women's portfolio would be appointed to a council, but the key positions of executive power and decision making remained in the hands of men. The imbalanced gender ratio has meant that the implementation of the reforms on the status of women instituted by the imam depended on institutions comprised of predominantly male appointees, many of whom, either consciously or unconsciously, still adhered to patriarchal attitudes and norms. Consequently, at the institutional level, the attainment of substantial equality between men and women was not given as high a priority as it would have if there had been more women in positions of leadership. It is only in the last decade, at the insistence of the current Aga Khan, that the gender imbalance in the community's institutional leadership is being corrected, with the appointment of a growing number of professional and highly educated Ismaili women to various institutions governing the community. For institutions in countries with a large number of qualified women, the goal is to have at least forty to fifty percent of the positions held by women. Not surprisingly, as more women are being appointed to positions of leadership, women's issues are once more in the forefront of institutional agendas after several decades of neglect.

The success of the Aga Khans' reforms was also, to a large extent, dependent on the extent to which states in which Ismaili communities reside recognized the Aga Khans' authority to legislate for their followers on matters of personal law. Since the Nizari Ismaili community is spread over twenty-five different countries with varying legal and political structures, the legal impact of the imams' reforms and the extent of their ability to enforce them through the community's institutional structure also varies. In countries such as Kenya, Uganda, and Tanzania traditions of legal pluralism are practiced. As a result, different races and religions are constitutionally permitted to have their own systems of personal law. Therefore, in these states, the imam's role as legislator within the Ismaili community has complete legal sanction. Rules and regulations governing the Ismaili community are legally binding with the proviso that the administration of the rules "be reasonable, just and... not offensive in any way against morality, natural justice and the law of the land."[35] Indeed, in some instances, the secular courts have even enforced the judgments and awards made by the community's institutions when these have been disputed outside the community.[36] A similar circumstance prevails in India, where the constitution recognizes the jurisdiction of institutions of individual religious communities over matters of personal law. By contrast, in Muslim majority countries governed by personal law that is Sunni Islamic law in content and interpretation and that typically does not enforce decisions of institutions internal to various minority Muslim groups, the state Shariʿa court can provide an alternative to the Ismaili community's institutions. Thus, an Ismaili male can choose to bring a divorce case before such a Shariʿa court as opposed to the community's own bodies in the hope of obtaining a decision less stringent for him than one based on Ismaili personal law, which in most cases accords greater protection to women. Not surprisingly, among Ismailis of Pakistan, instances of polygamy, a practice outlawed by the imams' edicts and hence illegal under Ismaili law, are still found since polygamy is legally valid according to Shariʿa law as implemented in that country.

The legal scenario for Ismailis residing in western countries such as the United States or Canada is slightly different.[37] In these countries, a general predominant civil law almost always overwhelms religious communities' distinct personal laws. In such situations, where legal enforcement of community laws and rulings is not available, social disapprobation by the community plays an important role in determining the extent to which an individual will conform to the authority of the imam and the rulings of the community's institutions.

The Ismaili community's minority status within the larger Muslim community has also imposed limitations on the Imamate's ability to institute change. This is especially true in countries such as Pakistan where the ideological forms of Islam that control public and political discourse have become increasingly less tolerant of diversity and divergent interpretations of the faith. Islamist groups such as the Jamaʿat-i Islami and right-wing extremists such as the Sipah-i Sahaba question the identity of the Ismailis as Muslims since their ritual practice does not conform to the orthopraxic norms as defined by Sunni theology and because they are Shiʿa.[38] The fact that Ismaili women in cities like Karachi participate in congregational prayers without strict veiling alongside males in Ismaili houses of congregation has led such groups to consider Ismaili women to be "improper" Muslims since they abide by neither the dress codes nor dictates of most Muslim communities that restrict female presence and participation in the public spaces of worship. Clearly, such restrictive attitudes run counter to the imams' guidance and make it difficult for Ismaili individuals and groups to sustain a different status for Ismaili women. Indeed, in the rural areas of the Punjab and the Northwest Frontier, some Ismailis have adopted a policy of compromise verging on pseudo-*taqiyya* (the Shiʿi practice of concealing one's faith in the face of persecution).[39] In the interests of maintaining good relations with the surrounding conservative Sunni Muslim population, the Ismailis ostensibly follow Hanafi Sunni law and their marriage and burial ceremonies are solemnized by Sunni mullahs.[40] In these regions, Ismaili women also wear the traditional *burqa* (outer garment covering the head and body) whenever they appear in public.

## Conclusion

In an age when Islamic religious institutions have been popularly regarded as reactionary and anti-feminist, the Imamate of the Ismaili community and the reforms it initiated in marriage contract law provide a powerful example to the contrary. Given an enabling social and legal environment, the Aga Khans have been able to use their authority at the apex of a hierarchy to institute change. The case of the Nizari Ismaili community and its Imamate demonstrates that not all of the obstacles to attaining an equality of status for women are based in religion. A complex combination of cultural, social, legal and political elements can also become a hindrance. Even when religious doctrines and institutions fervently mandate reform, resistance to change can still persist.

NOTES

1 Hassan 1991, 41.
2 Aga Khan III 1998, 7–10.
3 Aga Khan III 1950, 124.
4 Idem.
5 Quoted in Malick 1954, 141–142.
6 Aga Khan III 1998, 210–211.

[7] Soofi 1954, 4.
[8] Aga Khan III 1998, 112–113.
[9] Agh Khan III 1950, 83.
[10] Idem.
[11] Idem, 335–337.
[12] Aga Khan III 1918, 258.
[13] Ismaili Constitution 1905, 9.
[14] According to the 1946 constitution, a person could marry a second wife for reasons of serious illness, insanity, cruelty, or infertility of his first wife. He had to produce a medical certificate certifying any of the above reasons. The first wife had the right to contest such an application. If the man was permitted by the Ismaili Council to marry a second wife, he had to deposit with the Council a sum of money which would be invested and its income used to guarantee support for the first wife. Ismaili Constitution 63–64 (1946).
[15] Anderson 1964–65, 26.
[16] Ismaili Constitution 57.
[17] Ismaili Constitution 1925, 44.
[18] Anderson 1964–65, 26.
[19] Ismaili Constitution 61.
[20] As quoted in Malick 1954, 139.
[21] Anderson 1964–65, 29.
[22] Ismaili Constitution 1962, 276.
[23] Anderson 1964–65, 30.
[24] Shia Ismailia Association for Africa 1948, 17.
[25] Asani 1994, 22.
[26] As quoted in Malick 1954, 138–139.
[27] Idem.
[28] Ali and Musani 2006.
[29] Aga Khan 1997.
[30] Amiji 1982, 184.
[31] Aga Khan III 1955, 30–32.
[32] Idem.
[33] Walji 1974, 217.
[34] Asani 1994, 22–23.
[35] Anderson 1964–65, 36.
[36] Shariff 1989, 29–31.
[37] For a detailed discussion of the situation of Ismaili personal law in the Canadian legal context, see idem, 53–80.
[38] See Asani 2005, 181–190.
[39] I am using the term "pseudo-*taqiyya*" because, although the religious identity of Ismailis is not concealed, in their practice they are under pressure to conform to what are considered to be mainstream Sunni norms.
[40] Lokhandwalla 1971, 387.

# *Part Four*

## THE MUSLIM MARRIAGE CONTRACT IN WESTERN SECULAR LEGAL SYSTEMS

# *Fourteen*

# MARRIAGE CONTRACTS OF MUSLIMS IN THE DIASPORA: PROBLEMS IN THE RECOGNITION OF *MAHR* CONTRACTS IN GERMAN LAW

Christina Jones-Pauly

This chapter deals with the intricacies of how the Islamic institution of dower (*mahr*) is dealt with in German case law. Since the majority of court cases stem from conflicts between Muslims living in Germany who are not citizens of that country, the first part of this essay discusses the problems posed by the application of the Islamic law of *mahr* as a "foreign law." As the number of Muslim immigrants who become German citizens increases and more German citizens are converting to Islam, the second part of this chapter also analyzes the approach courts take when applying the Islamic rules of *mahr* as part of German law. In the conclusion are suggestions as to how the institution of *mahr* could be better understood by German courts.

## German Conflict of Laws Principles in Private International Law

As *mahr* is part of the marriage contract, it is important by way of background to summarize two basic characteristics of German law that are relevant to recognizing Islamic marriage contracts. The first relates to the conflict of laws rules, the second to the general recognition of marriage contracts. First we turn to the principles of conflict of laws.

The basic conflict of law rule in German marriage law is that it is *not* the law of domicile that primarily determines which law applies to the marriage (as it is in the common law system),[1] but rather the law of the parties' citizenship.[2] This fundamental difference between the common law system and the Continental systems has a long history, going back to the role of Roman law in Europe. This is not the place to dwell on this history. Suffice it to say that in terms of the current debates on immigration in Europe, the domicile rule has certain advantages which the British courts have long prized. British case law regards the *lex domicili* as more integrative than the citizenship principle, which stems from the *lex sanguinis*. To quote Lord Stowell, the citizenship principle is "Oriental," as keeping up an "immiscible character [...] [so that] foreigners [...] continue

[as] strangers as all their fathers were."[3] Whether in reality the *lex domicili* approach proves to be more integrative than the *lex sanguinis* is naturally subject to debate.

German law admits certain exceptions to the rule of citizenship as, for example, in maintenance claims for children.[4] When spouses have differing citizenships, domicile can play a role in determining which law shall apply, or the spouses may choose which law of citizenship shall apply. The choice of law is made basically in three steps. In the first step the courts decide upon the citizenship of the parties, or, exceptionally, the domicile, or allow the parties as a last resort in complicated cases of plural citizenships or residences to choose which of these laws they want to apply. The second step is to determine the nature of the case, that is, whether the conflict can be classified in one of the following categories: (1) validity of marriage, (2) conjugal rights and duties, (3) community of property or separation of property, (4) divorce, (5) access to the conjugal home and household goods, (6) maintenance of a former spouse, (7) maintenance of children, and (8) inheritance. The third step is to decide whether for the particular above-named category chosen, it is primarily the law of citizenship or domicile that applies as demanded by the German code. If a case falls outside any of the categories listed above and cannot be easily squeezed into a category, then problems arise, as we shall see in connection with the question of *mahr*.

The determination of the category of a foreign law has important procedural consequences. If a foreign rule fits into one of the above eight categories, then the division of the court that handles the case is the Family Law Chamber. If it is found to fall outside these categories, then the case could go to the Civil Law Chamber, which handles all non-family civil matters, such as contracts and torts.

The one escape hatch that the German courts have is the notion of *ordre public*, which basically means that a foreign law is repulsive to the essential principles of German law and, in particular, rights specified in the constitution.[5] The court is not to confine itself to comparing the contents of the foreign law with the contents of the German law; rather, it must concentrate on the question of whether the application of the foreign law will have consequences that lead to violating the basic principles of German law.[6] If the applicable law of citizenship is deemed to be against the *ordre public*, then it is not applicable. In that case only German law would apply.

Because most foreigners in Germany—and even German citizens—are not aware of the rule that a foreigner's own law continues to apply to them in Germany, it can come as a rude shock for some when they have marital disputes. For example, many Iranians who had fled to Germany under the Shah's regime, or later under Ayatollah Khomeini's regime, who have resided legally in Germany for as long as thirty years and want to divorce before German courts, are suddenly faced with the application of the very Islamic laws that they wished to escape. The fact that they have retained their Iranian citizenship—until recently it has not been easy to obtain German citizenship—means that they are considered "guests," who are entitled to have their own law apply in matrimonial disputes.

About 8.9 percent of the population in Germany is non-citizens; of this number, about 3.1–3.5 million originate from Muslim countries. This means that in matrimonial disputes between foreign Muslims, German judges must apply the law of their respective Muslim countries. Since the German judges are not schooled in Islamic law—or any foreign law for that matter—they rely on expert opinions as to the family law of the Muslim country involved. Otherwise, the judges try to decipher translations of the foreign law to the best of their abilities. The court may initiate a referral to an expert, or the parties may apply to bring in their own expert.

Of the Muslim residents in Germany, only the Iranian Muslims have special status because Iran is the only Muslim country that has a treaty with Germany, signed in 1929, which assures the application of Iranian personal status law for Iranian citizens in Germany (and vice versa for German citizens residing in Iran).[7] The treaty requires German courts to apply Iranian law in matters of marriage, community property, divorce, dissolution of marital status, dower, paternity, and inheritance.[8] The existence of a treaty has made a difference insofar as some judges have felt obliged to construe the notion of German *ordre public* as narrowly as possible in order to avoid declaring the application of the Iranian law repugnant to basic constitutional rights.[9]

## Application of German Conflict of Laws in the Case of Marriage Contracts

The marriage contract itself is not foreign to German judges. The Prussian Code of 1794 admitted contractual agreements between spouses regulating their separate properties and the dower promised by the husband. If the wife did not make a contract granting herself control over her properties, her husband was automatically given control over them.[10] The contract could not regulate the non-property substantive rights and duties of the spouses (in contrast to Islamic law); that was left to the state. For example, the only reasons that a spouse could be absent from the company of the other were reasons of public business, urgent private matters, or health trips.[11] The marriage was seen as a community where the division of labor had to be strictly regulated by state law.[12] The husband had a duty to maintain the wife; the wife had a duty to run the household.[13]

The family law chapter of the current German Civil Code continues this schema but with a difference. It is now left to the spouses to make a contractual agreement, whether oral or written, regarding which spouse shall be responsible for earning a living and which for running the household. The one who runs the household or rears the children is deemed by law to be contributing to the upkeep of the family and therefore is exempt from earning a living.[14] If, for example, the wife wishes to run the household and rear the children in a place other than the place of work of the husband, this can also be the subject of a contractual agreement between the spouses. If there are misunderstandings about the terms of such an agreement, the courts may decide on its fairness and equity. In one such case, the appellate court reversed the lower court and allowed a wife to claim maintenance from her husband. It held that she was not acting irrationally when she insisted on running the household in a location other than the husband's place of work because she did not want to leave her half-time job or her mother, who was caretaker of her daughter, even though the husband insisted that he was earning more money and therefore should be able to determine the location of the marital household.[15] In another recent case an unusual marital contract between a German citizen and an Algerian citizen twenty-three years her junior was recognized by the courts. Under the contract the husband was denied the right to the wife's pension, both spouses were to keep their properties separate, and both were exempted from claims of maintenance. Furthermore, the contract regulated the husband's access to the flat leased by the wife.[16] The couple's common sexual life was very short and the wife even declared before the court that she treated the marriage as one of convenience. Such a contract is not uncommon for marriages between immigrants and German citizens.[17] There has been some discussion, in fact, about whether courts should recognize marital contracts that perpetuate inequalities between the spouses.[18]

In Islamic law the *mahr* is seen as an integral part of the marriage contact, either as an explicit or implied term. However, when a marital conflict arises in German courts involving a *mahr*, the courts have not automatically or consistently treated it as part of the marriage contract. This is because the *mahr* is not easily classified into one of the eight categories of substantive law to which the rules of conflict of laws apply.[19] The courts ask themselves: Does the *mahr* concern the validity of the marriage, conjugal duties, access to the conjugal home and household goods, post alimony support, or inheritance? In the view of a major commentator on German conflict of laws, Gerhard Kegel, the Islamic legal institution of *mahr* falls "outside the law" since does not fit neatly into any of these categories.[20] Kegel likens the *mahr* to the English law of trusts, the African law of "substitute" marriage between two women, and the Jewish law of "get," which requires the wife to obtain a divorce certificate from the husband. Kegel considers all these examples of foreign laws as not fitting easily, if at all, within German categories. In light of such difficulties, one would think that in order to overcome the problem the German court must either decide that there is a possible category, devise some creative combination of categories, declare the foreign legal construct contrary to German *ordre public*, or, finally, decide simply to leave the parties without a remedy.

## Marital Contracts of Muslim Residents (Non-Citizens) in German Case Law

Practically all of the reported cases in Germany involving Muslim marital contracts concern claims by a wife for payment of her *mahr*. A chronological review of the case law will illustrate the evolution in attitude of the German courts towards the Islamic marriage contracts involving Muslim non-citizen residents.

### A. *1970–1977: What is* Mahr?

In a 1970 case involving a marriage contract between a German wife and a Jordanian husband concluded under Jordanian law, the husband had agreed to a *mahr* of 1 dinar (approximately DM 10.30 or 5 euros), payable immediately, and a deferred *mahr* of 1,000 dinars (DM 10,300, or 5,150 euros), payable in cash upon divorce or the death of the husband. After four years of marriage the wife sued in Germany for divorce and payment of the *mahr*. The German court sought expert advice on how to classify the nature of the latter claim: Was it an action in divorce? Was it an action arising from marriage without community of property (i.e., each spouse retained control over her/his own property)? Was it an action in post-divorce maintenance? Was it an action for contractual performance? Was it a debt action? Or was it a contract to buy a woman? It was important for the court to establish the category of action for two reasons: first, because the cause of action determined which law applied—that of either the nationality of the parties or that of the marital domicile; and second, because the nature of the action determined which court would have jurisdiction, the Family Law or the Civil Law Chamber.

The expert opinion submitted to the court first noted how the *mahr* is treated in Jordanian law: it is part of the marriage contract, separate from a claim for maintenance, and it is part of the wife's property, separate from that of her husband.[21] Because *mahr* is regulated in the Jordanian Family Code and not the Civil Code, it was concluded that *mahr* is not a debt action. Having concluded what the *mahr* is *not*, there still remained the question of what it *is*. The answer was sought by constructing what was thought to be the social function of *mahr*. It was opined that *mahr* is intended to function as a financial security for the wife in case of divorce or death. The expert opinion drew parallels to the former German law of dowry and the Roman law of *donatio propter nuptias*, which classified dowry as an agreement between spouses about dividing their property into that which belonged jointly to both and that which remained the individual property of each. Since the contractual agreement between Muslim spouses on *mahr* was deemed comparable to former German and Roman legal institutions, it was recommended that it not be treated as repugnant to German *ordre public*, that is, it should not be considered to be a contract to purchase a woman. *Mahr* was classified as a matter of community of property regime which serves the financial security of a woman upon dissolution of the marriage. This functional approach has served as the basis of subsequent court decisions, as illustrated below.[22]

Besides the issue of categorizing the *mahr* for purposes of German law, the Jordanian case raises the issue of the validity of the stipulation for payment of the most valuable part of the *mahr* upon termination of the marriage. The possibility that the validity of the stipulation could be put in question seems to have escaped the attention of the commentators. In my view, Islamic law allows the wife to claim the *mahr* any time she chooses after consummation of the marriage, and a contract term modifying this important right could be called into question.[23] We shall return to this issue later in relation to marriage contracts between German-born Muslim citizens.

B. *1980, Bremen:* Mahr *as Civil Law Claim or Family Law Claim?*

In 1980, the Higher Regional Court of Bremen (Oberlandesgericht, OLG) was faced with the question of how to classify an action on the marital agreement for payment of the *mahr*.[24] A German Muslim husband had agreed at marriage to pay a "bride price"—to use the literal words of the Court, *Brautpreis*—to his Muslim Iranian wife of 8,000 tuman (approximately 1,125 euros). The marriage contract stipulated that this sum was to be paid upon divorce, or any time the wife requested it. At first the wife claimed the *mahr* separately in connection with a divorce action. As she laid her claim before the Family Law Chamber of the court of first instance (Amtsgericht, AmtsG), the judge had doubts about hearing the matter, holding that it was instead a contractual claim, a civil matter. The court decided to remove the claim to the Civil Law Chamber, and the husband appealed this decision. The appellate Higher Regional Court in Bremen noted that the Iranian Islamic law on *mahr* had no counterpart in German law. Because an institution like *mahr* is not regulated in German law, the court held—in conformity with preceding expert opinions—that it had to determine the function for which the *mahr* is intended in order to classify its legal nature. Because the *mahr* was a large sum of money, the court deemed it to be substantial property which functioned to give financial security to the wife, especially since she had no claim under Iranian law at the time to post-divorce alimony or to her share of the profits accruing to the marital property. In other words, the *mahr* was to be treated in German law as a substitute for post-divorce maintenance and division of the surplus of marital profits. Hence the court declared that jurisdiction was proper in the Family Law Chamber.

We should note here that the new Iranian law, in place since 1992, undermines the Bremen court's view of the function of the *mahr*. Since 1992, Iranian law allows a divorced woman to make a claim in court for the increase in family wealth or her husband's business to which she contributed with her labor.[25] The action is separate from a claim for *mahr* in the marriage contract. This new Iranian law will complicate matters further for the German case law.

The tendency of German courts to treat claims for *mahr* as a family law matter and not as a civil contract matter has been rejected by some litigants. For example, a German woman married to a Jordanian husband challenged the German case law regarding the nature of her *mahr*.[26] She argued that the agreement has the nature of a gift (*ṣadaqa*) agreement. Accordingly the woman sued for her *mahr* as a civil matter in the Civil Law Chamber. The court decided against the wife, holding that the matter was a family law issue. The court gave two reasons for its decision. The first was doctrinal: *mahr* cannot be treated solely as a matter of contractual law, because it would be payable even without an express contract (i.e., it is payable also as *mahr mithl*, the estimated proper *mahr*). The second reason was functional: a large *mahr*, so the court estimated, functions as a deterrent against arbitrary divorce by the husband. Thus, it can be construed as a measure for protecting the stability of the marriage, a value that is also enshrined in the German constitution.[27] Finally, another function of the *mahr*, opined the court, is that because in practice it is usually paid upon divorce, it serves as a post-divorce maintenance agreement.

### C. *1983, Cologne: Repugnancy of the* Mahr *Contract as Unjust Enrichment of the Wife?*

Three years later, in 1983, an Iranian wife sued her German husband for the *mahr* fixed in a marriage contract at four million rials (DM 42,000, or 21,000 euros).[28] She wanted, in addition, interest at four percent since the date of filing the claim. The court did not challenge the claim for interest as being un-Islamic.[29] Nor did it make clear whether the marriage contract had stipulated that the wife could request compensation for delayed payment of the *mahr*. The notarized marital contract specified that the wife had been given a Qur'an worth 1,000 rials and jewelry worth 88,000 rials in addition to the promised four million rials. The four million rials were specifically referred to as a "debt" on the husband, payable at any time the wife requested. The marriage lasted only five years before the wife won a divorce order in a German Family Law Chamber.[30] She sued separately before the Civil Law Chamber for the *mahr* and interest. Her former husband disputed the contract and presented an expert opinion which concluded that the contract would be repugnant to German *ordre public* because of its unjust enrichment of the wife. The Civil Law Chamber agreed and refused to enforce the contract.

The wife then appealed. The appellate court rejected the argument that the *mahr* contract is repugnant as such, because previous courts had upheld the *mahr* as a function of the marital property regime or as post-alimony for the wife.[31] As a result, the court upheld the contract. In order to bring some "order" or uniformity to the case precedents, the appellate court decided to attempt to reconcile the differing approaches as to how to classify *mahr*. In its resolution, the court reconstructed the nature of mahr itself, and concluded that the *mahr* agreement is an agreement conferring exclusive ownership of the *mahr* to the wife (comparable to the Prussian law), but for purposes of maintenance. Since the purpose of *mahr* was to provide the wife with post-divorce maintenance, the court then took the law one step further: the maintenance agreement would have to meet the German standards of equitableness. This meant that enforcing its full amount—here a substantial sum—could be repugnant to German principles of justice. For this reason the amount would have to be counted against any maintenance which the husband might be ordered to pay under German law to avoid the wife becoming a social welfare burden on the state. In this roundabout way the husband's argument of "unjust enrichment" found favor with the court.

To establish exactly how much of the 21,000-euro *mahr* would be awarded to the divorced wife, the court decided to send the matter back to the trial court. But which court, the Family Law Chamber or the Civil Law Chamber? To answer this question, the court turned to the applicable Iranian law for guidance. Because *mahr* is regulated in the Iranian Family Law Code, the court reasoned, it transferred the matter to the Family Law Chamber. What is rather remarkable about this reliance on Iranian law is that there appears to have been no discussion in the German court about the legal significance of the explicit stipulation in the *mahr* contract that the *mahr* constituted a debt on the husband, and whether the Iranian provisions on *mahr*, though found in the family code, would have treated the *mahr* as a legal debt.

### D. *1983, Hamburg*: Mahr Mithl *vs.* Mahr *Debt Contract Created by a Third Party*

In the same year, in a Hamburg court of first instance (AmtsG), a divorced Iranian wife sought payment of *mahr* without a written marital contract from her Iranian husband.[32] The husband had given the wife a symbolic *mahr* consisting of a Qur'an and a piece of sugar cane candy symbolizing the sweetness of married life. Upon divorce, the wife claimed a more substantial *mahr*: DM 150,000 (75,000 euros) plus four percent interest. That amount would have been appropriate for a woman of her status, she stated, since she was educated and belonged to a well-off merchant family. The husband asserted that it should be much lower, because she was thirty-four years old at the time of marriage, thus reducing her worth as a child-bearer. The wife then presented witnesses who testified that the *mahr* had actually been orally agreed upon at DM 100,000 (50,000 euros), but because the groom did not have that much money, her father had "loaned" the amount to the husband on condition that the husband pay it back not to the father-in-law but to the wife as her *mahr*. The husband disputed the nature of the transaction, alleging that the wife's father had written a check of DM 100,000 to both of the newlyweds as a wedding gift. Besides, the husband had already spent the money, mainly to pay for the wife's various needs.

Because of the complexity of proving whether there had been an oral agreement and the substance of that agreement, the court decided first that this was primarily a family law matter. More specifically, in Islamic legal terminology, this was a matter of an "estimate *mahr*," or *mahr mithl* (i.e., a *mahr* that is customary for women of similar status), and thus was governed by the family law provisions of the Iranian Civil Code. The Hamburg court ultimately decided to award the higher amount, the *mahr mithl*, and explained in detail what factors determined the decision. Following German case law, the court held that the *mahr* is intended functionally to provide financial security for the divorced wife since she would have no claim to post-divorce maintenance once the *ʿidda* (post-divorce waiting period) expired. This meant that the German legal institution most comparable to *mahr* would be that of maintenance. Since Germany has no rule of thumb by which the courts could ascertain the normal *mahr mithl* appropriate for the area of Hamburg, the court decided that it would have to use criteria for an award of maintenance to the average divorced German citizen living in Hamburg, as the parties had originally planned to stay in that city.[33] The court took into account what it thought was the young age of the woman, the absence of children, and her good prospects for getting a job as a translator in about ten months. Given her high social status, a monthly amount of DM 2,000 (1,000 euros) was deemed appropriate for supporting her according to her social status until she got a job in ten months.[34] In the end, the award was equal to only DM 20,000 (2,000 x 10 months), one-fifth of the original claim.

The court was not prepared to break with precedent and consider the *mahr mithl* as a civil debt, which would have allowed interest or compensation from the husband for having profited from the use of the *mahr* during the marriage. It is also interesting to note that the court did not use as the measure of the *mahr mithl* the amount that would have been awarded under Iranian law, for it seems to have believed that such awards are based on the standard of living at the place of domicile of the parties.

After awarding the wife a *mahr mithl* of DM 20,000 the court then returned to the issue of her claim for repayment of the DM 100,000, plus interest—the amount her father had given to the husband. The court held that although the wife alleged that this was a *mahr* claim, it was preferable to classify it under German law as a loan. This would render the matter to a debt claim, which did not fall under the jurisdiction of the Family Law Chamber. The Civil Law Chamber would instead have jurisdiction.

This was the first reported decision in which the courts admitted even the possibility of a woman claiming the *mahr* as a civil law debt as part of a third party (here the father's) debt transfer. Thus, it seems that as long as the German courts continue to treat a *mahr* agreement as a family law matter connected to division of marital property for purposes of maintenance, the only way a woman can bring a suit on the *mahr* as a civil debt is by way of a loan agreement with a third party who in turn transfers the debt.[35]

The academic commentaries on the Hamburg decision have introduced even more complexity to the subject. The commentaries accept the treatment of the *mahr* as a family matter involving a division of marital property[36] and a one-time post-divorce maintenance payment.[37] It has been assumed that the *mahr* is payable mainly in connection with the termination of the marriage, even though in some cases it has been clearly shown that the parties agreed that the *mahr* is payable at any time during the marriage at the option of the wife, totally separate from the matter of maintenance. It has also been assumed that in case of death of the husband, a widow's claim for *mahr* out of the estate is to be treated as an inheritance agreement whereby the wife gets the sum stipulated as *mahr* as her part of the inheritance.[38] This is a misunderstanding of the nature of the *mahr*. The Islamic legal institution of *mahr* is separate from the wife's inheritance or maintenance claims, maintenance during the marriage being related to the concept of obedience of the wife and the duration of post-divorce maintenance to the issue of paternity in case the divorced woman is pregnant. The courts have not examined the treatment of the *mahr* as a debt on the estate like any other. This is notwithstanding the decisions of other courts around the world that reject "unjust enrichment" arguments put forth to try to prevent a Muslim widow from claiming both her *mahr* and inheritance.[39]

### E. *1986, Zweibrücken: Is* Mahr *a Debt Contract After All?*

In 1986, one of the appellate Higher Regional Courts was asked to take another look at the *mahr* issue. In the resulting opinion, the court laid down new criteria for testing the terms of a *mahr* contract.[40] In this new case, a Muslim Iranian husband had signed a contract notarized in Germany in which he was obliged to pay a *mahr* of DM 235,000 (117,000 euros), payable upon conclusion of the marriage or any time the wife requested it. The Muslim Iranian wife explicitly acknowledged her husband's obligation towards her. The spouses later separated, but did not divorce.

Upon separation, the wife made good on her acknowledged right to claim the *mahr*. She demanded a lump sum payment of only part of the *mahr* (DM 50,000, or 25,000 euros) and requested that her husband pay the remainder in installments. In response, he initiated proceedings in an Iranian court for a declaration that he was not obliged to pay the *mahr*. The wife continued her proceedings in Germany. For the first time in the reported case record, a German court was faced with a situation in which there was no divorce, so that the claim for the *mahr* could not be treated as an indirect claim for post-divorce alimony as part of the division of marital property. For our purposes, this case is especially interesting because of the expert opinion published in connection with it.[41]

The lower court (Kaiserslautern AmtsG) had ordered an expert opinion on when a wife can lose her right to the *mahr*, such as by statute of limitations, or because of some mistake about the social and economic class status of her family.[42] As a result of the testimony, the following conclusions were reached about the nature of a *mahr* agreement: (1) The agreement is a matter of contract, therefore all parties must have contractual capacity. (2) There is no statute of limitations on a claim as long as the parties have not specified any deadlines. (3) The *mahr* may be paid in a lump sum or in installments. (4) Iranian codified Islamic law does not set any limit on the amount of *mahr* to which the parties may agree. (5) The wife may not specify how the *mahr* may be paid. (6) The husband may not condition paying the *mahr* on the good conduct of the wife, such as refusing to pay if she leaves the conjugal home without his permission. (7) The wife may voluntarily renounce her right to the *mahr* in full or in part at any time or in connection with a *khulʿ* divorce. Unfortunately, the question of whether the sum could be reduced because of a mistake about the social or economic class of the bride was not addressed.

In this expert opinion, the *mahr* agreement was correctly characterized as a contractual matter. An acknowledgment that a *mahr* paid out before divorce can no longer be intended as a maintenance payment illustrates the chameleon nature that the *mahr* has assumed in German case law. What the courts determine the *mahr* to be depends on timing: after divorce it is a family law matter of maintenance, but before divorce it could be a contractual debt or gift. Despite having the benefit of the expert opinion, the appellate court bowed to precedent by remanding the case to the Family Law Chamber, thus confirming the function of the *mahr* as a means of financial security for the wife if it involves a substantial sum and has not been paid out before separation or termination of the marriage by divorce.

### F. *1988, Frankfurt: Is* Mahr *a Post-Divorce Contract?*

Three years after the Zweibrücken case, the first instance Family Law Chamber in Frankfurt (AmtsG)[43] approved an agreement between two

Iranian spouses to dissolve their marriage contract, in which the husband had agreed to give a Qur'an and 1,500 rials (approximately 1 euro) to the wife as *mahr*. In place of the original *marriage* contract the parties entered into a *divorce* contract. The husband committed himself as father to pay DM 400 (200 euros) monthly to support their son, who was living with the mother. The spouses agreed to forego any post-divorce alimony claims available under German law in exchange for an agreement by the husband to pay a lump sum of DM 15,000 (7,500 euros) to the wife. The case raises the interesting issue of whether Muslim parties should regulate not only marital life but also the post-divorce life in a marriage contract specifying what is *mahr* and what is maintenance.

G. *1988, Berlin: Fluctuating Value of the* Mahr

The peculiarities of the currency in which the *mahr* agreement is made are illustrated in the next case.[44] An Iranian Muslim couple was divorced by a German court applying Iranian Islamic law. Thereupon the wife claimed an agreed *mahr* of 1,500,000 rials, calculated according to the exchange rate at the time of the agreement to be worth DM 42,000 (22,000 euros), plus interest. The husband countered that the calculation had to be made according to the rate of exchange at the time the *mahr* was actually paid, in which case the agreed sum was worth only DM 5,000 (2500 euros) (there is no mention in the judgment as to whether he contested the payment of interest). Because the claim arose after a divorce, the court felt justified in following precedent by treating the *mahr* issue as a maintenance claim. Since the function of maintenance is to meet the needs of the person entitled to assistance, the court chose the higher sum to match the cost of living in Germany. The wife had also claimed four percent interest. This was rejected by the court because Iranian law applied (both parties were Iranian citizens), and a payment of interest would violate the basic Iranian sense of justice (*ordre public*).[45]

H. *1987–1988, Federal High Court: What Do the Parties to a* Mahr *Agreement Intend?*

The superior court in Germany, the Federal High Court (Bundesgerichtshof, BGH), cemented the treatment of the *mahr* contract as a matter of family law with a decision in 1987.[46] In that case a Muslim woman, a Palestinian student (who originally held an Israeli passport but after the marriage held a document for stateless persons), married a German Muslim convert in the Munich mosque. The marriage certificate issued by the mosque said: "The bride price has been fixed at DM 100,000 [50,000 euros]," a handsome sum. Three years later the marriage ended in divorce by way of a decree from the Family Law Chamber. Two years later the husband submitted to the mosque a written certification of *ṭalāq* (declaration of divorce) and final divorce. He declared unilaterally, without agreement from the wife, that financial claims from either spouse were excluded. The wife then took him to the Family Law Chamber to claim the *mahr* plus four percent interest. She won her suit. The contract was seen as an agreement on maintenance in a case of divorce. A maintenance agreement like this one needs no particular notarized form in order to be legitimate under German law. As for the amount, the court did find it to be too high when compared to the amount the husband would have had to pay had there been an agreement for lifetime support for the wife upon divorce.

On appeal before the Higher Regional Court (OLG), the husband won. The wife then appealed to the Federal High Court. The court admitted that it had difficulties deciding how to classify the *mahr* in terms of German law. The court recapitulated the intricate problems that *mahr* posed for the German conflict of law rules: If the *mahr* is seen as a result of marriage or in connection with the effects of marriage, then the law of the marital domicile is to be applied; but if it is seen as a matter of the financial security of the wife during the marriage, the law of domicile of the claimant also applies. Further, if the *mahr* is seen as a matter of post-divorce maintenance or a division of marital property, then the law of the nationality of the parties applies; but if it is seen as a debt claim based on a contract, the German law can apply instead of the law of nationality.

The court then proceeded to analyze the reasoning behind the lower appellate court's ruling in favor of the husband. The lower appellate court had treated the *mahr* agreement as a civil contractual transaction. However, it rejected the husband's assertion that he had only signed the marriage certificate as a formality without believing that he was taking on a legal obligation to pay the *mahr*. The marriage contract could have been nullified under German law only if both spouses were aware that one or the other was not taking its terms seriously. The lower appellate court also found that the contract could not be nullified on grounds of the husband's ignorance of Islamic law. As a religious convert he was presumed to be aware of his obligations under Islamic law. Furthermore, in terms of equity, he had waited much too long after the divorce to give written notice of his intention not to accept the obligation of the *mahr*. If he had never taken the *mahr* contract seriously, he should have made this known much earlier. In other words, he had slept on his rights.

Having held that the *mahr* agreement was to be treated under German civil law, the lower appellate court found the contract invalid for the following reasons: (1) it was an agreement made in connection with a religious marriage ceremony. Religious ceremonies have no legal consequences in Germany (a marriage is valid only if concluded before the state authorities after or before the religious ceremony), and, besides, in this case there had been a civil marriage; (2) the *mahr* agreement constituted a marriage contract, which is valid only if notarized in the form prescribed by the German family law regulating marital property and social security payments, especially when the contract involves a woman who becomes economically dependent on the husband because it is agreed that she care for the household and he earn the money; (3) because the wife may claim the *mahr* from the estate of her husband in the case of his death, the agreement is to be treated as an inheritance agreement which must also be in a prescribed form; and (4) if the *mahr* is to be taken as a promise of a gift, that is, a promise without consideration, the mosque agreement between the spouses in this case did not meet the notarization requirements.

The Federal High Court rejected the foregoing arguments of the lower appellate court on the ground that it had reached its legal conclusions without sufficient factual evidence. The Federal High Court remanded the case to establish what exactly the parties intended to achieve subjectively with the agreement on the *mahr*: specifically, was it intended that the wife have the right to a large sum of money as *mahr*, and is that sum meant to be added to or subtracted from her rights in profits earned from the marital properties, or is it a post-divorce lump sum of maintenance? The court then indicated what legal conclusions should follow once the facts were established. If it were found that the parties intended the *mahr* as a sum additional to the wife's normal share of the marital property, then the agreement could be treated as a simple marriage contract, and thus not as a property contract in need of notarization. If it found that the parties had intended it to be a maintenance agreement, then the court had the authority to interfere with the agreement and reduce the amount due, given that the length of the marriage was just a few months longer than what is called a "short marriage" in German law.[47] Divorces after short marriages are deemed under German family law to be inequitable and are therefore "punished" by reduced or no maintenance awards.[48] So it was necessary to further establish whether the marriage could be treated as "short" because it seemed that the husband had threatened to end the marriage sooner than actually happened, but did not because the wife was under a deportation threat.

In terms of legal doctrine, the Federal High Court further confirmed the chameleon treatment of *mahr*. It held that the nature of the claim for *mahr* under a marriage agreement should depend on when the claim is made. If the claim is made during the marriage, then it is a matter of marital maintenance and division of marital properties; if made after divorce, then it is a matter of post-divorce maintenance. Despite offering this solution, the court cautiously left the doctrinal door open. It declared courts free in the future to reclassify the nature of the *mahr* claim, depending on the circumstances and the intent of the parties.

The court's decision to base the test of validity of the *mahr* terms of a marriage contract on the subjective intentions of the parties does not make life for Muslim couples any easier.[49] Certainly lawyers and notaries could advise their clients to enter into only notarized agreements and to specify what the wife is to do with the *mahr*. Such specifications do not conform to the classical Islamic legal notion that the *mahr* is simply the possession of the wife, however, who does not have to specify how she will use it.[50] In trying to ascertain the intentions of the parties in *mahr* agreements, it may be that the German courts will be forced to rely on cultural expectations as best explaining the intentions of the parties.

One issue the court failed to mention, even as dicta, is whether the German courts could eventually recognize the *mahr* as a separate legal category. Certainly this would be possible under the German-Iranian Treaty, in which dower is listed as a separate legal category. The judges may also have to acquaint themselves again with Prussian law, which allowed spouses to make their own contractual agreements about the dowry. There seems to be an unarticulated reluctance of the German courts to treat dower as a category of debt. This is true even without considering it as a gift (*ṣadaqa*) that the Iranian husband should give upon divorcing the wife under the reformed Iranian family law as a compensation for her having cared for him and contributed to his wealth. It seems from the German point of view that if the *mahr* were seen as arising from a debt contract it would tend to be seen as mere consideration for marital sexual intercourse.[51] Such a result might well render the *mahr* contrary to *ordre public* and the principle of gender equality (as has been decided in Canada).[52]

### I. *1987–88, Hamm:* Mahr *is a Debt Contract*

Eight months after the Federal High Court decision, a Higher Regional Court (OLG) issued an interesting decision on the nature of *mahr*, which comes closest to the traditional Islamic law understanding.[53] In 1979 a Tunisian citizen had married a German citizen. They entered a notarized marriage contract just before the marriage, in which they specified: (1) that the marriage was unlimited (to distinguish it from a temporary or *mutʿa* marriage); (2) that the spouses would not have community property, but rather keep their fortunes separate (which also conforms to the Qurʾanic injunction that the wife has control over her own property and earnings);[54] and (3) that if the marriage ended in divorce, the husband was obliged to pay the wife DM 5,000 (2,500 euros) as settlement/compensation and as dower (which seems to refer to not only *mahr* but also the classical Islamic gift on divorce, or *mutʿa*). In the course of the marriage the wife, a schoolteacher with permanent civil service status, used her salary to maintain the family, to pay for her husband's further education, and to buy a building site in which she gave him one-half interest. In the course of the divorce proceedings, the two spouses disagreed on two issues: (1) whether the husband, as the financially weaker partner, was to receive a settlement; and (2) whether the husband should pay the *mahr*. On the issue of settlement, the court held that under the conflict of laws rules, German law should apply. It explained the function of a settlement as an instrument of equity to compensate the financially weaker marriage partner, who was disadvantaged by foregoing independent financial earnings for the sake of the marriage. The court rejected the husband's argument that he was the "house-husband" and therefore was disadvantaged. The court found that the wife had not only earned the family income, but also had taken care of the household and the three children.

On the issue of *mahr*, the court found itself in the same quandary as other German courts had. Because the German conflict of laws statute does not regulate *mahr* specifically, the courts have felt that they had the responsibility to try to fit *mahr* into one of the general categories named in the statute. Yet no one category had been fixed. The Higher Regional Court interpreted the most recent decision of the Federal High Court to mean that the "authentic" nature of *mahr*, for purposes of conflict of law, remained open. Accordingly, this court observed that whether German or Tunisian law applied depended on whether the *mahr* was to be classified as an element of the marriage (in which case the law of domicile would apply), or an element of divorce (in which case the law of nationality would apply), or a matter of separation of property (which could depend on the spouses' choice of law). The court then systematically listed the facts that would speak for a choice of German law: the marriage had taken place in Germany, the marital home was in Germany, and the wife had a civil service job in Germany. What spoke for the choice of Tunisian law was that the *mahr* represented a desire of the parties that their marriage be equally recognized in Tunisia. The court then found that it really did not have to decide between applying either German or Tunisian law because the results of both laws would be the same. Under Tunisian law, the husband would have been obliged to pay the *mahr* upon divorce. Under German law, the husband would be held to his promise to pay.[55] The wife as creditor needed only to base her claim on the husband's promise to pay, and this existed regardless of the economic and legal context in which the promise was made. Thus, in the end the husband was required to pay the agreed-upon amount of *mahr*.

Of the cases discussed above, this decision is the clearest treatment of *mahr* as a legal debt and contractual institution in itself. One commentator criticized it as a deviation from the usual classification of *mahr* as a maintenance issue.[56] But this critique ignores the careful delineations the spouses had made in the written contract setting forth the details of their married life. They had rejected community property (they kept their own earnings separate), and the *mahr* was not confused with this legal institution. The *mahr* was specifically named as dower and as compensation for divorce. Under Islamic law such a combination could be called into question, since these are two separate legal conceptions. Nonetheless, for purposes of German legal understanding of *mahr*, the fact that the spouses had clearly distinguished it from maintenance and from community property prevented the *mahr* from being classified as maintenance. Thus, this position of the Hamm Higher Regional Court can be said to have brought some clarity to the German legal understanding of *mahr*. But as we shall see in an analysis of the case law for parties who are German-born, this clarity has again been undermined.

## Mahr Agreements of Muslim Turkish Citizens in Germany

As is clear from the foregoing examples, most of the reported cases on *mahr* involve Muslim parties coming from countries other than Turkey. Yet most of the Muslims in Germany originate from Turkey. The Turkish law applied by the German courts to family disputes is based on Swiss law. The Turkish superior courts are divided on the question of whether monies paid by the husband on the wedding day should even be legally justiciable, since in the opinion of some judges it appears that the man is purchasing sexual rights over the woman.[57]

German courts often deal with gifts of wedding jewelry from the husband to the wife.[58] The jewelry is considered distinct from the *mahr*, as custom in the Turkish German community holds that the husband "lends" the gold jewelry to the wife only for the duration of the marriage.[59] This is consistent with the Turkish Family Law Code, which entitles each spouse to the return of personal property upon dissolution of a marriage, regardless of whether the parties lived in or out of community property.[60] Probably, if a *mahr* agreement included reference to valuable jewelry, courts would presume that the parties intended not to make the jewelry part of the *mahr*.[61] Any enforcement of *mahr* agreements reached by Turkish couples would have to be done not through the German courts, but through arbitration led by the imam of their local German mosque.

There is one unusual German court decision which has added fuel to the fire about whether Turkish law as understood by German judges allows for state enforcement of a *mahr* agreement between Turkish citizens living in Germany. In 1997 the Higher Regional Appellate Court (OLG) in Düsseldorf[62] tried to distinguish the *mahr* (*mehir* in Turkish, payable to the bride) and the bride price (*baslik* in Turkish, payable to the parents of the bride) based on the intentions of the parties, who were Turkish citizens. In a written agreement, the husband had stated that he would pay the bride DM 5,000 (2,500 euros). The parties divorced in Germany under Turkish law without consummating the marriage. The wife then sued for fulfillment of the husband's promise to pay he DM 5,000. The husband contended that the *mahr* is not obligatory under Turkish law as it does not determine the validity of the marriage. The German court rejected his arguments, holding that as long as the German Federal High Court had accepted the validity of the *mahr* under Islamic religious law, and the parties had indeed undergone a religious marriage ceremony, then why should Turkish law be construed to involve religious law any less than German law does? Alternatively, the husband contended that his promise to pay was a promise of a gift, and therefore the *mahr* obligation had been fulfilled when he had given his wife many marriage gifts. The court again rejected these arguments. On the contrary, it asserted, marriage gifts had nothing to do with the *mahr*. The court concluded by applying the Islamic law that provides for the return of the *mahr* upon termination of an unconsummated marriage but with one-half of the agreed-upon *mahr* retained by the wife.

Turkish jurist Bilge Özlan commented critically on the German court's decision.[63] The court should not have applied Islamic law as Turkish law, she said. Özlan asserted that in the religious ceremony men promise to pay a given sum of money only in order to get through the ceremony, but both spouses know that the promise has no legal significance. Özlan further pointed out that the question remains open whether an agreement to pay a *mahr* would be valid as part of a civil marriage ceremony in Turkey. Some courts have decided positively and others negatively. When the parties intend that the *mahr* should constitute the promise of a gift only,[64] then Turkish law allows the donor to withdraw from the promise at any time. If the parties intend that the promise of money constitute a contract, then unilateral withdrawal requires a legally valid reason.

## Application of German Contract and Family Law to Marriage Contracts in the Case of German-Born Muslim Citizens

There is a growing body of case law on claims for *mahr* by both German-born and naturalized Muslim citizens. Reported decisions indicate that in these cases German courts are applying the concepts and doctrines that were developed for foreigners under the conflict of laws rules. This approach is questionable for Muslim German citizens, for whom the Islamic law sought to be applied is not a foreign state law. Instead, it takes on the character of a religious law. The issue should therefore be whether state law can recognize religious law as binding. The following case from 1997–1998, respecting a contractual agreement on *mahr* involved two German-born spouses who had converted to Islam, illustrates the problem.[65]

### J. *1997–1998, Celle*: Mahr *as Maintenance*

In the city of Celle, as part of their religious marriage ceremony, the couple entered into a contract specifying that the husband would pay DM 30,000 (15,000 euros) as a lump-sum payment upon divorce, if it were to occur. The parties later divorced. The wife then sued for the lump-sum payment in the Civil Law Chamber, citing a Qur'anic verse granting women a dower from their husbands.[66] She argued that the function of the dower is to protect the wife against the arbitrary decision of the husband to divorce her, since a financial obligation would make him think twice before divorcing. It was with this intention that the two had entered into the contract. This implied that her husband, despite the intended deterrent, had divorced her arbitrarily and that the agreement was intended to punish him for an inequitable decision by compensating her for the inequity.

The Higher Regional Court did not have to determine (unlike in the typical *mahr* dispute in Germany) which of the foreign Islamic laws was applicable, since both parties were German. This is the first reported case in which the parties cite the Qurʾan as a legal authority. The final decision of the court was to dismiss the cause of action. Two grounds were given, one jurisdictional and the other substantive. First, the Civil Law Chamber was denied jurisdiction of the first instance because the cause of action should have been classified as a family matter. Second, in terms of the substantive law, the court held that the wife had no cause of action based on the marriage contract. The reasons were twofold: (1) the *mahr* has the objective function of a maintenance agreement, independent of what the parties perhaps intended; and (2) the wife had already received an award from the Family Law Chamber as part of the divorce proceedings, a lump sum of DM 37,000 for maintenance. Thus, the court reasoned, she could not in all equity make a claim for an additional *mahr* of DM 30,000 based on the marriage contract.

The court then addressed the wife's argument that the *mahr* contract could serve as an agreement on division of profits from marital property. The husband counter-argued that if the agreement was treated as a marital property agreement it was still invalid because it was not notarized as required by the German law governing marital property. Because the husband was a lawyer, the court observed that in all fairness he could have been denied the right to oppose the claim for payment of the *mahr* on grounds of form because as a lawyer he should have known that the agreement was not in proper form as a property agreement. The court nonetheless pardoned him on the ground that it cannot be expected of a German lawyer, even a Muslim, to know without arduous research that his Islamic marriage agreement, pursuant to German law, had the same character as a marital property agreement in need of notarization.

Unfortunately, the Celle court did not refer to the Federal High Court decision of 1986 regarding the need to determine the parties' intention. Hence, it was not factually ascertained what the parties had subjectively intended when signing the marriage contract. Nor was there an analysis of or credence given to the arguments of the wife to the effect that the agreement was intended as a civil contract to compensate the wife and punish the husband for inequitable divorce.

K. *1998, Federal High Court:* Mahr *is Not a Debt Contract*

Since the Celle decision, another case has given the Federal High Court occasion to return to the question of *mahr* agreements.[67] The facts of the case were as follows:[68] A then-Syrian citizen had entered a notarized marriage contract in Frankfurt with his German wife-to-be in 1976. In it, he was obliged to pay a *mahr* of DM 20,000 (10,000 euros), one half at the wedding and the other half payable upon divorce. He also conferred on the wife the conditional right of *ṭalāq* (delegating to her a unilateral right to pronounce a final divorce) if he entered a polygamous marriage, had an adulterous relationship, did not maintain her, undermined her authority over the children, or gave her grounds for divorce under German law. In fact, he never paid any of the *mahr* and she never claimed the first half in nineteen years of marriage. In the meantime the husband became a German citizen. In 1995 the wife applied for and was granted a divorce decree under German law, which recognizes "breakdown of the marriage" as the sole ground for divorce. Three months after the decree, she remarried. Six months after the decree, she entered an action in the Family Law Chamber for the DM 20,000 (10,000 euros) dower plus four percent interest since the date of the proceedings. The husband submitted four defenses: (1) the wife had forfeited the first half of her dowry because she had not claimed it upon marriage; (2) even if it could not be said that she forfeited it, she had received it in the form of gifts from him (in addition to everyday maintenance) worth more than DM 10,000 (5000 euros); (3) in any case, the terms of the marriage contract were invalid because such stipulations are against good morals or local custom (*gute Sitte*); and (4) even if the contract were deemed valid, paying the dowry was conditioned on the husband being the cause of the marital breakdown. He had not given her cause to divorce him, so the condition for receipt of the dower had not been fulfilled.

The trial court of the Family Law Chamber agreed in part with the husband that the wife had forfeited the first half of the *mahr*. The court cited equity as its reason: the wife had slept on her rights for nineteen years and had indeed enjoyed various gifts during the marriage. Furthermore, she could not treat the claim as separate from the divorce litigation. As the latter had already been closed, procedurally she would be reopening the divorce matter with an action on the *mahr*. There was no mention of the point that Islamic law in effect recognizes no statute of limitations on the claim for *mahr*.[69] Also, the court may have too readily accepted the husband's argument that the first half of the *mahr* had already been paid in the equivalent form of various gifts during the marriage: under Islamic law, the *mahr* cannot be replaced by or confused with gifts.[70] As for the second half of the *mahr*, the court found that the contract was not immoral or bad custom.

The husband appealed to the Higher Regional Court.[71] Relying on the precedent set by the Federal High Court of 1987,[72] the husband took another tack. He no longer argued that the contract was invalid. He instead argued that the trial court had failed to analyze the intentions of the parties to the marriage contract as required by case law. They had agreed upon two legal matters—*mahr* and *ṭalāq*—which are matters of Islamic religious law. Hence their intention was that Islamic law is applicable. Therefore one has to go to the Qurʾan—just as the German Muslim wife had argued in the Celle case above—to find out the conditions of *ṭalāq* and *mahr*. *fialāq* had to be pronounced three times, whereupon dower was payable. On the facts, however, the thrice-pronounced *ṭalāq* had not occurred. Hence, there was no Islamic religious divorce and ergo, there could be no enforcement of the *mahr* payment. The wife countered with the argument that the contract did not limit itself to Islamic law only. The contract gave her the alternative of applying the German divorce law, whereupon she could also claim the DM 10,000.

The appellate court first found that German law applies, not foreign law as in preceding case law concerning non-citizens. And it agreed with the trial court that the *mahr* agreement was a contract without an immoral purpose. It explained why it had to treat the matter as one involving a civil contract rather than one of family maintenance or community property. The conflict of laws statute, the EGBGB, had no definitive rule on *mahr*. Neither did any other German law. Up to now the courts had tried to subsume *mahr* into family law in general and, more specifically, into the subcategories of post-divorce maintenance, community property, and inheritance. For lack of a definitive statutory definition of *mahr*, even for German citizens, the court held that it could be subsumed into the German law for notarized contracts for payment, as the parties had so intended under the principle of contractual freedom. The *mahr* agreement was to be deemed a debt contract, as the Hamm Higher Regional Court had done in 1987 in the case of the Tunisian husband.[73] It also appeared to the court that the previous Federal High Court in the case of the Palestinian wife[74] had also construed the *mahr* agreement as a contractual matter because it had cited provisions in the Civil Code governing state of mind for purposes of contract.[75]

The court upheld the award of DM 10,000 deferred dower plus interest to the wife.[76] The husband persisted and appealed to the Federal High Court. While it agreed with the lower courts that a *mahr* contract is not immoral, the court found that in the absence of German statutory regulation of *mahr*, there is sufficient case law defining this legal institution. Even though the case law had been developed in the context of international private law for foreigners, the doctrine could be applied by analogy to German citizens. The case law had usually treated the *mahr* as a family law institution, largely comparable to post-divorce maintenance. Nonetheless, as the court remarked, some judges have treated a *mahr* agreement as a civil contract of debt, as the lower appellate court and the Hamm Higher Regional Court[77] had done. Hence, the Federal High Court felt compelled to examine the nature of the German law of debt contracts and decide whether a *mahr* contract met the same requirements.

A contract under the German Civil Code[78] consists of an abstract promise to perform and a description of what is to be performed, independent of motives, economic circumstances or legal considerations. A measure of abstractness lies in the absence of a motive for the performance in the written contract.[79] The *mahr* agreement as written in the case at hand thus could not be a debt contract, said the court, because the husband had specified the reasons or motives for agreeing to pay the *mahr* and had done so in consideration of Islamic legal rules. There were no other indications that the parties would have entered into the *mahr* contract for reasons other than those given—a sign that the contract failed the test of abstractness. In effect, a *mahr* contract specifying payment after divorce upon the petition of the wife is not a debt contract in the German understanding of a contract as an economic or commercial dealing. Even though the Federal High Court categorically refused to recognize the *mahr* agreement as a debt contract under German law, it still recognized the contract as a potentially enforceable marriage agreement if all the circumstances intended by the parties were fulfilled, as it had done in its 1987 decision (though it did not refer in detail to that case). The court went on to say that the lower appellate court had not properly construed the intentions of the parties. The fact that they had made an agreement with regard to the non-German legal institution of *mahr*—an Islamic institution—meant that they intended that the terms of the contract be interpreted within the context of Islamic law. Without being specific about whether a debt is intended to be created by *mahr* or not under Islamic law, the court then leapt to the conclusion that the spouses could have thought that they were intending to regulate spousal maintenance under Islamic law. The court did not ask itself whether this would have been possible, since Islamic law distinguishes *mahr* from post-divorce maintenance such as *ʿidda* maintenance and *mutʿa* maintenance.

The Federal High Court then remanded the case for a factual determination of what the parties had intended with the *mahr* agreement. In other words, if it were found that the parties intended it to be a maintenance contract, it might still be unenforceable. For one, the wife had remarried, meaning that she was being maintained by another man. This was relevant because if the *mahr* were intended to be a post-divorce maintenance contract, it could be that the parties did not intend for the wife to receive maintenance from two sources: her divorced husband and her second husband. No mention was made of the "Islamic law context" which allows a divorced wife to claim the *mahr* as a debt even if she is remarried by the time she makes her claim. The second factor that the lower court was to address was the spouses' divorce mutual agreement to forego post-divorce alimony. The implication was that the release from alimony claims amounted to a retraction of the original *mahr* agreement, assuming that the parties intended the *mahr* to be a maintenance agreement. From this it appears that it is difficult for the judges to imagine that Islamic law puts the divorced woman in a much more favorable position than German law ever could achieve, since she could end up with her *mahr* from her former marriage, her *ʿidda* payments, her *mutʿa* gift[80] and, if remarried, a new *mahr* and daily maintenance from her new husband.

In light of an opinion from the classical Hanbali jurist Ibn Taymiyya, it is also questionable whether a wife's agreement to renounce the *mahr* is valid.[81] Ibn Taymiyya surmised that a woman is likely to agree to the opposite of what was in the marriage contract either out of fear or as the price to be paid for an untroubled divorce. He agreed that her renunciation would be acceptable only when totally independent of a divorce or when provision is already made in the marriage contract for the conditions of renunciation. This position strengthens the point of view that *mahr* claims should be handled completely separately from divorce proceedings in the German courts.

Interestingly, the issue of four percent interest on a delayed *mahr* payment seems not to have raised any eyebrows in the Federal High Court. As in most of the foregoing case law, there was no discussion about whether the wife could claim interest on the *mahr* in an Islamic law context.[82] Muslim women in Germany may have to reflect on whether they wish to make a provision in a *mahr* agreement for reimbursement from the husband for the costs incurred in payment if the husband has no genuine reasons for withholding it under Islamic law. According to some modern Islamic scholars, even a compensatory fine could be fixed, for the sayings of the Prophet (*ḥadīth*) clearly lay down the principle that a man who is more than capable of paying a debt is to be morally condemned for delaying payment.[83] Or the contract could specify that the deferred *mahr* shall be treated as a benefit from the wife to her husband, since he receives the benefit of holding on to that money until it is requested. For this benefit the husband should repay the wife an extra compensation out of gratitude.[84] One could argue that it is analogous to a controversy that arose in twelfth-century Andalusia, where the jurists argued about whether a wife could claim rent from her husband who had received a benefit by choosing to live in her home as the seat of the marriage.[85]

## Mahr Practices of German-Born Muslims Outside of Case Law

Outside of the courtroom, German-born Muslims are entering into marriage contracts regulating the payment of *mahr* without any thought of what the courts are deciding, just as the courts seem to make decisions about the nature of *mahr* without considering the practice of Muslims in Germany. In two reported decisions on *mahr* contracts between non-immigrants, for example, the courts did not call for an expert opinion on the actual practices of German-born Muslims to help them understand what Muslim couples generally intend with the institution of *mahr*. Yet it is not difficult for courts to determine these practices. Information is available from one of the largest non-immigrant Muslim associations in Germany, led by a German-born imam who has studied Islamic theology and Shariʿa.[86] He reports that, as a rule, when he performs a marriage ceremony there is no written contract, as in the Turkish community. But the German imam insists that the full *mahr* be paid on the day before the marriage ceremony or at the ceremony itself. He argues that the early practice in the time of the Prophet Muḥammad was immediate payment of the *mahr*. It was only under later practice that part of the *mahr* was paid upon marriage and the larger portion deferred until the time of divorce or death of the husband.[87] While the intention might have been to discourage men from divorcing their wives at the slightest disagreement, he says, the deferred dower was also abusive to women. Husbands placed all possible obstacles in the way of women seeking a divorce so that she would be forced to agree to forfeit the deferred dower as the price for divorce. This practice is against the rule in Islamic law, which treats *mahr* as the exclusive property of the wife, payable at any time she wants without any statute of limitations, and as a debt on the estate of the deceased husband if he does not pay upon request. All other gifts from the husband to the wife during the marriage do not count as *mahr*.

*Mahr* sizes in the German Muslim community range from DM 10 (5 euros) to DM 50,000 (25,000 euros), with an average of perhaps DM 2,000 (1,000 euros). The imam discourages husbands from borrowing money to pay the *mahr*, because if the husband fails to pay back the credit during the course of the marriage, he may pressure his wife to give back the *mahr*. While under Islamic law the *mahr* is the exclusive property of the wife, it does happen in practice that sometimes the wife gives the *mahr* to her parents for covering the costs of the wedding, or she buys household goods that belong exclusively to her.

The *mahr* is not regarded as maintenance under Islamic law. Once it has been given to the wife, the imam informs the marrying parties that the husband is exclusively responsible for maintenance during the marriage, including providing the wife with household help. Maintenance during the marriage is separate from the *mahr*. As for post-divorce alimony, in addition to the payment of maintenance during the *ʿidda*, the couple is counseled to regulate this issue in the marriage contract, whereby the husband is obliged to pay the Qurʾanic divorce portion, the *mutʿa*.[88]

## Lessons from Other Jurisdictions

The German courts have tried to make the best of a bad situation in regard to defining what a *mahr* agreement actually is. They have no statutory guidance. Technically, the German courts could simply decide there is no remedy for an action on *mahr*, since there is no provision in the conflict of laws rules for such a legal institution. Instead the courts have decided to give a remedy by putting the round peg of *mahr* into the square hole of the scheme of conflict of laws rules. The *mahr* has been squeezed into two squares: (1) the regulation of marital property, since *mahr* is the property of the wife but usually remains in the possession of the husband, benefiting him until divorce or death; and (2) post-divorce alimony, since the practice of deferred dowry has led to most claims on the *mahr* being made as a consequence of divorce, thus causing the German courts to associate *mahr* more with divorce than with marriage.

One of the reasons why the German courts seem to fall into the trap of seeing the *mahr* as part of post-divorce maintenance lies in the very methodology used to determine foreign or religious law. Judges rely primarily on translated statutes of the respective Muslim countries involved. Thus, they ignore academic jurisprudence and case law, partly because this would mean an increase in the costs of litigation. Yet if German judges sought more information about how other countries distinguish between *mahr* and maintenance, they might avoid misunderstanding the *mahr*. Few German courts realize that Islamic law does provide for post-divorce maintenance: there exist both maintenance for the three months after divorce or for the duration of a pregnancy (which theoretically can last up to seven years in some jurisdictions), and the *mutʿa* maintenance. Moreover, German courts have not kept abreast of the changes in the laws in various Muslim countries. Egyptian courts, for example, have recently used the *mutʿa* to award a woman post-divorce alimony.[89]

German courts would do well to read the Indian constitutional case law on how to distinguish the *mahr* from maintenance. As the Indian Supreme Court held in a claim from a woman divorced after forty-three years of marriage, *mahr* is not occasioned by the divorce.[90] It is instead an amount the wife is entitled to receive in consideration of the marriage. This is the very opposite of an amount paid in consideration of divorce. Instead, the *mahr* is imposed on the husband as a mark of respect for his wife. This is quite different from providing the wife, once divorced, with maintenance beyond the *ʿidda*. The Supreme Court found authority for the maintenance after divorce in the Qurʾanic verse: "For divorced women maintenance should be provided on a reasonable scale. This is a duty on the righteous."[91] In answer to the explanation put forth by the All India Muslim Personal Law Board that the obligation is only on the more pious Muslim husband, the court cited another verse that encourages the use of common sense.[92] There appears to have been no explanation as to why the *mahr* verse has been interpreted as obligatory, but not the verse about *mutʿa*.

The Shah Bano Begum decision[93] rendering *mutʿa* obligatory attracted the ire of the Muslim Personal Law Board and led to the enactment of a new law, the Muslim Women (Protection of Rights on Divorce) Act.[94] Under this law the divorced husband is still responsible for paying the *mahr* as a contractual obligation "at the time of her marriage or any time thereafter"[95] but is no longer responsible for paying maintenance beyond the *ʿidda* or two years after the birth of a child. Instead, the courts must issue orders against the relatives of the needy wife. These blood relatives are defined as those who have a right to inherit from her, for example, her grown children or her parents.[96] Failing such relatives, the State Waqf Board (religious charity trust) shall be ordered to maintain the divorced wife.[97] This position corresponds to that of the classical Maliki school of Islamic law.[98] Whether it is reasonable and compatible with German *ordre public* to expect a needy divorced woman to go in search of relatives or to apply for public charity funds may be a question a German court would pose. Answering this question would require not only an understanding of the Islamic law of *mahr*, but also the controversial nature of spousal maintenance in Islamic law in general.[99]

**Conclusion**

This survey of German case law on *mahr* as an aspect of the Muslim marriage contract reveals a jarring cacophony of judicial voices. Yet there is one dominant melody: the *mahr* is to be construed as an agreement to regulate marital property but for the functional purpose of providing the wife with post-divorce alimony. On the fringes of this doctrinal melody are some discordant notes, however. Some believe that the *mahr* is per se evidence of a purchase of sexual services of the wife because it is paid only by the husband. If true, this violates the *ordre public* and principle of equality in German society. According to another group, the *mahr* should be construed through the social-functional lenses of the average German marriage pattern, in which it is usually the man who is the financial provider in exchange for the wife providing household and conjugal comfort. On the other hand, some voices argue that *mahr* has no direct equivalent in German law, irrespective of social function. It is an institution of Muslim religious law, and as such the state has no business enforcing it. The parties should rely on their own religious authorities to mediate and resolve conflicts between spouses over payment of the *mahr*. Nonetheless, others see the *mahr* as part of an agreement between spouses who have the freedom under contract law to regulate their own affairs. Any dispute arising from such agreements is fully justiciable as long as the formal German notarization requirements for contracts or debt or gift agreements are met. The role of the courts, then, would be to interpret the intention of the parties.

What changes are then possible in the law given these disparate approaches to *mahr*? Basically there are two possibilities. First, the legislature could pass a statute regulating the *mahr* as a legal institution and formally add it to the categories of family law topics that fall under the conflict of laws rules. Alternatively, the courts could reconfigure their understanding of *mahr* by classifying it as a debt or gift agreement and treat it as a civil issue rather than one of family law.

If these two solutions are not adopted, litigating parties will have to hire legal experts who write water-tight agreements that anticipate as far as possible all of the courts' points of view. It is doubtful that any of the above options will be adopted or are practical. The reason, I believe, is an underlying unease about the consequences of applying the Islamic law of *mahr* in German courts.

A comprehensive system upholding *mahr* agreements contains the seeds of upsetting the German social and political concept of how best to prevent women from overburdening men, but at the same time not burdening the state with the support of financially insecure women.[100] I assert this because a consistent theme in the German case law is that a woman who has been promised a large substantial sum in the form of the *mahr* will end up in a far better financial position than her average German non-Muslim sister. A divorced Muslim woman could get not only the *mahr* and *ʿidda* maintenance, but also possibly a post-divorce *mutʿa* gift, plus a second *mahr* and continuing maintenance from her second husband if she remarries. In addition, she could keep any expensive gifts received from her ex-husband during their marriage. By contrast, her "poor" divorced husband is stuck with paying not only the *mahr* to the ex-wife, but also a second *mahr* to the new wife if he remarries and her continuing maintenance costs. It could be feared that the man could become so indebted that he could become a welfare case for the state (rather than the woman, which is usually expected in a divorce situation). Social expectations are thus turned upside down by the *mahr*.

The explanation I have given above about underlying fears of the consequences of a *mahr* may also explain why the courts apply a functional lens. They do not examine the question of whether Islamic jurisprudence would use the same functional lens. Is *mahr* a sign of respect for the woman[101] or is it a form of financial security against a husband's unreasonable use of his *ṭalāq* power? Or is it a private instrument for rearranging the inequities in the job market? Perhaps both the German courts and modern Islamic jurists have to rephrase the debate and ask to what extent German law and Islamic family law perpetuate inequalities between men and women which the partners themselves try to overcome through their own marriage contracts.

NOTES

[1] *Lex domicili* has a long tradition in English law. See, e.g., Bombay High Court *Fall Queen Empress v. Rego Montopoulo*, (1849) 19 I.L.R. Bombay Series 741, 746 (citing Coke in Calvin's Case, 7 Coke's Rep. 6a).

[2] Einführungsgesetz zum Bürgerlichen Gesetzbuche [EGBGB], ch. 2 (prologue, Civil Code) (discussing international private law).

[3] The Indian Chief, (1801) 3 Chr. Rob. Admir. Rep. 29.

[4] Domicile applies as the primary law only in cases of maintenance claims for children. EGBGB Art. 18(1). A post-divorce alimony claim, in contrast, is subject to the law governing the divorce, EGBGB Art. 18(4), which in turn is governed by the law that determines conjugal rights. The law of conjugal rights is governed primarily by citizenship; in the case of plural citizenships, the law of residence applies or the parties are allowed to choose which law of citizenship should apply. EGBGB Art. 14.

[5] EGBGB Art. 6. See judgment of the Frankfurt First Instance Court (AmtsGericht), which held that a husband's divorce right (*ṭalāq*) is arbitrary and therefore contrary to the German constitutional provisions for gender equality. In IPRspr. 1988, no. 75, also in NJW 1989, 1414.

[6] EGBGB Art. 6.

[7] Niederlassungsabkommen zwischen dem Deutschen Reich und dem Kaiserreich Persien of 17 December 1929, Reichsgesetzblatt Jg. 1930, Teil II, p. 1002, p. 1006 (confirmed by the Federal Republic of Germany on 15 August 1955, BGBl. Teil II, No. 19, 25 August 1955, p. 829). The treaty foresees the application of the law of citizenship basically only in cases where both parties are of the same citizenship. Presumably in a mixed German-Iranian marriage, the normal statutory rules of conflict of law of the country where the case is being heard would apply. See Kegel 1996, 44–46.

[8] Schlussprotokoll Art. 8(3).

[9] BundesGerichtsHof [BGH] (Federal High Court) Oct. 14, 1992, Das Standesamt (StAZ), 1993, 5, and Praxis des internationalen Privat- und Verfahrensrechts (IPRax) 1993, 102. See also Amts Gericht Kerpen Mar. 2, 2001, *Zeitschrift für das gesamte Familienrecht* (FamRZ) 2001, 1526–1527 (where it was held that a treaty is the primary source of law even above the codes of law. I have not yet investigated the actual history of the treaty and the motives behind it).

[10] Hattenhauer 1994, Arts. 204ff.

[11] Idem, Art. 177.

[12] Ganghofer and Poughon 1995, 357–370.

[13] Hattenhauer 1994, Arts. 185, 194.

[14] Bürgerlichesgesetzbuch [BGB] § 1360.

[15] BundesGerichtsHof, FamRZ 1987, 572–576.

[16] OberLandesGericht [OLG] Zweibrücken, FamRZ 1997, 1212–1213.

[17] This is based on my consultative work with a women's immigrant organization in Nuremberg (Kofiza) which specializes in the problems of marriages plagued with conflict of laws problems.

[18] Pawlowski 1983, 7. Up to now there has been no reported case on the validity or invalidity of unequal terms or contracts.

[19] See infra n. 20.

[20] Kegel and Schurig 2000, 283ff.

[21] The opinion was published separately from the court decision in *Gutachten zum internationalen und ausländischen Privatrecht* 1971 (IPR Gutachten), no. 38.

[22] See also Krüger 1977, 114–118.

[23] Here I am casting doubt on the correctness of the hornbook Islamic law that allows a deferred dowry, contrary to the primary principle in Islamic law that the wife may claim the dower anytime since it is her property. Jones 1996, 322–328.

[24] OLG Bremen, FamRZ 1980, 606.

[25] Elwan 1992, 326.

[26] KG (Berlin), 12 November 1979, FamRZ, 1980, 470.

[27] Grundgesetz für die Bundesrepublik Deutschland (federal constitution) (GG) Art. 6.

[28] OLG Koeln, IPRax 1983, 73.

[29] Traditionally, interest is not allowed under Islamic financial law.

[30] The judgment did not make clear under what law this divorce order was made.

[31] This could raise some questions about the principle of equality under German law, since the *mahr* has not yet been regarded equally as alimony for a poor needy husband who might not be earning as much as his wife.

[32] See IPRax 1983, 74–77 and 64–65. It is significant to note that all the other reported cases up to this point had involved written contracts.

[33] The parties resided in Hamburg, but it was not noted where they had married.

[34] For a discussion of the role of social status in German law, see Battes 1992, 69ff, 89.

[35] The legal construct to achieve this end would look like the following: a third party contracts with the husband to loan him money, but specifies that the loan is to be paid back to the wife. In effect, the claim to the debt is transferred to the wife. The husband retains the full amount of the loan throughout the marriage. Upon divorce, the loan becomes due. The wife then may sue the husband as the transferee of the debt. In this way, the *mahr* could be recognized under German law as a civil debt transaction rather than a matter of family law.

[36] Heldrich 1983, 64–65.

[37] Böhmer 1986, 216–218.

[38] See Jones 1996, 322–328.

[39] See idem.

[40] OLG Zweibrücken, Die deutsche Rechtsprechung auf dem Gebiete des Internationalen Privatrechts im Jahre 1986 (IPRspr 1986), no. 150.

[41] For procedural reasons, which we will not discuss in detail here, the appellate court sent the case back to the trial court, which was to treat it as a family law matter. The disposition of the case has not been reported.

[42] IPR Gutachten 1985/86, no. 31.

[43] AG Frankfurt, IPRspr. 1988, no. 75.

[44] KG (Berlin), FamRZ 1988, 296.

[45] Contrast this with the case law of the Indian courts when the delay is inequitable to the wife: Qureshi 1993, 157–158. This holding would also be in conformity with some of the early Egyptian case law, which has invalidated actual stipulations in the *mahr* contract that the husband is to compensate the wife for delayed payments. Shaham 1997, 150.

[46] BGH Judgment of 28 Jan. 1987, in IPRax 1988, 109–113.

[47] A short marriage is one that lasts three years or less. In this case, the parties had been married three years and four months.

[48] See, e.g., Bürgerliches Gesetzbuch [BGB] § 1576.

[49] Hessler 1988, 95–97.

[50] Such an approach would conform to an East African Islamic notion that a wife is expected to use the *mahr* for doing business in her own name. Bi Hawa Mohamed and Ally Sefu, Court of Appeal of Tanzania at Dar es Salaam, Civil Appeal No. 9/1983 (unreported).

[51] Siddiqui 1995, 16, 25.

[52] See *Vladi v. Vladi*, [1987] 7 Rep. Fam. L. (3d) 337 (Nova Scotia); Münchener Kommentar zum EGBGB 1990: Art. 15, 4, p. 882, n. 7.

[53] FamRZ 1988, 516.

[54] Qur'an 4:32. See also interpretation by Haddad 1985, 50.

[55] BGB § 780.

[56] Editor's note, Fam RZ 1988, 518.

[57] Krüger 1990, 313–325.

[58] E.g., OLG Hamm, Fam RZ 1994, 1259–1261.

[59] Krüger 1990, 313–325.

[60] Turkish Family Law Code Art. 146.

[61] This presumption would not necessarily apply to Omani Arabs living in Germany. See *Hafsa Saleh Mahmoud v. Abdul Aziz Ali Salim*, High Court, Zanzibar, Civil Case 30/1990; Abdul Aziz Ali Salim and Hafsa Saleh Mahmoud, Court of Appeal of Tanzania at Zanzibar, Civil Appeal 4/1992 (both unreported). The husband's contention that he only "loaned" the valuable wedding jewelry to the wife was rejected as contrary to the Maliki law of gifts.

[62] OLG Düsseldorf, FamRZ 1998, 623–624.

[63] Özlan 1998, 624–626.

[64] See OLG Nürnberg, FamRZ 2001, 1613, classifying the Turkish *mehir* as a promise of a gift, which does not serve the function of maintenance, which rests on the principle of women's need for financial security. Gifts are not related to this need.

[65] OLG Celle, FamRZ 1998, 374.

[66] Qur'an 4:24.

[67] BGH Judgment of 14 October 1998, reported in *Neue Juristische Wochenschrift* (NJW) 1999, 575.

[68] OberLandesGericht Bamberg, Judgment of 13 February 1997, 2 UF 257/96; F 224/96 AG-FG-Obernburg (unreported).

[69] OLG Zweibrücken, IPRspr 1986, no. 150.

[70] Qureshi 1995, 98.

[71] OLG, Bamberg, 1997.

[72] BGH, 28 Jan. 1987, in IPRax 1988, 109–113.

[73] OLG Hamm, FamRZ 1988, 516.

[74] BGH, 28 Jan. 1987, IPRax 1988, 109–113.

[75] BGB §§ 116–118.

[76] The Islamic legality of the interest award was not discussed. While it has been deemed in conflict of laws cases as contrary to the Islamic sense of justice, it should also be pointed out that the Indian Muslim case law approves of awards of interest on sums of *mahr* due when the delay is inequitable towards the wife. See Qureshi 1995, 157–158.

77 OLG Hamm, FamRZ 1988, 516.

78 BGB § 780.

79 Cf. supra n. 49, on the Tanzanian Bi Hawa case.

80 No *mutʿa* (maintenance) would be due, only half of the *mahr*, if the marriage has not been consummated before the divorce, according to a rule from Caliph ʿUmar in the traditions of Mālik. See Malik ibn Anas 1989, on *ṭalāq: mutʿa.*

81 Ibn Taymiyya 1987, 256–257. While his opinion is not binding on all jurists, it has great weight, and challenges us to recast some Islamic legal issues.

82 There is one exception in AmtsG Frankfurt, IPRspr 1988, no. 75.

83 Mālik ibn Anas 1989, *buyūʾ: dayn.*

84 As in the *ḥadīth* of the man who borrowed a young camel but repaid with a grown camel. See *Ṣaḥīḥ Muslim* 1994, *musāqāh, bāb: salaf*; Malik ibn Anas 1989. One may also have to reopen the debate on whether the dowry is compulsory or morally recommended, similar to the debate about whether the post-divorce *mutʿa* payment is compulsory or not.

85 Shatzmiller 1995, 219–257.

86 Murad Wilfried Hofmann, Haus des Islams in Rheinland, located in Lützelbach. Since 1982 Hofmann has been performing pastoral work, organizing youth work as well as the hajj trips. Haus des Islams has about 2,500 members. Interview with Murad Wilfried Hofmann, Chair, Haus des Islams (April 1999).

87 On the difficulties Tunisian women began to face from the tenth century onwards, see Labidi 1989, 156.

88 Qurʾan 2:241.

89 See 1993 report in Sonbol 1996, 284. This applies if the husband bears the fault for the breakdown of the marriage.

90 *Mohd. Ahmed Khan v. Shah Bano Begum*, A.I.R. 1985, S.C. 951. This decision overturned the prior case law, under which the *mahr* was treated as maintenance. See *Bai Tahira v. Ali Hussain Fiddali Chotia*, A.I.R. 1979 S.C. 362.

91 Qurʾan 2:241.

92 Qurʾan 2:243.

93 *Mohd. Ahmed Khan v. Shah Bano Begum*, A.I.R. 1985, S.C. 951.

94 No. 25 of 1986.

95 Muslim Women (Protection of Rights on Divorce) Act, 1986, § 3(c) (F.R.G.).

96 Muslim Women (Protection of Rights on Divorce) Act, 1986, § 4 (F.R.G.).

97 Muslim Women (Protection of Rights on Divorce) Act, 1986, § 4 (F.R.G.).

98 Mālik 1863. See also Tunisian Law No. 93–65 of 5 July 1993 (JORT, 6 July 1993, p. 931); Decree No. 93–1655 of 9 August 1993 (JORT, 20 August 1993, p. 1301), which creates a state fund for maintenance for divorced wives.

99 The classical jurists do not uniformly treat the maintenance obligation of the husband as comprehensive: it was limited to a minimum of clothing, food, and shelter. The wife had to meet her own medical costs and the costs of her ritual needs. See Meron 1971, 17–18, 22, 225–226. It would seem that this limited obligation was justified by the rule that each spouse retained control over her/his own properties. Qurʾan 4:32. This contrasts with the European approach, which transferred the wife's property to her husband's control with the corresponding obligation of comprehensive maintenance.

100 See Heinrich 2004, 399. There is also a recent Indian Supreme Court decision on a basic socio-political assumption made about the place of women: "Our society is male dominated both economically and socially and women are

assigned, invariably, a dependent role, irrespective of the class of society to which she belongs." *Danial Latifi and Anor. v. Union of India*, Judgments Today, 2001 (8), Oct. 31, 2001, Taxation Publishers, SC 231 (JT 2001 (8) SC).

[101] E.g. *Mohd. Ahmed Khan v. Shah Bano Begum*, A.I.R., 1985 SC 951.

# *Fifteen*

## THE SHARIʿA AND ENGLISH LAW: IDENTITY AND JUSTICE FOR BRITISH MUSLIMS

Richard Freeland and Martin Lau

Of the estimated 1.5 million Muslims now living in the United Kingdom, the majority traces their ancestry to the Indian subcontinent, but there are also substantial numbers from the Middle East, Africa, and South East Asia.[1] Large-scale immigration began after the Second World War and although the migration of Muslims to Britain still continues, there is now emerging a culturally distinct body of British Muslims. They are British citizens either by birth or by naturalization and are therefore subject to the same laws as non-Muslim British citizens.[2] The subjection of British Muslims to English law has drawn criticism from some Muslim organizations, who perceive a failure to acknowledge the importance of Islamic law to Muslims living in Britain. This is most apparent in the context of family law because this is the area where there is the most scope for recognition of the religious identity of foreign and British Muslims.[3]

In 1983 the Union of Muslim Organisations published a paper entitled "Why Islamic Family Law for British Muslims?" It demanded a separate legal system based on the Shariʿa for British Muslims; however, nothing has come of the proposal. The obvious justification for the government's antipathy is the apparently secular and uniform character of the English legal system, through which justice is achieved by treating all individuals equally. In contrast, many Muslims feel that justice would be better served if they were permitted their own personal laws, and they see official refusal as a matter of straightforward discrimination. However, the viability of a distinct system of Islamic personal law is more complicated than a simple choice between secular/uniform and religious/plural legal systems. Marriage still holds an ambiguous status in English law, and the inconsistencies that persist there may be traced to the complex interaction between secular and religious authority in English history. English matrimonial law is a peculiar mixture of religious and secular elements, and thus reflects the Islamic legal approach to marriage in an interesting way. The religious aspects of English marriages contradict the impression that English law is an exclusively secular system. Similarly, the Islamic law of marriage is largely a matter of civil contract, and it would be wrong to overemphasize its religious elements.

In the second part of this chapter we will look at how the history and development of English matrimonial law has given it such a peculiar character, and why there has been a refusal to incorporate parts of the Shariʿa into English law. But first we will show what the legal status of an Islamic marriage contract is in England, whether it is made abroad or in the United Kingdom. This will require a brief survey of English matrimonial law, and how English courts treat Islamic marriage contracts when such issues do arise.

## English Matrimonial Law

The law applied in English courts is generally the same for all individuals regardless of their religion.[4] Family law is primarily based upon legislation, which is usually drafted in terms sufficiently wide to give courts considerable latitude in individual cases. A series of Marriage Acts from 1949 to 1996 regulate the legal formalities of marriage. There are strict rules regarding where and when legitimate marriages may take place, who can conduct a marriage ceremony, and the correct procedure to be followed. Marriages can take place in an Anglican church, a civil registry office, or a "registered building."[5] This can include any non-Anglican place of worship, and several mosques have been registered. The only exceptions to these rules are enjoyed by Jews and Quakers who are permitted to conduct marriages in accordance with their own religious practices.[6]

The personal capacity of an individual to marry is controlled by the Matrimonial Causes Act of 1973, which states that a marriage is null and void if either of the parties is under sixteen years of age, is already married, or is within the prohibited degrees of consanguinity. A marriage must be entered into with the free consent of the parties, and an annulment may be sought within three years if either party was forced into the agreement to marry.[7] The issue of forced marriages has been dealt with on several occasions by English courts and they have given a broad construction of duress in this context, so any threat made to an individual which destroys the reality of that person's consent will compromise the legitimacy of the marriage.[8] There is nothing legally wrong with arranged marriages, in principle, provided the parties also give their consent.

A divorce may only be sought by court order on the basis of the irretrievable breakdown of the marriage.[9] No other method of divorce is acceptable to English law so a *ṭalāq* divorce (unilateral declaration of divorce by the husband) in England would not be sufficient to end an English marriage. Upon divorce or separation the court has wide discretion within statutory guidelines to make orders for financial provision.[10] The court also retains extensive powers to supervise and vary individual arrangements that couples may have made, such as maintenance agreements.[11] Pre- and post-nuptial settlements are also subject to comprehensive powers of review and all aspects of such contracts may be varied according to the judgment of the court.[12] These may include lump sums, regular payments, settlements of property, trusts, and outright gifts.[13]

This expansive scope for the judicial resolution of family disputes is partly due to the emergence of English law as a singular and unified system. English law observes the principle that only one single body of rules is applicable to all individuals inside the jurisdiction,[14] and within that framework no other system of law is acknowledged as legally effective. Thus, in 1947 the House of Lords held:

> The fact is that the law of the land cannot be co-extensive with the law of morals; nor can the civil consequences of marriage be identical with its religious consequences. What marriage means to different persons will depend upon their upbringing, their outlook and their religious belief. We must remember, as Scott L. J. says, that marriage, whether solemnised in a church or a registry office, whether contracted between Christians or between those who have different or no religious beliefs, must in each case have the same legal consequences.[15]

A marriage or a divorce that does not conform strictly to the requirements of English law will therefore not be legal. In order for Muslims to marry according to English law they either have to supplement their religious ritual with a civil marriage at the registry office, or marry in a mosque that is designated as a "registered building."[16] A Muslim marriage ceremony not performed according to these rules is not only legally ineffective but is positively discouraged by the law. Under the Marriage Act of 1949, it is a criminal offense to knowingly and wilfully solemnize a marriage in a place other than a registered building.[17] In *R. v. Bham*[18] an imam (Muslim community leader) was convicted of this offense after conducting a Muslim marriage ceremony in a private house that was not a registered building. The Court of Appeal overturned the conviction because the ceremony was not and did not purport to bring about a marriage of the kind allowed in English law. However, the court stressed that it may have decided differently had there been evidence that the imam conducting the ceremony asserted that the marriage was legally valid. Although this decision seems to permit some religious freedom for Muslims, in that the performance of the religious marriage ceremony was insufficient in itself to establish liability, it nevertheless confirms the absolute refusal of English law to approve of marriages outside its established legal boundaries.

## Islamic Marriage Contracts in English Courts

The only context in which an English court would accept the validity of an Islamic marriage is if the marriage was undertaken in an Islamic state[19] and is thus recognizable as foreign law. English rules of private international law require English courts to deal with issues of foreign marriages which can arise in a variety of circumstances, for instance, immigration, inheritance, or financial disputes.[20] Although a distinction can be made between Islamic law within the English jurisdiction (where it is not recognized) and Islamic law as foreign law (where it is recognized under rules of private international law for limited purposes), in practice this division can become blurred. When English law recognizes a foreign marriage, divorce, or an order for ancillary relief, it then becomes English law and the legal relationship between the parties changes accordingly. Therefore, some concepts and practices quite alien to English law, such as polygamy, the marriage of cousins, or *ṭalāq* divorces may attain legal validity by an indirect route.

The prevalence of international connections among British Muslims has become the channel through which Islamic law is imported into Britain. For example, a British Muslim may marry in an Islamic state but seek a divorce in Britain, divorce abroad but possess matrimonial property in England, or possess property abroad but provide for the settlement of disputes by an English court.[21] In all these scenarios an English court will have to decide upon issues of Islamic law according to the law of another state. Although this should be a straightforward matter of evidence, usually provided by expert opinion, it can cause English judges problems. Determining the law of a foreign country may test forensic resources, particularly in older cases where information on distant legal systems is scarce.[22] Even today, the absence of registration schemes in some countries means that a certain number of Islamic marriages are difficult to prove.[23] These difficulties are compounded by the often complex facts and the novel legal issues that arise in these cases.[24]

The leading cases in English courts on Islamic marriage contracts all involve foreign law. Examples that best illustrate the treatment of Islamic marriage contracts relate to disputes over dower, as this is regarded as a contractual right under Islamic jurisprudence. In *Shahnaz v. Rizwan*[25] a Muslim couple had been married in India in accordance with Islamic law and subsequently divorced. Having moved to England, the wife sought to enforce her right under Islamic law to dower (*mahr*)[26] in an English court. The husband argued that the dower was a matrimonial right that the court should refuse to enforce because no such right had ever been recognized in English law. The court rejected this argument and enforced the deferred dower, not as a matrimonial right, but as a contractual obligation pursuant to the Islamic marriage contract. The court held:

> In my judgment, it [*mahr*] is quite different in essence from maintenance as understood in English or Mohammedan [Muslim] law. This right is far more closely to be compared with the right of property than a matrimonial right or obligation, and I think that, upon the

> true analysis of it, it is a right ex contractu, which, whilst it can in the nature of things only arise in connection with a marriage by Mohammedan law (which is ex hypothesi polygamous) it is not a matrimonial right. It is not a right derived from the marriage but is a right in personam, enforceable by the wife or widow against the husband or his heirs.[27]

The court actively sought a solution and expressed its concern that British Muslim women should not be left without a legal remedy, stating that:

> As matter of policy, I would incline to the view that, there being now so many Mohammedans resident in this country, it is better that the court should recognize in favour of women who have come here as a result of a Mohammedan marriage the right to obtain from their husband what was promised to them by enforcing the contract and payment of what was promised, than that they should be bereft of those rights and receive no assistance from the courts.[28]

In this case the dower was a specified sum, and therefore the court could enforce the contract without considering Islamic law in any depth.[29] Had the dower not been specified, however, the case would have taken a different tone because the English court would then have been obliged to consider whether it was able to calculate the amount of proper dower, and if so, what that figure should be. An Islamic court would assess the proper dower on the basis of the principles of Islamic law, and an English court may have to do the same in order to construct the terms of the contract. David Pearl, an English judge and noted writer on Islamic law, has argued that there is no reason why an English court should not be able to assess proper dower. The hesitation of English judges to do this in older cases on Greek dower was unjustified, as English courts regularly deal with contracts where the sums payable are not specified.[30]

The principle that dower can be enforced as a purely contractual right was confirmed in *Qureshi v. Qureshi*.[31] In that case two Muslims married in England according to English law but they also agreed to a Muslim marriage, including a specified dower. The husband later divorced his wife in Pakistan by *ṭalāq*, which was a valid divorce under Pakistani law. The wife petitioned an English court for a declaration that the marriage still subsisted and for maintenance, and alternatively, if the marriage had been validly dissolved, that she was entitled to dower. The court held that there had been a valid divorce and that she was therefore not entitled to maintenance as a wife, but she was entitled to her dower. The court refused to elaborate on this decision because the husband had conceded that if the marriage was validly dissolved by *ṭalāq* the dower would be automatically payable. *Qureshi v. Qureshi* takes the recognition of Islamic law as English law one step further, in that the marriage contract under consideration was created solely within the English jurisdiction.

Some aspects of traditional Islamic marriage have therefore found expression in English law, but rather than simply applying Islamic law, English courts have used an oblique method. With respect to dower, the Islamic marriage contract entered into by British Muslims is not recognized as part of English family law but is given legal efficacy as part of the law of contract. As a convenient template exists, namely, a notion of contractual rights, the courts have been willing to respect some fundamental aspects of the Shariʿa, provided that there are public policy grounds that justify such action. This approach is partly because the refusal to incorporate a separate system of Islamic personal law into English law limits the courts' options. The peculiar structure of English law also separates different causes of action, while still allowing for flexibility within these channels. English courts will not even consider issues unless they fall within a recognized cause of action, but appropriate remedies can be improvised if justice demands it; hence the court's preference for using the principles of contract law. Matrimonial matters have always held an ambiguous position within this arrangement, perhaps because it has never been clear what exactly the legal status of marriage is.[32] The mixture of religious and contractual elements in English matrimonial law make an interesting parallel with Islamic law, and also help to answer why the English judiciary is reluctant to incorporate parts of the Shariʿa into English law.

## Marriage in English Legal History: Status or Contract?

Islamic law shares with English law some ambiguity over the nature of marriage. Marriage is consistently described in English case law as being itself a contract, and wedding vows from the eighteenth century refer to a "contract of marriage."[33] Blackstone wrote:

> Our law considers marriage in no other light than a civil contract [...] and taken in a civil light, the law treats it as it does all other contracts: allowing it to be good and valid in all cases, where the parties at the times of making it were, in the first place willing to contract; secondly able to contract; and lastly actually did contract, in the proper forms and solemnities required by law.[34]

This view was not new, as in the seventeenth century the jurist John Selden treated marriage as "nothing more than a civil contract."[35] There are certainly similarities between contracts and marriage in that marriage involves a sort of offer and acceptance, and an exchange of rights and duties.

It is understandable that jurists in the seventeenth and eighteenth centuries would make such a comparison as their conception of a contract significantly differed from ours, and the meaning of words changes over time. "Contract" was one of a number of terms, along with "covenant," "pact," and "promise," used to describe various legal relationships concerning personal obligations. The law of contract had not developed into the singular body of rules we recognize today,[36] and Blackstone himself hardly refers to "contracts" in his *Commentaries*. We really use the expressions "contract a marriage" and a "marriage contract" idiomatically, as these terms developed before "contract" came to mean a legal relationship. It derives from Old French *contractus* meaning "draw together" and was used in England in the late fourteenth century as a noun, and became a verb soon after.[37] In the mid-sixteenth century it emerged as a term applicable to both commercial agreements and marriage, but was used imprecisely in each case.

The view that marriage was simply a contract would find little favor today, and even in the seventeenth and eighteenth centuries Blackstone's and Selden's analysis would have been controversial. Marriages have always been a discrete legal entity and there are some obvious differences between marriages and other types of legal contracts. The fundamental distinction was pointed out by Joel Prentiss Bishop, who asserted that they are separate causes of action, and divorce is not an action upon a contract but a *sui generis* proceeding.[38] An important discrepancy relates to freedom of contract, as the entire purpose of a contractual agreement is to negotiate terms freely. In contrast, marital obligations can rarely be modified by agreement, and on the dissolution of marriage the courts have retained almost complete discretion. In addition, a protective framework of public policy renders unenforceable contracts that prevent marriage or encourage divorce.[39] The reluctance to regard marriage as a contract extends to pre-nuptial agreements: in England they are rarely enforceable and are discouraged by lawyers and judges.[40] English law has adopted the pragmatic approach that marriages are related to contracts but are not quite the same thing. Jeremy Bentham regarded marriage as a special form of contract that had the purpose of legitimizing children, and could be distinguished from ordinary contracts by sacramental or restrictive characteristics, such as monogamy.[41] The most credible case law has reached similar conclusions:

> In truth, very many and serious difficulties arise if marriage be regarded only in the light of a contract. It is indeed based upon the contract of the parties, but it is a status arising out of a contract to which each country is entitled to attach its own conditions, both as to its creation and duration.[42]

Whether marriage is purely a contract or something more than this is part of a wider confusion as to the very nature of marriage. The character of English matrimonial law has developed over time in accordance with the changing roles of parliament, the courts, and the church. The most important event was the 1753 Clandestine Marriages Act,[43] which regularized the performance and registration of marriage by giving the Anglican Church sole authority to solemnize marriages, but reserving for the state the right to determine correct preliminaries. The Act was a watershed in the development of matrimonial law, because with it the state assumed the power to determine the validity of marriages. It had previously been left to the church and canon law to regulate matrimonial affairs, but from 1753 onward, a marriage could only be conducted in accordance with the new statutory framework.[44] The Act was passed to prevent the proliferation of clandestine marriages, as Georgian society was being scandalized by the easy opportunities for young men and women to elope and marry without registration or parental consent.[45] The Act required parental consent if a party was under the age of twenty-one, and obligated the parties to record the union in the parish register. The stipulation that the ceremony had to be conducted in an Anglican church effectively abolished all other forms of marriage, including Catholic ceremonies and common-law marriages. The only exemptions were granted to Jews and Quakers who are to this day allowed to marry in accordance with their own religious laws and customs.

Two acts of Parliament, passed in 1836 and 1857, largely secularized marriage and divorce laws and laid the foundations for the modern law in use today. The registry offices established by the Marriage Act of 1836 broke the Anglican monopoly on marriage, and enabled men and women of all faiths to enter into a legally valid marriage. Church of England ceremonies were still the preferred form, but after 1836 the parallel system of civil registration supplemented conventional Anglican weddings, and was an important step towards emancipating Catholics and Nonconformists. The authority of the Anglican Church was further undermined by the Matrimonial Causes Act of 1857, which transferred responsibility for divorce from the ecclesiastical to the common-law courts. Parliament took this step because there was a growing demand for judicial recognition of the breakdown of marriage, but the ecclesiastical courts refused to reform the canon law of divorce. The Church still regarded marriage as a sacrament that could only be dissolved in the most exceptional circumstances.[46]

The role of ecclesiastical courts may have been permanently undermined, but religion and the Anglican Church continued to exert a powerful influence over the substantive law of marriage. The two Acts did not wholly secularize matrimonial law, and it was never the intent of Parliament to entirely disempower the Church of England. The Church of England is established, holds—and has always held—a privileged position, and retains some autonomy. For example, the refusal to allow divorcees to remarry in an Anglican church still forces them to resort to civil registration for a second marriage. Until relatively recently, marriage was defined by its Christian qualities, and any union that did not conform to these values was not regarded as a marriage at all.[47] It was only after the Second World War that English law started to recognize polygamous marriages abroad, and there were even doubts over the validity of potentially polygamous marriages until 1996.[48]

The first records of English courts dealing with Islamic marriages appear in the twentieth century. Prior to this, there were very few Muslim couples resident in England, and their marriages could only be solemnized under English law after 1836.[49] The first permanent embassies from Islamic countries were established in London in the 1790s. As the century progressed, more sailors, servants, and students settled in London and Liverpool.[50] The first English mosque was opened in Woking in 1889, but British Muslims remained low-profile until the end of the Second World War. There were only a few examples of inter-faith marriages in Britain, but the ones that did exist illustrate the diversity of Muslim lives in England. Henry Mayhew's classic description of Victorian poverty, *The London Labour and the London Poor*, mentions a Muslim beggar who married a Christian English woman, and at the other end of the social spectrum, a professor of Hindustani at University College London was an Indian Muslim who also married a Christian English woman.[51]

As mentioned above, the only two communities that have ever been allowed to retain some of their own religious family laws and rituals are the Jews and the Quakers.[52] This fact has prompted British Muslims to demand similar recognition. However, the exemptions granted to Jews and Quakers in the mid-eighteenth century never amounted to a genuine concession because their ambit was so narrow. Although Jews are allowed to marry according to Mosaic law, they are—quite irrationally—not allowed to divorce under it. This has not only led to difficult questions of jurisdiction between different English courts but has also left many Jews trapped between two systems of law.[53] The concessions were only given to Jews and Quakers because they served the interests of the ruling elites of Georgian England, and have to be seen in the context of anti-Catholic prejudice of the time. In the eighteenth century, Protestant England had embarked on a campaign to disempower Catholics. The exemption of Jews and Quakers was not an act of parliamentary largesse but simply an attempt to confine discrimination to the primary enemy. This focus on Catholics as the enemy is reflected in the 1701 Succession Act, which not only barred Catholics from the throne but also prevented the succession of anybody who married a Catholic.[54]

At the time, there would have been no question of including Muslim marriages in any English legislation. Islamic marriages were not even recognized in English law, even if they were solemnized abroad, until the middle of the twentieth century. This was due to the fact that they were often potentially polygamous, and this offended the European Christian notion that marriages had to be monogamous. Polygamy was not simply seen as a consequence of Islamic social practices, but was regarded as the defining element of the Islamic concept of marriage.[55] Knowledge of Islam was surprisingly widespread in some circles for some centuries,[56] but in general characteristics such as polygamy and easy divorces invited substantial criticism from Europeans.

## The Demand for a Parallel System of Islamic Law

The 1983 publication by the Union of Muslim Organisations entitled "Why Muslim Family Law for British Muslims?" articulated the demand of one section of the British Muslim community for a separate system of family law based on the Shariʿa (Islamic law) to be applied to them in England. The paper was presented to the government on several occasions in the 1980s but was met with a lukewarm response. The importance of family law to British Muslims was never disputed, but the reasons for demanding a separate system were insufficient to convince the government to take the proposals any further. Proponents of the paper argued that it is a matter of religious freedom, which Muslims claim to have given Christians in the past, and should now be reciprocated. At the time there was also a feeling that the secularization of some Islamic countries was undermining the Shariʿa, and the erosion and weakening of Islam could be combated by adherence to the Shariʿa even in non-Muslim countries. Such threats to cultural and religious identity are keenly felt by an isolated Muslim community, which not only has to protect its identity outside its traditional homeland, but also acts in opposition to what is perceived as a hostile and "Islamophobic" society.

British Muslims have been prompted to demand their own laws by their familiarity with other pluralistic regimes. Many countries apply separate laws for different communities, including Pakistan, Bangladesh, and India, to where most British Muslims trace their ancestry. Despite shortcomings, these parallel systems of personal law have been relatively successful in appeasing each community's desire for the preservation of its cultural identity. This point is given more force by the fact that a dual-law system was officially endorsed by the British in India as early as 1772. Regulation II provided that "in all suits regarding inheritance, succession, marriage and caste and other usages and institutions, the laws of the Koran [Qurʾan] with respect to Mahomedans [Muslims], and those of the Shaster with respect to the Gentoos [Hindus], shall be invariably adhered to."[57] In the middle of the nineteenth century a British judge in

India made the point that if European laws are taken to India to govern Christians, the same principle should apply in reverse to Muslims residing in England: "On very many questions, such as marriage, divorce, succession, and, possibly, adoption, there seems no reason to doubt that the proper law to be referred to for the decision of any controversy would not be the law of the Christian community but the law and usage of the peculiar non-Christian class."[58]

The most compelling argument put forward by the Union of Muslim Organisations is that a separate system of personal law is the only way British Muslims can create a stable community. There is a feeling among British Muslims that English law has failed to create the kind of moral society in which Islam can thrive, and many social problems are blamed on its secular and permissive legal system. High rates of divorce and single parent families have produced what Muslims perceive to be a decadent society, in which crime is more likely to flourish and individuals are more likely to resort to unacceptable behavior such as adultery and alcoholism.[59] Despite these claims, it is doubtful that the British government would allow the incorporation of the Shariʿa into English law. This is partly based on principle and partly on the practical difficulties in implementing such a fundamental change to the English legal system.

A separate system for Muslims would contradict the explicit policy of creating a non-discriminatory society through a unified and single legal system.[60] The concession given to Jews and Quakers is a historical anomaly, which rather tends to undermine any claim to a separate system. As we have seen, the interaction between Jewish and English law has been tense and can hardly be used as a blueprint for an effective representation of minority rights. Furthermore, the Jewish example suggests that any concession may inhibit the development of English law because once implemented it would be very difficult to abolish. Reform of Islamic family law would be deeply problematic given the discrepancy between the *fiqh* (legal doctrine) of the Shariʿa and the methodologies of the British Parliament and the courts. The sources of Islamic law are religious, and as such are outside the competence and control of the lawmakers in England. It is arguable that it would amount to an abdication of sovereignty for Parliament to accept the authority of the Qurʾan over the lives of some of its subjects.

Furthermore, some aspects of traditional Islamic family law would be difficult to reconcile with the standards for the protection of women's rights now found in English law. There is an implicit recognition of gender equality, which natural justice has implied into the common law during the course of the twentieth century. This trend is complemented by Britain's international obligations to guarantee equality in its domestic laws. The European Convention on Human Rights and the International

Covenant on Civil and Political Rights establish agreed norms for gender equality, and are supplemented by other United Nations treaties such as the International Convention on the Elimination of all Forms of Discrimination against Women[61] and the Convention on Consent to Marriage, Minimum Age for Marriage, and Registration of Marriages. Although many Islamic countries have also ratified these agreements, there is little doubt among the academic and professional community that the legal systems of these countries fail to implement satisfactory legal safeguards.[62]

There are three features of the Shariʿa that most obviously conflict with the right to equality between the sexes. A man is permitted to take four wives while a woman is limited to one husband—a clear example of unequal treatment.[63] *Ṭalāq* divorces are also discriminatory since the right vests solely in the husband, whereas a woman's right to divorce follows a more restrictive and complicated procedure.[64] Additionally, in contrast to men, who are allowed to marry Jewish or Christian women, there is a blanket prohibition on Muslim women marrying non-Muslims. The existence of these discrepancies is justified by some commentators on the basis that women are on the whole treated very well by Islam.[65] While the contribution of Islam to the development of women's rights over the centuries cannot be denied, claims to proto-feminism are insufficient to justify the application of such laws in England. The issue of equality is not one that is simply restricted to Muslim couples, but extends to the treatment of Muslim women vis-à-vis non-Muslim women. The European Convention on Human Rights was incorporated into English law under the Human Rights Act of 1998; there would be a clear potential for Islamic family law in England to be challenged under this legislation.

The practical difficulties of amalgamating the Shariʿa into the English legal system would be immense, howsoever implemented. One alternative is to subject all British Muslims to a British version of the Shariʿa on a compulsory basis; the other is to give individual Muslims the choice of whether to submit themselves to the Shariʿa or secular English law. Either way, there would be a section of the Muslim community contesting the legitimacy of any particular method. Two problems most obviously present themselves. First, Islamic law is a diverse system of law and it is by no means clear which version an English court should enforce. The four Islamic schools of law differ over certain details, and most Islamic states have substantially altered the classical Shariʿa by blending it with modern legislation.[66] It has been suggested that the most usable parts of the various schools be selected and molded into a novel body of British-Islamic law, but it is difficult to imagine the United Kingdom Parliament managing to see through such a tortuous project.[67]

The second obstacle concerns court structure and personnel. A separate system of Islamic tribunals could be established or existing courts might be retained. In either case, it would have to be decided whether to employ present judges or train new Muslim ones. Muslims may dispute an English judge's authority or ability to interpret Islamic jurisprudence,[68] and the independence and integrity of a Muslim arbitrator will always have to be compromised by the right to appeal from any Shariʿa court to a conventional English tribunal.[69] The ethnic, cultural, and religious tensions between British Muslims might also be an impediment to cooperation; for example, a Sunni Muslim may possibly object to the authority of a Shiʿi judge.[70]

British Muslims have responded to the refusal to assimilate a separate system of Islamic law into English law by establishing voluntary tribunals, which can be referred to for advice on family law matters.[71] These tribunals are centered around mosques or colleges and are used by British Muslims if they feel that English courts are unresponsive to their religious needs. They are voluntary and all advice is carefully tailored so as not to conflict with English law. For example, the Sharia Council of Great Britain and Northern Ireland was established in 1982 to "safeguard the identity of Islamic personal and family laws and to encourage their recognition for the Muslim community by the British legal system," and "to establish a bench to make decisions on personal matters referred to it by Muslims."[72] In 1985, the Muslim Law (Shariʿa) Council was established by the Imams and Mosques Council;[73] it has since assumed the power to grant Islamic divorces and to draft marriage contracts. It appears that these institutions have enjoyed some success despite being unofficial and having no formal legal powers. This parallel system of unofficial Muslim personal law has acquired some weight among the Muslim community, as it is completely voluntary and independent of the state.[74]

## Conclusion

It is likely that these informal systems for matrimonial dispute resolution will continue to flourish in Britain. Beyond these, there is likely to be vocal opposition to a "British Shariʿa" from those Muslims who feel that religion is a matter of individual choice and would resent the imposition of the Shariʿa on them. Objections are also likely to be raised by Muslim women who might anticipate the undermining of the rights they have been given in England and fought for within their own communities. In any case, no workable model for a "British Shariʿa" has been suggested. Theoretically, some parts of Islamic family law could be incorporated into English law. However, the practical difficulties, such as the conflict with human rights standards, make it unlikely that the introduction of a separate system of Islamic personal laws will ever be achieved in the English legal system.

## NOTES

Editors' Note: This chapter is based upon the state of the law in 1999. Insofar as the recognition of Muslim marriages in English law is concerned, the statements made in this chapter remain correct.

[1] The official census data in the UK does not include information on the religious affiliations of individuals and precise figures are therefore not available. See Pearl and Menski 1998, 60.

[2] Religion per se does not give rise to protection under the Race Relations Act of 1976 although the Human Rights Act of 1998 provides for the right to protection from discrimination on the grounds of religion.

[3] Union of Muslim Organisations 1983. The Union aims to coordinate the activities of all Muslim organizations in the UK and Ireland, and to be the representative body of British Muslims in negotiations with the British government and other governments and international bodies. It runs the National Muslim Education Council, which advises on the role of Islam in education in Britain, and teaches how individual Muslims can practice the tenets of Islam while at work.

[4] The legal system of the United Kingdom is fragmented into three geographical areas. Scotland and Northern Ireland have distinct legal systems. In this essay we will only deal with England and Wales, as the vast majority of British Muslims live in England.

[5] The Marriage (Registration of Buildings) Act, 1990 (Eng.).

[6] This has been the case since at least 1753; more will be said on this later.

[7] Matrimonial Causes Act, 1973, §§ 12, 13 (Eng.).

[8] See *Hirani v. Hirani*, [1983] 4 F.L.R. 232 (Court of Appeal).

[9] Family Law Act, 1998, § 3 (Eng.).

[10] See Matrimonial Causes Act, 1973, as amended by the Matrimonial Finances and Provisions Act, 1984 (Eng.). See also the Domestic Proceedings and Magistrates' Court Act, 1978 (Eng.).

[11] Matrimonial Causes Act, 1973, §§ 34 and 35.

[12] See Foskett 1996, 279.

[13] Comparing the brief nature of English family law with Islamic family law, it is an interesting reversal of the popular impression that Islamic law lacks rules compared to our own law; in fact, Islamic law lays down a more comprehensive system of family law than some Western legal systems. See Edge 1995, 127.

[14] There are many legal systems in the world today which have obtained some flexibility by applying different family laws to different religious communities; see, for instance, Pakistan, Israel, India, and Nigeria. See Lau 1996.

[15] *Weatherley v. Weatherley*, 1947 A.C. 628, at 633 (House of Lords). In *R v. The Superintendent Registrar of Marriages, Hammersmith ex p. Mir-Anwaruddin*, 1917 KB 634 (Court of Appeal), Viscount Reading made a similar reference in the context of divorce: "Neither authority nor principle can be found in English law to establish the proposition that a marriage contracted in England is dissolved according to the laws of England by mere operation of the laws of the religion of the husband and without the decree of a court of law." (Idem, 642).

[16] There has been little need to register mosques as "registered buildings," as most Muslims still combine a civil ceremony in a registry office with an Islamic ceremony in a mosque. This is due to the fact that before 1990 a mosque could not be a "registered building" at all.

[17] Marriage Act (1949) (Eng.), § 75.

[18] [1965] 3 All E.R. 124 (Court of Appeal).

[19] In the context of this article, the term "Islamic state" does no more than to refer to a jurisdiction that allows for the application of Islamic law in the area of family law.

[20] See Pearl 1995.

[21] Generally English courts have jurisdiction if either party is domiciled in England or either party is habitually resident there for at least one year.

[22] See, for instance, *Colliss v. Hector*, [1875] Law Reports 19 Equity Cases 334 Equity where the court was unsure of "Turkish" matrimonial law despite expert submissions received from the Patriarch of Babylon.

[23] See Hasan 1999.

[24] See, for instance, *Kassim v. Kassim*, [1962] 3 All. E.R. 426, where the court had to decide on complex issues of South Rhodesian family law.

[25] [1965] 1 Q.B. 390.

[26] Dower, or *mahr*, is a payment of money (or property) to the wife at the time of the completion of the marriage contract. Without a dower provision, the marriage itself is invalid under Islamic law. The payment of dower can be deferred, but it will always become payable in the event of the wife being divorced by her husband or her husband's death. See Pearl and Menski 1998, 177–178.

[27] Ibid., 401.

[28] Ibid.

[29] I.e., in this case, the Indian version of Islamic law.

[30] See Pearl 1972, 135.

[31] [1971] 2 W.L.R. 518.

[32] A useful discussion can be found in James 1957.

[33] Ibid., 27.

[34] Blackstone's Commentaries, vol. 1 ("Of Husband and Wife"), 421.

[35] Selden 1892, 109. Selden knew Arabic and collected Oriental manuscripts. His treatise on Jewish matrimonial law, the Uxor Ebraica (1646), was considered sufficiently authoritative to be used in court in the late eighteenth century.

[36] It has been argued that the very notion of a distinct body of contract law only emerged in the beginning of the nineteenth century. See in general Atiyah 1979.

[37] Mellinkoff 1963, 101.

[38] See Bishop 1881, 30ff., writing from a U.S. perspective. The same view has been upheld by the English courts: "While habitually speaking of a marriage as a contract English lawyers have never been misled by an imperfect analogy into regarding it as a mere contract [...]." *Moss v. Moss*, [1897] P. 263, 266.

[39] See Beale 2004, ¶¶ 16–72 [p. 979].

[40] See Milligan 1999 and Wilson 1999.

[41] See Bentham 1823, ch. 60, ¶¶ 51–53.

[42] *Sottomayer v. De Barros*, (2) [1879] Law Reports 5 Probate Division 94.

[43] Also known as Lord Hardwicke's Act.

[44] In 1843 the House of Lords in *R. v. Millis*, 10 Clark and Finnely 534 not only confirmed that common law marriages were invalid but also stated that they had never been legitimate even before 1753. The judgment has been considered controversial ever since; see, for instance, the criticism in the Australian case of

*McLean v. Cristall* (1849) contained in Perry 1853, 75. See also Justice Hodson 1958, 209.

[45] See Stone 1992, 57.

[46] Wealthy individuals could circumvent the ecclesiastical courts by paying for a private parliamentary Act of Divorce. However, such privileges were difficult to obtain, and between 1670 and 1857 only 325 divorces were granted in this way. See Stone 1992, 84ff.

[47] See for instance *Hyde v. Hyde*, 1 P&D 130 (Court of Probate and Divorce, 1866) at 134, which concerned the polygamous marriage of Mormons in America.

[48] See the Law Reforms (Miscellaneous Provisions) Act (1996) (Eng.).

[49] However, anyone could have a common law marriage before 1753.

[50] Precise figures and the roles of Muslims in British history are controversial issues. For many years the orthodox view was that Muslims played a peripheral role in domestic British history; see Lewis 1982. This view is now being challenged; see Matar 1998.

[51] See Mayhew 1861 and Salter 1873. Salter, a missionary, was active in promoting the welfare of Muslims in the Victorian docks.

[52] The Jews were allowed their own courts in England between their arrival with William the Conqueror in 1066 to their exclusion from the British Isles in 1291. From their re-entry to Britain in 1660, their religious practices were informally tolerated, culminating in formal recognition in 1753. See *Lindo v. Belisario*, 1 Hag Con 216 (1795), and Jacobs 1893, 212–215. King John's Charter of the Jews of England (April 10, 1201) stated that this liberty extended to all matters except "those which belong to our crown and justice, as homicide, mayhem, premeditated assault, burglary, rape, theft, arson, and treasure trove, [...]." Quoted from Jacobs 1893, 212–215.

[53] A Jewish woman married under Mosaic law in England will have to divorce under English law. However, some Jewish authorities, especially the Orthodox ones, will not recognize the English divorce, thereby preventing her remarrying under Mosaic law. See Katzenberg and Rosenblatt 1999, 165.

[54] This act is still in force. There is nothing to prevent the monarch or heir marrying a Muslim.

[55] See, for instance, *Warrender v. Warrender*, (1835) 2 Clark and Finnely 488, where polygamy was described as the "essence" of Muslim marriage.

[56] The Middle Ages' most popular travel book, *Mandeville's Travels* (mid-fourteenth century), referred to the condition that a Muslim wife receives her dower after a divorce. See Daniel 1960, 140.

[57] Quoted from Fyzee 1997, 49.

[58] Perry 1853, 128.

[59] The best discussion of these issues can be found in Poulter 1998a.

[60] In the 1960s the British government adopted the policy of multiculturalism; see Poulter 1995.

[61] Article 16 provides that "States' parties shall take all appropriate measures to eliminate discrimination against women in all matters relating to marriage and family relations and in particular shall ensure, on a basis of equality of men and women: a. the same right to enter into marriage, b. the same right freely to choose a spouse and to enter into marriage only with their free and full consent, c. the same rights and responsibilities during marriage and at its dissolution. [...]"

[62] See Mayer 1995.

[63] While polygamous marriages by non-British Muslims domiciled abroad are recognized in limited circumstances, the European Court of Human Rights has upheld a decision by the Immigration Appeals Tribunal that bans the formation of polygamous households in England through immigration, see *Bibi v. the United Kingdom*, Appl 19628/92, 29 June 1992 (Eur. Comm. H.R.).

[64] Under Islamic law, a wife can divorce her husband only through a judicial process called *faskh* or with consent of the husband called *khulʿ* (release). See Pearl and Menski 1998; Nasir 1986.

[65] See for instance Brohi 1982.

[66] El Alami and Hinchcliffe 1996.

[67] Poulter 1998.

[68] A significant problem is the translation of Arabic terms into English. For example, the term *mahr* is rendered as "dower," but the word dower has its own meaning in English law which is quite different from the Arabic. For the way in which such translations construct Islamic ideas in an English context, see Strawson 1995. Problems of translation were alluded to in *Hyde v. Hyde*, 1 P&D 130 Court of Probate and Divorce, 1866, at 134.

[69] Any public body is susceptible to judicial review by the High Court. See section 31 of the Supreme Court Act (1981) (Eng.) and RSC [Rules of the Supreme Court] order 53, rule 1.

[70] There is dispute among Muslims themselves as to what constitutes adherence to the faith. Some sects, such as the Ahmadiyya, are not regarded as Muslims by some sections of the orthodox hierarchy. The controversies surrounding the question of Muslim status would eventually require parliamentary or judicial intervention since legal consequences flow from it.

[71] Lewis 1994, 118.

[72] Quoted in Surty 1991, 60.

[73] The Imams and Mosques Council is affiliated with The Muslim College in Ealing, West London.

[74] The degree of state involvement in Islamic organizations is considered controversial. The late Zaki Badawi, a prominent British Muslim, argued that state funding for these bodies is unwelcome because it may politicize them and undermine their independence.

# BIBLIOGRAPHY

**Abbreviations**

| | |
|---|---|
| A.I.R.: | All India Reports |
| C.L.J. (Sya): | *Current Law Journal (Syariah)* |
| FamRZ: | *Zeitschrift für das gesamte Familienrecht* |
| IPR Gutachten: | *Gutachten zum internationalen und ausländischen Privatrecht*, no. 38 (1971). Berlin: W. de Gruyter; no. 31 (1985–86). Frankfurt am Main: A. Metzner |
| IPRax: | *Praxis des internationalen Privat- und Verfahrensrechts* |
| IPRspr 1986: | Die deutsche Rechtsprechung auf dem Gebiete des Internationalen Privatrechts im Jahre 1986, no. 150 |
| IPRspr 1988: | Die deutsche Rechtsprechung auf dem Gebiet des Internationalen Privatrechts im Jahre 1988. No. 75 |
| J.H: | *Jernal Hukum* |
| M.L.J.: | *Malayan Law Journal* |
| StAZ: | Das Standesamt |

**Cases and Court Records**


Abdul Aziz Ali Salim and Hafsa Saleh Mahmoud, Court of Appeal of Tanzania at Zanzibar, Civil Appeal 4/1992 (unreported).

Aisny v. Haji Fahro Rozi [1990] 2 M.L.J. xxvi.

Amtsgericht Frankfurt, IPRspr 1988, no. 75.

Amtsgericht Hamburg, IPRax 1983, 74–77, 64–65.

Amtsgericht Kerpen, judgment of 2 March 2001, FamRZ 2001, 1526–1527.

Avitzur v. Avitzur, 446 N.E.2d 136 (N.Y. 1983), *cert. denied*, 464 U.S. 817 (1983).

Bai Tahira v. Ali Hussain Fiddali Chotia, A.I.R. 1979 S.C. 362.

Bi Hawa Mohamed and Ally Sefu, Court of Appeal of Tanzania at Dar es Salaam, Civil Appeal No. 9/1983 (from unreported unabridged version).

Bombay High Court, Fall Queen Empress v. Rego Montopoulo, [1849] 19 I.L.R. Bombay Series 741.

Bundesgerichtshof, IPRax 1988, 109–113.

Bundesgerichtshof, Neue Juristische Wochenschrift (NJW) 1999, 575.

Bundesgerichtshof, FamRZ 1987, 572–576.

Bundesgerichtshof, StAZ 1993, 5, and IPRax 1993, 102.

Daniel Latifi and Anor. v. Union of India, *Judgements Today* 2001 (8), 31 Oct. 2001, Taxation Publishers, SC 231 (JT 2001 (8) SC).

Dār al-Wathāʾiq al-Qawmiyya.

Alexandria, sijill 1:11–50, 34–157, 99–470 (957 AH/1550 CE); 51:146, 147–325 (1046 AH/1637 CE); 95:285–408 (1182 AH/1769 CE); 108:81–153 (1219 AH/1804 CE).

Alexandria Ishhādāt, sijill 1:24–38, 1:6–40 (1273 AH/1857 CE); 51:91–220 (1074 AH/1663 CE).

Alexandria Mubāyaʿāt, sijill 120:281–908 (1230 AH/1814 CE).

Alexandria Wathā'iq, sijill 1:481–1974, 1:51–2227, 975 (958 AH/1551 CE).
Bab al-ʿĀlī, sijill 106:342–1034 (1229 AH/1813 CE); 123:248–1291 (1056 AH/1646 CE).
Dishnā Ishhādāt, sijill 17:1–9, 3–15, 2–16, 3–25, 8–44 (1283 AH/1865 CE); 1:15–92, 1:1–9 (1273 AH/1857 CE).
Dumyāṭ, sijill 9:116–251, 9:180–3821(1215 AH/1800 CE), 40: 32–83.
Isna, sijill 30:11–43 (1193 AH/1777 CE).
Manfalūṭ, cases 118, 119, 121, 136 (1222–1224 AH/1808–1810 AD), sijillat 5:26–136, 244–651, 5:26–122, 5:38–136 (1228–29 AH/1812–13 CE).
Miṣr, Iʿlāmāt, sijillat 23:244–651, 237–635 (1266–67 AH/1850–51 CE).
Miṣr al-Qadīma, sijill 103:95–221(1079 AH/1669 CE).
Egyptian Courts.
Egyptian Supreme Court Judgment of Mar. 29, 1967, Technical Office Compilation.
Egyptian Supreme Court Judgment of Nov. 1, 1978.
Egyptian Supreme Court Judgment of Nov. 9, 1977, Technical Office Compilation.
Egyptian Supreme Court Judgment of June 11, 1991, Appeal No. 36 for 59J.
Egyptian Supreme Court, Case No. 129 for Year 59J of Mar. 5, 1991.
Maḥkamat Bāb al-Sharʿiyya, sijills 582:29–136 (955 AH/1548 CE); 588:309–1266 (999 AH/1561 CE); 590:69–259 (972 AH/1564 CE).
Maḥkamat Miṣr al-Jadīda al-Juz'iyya. 1956 (case 98, July 23).
Maḥkamat al-Ṣāliḥiyya al-Najmiyya, sijill 446:121–289 (964 AH/1557 CE).
Fakhariah v. Johari [1993] 1 M.L.J. lxxvii.
Golding v. Golding, 581 N.Y. Supp. 2d 4 (N.Y. App. Div. 1992).
Hairun v. Omar [1990] 8 J.H. 289.
Hafsa Saleh Mahmoud v. Abdul Aziz Ali Salim, High Court, Zanzibar, Civil Case 30/1990 (unreported).
Hamzah v. Fatimah Zaharah [1982] 1 M.L.J. 361.
Kammergericht (Berlin), FamRZ 1980, 470.
Kammergericht (Berlin), FamRZ 1988, 296.
Maḥkamat Nābulus (Nablus Islamic Court), sijills no. 4 (1134–1138 AH/1722–1726 CE); no. 5 (1139–1141 AH/1728–1729 CE).
Maḥkamat al-Quds (Jerusalem Islamic Court), sijills no. 226 (1145–1146 AH/1732–1734 CE); no. 230 (1151–1152 AH/1738–1740 CE).
Mansjur v. Kamariah [1988] 3 M.L.J. xliv.
Mohd. Ahmed Khan v. Shah Bano Begum, A.I.R. 1985, S.C. 951.
Noraini Mokhtar v. Abd Halim Samat [2005] 1 C.L.J. (Sya) 21.
Oberlandesgericht Bamberg, Judgment of 13 February 1997, 2 UF 257/96; F 224/96 AG-FG-Obernburg (unreported).
Oberlandesgericht (OLG) Zweibrücken, FamRZ 1997, 1212–1213.
Oberlandesgericht Bamberg, 1997.
Oberlandesgericht Bremen, FamRZ 1980, 606.
Oberlandesgericht Celle, FamRZ 1998, 374.
Oberlandesgericht Düsseldorf, FamRZ 1998, 623–624.
Oberlandesgericht Hamm, FamRZ 1988, 516.
Oberlandesgericht Hamm, Fam RZ 1994, 1259–1261.
Oberlandesgericht Köln, IPRax 1983, 73.

Oberlandesgericht Nürnberg, FamRZ 2001, 1613.
Oberlandesgericht Zweibrücken, IPRspr 1986, no. 150.
Piah v. Che Lah [1983] 3 J.H. 220.
Rojmah bte Abdul Kadir v. Mohsin bin Ahmad [1991] 3 M.L.J. xxx.
Rokiah v. Mohamed Idris [1989] 3 M.L.J. ix.
Rosilah v. Abdul Rahman [1991] 8 J.H. 249.
Sakamah v. Tasmin [1938] M.L.J. Rep. 38.
Salemewegam v. Mohd Anuar [1983] 5 J.H. 109.
Talib v. Sepiah [1979] 1 J.H. (1) 84.
The Indian Chief, 3 Chr. Rob. Admir. Rep. 29.
Vladi v. Vladi [1987] 7 Rep. Fam. L. (3d) 337 (Nova Scotia).
Zainab binti Mahmood v. Abd Latif bin Jusoh [1991] 8 JH 297.

**Religious Documents**

Babylonian Talmud, Baba Kamma 87a.
Babylonian Talmud, Arakhin 22a.
Babylonian Talmud, Baba Kamma 89a–b.
Babylonian Talmud, Baba Kamma 113a–b.
Babylonian Talmud, Gittin 10b.
Babylonian Talmud, Ketubbot 56a.
Babylonian Talmud, Kiddushin 12b.
Babylonian Talmud, Nazir 24b.
Babylonian Talmud, Nedarim 28a.
Babylonian Talmud, Yevamot 107b–108a.
Deuteronomy 24:1.
H. Hirschenson, Malki BaKodesh, Responsum No. 2.
Hoshen Mishpat, 26:1.
Maimonides, Mishneh Torah, Introduction to Laws of Divorce.
Maimonides, Mishneh Torah, Introduction to Laws of Marriage.
Maimonides, Mishneh Torah, Laws of Divorce 4:11.
Maimonides, Mishneh Torah, Laws of Marriage, 6:9.
Mishnah, Gittin 5:7.
Mishnah, Ketubbot 4:7.
Mishnah, Kiddushin 1:1.
Mishnah, Yevamot 14:1.
Mordecai, Gittin 455.
Nehemiah 13:30.
Palestinian Talmud, Kiddushin 1:1.
Rashi, Babylonian Talmud, Gittin 9b–10b.
Responsa of Hatam Sofer, Vol. 3, chapter 4, s.v. Yekarto.
Teshuvot Rosh 42:1.
Tosafot, Gittin 33a, s.v. Kol.
Tosafot, Ketubbot 47b, s.v. Zimnin.
Tosafot, Kiddushin 41a, s.v. Assur l'adam.

**Laws**

Bürgerlichesgesetzbuch (BGB).
Decree No. 93–1655 of 9 August 1993 (JORT, 20 August 1993, p. 1301).

Egyptian Law 10 of 1984.
Egyptian Law 25 of 1920.
Egyptian Law 25 of 1929, as amended by Law 100 of 1985.
Egyptian Law 44 of 1979, amending certain provisions of Law 25 of 1920.
Egyptian Law 51 of 1984.
Egyptian Law 84 of 1984.
Egyptian Law 100 of 1985, amending certain provisions of Law 25 of 1920.
Einführungsgesetz zum Bürgerlichen Gesetzbuche (EGBGB).
Islamic Family Law (Federal Territories) Act 1984 (Act 303).
Ismaili Constitution 1905. *Rules and Regulations of the Khoja Ismailia Council*. Zanzibar: Khoja Ismailia Council.
Ismaili Constitution 1925. *Rules of the Shia Imami Ismailia Councils of the Continent of Africa*. Zanzibar: The Shia Imami Ismailia Supreme Council of Zanzibar (rev. ed.).
Ismaili Constitution 1946. Mombasa: His Highness the Aga Khan Supreme Council for Africa.
Ismaili Constitution 1962. Nairobi: His Highness the Aga Khan Shia Imami Ismaili Supreme Council for Africa.
Malaysian Federal Constitution. Item 1 of List II (the state list) in the 9th Schedule.
Moroccan Family Code (Moudawana) of 2004.
Münchener Kommentar zum EGBGB. 1990. Article 15, 4, p. 882, n. 7. 2nd ed. München: C. H. Beck.
Muslim Women (Protection of Rights on Divorce) Act, 1986, no. 25 of 1986.
Niederlassungsabkommen zwischen dem Deutschen Reich und dem Kaiserreich Persien of 17 December 1929. Reichsgesetzblatt Jg. 1930, Teil II, p. 1002, at p. 1006 (confirmed by the Federal Republic of Germany on 15 August 1955, BGBl. Teil II, No. 19, 25 August 1955, p. 829).
N.Y. DOM. REL. LAW § 253 (McKinney 1986).
Schlussprotokoll of the Niederlassungsabkommen zwischen dem Deutschen Reich und dem Kaiserreich Persien of 17 December 1929, Reichsgesetzblatt Jg. 1930, Teil II, p. 1002, at p. 1006 (confirmed by the Federal Republic of Germany on 15 August 1955, BGBl. Teil II, No. 19, 25 August 1955, p. 829).
Tunisian Law No. 93–65 of 5 July 1993 (JORT, 6 July, 1993, p. 931).
Turkish Family Law Code.

## Primary Works and Studies

Abdal-Rehim, A. R. 1996. "The Family and Gender Laws in Egypt during the Ottoman Period," in Amira El Azhary Sonbol (ed.), *Women, the Family, and Divorce Laws in Islamic History*. Syracuse: Syracuse University Press. Pp. 96–111.
Abū Shujāʿ, Aḥmad. 1894. *Matn* embedded in al-Ghazzī, Ibn Qāsim, *Fatḥ al-Qarīb*. Ed. and French tr. L. W. C. van den Berg. Leiden: E. J. Brill.
Abū Yūsuf Yaʿqūb. 1938. *Ikhtilāf Abī Ḥanīfa wa-Ibn Abī Layla, li-l-imām Abī Yūsuf Yaʿqūb ibn Ibrāhīm al-Anṣārī*. Cairo: Maṭbaʿat al-Wafāʾ.
Afshar, Haleh (ed.). 1993. *Women in the Middle East: Perceptions, Realities and Struggles for Liberation*. New York: St. Martin's Press.
——. 1996. "Islam and Feminism: An Analysis of Political Strategies," in M. Yamani (ed.), *Feminism and Islam: Legal and Literary Perspectives*. New York: New York University Press. Pp. 197–216.

Aga Khan, Zahra. 1997. Speech to Ismaili Women's Forum, Toronto, Canada, May 9. Text available at http://www.ismaili.net/timeline/1997/970509.html (last visited June 19, 2008).

Aga Khan III. 1918. *India in Transition: A Study in Political Evolution*. London: Philip Lee Warner.

——. 1950. *Kalām-i Imām-i mubīn*, Vol. 2. Bombay: Ismailia Association for India.

——. 1955. *Mowlana Hazir Imam's Guidance and Advice in Spiritual and Worldly Matters to Ismailis of Africa*. Mombasa: Shia Imami Ismailia Associations for Africa.

——. 1998. *Selected Speeches and Writings of Sir Sultan Muhammad Shah*. Ed. K. K. Aziz. Vol. 1. London and New York: Kegan Paul International.

Ahmed, Leila. 1992. *Women and Gender in Islam: Historical Roots of a Modern Debate*. New Haven: Yale University Press.

——. 1999. *A Border Passage. From Cairo to America—A Woman's Journey*. New York: Farrar, Strauss, Giroux.

Alberigo, J. (ed.). 1982. *Conciliorum oecumenicorum decreta*. Bologna: Istituto per le scienze religiose.

Algar, Hamid. 1985. *Islam and Revolution: Writings and Declarations of Imam Khomeini*. Berkeley: Mizan.

Ali, Kecia. 2002. "Money, Sex, and Power: The Contractual Nature of Marriage in Islamic Jurisprudence of the Formative Period." Ph.D. diss., Duke University.

——. 2003. "Progressive Muslims and Islamic Jurisprudence: The Necessity for Critical Engagement with Marriage and Divorce Law," in Omid Safi (ed.), *Progressive Muslims: On Justice, Gender, and Pluralism*. Oxford: Oneworld. Pp. 163–189.

——. 2005. "Marriage," in Oliver Leaman (ed.), *The Qur'an: An Encyclopedia*. London: Routledge. Pp. 389–393.

——. 2006. *Sexual Ethics and Islam: Feminist Reflections on Qur'an, Hadith, and Jurisprudence*. Oxford: Oneworld Publications.

Ali, Sehreen Noor, and Farrah Musani. 2006. "Ismaili Muslim Women as Public Leaders in Canadian Government and Politics." Unpubl. paper presented at Women as Global Leaders Conference, Zayed University, Abu Dhabi, U.A.E., March 12–14 (on file with Ali Asani).

Ali, Shaheen Sardar. 1997. "Is an Adult Muslim Woman *Sui Juris*? Some Reflections on the Concept of 'Consent in Marriage' Without a *Wali* (With Particular Reference to the Saima Waheed Case)," in E. Cotran and C. Mallat (eds.), *Yearbook of Islamic and Middle Eastern Law* 3. London: Kluwer Law International. Pp. 156–174.

Al-Munajjed, Mona. 1997. *Women in Saudi Arabia Today*. New York: St. Martin's Press.

Altorki, Soraya. 1986. *Women in Saudi Arabia: Ideology and Behavior Among the Elite*. New York: Columbia University Press.

Amiji, Hatim M. 1982. "Islam and Socio-Economic Development: A Case Study of a Muslim Minority in Tanzania," in *Journal of the Institute of Muslim Minority Affairs* 4. Pp. 175–187.

Anderson, J. N. D. 1964–65. "The Ismaili Khojas of East Africa: A New Constitution and Personal Law for the Community," in *Middle Eastern Studies* 1. Pp. 21–39.

——. 1976. *Law Reforms in the Muslim World*. London: Athlone.
An-Naʾim, Abdullahi A. (ed.). 2002. *Islamic Family Law in a Changing World: A Global Resource Book*. London: Zed Books.
al-Anṣārī, ʿAnbara Ḥusayn ʿAbd Allāh. 1990. *Athar al-khādimāt al-ajnabiyyāt fī tarbiyat al-ṭifl*. Jiddah: Dār al-Mujtamaʿ li-l-Nashr wa-l-Tawzīʿ.
al-ʿAnsī, Aḥmad b. Qāsim. 1993. *al-Tāj al-mudhhab li-aḥkām al-madhhab*. Sanʿaʾ: Dār al-Ḥikma al-Yamaniyya.
Anwar, Zainah. 1987. *Islamic Revivalism in Malaysia: Dakwah Among the Students*. Petaling Jaya: Pelanduk Publications.
Asani, Ali S. 1994. "The Impact of Modernization on the Marriage Rites of the Khojah Ismailis of East Africa," in *Journal of Turkish Studies* 18. Pp. 17–24.
——. 2005. "On Muslims Knowing the 'Muslim' Other: Reflections on Pluralism and Islam," in Philippa Sturm (ed.), *Muslims in the United States: Identity, Influence, Innovation*. Washington: Woodrow Wilson Institute. Pp. 181–190.
Atiyah, P. S. 1979. *The Rise and Fall of Freedom of Contract*. Oxford: Clarendon Press.
Badr, ʿAbd al-Munʾim Muḥammad. 1985. *Mushkilātunā al-ijtimāʿiyya: usūs naẓariyya wa-namādhij khālijiyya*. Alexandria: al-Maktab al-Jāmiʿī al-Ḥadīth.
Badran, Margot. 1995. *Feminists, Islam and Nation: Gender and the Making of Modern Egypt*. Princeton: Princeton University Press.
Badri, B. 1989. "Attitudes and Behaviours of Educated Sudanese Women Concerning Legal Rights in Marriage and Divorce," in *The Afhad Journal: Women and Change* 6. Pp. 22–25. As quoted at http://www.bridge.ids.ac.uk/reports/R4%20Women%20Islam%202c.doc.
Bagley, F. R. C. 1971. "The Iranian Family Protection Law of 1967: A Milestone in the Advance of Women's Rights," in C. E. Bosworth (ed.), *Iran and Islam*. Edinburgh: Edinburgh University Press. Pp. 47–64.
Baker, H. E. 1968. *The Legal System of Israel*. Jerusalem: Israel Universities Press.
Bakhtiar, Laleh (adapter). 1996. *Encyclopedia of Islamic Law: A Compendium of the Major Schools*. Chicago: ABC International Group, Inc./Kazi Publications.
——. 1996a. "Women in the Heart of Muhammad s.a.w.," in Laleh Bakhtiar, *Shariati on Shariati and the Muslim Woman*. Chicago: ABC Group International, Inc. Pp. 3–34.
al-Bakrī, Muḥammad ʿAzmī. 1991. *Mawsūʿat al-fiqh wa-l-qaḍāʾ fī-l-aḥwāl al-shakhṣiyya*. Vol. 2. Cairo: Dār Maḥmūd li-l-Nashr wa-l-Tawziʿ.
Battes, Robert. 1992. "Rechtsvergleichendes zum Unterhaltsanspruch des geschiedenen Ehegatte," in Hans F. Gaul (ed.), *Familienrecht in Geschichte und Gegenwart*. Bielefeld: Gieseking. Pp. 69–92.
Beal, John P., James A. Coriden, and Thomas J. Green (eds.). 2000. *New Commentary on the Code of Canon Law*. New York: Paulist Press.
Beale, H. G. (ed.). 2004. *Chitty on Contracts*. 29th ed. Vol. 1. London: Sweet and Maxwell.
Beceiro, I., and R. Córdoba de la Llave. 1990. *Parentesco, poder y mentalidad*. Madrid: CSIC.
Bentham, Jeremy. 1823. *Introduction to the Principles and Morals of Legislation*. London: W. Pickering.
Bishop, Joel Prentiss. 1881. *Commentaries on the Law of Marriage and Divorce (with the Evidence, Practice, Pleading, and Forms; and also of Separations without Divorce, and of the Evidence of Marriage in all Issues)*. 6th ed. Boston: Little, Brown, and Company.

Blackstone, William. 1765. *Commentaries on the Laws of England. Book the First.* Repr. of 1st ed. Oxford: Clarendon Press.
Bleich, J. David. 1984. "Jewish Divorce: Judicial Misconceptions and Possible Means of Civil Enforcement," in *Connecticut Law Review* 16. Pp. 201–290.
Böhmer, Christof. 1986. "Prozesskostenhilfe und internationales Unterhaltsrecht," in IPRax. Pp. 216–218.
Breitowitz, Irving A. 1993. *Between Civil and Religious Law: The Plight of the Agunah in American Society.* Westport, Conn.: Greenwood Press.
Brohi, A. K. 1982. "The Nature of Islamic Law and the Concept of Human Rights," in International Commission of Jurists, Kuwait University, and Union of Arab Lawyers, *Human Rights in Islam: Report of a Seminar Held in Kuwait, December 1980.* Geneva: International Commission of Jurists. Pp. 43–60.
Brown, Raymond E., Joseph A. Fitzmyer, and Roland E. Murphy (eds.). 1990. *The New Jerome Biblical Commentary.* Englewood Cliffs, New Jersey: Prentice Hall.
Brundage, James A. 1987. *Law, Sex and Christian Society in Medieval Europe.* Chicago: University of Chicago Press.
al-Bukhārī, Muḥammad b. Ismāʿīl. 1974. *al-Ṣaḥīḥ.* Ed. and tr. Muḥammad Muḥsin Khān. Vol. 7. Medina: Islamic University.
Butaye, Émile, and Gaston de Leval. 1918. *A Digest of the Laws of Belgium and of the French Code Napoléon.* London: Stevens and Sons.
Būtshīsh, Ibrāhīm al-Qādirī. 1993. *al-Maghrib wa-l-Andalus fī ʿaṣr al-murābiṭīn.* Beirut: Dār al-Ṭalīʿa.
Calder, Norman. 1988. "Ḥinth, Birr, Tabarrur, Taḥannuth: An Inquiry into the Arabic Vocabulary of Vows," in *Journal of the School for Oriental and African Studies* 51. Pp. 214–239.
Capel, Anne K., and Glenn E. Markoe (eds.). 1996. *Mistress of the House, Mistress of Heaven: Women in Ancient Egypt.* New York: Hudson Hills Press with Cincinnati Art Museum.
Carmona, A. 1993. "Aportación al estudio del contrato matrimonial en el occidente islámico medieval," in *Orientalia Lovaniensia Analecta* 52. Pp. 53–66.
Carroll, Lucy. 1996. "*Ṭalāq-i-Tafwīḍ* and Stipulations in a Muslim Marriage Contract: Important Means of Protecting the Position of the South Asian Muslim Wife," in idem and H. Kapoor (eds.), *Ṭalāq-i-Tafwīḍ: The Muslim Woman's Contractual Access to Divorce.* Grabels: Women Living Under Muslim Laws (WLUML). Pp. 53– 84.
——, and H. Kapoor (eds.). 1996. *Ṭalāq-i-Tafwīḍ: The Muslim Woman's Contractual Access to Divorce.* Grabels: Women Living Under Muslim Laws (WLUML).
Chalmeta, P. 1995. "El matrimonio según el *Kitab al-Wathāʾiq* de Ibn al-ʿAṭṭār (s. X). Análisis y observaciones," in *Anaquel de Estudios Árabes* 6. Pp. 29–70.
Cohen, Boaz. 1966. *Jewish and Roman Law.* New York: Shulsinger Bros., Inc.
Cohn, Haim H. 1971. "The Secularization of Divine Law," in Haim H. Cohen (ed.), *Jewish Law in Ancient and Modern Israel.* New York: Ktav Publishing. Pp. 1–49.
Comaroff, John L. 1980. "Introduction," in John L. Comaroff (ed.), *The Meaning of Marriage Payments.* London, New York: Academic Press. Pp. 1–47.
Dāmād, Sayyid Muṣṭafā Muḥaqqiq. 1986. *Barrasī-yi fiqhī-yi ḥuqūq-i khānavāda* (Investigation of the Islamic Jurisprudence of Family Law). Tehran: Nashr-i ʿUlūm-i Islāmī. Pp. 341–443.

Daniel, Norman. 1960. *Islam and the West. The Making of an Image*. Edinburgh: The University Press.
De Bellefonds, Yves Linant. 1965. *Traité de droit musulman comparé*. Paris: Mouton and Co.
Donahue, Charles. 1976. "The Policy of Alexander the Third's Consent Theory of Marriage," in Stephen Kuttner (ed.), *Proceedings of the Fourth International Congress of Medieval Canon Law* (Monumenta Iuris Canonici C:5). Città del Vaticano: Biblioteca apostolica vaticana.
——. 1982. "The Dating of Alexander the Third's Marriage Decretals: Dauvillier Revisited After Fifty Years," in *Zeitschrift für Rechtsgeschichte (Kanonistische Abteilung)* 99 (68). Pp. 70–124.
——. 2006. "Genesis in Western Canon Law," in *Jewish Law Annual* 16. Pp. 155–184.
Dorff, Elliot N., and Arthur Rosett. 1988. *A Living Tree: The Roots and Growth of Jewish Law*. Albany: State University of New York Press.
Duby, G. 1994. *Love and Marriage in the Middle Ages*. Tr. Jane Dunnett. Chicago: University of Chicago Press.
Durant, Will. 1962. *Histoire de la Civilization*. Vol. 1. Lausanne: Editions Rencontre. (= *Our Oriental Heritage: Being a History of Civilization in Egypt and the Near East to the Death of Alexander, and in India, China and Japan from the Beginning to our Own Day*. New York: Simon and Schuster, 1954).
Echevarría Arsuaga, A. 2000. "Mudéjares y moriscos," in M. J. Viguera Molíns (ed.), *El Reino Nazarí de Granada (1232–1492). Sociedad, vida y cultura*. Madrid: Espasa Calpe. Pp. 367–440.
Edelman, Martin. 1994. *Courts, Politics and Culture in Israel*. Charlottesville: University of Virginia Press.
Edge, Ian. 1995. "The Middle East: Legal System or Legal Vacuum?" in *Middle Eastern Commercial Law Review* 4. P. 127.
El Alami, Dawoud S. 1991. "Legal Capacity with Specific Reference to the Marriage Contract," in *Arab Law Quarterly* 6:2. Pp. 190–204.
——. 1992. *The Marriage Contract in Islamic Law*. London: Graham and Trotman.
——, and D. Hinchcliffe. 1996. *Islamic Marriage and Divorce Laws of the Arab World*. London: Kluwer Law International.
Elon, Menahem. 1994. *Jewish Law: History, Sources, Principles*, Vol. 1. Philadelphia: Jewish Publication Society.
Elwan, Omaia. 1994. "Neues iranisches Scheidungsgesetz vom 26.11.1992," in IPRax. P. 326.
Esposito, John L. 1982. *Women in Muslim Family Law*. Syracuse: Syracuse University Press.
——, with Natana J. DeLong-Bas. 2001. *Women in Muslim Family Law*. 2nd ed. Syracuse, NY: Syracuse University Press.
Ezzat, Heba Ra'uf. 1994. "An Interview with Heba Ra'uf Ezzat," in *Middle East Report* 191 (Nov.–Dec.). Pp. 26–27.
Fakhry, Majid (tr.). 1997. *The Qur'an: A Modern English Version*. Reading: Garnet.
Falk, Ze'ev W. 1966. *Jewish Matrimonial Law in the Middle Ages*. Oxford: Oxford University Press.
——. 1981. *Law and Religion: The Jewish Experience*. Jerusalem: Mesharim Publishers.
*Al-Fatāwā al-islāmiyya* 6 (1982).

Flannery, Austin (ed.). 1975. *Vatican Council II: The Conciliar and Post Conciliar Documents*. Boston: St Paul Editions.
Foskett, David. 1996. *The Law and Practice of Compromise*. 4th ed. London: Sweet and Maxwell.
Friedman, M. A. 1980. *Jewish Marriage in Palestine: A Cairo Geniza Study*. 2 vols. New York: The Jewish Theological Seminary of America.
Fyzee, Asaf. 1997. *Outlines of Muhammadan Law*. 4th ed. Delhi: Oxford University Press.
Galanter, Marc and Jayanth Krishnan. 2000. "Personal Law and Human Rights in India and Israel," in *Israel Law Review* 34. Pp. 101–33.
Gallego Burín, A., and Gámir Sandoval, A. 1968. *Los moriscos del Reino de Granada según el sínodo de Guádix de 1554*. Granada: Universidad.
Ganghofer, Roland, and Jean-Michel Poughon. 1995. "Le Droit de la femme dans le code civil et l'ALR," in Barbara Dölemeyer and Heinz Mohnhaupt (eds.), *200 Jahre Allgemeines Landrecht für die preussischen Staaten: Wirkungsgeschichte und internationaler Kontext*, Frankfurt am Mein: Vittorio Klostermann. Pp. 357–370.
Geertz, Clifford. 1983. *Local Knowledge*. New York: Basic Books.
Gelder, Geert Jan van. 2005. *Close Relationships: Incest and Inbreeding in Classical Arabic Literature*. London: I. B. Tauris.
al-Gharnāṭī, Abū Isḥāq. 1988. *al-Wathā'iq al-mukhtaṣara*. Ed. Muṣṭafā Nājī. Rabat: Markaz Iḥyā' al-Turāth al-Maghribī.
Gómez Moreno, M. 1944. "Carta de dote que se dio en tiempo que eran moros en Hornachos," in *Al-Andalus* 9. Pp. 503–505.
Grohmann, Adolf. 1994. *Awrāq al-bardī al-ʿarabiyya bi-Dār al-Kutub al-Miṣriyya*. Vol. 1. Cairo: Maṭbaʿa Dār al-Kutub al-Miṣriyya.
Guichard, P. 1977. *Structures sociales "orientales" et "occidentales" dans l'Espagne musulmane*. Paris: Mouton.
Ḥaddād, al-Ṭāhir. 1930. *Imra'atunā fi-l-sharīʿa wa-l-mujtamaʿ*. Tunis: Dār al-Tūnisiyya li-l-Nashr.
Haeri, Shahla. 1989. *Law of Desire: Temporary Marriage in Shiʿi Iran*. Syracuse, NY: Syracuse University Press.
——. 1996. "Mutʿa: Regulating Gender and Sexuality in Postrevolutionary Iran," in Muhammad Khalid Masud, Brinkley Messick, and David S. Powers (eds.), *Islamic Legal Interpretation: Muftis and Their Fatwas*. Cambridge: Harvard University Press. Pp. 251–261.
Hallaq, Wael. 1995. "Model *Shurūṭ* Works and the Dialectic of Doctrine and Practice," in *Islamic Law and Society* 2. Pp. 109–134.
——. 1997. *A History of Islamic Legal Theories: An Introduction to Sunnī Uṣūl al-Fiqh*. Cambridge: Cambridge University Press.
——. 2001. *Authority, Continuity, and Change in Islamic Law*. Cambridge: Cambridge University Press.
——. 2004. "Can the Shariʿa be Restored?," in Yvonne Yazbeck Haddad and Barbara Freyer Stowasser (eds.), *Islamic Law and the Challenges of Modernity*. Walnut Creek, Calif.: AltaMira Press. Pp. 21–53.
Hamadeh, Najla. 1996. "Islamic Family Legislation: The Authoritarian Discourse of Silence," in Mai Yamani (ed.), *Feminism and Islam: Legal and Literary Perspectives*. Reading: Garnet Publishing Ltd. Pp. 331–349.

Hamid, Mohamed El Fatih. 1976. "The Freedom to Make Stipulations in the Islamic Law of Contract," in *Journal of Islamic and Comparative Law* 6. Pp. 22–32.

Hasan, Ayesha. 1999. "Marriages in Islamic Law: A Brief Introduction," in *Family Law* 29. Pp. 164–165.

Ḥaṣkafī, Muḥammad b. ʿAlī. 1992. *The Durr-ul-Mukhtar, Being the Commentary of the Tanvirul Absar of Muhammad Bin Abdullah Tamartashi.* Trans. B. M. Dayal. New Delhi: Kitab Bhavan.

Hassan, Riffat. 1987. "Equal Before Allah? Woman-Man Equality in the Islamic Tradition," in *Harvard Divinity Bulletin* 17. Pp. 2–4 (also in idem, *Selected Articles*, Women Living Under Muslim Law, n.d. Pp. 12–17).

——. 1991. "Muslim Women and Post-Patriarchal Islam," in Paula M. Cooey, William R. Eakin, and Jay B. McDaniel (eds.), *After Patriarchy: Feminist Transformations of the World Religions.* Maryknoll, NY: Orbis Books. Pp. 39–64.

——. 1996. "Feminist Theology: Challenges for Muslim Women," in *Critique: The Journal for Critical Studies of the Middle East* 9 (Fall). Pp. 53–65.

Hattenhauer, Hans. 1994. *Allgemeines Landrecht für die Preussischen Staaten von 1794.* 2nd ed. Neuwied: Luchterhand.

Hawting, Gerald. 1994. "An Ascetic Vow and an Unseemly Oath? *Īlāʾ* and *Ẓihār* in Muslim Law," in *Journal of the School for Oriental and African Studies* 57. Pp. 113–125.

Heinrich, Dieter. 2004. "Die Morgengabe und das Internationale Privatrecht," in Michael Coester et al. (eds.), *Privatrecht in Europa: Vielfalt, Kollision, Kooperation. Festschrift für Hans-Jürgen Sonnenberger zum 70. Geburtstag.* Munich: Beck. Pp. 389–400.

Heldrich, Andreas. 1983. "Das juristische Kuckucksei aus dem Morgenland," in IPRax. Pp. 64–65.

Helmholz, R. H. 1974. *Marriage Litigation in Medieval England.* Cambridge: Cambridge University Press.

Hessler, Hans-Joachim. 1988. "Islamisch-rechtliche Morgengabe: vereinbarter Vermögensausgleich im deutschen Scheidungsfolgerecht," in IPRax. Pp. 95–97.

Ḥillī, ʿAllāma. 1364 (1985). *Sharāʾiʿ al-Islām.* Vol. 2. Persian tr. A. A. Yazdi, compiled by Muhammad Taqi Danish-Pazhuh. Tehran: Tehran University Press.

——. 1999. *Taḥrīr al-iḥkam (aḥkām) al-sharʿiyya ʿalā al-madhhab al-imāmiyya.* Qum: Maktab al-Tawḥīd.

Hinchcliffe, D. 1968. "The Iranian Family Protection Act," in *International and Comparative Law Quarterly* 17. Pp. 516–521.

Hodson, Justice, 1958. "Common Law Marriage," in *The International and Comparative Quarterly* 7. Pp. 205–216.

Hoenerbach, W. 1965. *Spanisch-Islamische Urkunden aus der Zeit der Nasriden und Moriscos.* Bonn: Selbstverlag des Orientalischen Seminars der Universität.

Hoodfar, Homa. 1991. "Return to the Veil: Personal Strategy and 'Public' Participation in Egypt," in N. Redclift and M. T. Sinclair (eds.), *Working Women: International Perspectives on Labour and Gender Ideology.* London: Routledge. Pp. 104–124.

——. 1997. *Between Marriage and the Market: Intimate Politics and Survival in Cairo.* Berkeley: University of California Press.

Hourani, Albert. 1992. *A History of the Arab Peoples.* New York: Warner Books.

Human Rights Watch. 2004. *Divorced from Justice: Women's Unequal Access to Divorce in Egypt*. Vol. 16, no. 8. Available at http://hrw.org/reports/2004/egypt1204/egypt1204.pdf.
Ibn ʿAbd al-Barr. 1987. *al-Kāfī fī fiqh ahl al-Madīna*. Beirut: Dār al-Kutub al-ʿIlmiyya.
Ibn ʿAbd al-Rafīʿ. 1989. *Muʿīn al-ḥukkām*. Ed. Muḥammad ibn Qāsim ibn ʿIyād. Beirut: Dār al-Gharb al-Islāmī.
Ibn ʿAbd al-Raʾūf, Aḥmad b. ʿAbd Allāh. 1955. *Risāla fī adab al-ḥisba*, in E. Lévi-Provençal (ed.), *Documents arabes inédits sur la vie sociale et économique en occident musulman au moyen age*. Cairo: Institut Français d'Archéologie Orientale.
Ibn ʿĀbidīn, Muḥammad Amīn ibn ʿUmar. 1994. *Radd al-muḥtār ʿalā al-Durr al-mukhtār sharḥ Tanwīr al-abṣār*. Beirut: Dār al-Kutub al-ʿIlmiyya.
Ibn ʿĀṣim. 1882. *La Tohfat d'ebn Acem. Traité de droit musulman*. Ed. and tr. O. Houdas and F. Martel. Argel: Gavault Saint-Lager.
Ibn al-ʿAṭṭār. 1983. *Kitāb al-Wathāʾiq wa-l-sijillāt. Formulario notarial hispano-árabe por el alfaquí y notario cordobés Ibn al-ʿAttar (s. X)*. Ed. P. Chalmeta and F. Corriente. Madrid: Instituto Hispano-Arabe de Cultura-Academia Matritense del Notariado.
Ibn Juzayy, Muḥammad b. Aḥmad. 1982. *al-Qawānīn al-fiqhiyya*. Tunis: al-Dār al-ʿArabiyya li-l-Kitāb.
Ibn Mughīth al-Ṭulayṭulī, Aḥmad. 1994. *al-Muqniʿ fī ʿilm al-shurūṭ (Formulario notarial)*. Ed. F. J. Aguirre Sádaba. Madrid: CSIC.
Ibn al-Naqīb al-Miṣrī, Aḥmad. 1999. *Reliance of the Traveller: A Classic Manual of Islamic Sacred Law*. Tr. and ed. Nuh Ha Mim Keller. Rev. ed. Beltsville, Maryland: Amana Publications.
Ibn Qudama, Muwaffaq al-Dīn. 1950. *Le Précis de droit d'Ibn Qudāma*. Tr. Henri Laoust. (= *ʿUmda fī aḥkam al-fiqh*). Beirut.
——. 1994. *al-Kāfī fī fiqh Aḥmad ibn Ḥanbal*. Beirut: Dār al-Kutub al-ʿIlmiyya.
Ibn Rushd, Abū l-Walīd. 1992. *Masāʾil*. Ed. M. al-Ḥabīb al-Tijānī. 2 vols. Casablanca: Dār al-Āfāq al-Jadīda.
——. 1994–1996. *The Distinguished Jurist's Primer: A Translation of* Bidāyat al-Mujtahid. 2 vols. Tr. Imran Ahsan Khan Nyazee. Reading: Centre for Muslim Contribution to Civilization; Garnet Publishing.
——. 1415 [1995]. *Bidāyat al-mujtahid wa-nihāyat al-muqtaṣid*. Ed. Muḥammad Ṣubḥī Ḥasan Ḥallāq. Cairo: Maktabat Ibn Taymiyya.
Ibn Salmūn al-Kinānī. 1885. *Kitāb al-ʿiqd al-munaẓẓam li-l-ḥukkām fī-mā yajrī bayna aydihim min al-ʿuqūd wa-l-aḥkām*. Printed on the margins of Ibn Farḥūn, *Tabṣirat al-ḥukkām fī uṣūl al-aqḍiya wa-manāhij al-aḥkām*. Cairo: Maṭbaʿat al-ʿĀmira al-Sharqiyya.
Ibn Taymiyya, Aḥmad b. ʿAbd al-Ḥalīm. 1948. *al-Fatāwā al-kubrā*. Cairo: Kurdistān al-ʿIlmiyya.
——. 1987. *Fatāwā al-nisāʾ*. Book 5. Beirut: Dār al Kalām.
Ibrahim, Ahmad. 1975. *Islamic Law in Malaya*. Ed. Shirle Gordon. Kuala Lumpur: Malaysian Sociological Research Institute.
——. 2000. *The Administration of Islamic Law in Malaysia*. Kuala Lumpur: Institute of Islamic Understanding Malaysia.
Idris, H. R. 1970. "Le Mariage en occident musulman d'après un choix de fatwas médiévales extraites du *Miʿyar* d'al-Wanžarīsī," in *Studia Islamica* 32. Pp. 157–167.

al-ʿImādī, Ḥāmid. 1881–82 (1300 AH). *al-ʿUqūd al-durriya*. Ed. Ibn ʿĀbidīn, Muḥammad Amīn. Vol. 1. Bulāq: al-Maṭbaʿa al-Āmira al-Mīriyya.
Imam Aḥmad. *Ikhtiyārāt*. Ms.
al-Iryānī, ʿAlī ʿAbd Allāh. N.d. *Najāḥ al-ṭālib fī ṣifat mā yaktub al-kātib*. Ms. Jāmiʿ al-gharbiyya, Ṣanaʿāʾ, 64 fiqh.
Jacobs, Joseph. 1893. *The Jews of Angevin England: Documents and Records*. London: D. Nutt.
James, T. E. 1957. "The English Law of Marriage," in Ronald Harry Graveson and Francise R. Crane (eds.), *A Century of Family Law 1857–1957*. London: Sweet and Maxwell. Pp. 20–38.
*al-Jarīda al-Qaḍāʾiyya*. 1934, 1936 (19, year 5, 12, at 44; vol. 1, year 7, at 12–13).
al-Jazīrī, ʿAlī b. Yaḥyā. 1998. *al-Maqṣad al-maḥmūd fī talkhīṣ al-ʿuqūd (Proyecto plausible de compendio de fórmulas notariales)*. Ed. A. Ferreras, A. Madrid: CSIC.
Jones, Chris. 1996. "Die Anwendung des islamischen Rechts in der Bundesrepublik Deutschland," in *Deutsche Richterzeitung* 74. Pp. 322–328.
Kamāl, Ashraf M. 1993. *Al-Mushkilāt al-ʿamaliyya fī qānūn al-aḥwāl al-shakhṣiyya*. Cairo: A. M. Kamāl.
Kamali, Mohammad Hashim. 1991. *Principles of Islamic Jurisprudence*. Cambridge: Islamic Texts Society.
Kātūziyan, Nāṣir. 1368 (1989). *Ḥuqūq-i madanī-yi khānavāda* (Family Civil Law). Tehran: Tehran University Press.
Katzenberg, Simone, and Jeremy Rosenblatt. 1999. "Getting the Get," in *Family Law* 29 (March).
Kegel, Gerhard. 1996. *Sörgel—BGB Kommentar: Bürgerliches Gesetzbuch mit Einführungsgesetz und Nebengesetzen*. Stuttgart and Berlin: Verlag W. Kohlhammer. Vor Art. 3 Rdn. 44–46.
——, and Klaus Schurig. 2000. *Internationales Privatrecht: Ein Studienbuch*. 8th ed. Munich: C. H. Beck.
Khalīl ibn Isḥāq al-Jundī. 1919. *Il "Mukhtasar". Somario del diritto malechita di Khalil ibn Ishaq*. Tr. D. Santillana and I. Guidi. Milan: Hoepli.
——. 1980 [1916]. *Mâliki Law: Being a Summary from French Translations of the Mukhtaṣar of Sîdî Khalîl*. Ed. and tr. F. X. Ruxton. Westport, Conn.: Hyperion.
——. 2004. *Mukhtaṣar al-ʿAllāma Khalīl fī fiqh al-Imām Mālik*. Beirut: Dār al-Kutub al-ʿIlmiyya.
al-Khiraqī, ʿUmar b. al-Ḥusayn. 1982. *Mukhtaṣar al-Khiraqī fi-l-madhhab al-Ḥanbalī*. Riyadh: al-Maktaba al-Dawliyya.
Krüger, Hilmar. 1977. "Ehe und Brautgabe," in FamRZ. Pp. 114–118.
——. 1990. "Grundlage des türkischen Verlöbnisrechts," in StAZ. Pp. 313–325.
Labarta, A. 1980. "Inventario de los documentos árabes contenidos en los procesos inquisitoriales contra moriscos valencianos conservados en el Archivo Histórico Nacional de Madrid (legajos 548–556)," in *Al-Qantara* 1. Pp. 115–164.
——. 1983. "Contratos matrimoniales entre moriscos valencianos," in *Al-Qantara* 4. Pp. 57–87.
Labidi, Lilia. 1989. *Çabra hachma: Sexualité et tradition*. Tunis: Dār Annawras.
Lau, Martin. 1996. "Opening Pandora's Box: The Impact of the Saima Waheed Case on the Legal Status of Women in Pakistan," in *Yearbook of Islamic and Middle Eastern Law* 3. Pp. 518–533.

Lewis, Bernard. 1982. *The Muslim Discovery of Europe*. London: Weidenfeld and Nicolson.
Lewis, Philip. 1994. *Islamic Britain: Religion, Politics and Identity Among British Muslims. Bradford in the 1990s*. London: I. B. Tauris.
Linant de Bellefonds, Y. 1973. *Traité de droit musulman comparé III*. Paris and The Hague: Mouton and Co.
Lokhandwalla, S. T. 1971. "Islamic Law and Ismaili Communities (Khojas and Bohras)," in S. T. Lokhandwalla (ed.), *India and Contemporary Islam*. Simla: Indian Institute of Advanced Study. Pp. 379–397.
Lombard, Peter, Bishop of Paris. 1971–1981. *Magistri Petri Lombardi Parisensis episcopi Sententiae in IV libros distinctae*. 2 vols. in 3. 3rd ed. Specilegium Bonaventurianum 4, 5. Grottaferrata: Editiones Collegii S. Bonaventurae ad Claras Aquas.
López Ortiz, J. 1926. "Formularios notariales de la España musulmana," in *Ciudad de Dios* 145. Pp. 262–70.
——. 1927. "Algunos capítulos del formulario notarial de Abensalmún de Granada," in *Anuario de Historia del Derecho Español* 4. Pp. 319–375.
——. 1932. *Derecho musulmán*. Barcelona: Editorial Labor.
MacLeod, Arlene Elowe. 1991. *Accommodating Protest*. New York: Columbia University Press.
Māhir, Suʿād. 1978. "ʿUqūd al-zawāj ʿalā al-mansūjāt al-athariyya," in *Majallat Kulliyyāt al-Āthār: al-Kitāb al-dhahabī*. Pt. 1 (Cairo). Pp. 39–55.
Mahmood, T. 1972. *Family Law Reforms in the Muslim World*. Bombay: N. M. Tripathi.
*Majallat Muḥāmā al-Sharʿiyya*. 1929–1955. Egypt: Niqābat al-Muḥāmīn al-Sharʿiyyīn.
*Majallat al-Qaḍāʾ al-Sharʿī* 8 (August). 1926.
*al-Majmūʿa al-rasmiyya li-l-maḥākim al-ahliyya wa-l-sharʿiyya*. 1938. September 4. Bulaq, Cairo: Maṭbaʿa al-Amīriyya.
al-Mālaqī, Abū l-Muṭarrif al-Shaʿbī. 1992. *al-Aḥkām*. Ed. al-Ṣādiq al-Ḥalawī. Beirut: Dār al-Gharb al-Islāmī.
Malick, Qayyum A. 1954. *His Royal Highness Prince Aga Khan: Guide, Philosopher and Friend of the Islamic World*. Karachi: Ismailia Association for Pakistan.
al-Marghīnānī, ʿAlī ibn Abī Bakr. 1957, $^{2}$1975. *The Hedaya, or Guide: A Commentary on the Mussulman Laws*. Tr. Charles Hamilton. 2nd ed. Reprint. Lahore: Premier Book House.
——. 2006. *al-Hidāyah = The Guidance: A Translation of al-Hidāyah fi Sharḥ Bidāyat al-Mubtadī, a Classical Manual of Hanafi Law*. Tr. Imran Ahsan Khan Nyazee. Vol. 1. Bristol: Amal Press.
Matar, N. 1998. *Islam in Britain*. Cambridge: Cambridge University Press.
Mayer, Ann Elizabeth. 1995. *Islam and Human Rights: Tradition and Politics*. 2nd ed. London: Pinter Publishers.
Mayhew, Henry. 1861. *The London Labour and the London Poor*. London: Griffin, Bohn and Company.
Melchert, Christopher. 1997. *The Formation of the Sunni Schools of Law, 9th–10th Centuries C.E.* Leiden: Brill.
Mellinkoff, D. 1963. *The Language of the Law*. Boston: Little, Brown.
Mernissi, Fatima. 1991. *Women and Islam: An Historical and Theological Enquiry*. Tr. M. J. Lakeland. Oxford: Blackwell.

Meron, Ya'akov. 1971. *L'Obligation alimentaire entre époux en droit musulman hanéfite.* Paris: Librairie Générale de Droit et de Jurisprudence.

Messick, Brinkley. 1993. *The Calligraphic State: Textual Domination and History in a Muslim Society*. Berkeley: University of California Press.

——. 2001. "Indexing the Self: Intent and Expression in Islamic Legal Acts," in *Islamic Law and Society* 8:2. Pp. 151–178.

——. 2002. "Evidence: From Memory to Archive," in *Islamic Law and Society* 9:2. Pp. 231–270.

Migne, J. P. (ed.). 1880. *Patrologia latina cursus completus*. Paris: Migne.

Mihrpūr, Ḥusayn. 1379 [2000]. *Mabāḥisi az ḥuqūq-i zan*. Tehran: Iṭṭilā'āt Publications.

Milligan, Paul. 1999. "Pre-Nuptials Beware," in *Family Law* 29 (July).

Mir-Hosseini, Ziba. 1993. *Marriage on Trial*. London: I. B. Tauris.

——. 1993a. "Women, Marriage and the Law in Post-Revolutionary Iran," in Haleh Afshar (ed.), *Women in the Middle East: Perceptions, Realities and Struggles for Liberation*. New York: Palgrave Macmillan. Pp. 59–84.

——. 1996. "Stretching the Limits: A Feminist Reading of the *Shari'a*," in M. Yamani (ed.), *Islam and Feminism: Legal and Literary Perspectives*. London: Ithaca Press. Pp. 285–319.

——. 1996a. "Women and Politics in Post-Khomeini Iran: Divorce, Veiling and Emerging Feminist Voices," in H. Afshar (ed.), *Women and Politics in the Third World*. London: Routledge. Pp. 142–169.

——. 1998. "Gender and Islam: Debates with the *Ulama* in Iran," in *Critique: Journal for Critical Studies of the Middle East* 7 (Fall). Pp. 45–60.

——. 1998a. "Mariage et divorce: Une marge de négociation pour les femmes," in N. Yavari-d'Hellencourt, *Les Femmes en Iran: Pressions sociales et stratégies identitaires*. Paris: Harmattan. Pp. 95–118.

——. 1999. "Family Law. III. In Modern Persia," in *Encyclopedia Iranica* 9. Pp. 192–196.

——. 1999a. *Islam and Gender: The Religious Debate in Contemporary Iran*. Princeton: Princeton University Press.

——. 2000. "Ayatollah Khomeini and the Question of Women," in Richard Tapper (ed.), *Ayatollah Khomeini and the Modernization of Islamic Thought* (Occasional Paper 19). London: SOAS/CNMES. Pp. 27–34.

Misholov, David. 2001. "Pre-Nuptial Agreements" in *Tehumin* 21. Israel: Zomet.

Moghadam, Valentine M. 1992. "Revolution, Islam and Women: Sexual Politics in Iran and Afghanistan," in Parker, Russo, Sommer, and Yaeger (eds.), *Nationalisms and Sexualities*. New York: Routledge. Pp. 424–446.

Mohamad, Maznah. 1996. "Kes-Kes Nafkah dan Penceraian: Satu Analisis Social Mengenai Keberkesanan Mekanisme Undang-Undang Bagi Wanita" (Cases of Nafkah and Divorce: A Social Analysis on the Effectiveness of Legal Mechanisms for Women). Paper presented at the Workshop on Shari'ah Law, Legal and Counselling Experience of Muslim Women, Penang, Malaysia, October 25–26 (unpubl. transcript on file with Zainah Anwar).

Moors, Annelies. 1995. *Women, Property and Islam: Palestinian Experiences, 1920–1990*. Cambridge: Cambridge University Press.

——. 1996. "Gender Relations and Inheritance: Person, Power and Property in Palestine," in D. Kandiyoti (ed.), *Gendering the Middle East*. London: I. B. Tauris. Pp. 69–84.

Motzki, Harald. 1996. "Child Marriage in Seventeenth-Century Palestine," in M. Khalid Masud, Brinkley Messick, and David Powers (eds.), *Islamic Legal Interpretation: Muftis and their Fatwas*. Cambridge: Harvard University Press. Pp. 129–140.

——. 2001. "Marriage and Divorce," in *Encyclopaedia of the Qurʾān*. Leiden: Brill. Vol. 3. Pp. 276–281.

al-Muftī al-Ḥubayshī, Muḥammad b. ʿAlī. 1988. *Fatḥ al-mannān sharḥ Zubad Ibn Raslān*. Ed. ʿAbd Allāh al-Ḥibshī. Sanʿaʾ: Maktabat al-Jīl al-Jadīd.

Muhammad, Khaleel. 2008. "Marriage in Islam," in *Encyclopedia of Love in World Religions*. Santa Barbara, Calif.: ABC-Clio. Vol. 2. Pp. 396–397.

Mundy, Martha. 1995. *Domestic Government: Kinship, Community and Polity in North Yemen*. London: I. B. Tauris.

Murata, Sachiko. 1974. "Temporary Marriage in Islamic Law." M.A. Thesis, Tehran University. Available in revised form at http://www.al-islam.org/al-serat/muta/.

al-Muṭahhar, Muḥammad b. Yaḥyā. 1985. *Aḥkām al-aḥwāl al-shakhṣiyya min fiqh al-sharīʿa al-islāmiyya*. Vol. 1. Beirut: Dār al-Kitāb al-Lubnānī.

al-Muzanī, Ismāʿīl b. Yaḥyā. 1993. *Mukhtaṣar al-Muzanī*. Published as Vol. 9 of al-Shāfiʿī, *al-Umm*. Beirut: Dār al-Kutub al-ʿIlmiyya.

Nasir, Jamil J. 1986, [2]1990. *The Islamic Law of Personal Status*. London: Graham and Trotman.

National NGO Committee. 1994. *The Egyptian NGO Platform Document for the ICPD*, available at http://www.popline.org/docs/099431.

al-Nawawī, Muḥyī al-Dīn. 1977. *Minhaj et Talibin: A Manual of Muhammadan Law According to the School of Shafi*. Tr. E. C. Howard from French tr. by L. W. C. van den Berg. Lahore: Law Publishing Co.

Othman, Norani. 1996. "Shariʿa and the Citizenship Rights of Women in a Modern Nation State: Grounding Human Rights Arguments in Non-Western Cultural Terms." Paper presented at "The Growth of East Asia and its Impact on Human Rights: Cultural Sources of Human Rights in East Asia" workshop in Bangkok, Thailand, 24–27 March.

——. 1997. *Grounding Human Rights Arguments in Non-Western Cultural Terms: Shariʿa and the Citizenship Rights of Women in a Modern Nation-State*. Kuala Lumpur: IKMAS Working Paper Series No. 10.

Özlan, Bilge, 1998. "Anmerkung," in FamRZ. Pp. 624–626.

Pawlowski, Hans-Martin. 1983. *Die "Bürgerliche Ehe" als Organisation: Überlegungen zu den juristischen Arbeitsmitteln*. Hamburg: R. v. Decker.

Pearl, David. 1972. "Muslim Marriages in English Law," in *The Cambridge Law Journal* 30. Pp. 120–143.

——. 1995. "The Application of Islamic Law in the English Courts," in *Yearbook of Middle Eastern and Islamic Law* 2. Pp. 3–11.

Pearl, David and Werner Menski. 1998. *Muslim Family Law*. 3rd ed. London: Sweet and Maxwell.

Perry, Sir Erskine. 1853. *Oriental Cases*. London: S. Sweet.

Pesle, O. 1936. *Le Mariage chez les Malékites de l'Afrique du Nord*. Rabat: F. Moncho.

Pharaon, Nora Alarafi. 2004. "Saudi Women and the Muslim State in the Twenty-First Century," in *Sex Roles* 51: 349–366.

Poulter, Sebastian. 1995. "The Construction of an Islamic Identity in Western Europe," in Michael King (ed.), *God's Law versus State Law*. London: Grey Seal.

———. 1998. *Ethnicity, Law and Human Rights*. Oxford: Clarendon Press.
———. 1998a. "Muslims: The Claim to a Separate System of Personal Law," in Sebastian Poulter, *Ethnicity, Law and Human Rights*. Oxford: Clarendon Press.
Powers, D. S. 1990. "A Court Case from Fourteenth-Century North Africa," in *Journal of the American Oriental Society* 110. Pp. 229–254.
———. 1990a. "*Fatwas* as Sources for Legal and Social History: A Dispute over Endowment Revenues from Fourteenth-Century Fez," in *Al-Qantara* 11. Pp. 295–341.
al-Qayrawānī, Ibn Abī Zayd. 1968. *La Risâla ou Epître sur les éléments du dogme et de la loi de l'Islâm selon le rite malikite*. Ed. Leon Bercher. Argel: Jules Carbonel.
Qureshi, M. A. 1995. *Muslim Law of Marriage, Divorce and Maintenance*. New Delhi: Deep and Deep Publications.
Raḍwān, Zaynab. 1993. *Al-Islām wa-qaḍāyā al-marʾa*. 2nd ed. Dubai: Dār al-Qirāʾa.
al-Ramlī, Khayr al-Dīn ibn Aḥmad. 1856–1857 (1273 AH). *Kitāb al-Fatāwā al-kubrā li-nafʿ al-birriyya*. Vol. 1. Cairo: Bulaq.
Rapoport, Yossef. 2000. "Matrimonial Gifts in Early Islamic Egypt," in *Islamic Law and Society* 7. Pp. 1–36.
———. 2005. *Marriage, Money, and Divorce in Medieval Islamic Society*. Cambridge: Cambridge University Press.
Rosen, Lawrence. 1984. *Bargaining for Reality: The Construction of Social Relations in a Muslim Community*. Chicago: University of Chicago Press.
———. 1989. *The Anthropology of Justice: Law as Culture in Islamic Society*. Cambridge: Cambridge University Press.
Rowlandson, Jane (ed.). 1998. *Women and Society in Greek and Roman Egypt: A Sourcebook*. Cambridge: Cambridge University Press.
Russell, Mona. 2004. *Creating the New Egyptian Woman: Consumerism, Education, and National Identity, 1863–1922*. New York: Palgrave Macmillan.
*Ṣaḥīḥ Muslim*. 1976. Tr. Abdul Hamid Siddiqi. Lahore: Ashraf Publications.
Saḥnūn al-Tanūkhī. 1323H. *Mālik b. Anas. al-Mudawwana al-kubrā*. Beirut: Dār Sādir Publishers.
Said, Edward. 1978. *Orientalism*. New York: Vintage Books.
Saʿidzadeh, Muhsin, 1998. "The Foundation of the Equality Perspective in Modern Fiqh: The Case of Divorce," *Payām-e Ḥajar* 233 (Farvardin-Ordibehest 1377 [April–May 1998]). Pp. 51–53.
Salter, Joseph. 1873. *The Asiatic in England. Sketches of Sixteen Years' Work among Orientals*. London: Seeley, Jackson and Halliday.
Santillana, David. 1925/1926. *Istituzioni di diritto musulmano malichita con riguardo anche al sistema sciafiita*. Rome: Istituto per l'Oriente.
al-Sarakhsī, Muḥammad ibn Aḥmad. 2001. *Kitāb al-Mabsūṭ*. Beirut: Dār al-Kutub al-ʿIlmiyya.
Schacht, Joseph. 1964. *An Introduction to Islamic Law*. Oxford: Clarendon Press.
Schillebeeckx, Edward. 1965. *Marriage: Human Reality and Saving Mystery*. New York: Sheed and Ward.
Schweid, Eliezer. 1996. "'Beyond' All That—Modernism, Zionism, Judaism," in *Israel Studies* 1. Pp. 224–246.
Scott, Patti A. 1996. "Comment: New York Divorce Law and the Religion Clauses: An Unconstitutional Exorcism of the Jewish Get Laws," in *Seton Hall Constitutional Law Journal* 6. Pp. 1117–1191.

Seco de Lucena, L. 1961. *Documentos arábigo-granadinos*. Madrid: Instituto Egipcio de Estudios Islámicos.
Selden, John. 1892. *The Table Talk of John Selden*. Ed. Samuel H. Reynolds. Oxford: Clarendon Press.
Shaham, Ron. 1997. *Family and the Courts in Modern Egypt: A Study Based on Decisions by the Sharīʿa Courts, 1900–1955*. Leiden: E. J. Brill.
——. 1999. "State, Feminists and Islamists: The Debate over Stipulations in Marriage Contracts in Egypt," in *Bulletin of the School of Oriental and African Studies* 62. Pp. 462–483.
Shaheed, Farida. 1994. "Controlled or Autonomous: Identity and the Experience of the Network, Women Living Under Muslim Laws," in *Signs* 19. Pp. 997–1019.
Shariff, Shahilla. 1989. "Secular States and Religious Laws: Marital Disputes and Divorce in the Shia Imami Ismaili Muslim Community." On file with Ali Asani.
Shatzmiller, Maya. 1995. "Women and Property Rights in al-Andalus and the Maghrib: Social Patterns and Legal Discourse," in *Islamic Law and Society* 2. Pp. 219–257.
——. 2007. *Her Day in Court: Women's Property Rights in Fifteenth-Century Granada*. Cambridge, MA: Islamic Legal Studies Program, Harvard Law School.
al-Shawkānī, Muḥammad b. ʿAlī. 1985. *al-Sayl al-jarrār al-mutadaffiq ʿalā ḥadāʾiq al-azhār*. Beirut: Dār al-Kutub al-ʿIlmiyya.
al-Shaybānī, Muḥammad. n.d. *al-Jāmiʿ al-ṣaghīr*. Beirut: ʿAlam al-Kutub.
——. 1965. *Kitāb al-Ḥujja*. Hyderabad: Lajnat Iḥyāʾ al-Maʿārif al-Nuʿmāniyya.
——. 1967. *al-Jāmiʿ al-kabīr*. Lahore: Dār al-Maʿārif al-Nuʿmāniyya.
——. 1997. *Muwaṭṭaʾ al-Imām Mālik bi-riwāyat Muḥammad ibn al-Ḥasan al-Shaybānī*. Beirut: al-Maṭbaʿat al-ʿIlmiyya.
al-Shāfiʿī, Muḥammad ibn Idrīs. 1993. *al-Umm*. 9 vols. Beirut: Dār al-Kutub al-ʿIlmiyya.
Shia Ismailia Association for Africa. 1948. *Ami jarana: Mawlana Hazar Imam na 1899 thi 1945 sudhi pavitr farmanoni vishayvar taravni*. Mombasa: His Highness the Aga Khan Shia Ismailia Association for Africa.
Shochetman, Eliav. 1995. "On the Improvement of Divorce Agreements," in Eliav Shochetman and Shmuel Shilo (eds.), *Shenaton Ha-Mishpat Ha-Ivri* 18–19. Jerusalem: Institute for Research in Jewish Law (in Hebr.).
Siddiqui, Mona. 1995. "*Mahr*: Legal Obligation or Rightful Demand?," in *Journal of Islamic Studies* 6. Pp. 14–24.
——. 1996. "Law and the Desire for Social Control: An Insight into the Hanafi Concept of Kafāʾa with Reference to the Fatāwā ʿĀlamgīrī (1664–1672)," in Mai Yamani (ed.), *Feminism and Islam: Legal and Literary Perspectives*. New York: New York University Press. Pp. 49–68.
Silberg, Moshe. 1973. *Talmudic Law and the Modern State*. New York: Burning Bush Press.
SIS and AWL. 1996. *Memorandum on Reform of the Islamic Family Laws on Polygamy, submitted to the Prime Minister of Malaysia in December 1996 by Sisters in Islam (SIS) and Association of Women Lawyers (AWL)*. Available at www.sistersinislam.org .my/advocacy-memo.htm (last accessed May 2008).
SIS, NCWO, and AWL. 1997. *Memorandum on Reform of the Islamic Family Laws and the Administration of Justice in the Syariah System in Malaysia, submitted to the Government of Malaysia in March 1997 by Sisters in Islam (SIS), National Council of Women's*

*Organisations (NCWO) and Association of Women Lawyers (AWL)*. Available at www.sistersinislam.org.my/advocacy-memo.htm (last accessed May 2008).

Smith, Anthony D. 1991. *National Identity*. London, New York: Penguin Books.

Sonbol, Amira El Azhary (ed.). 1996. *Women, the Family, and Divorce Laws in Islamic History*. Syracuse: Syracuse University Press.

——. 1996a. "Adults and Minors in Ottoman Shariʿa Courts and Modern Law," in Amira El Azhary Sonbol (ed.), *Women, the Family, and Divorce Laws in Islamic History*. Syracuse: Syracuse University Press. Pp. 236–256.

——. 2001. "Rethinking Women and Islam," in Yvonne Yazbeck Haddad and John L. Esposito (eds.), *Daughters of Abraham: Feminist Thought in Judaism, Christianity, and Islam*. Gainesville: University Press of Florida. Pp. 108–146.

——. 2005. "History of Marriage Contracts in Egypt," in *HAWWA: Journal of Women of the Middle East and the Islamic World* 3. Pp. 159–196.

——. 2006. "Negotiating and Disputing Marriage and Business in Early Modern Egypt and Palestine," in *L'Homme* 17,2. Pp. 1–24.

Soofi, J. M. (ed.). 1954. "The Aga Khan's Message to All Pakistan Women's Association," in *Message of His Highness the Rt. Hon'ble Sir Sultan Muhammad Shah the Aga Khan to Muslim Women*. Nairobi: Ismailia Association for Kenya.

Stone, Lawrence. 1992. *Road to Divorce: England 1530–1987*. Oxford: Oxford University Press.

Stone, Suzanne Last. 1991. "Sinaitic and Noahide Law: Legal Pluralism in Jewish Law," in *Cardozo Law Review* 12. Pp. 1157–1214.

——. 1993. "In Pursuit of the Countertext: The Turn to the Jewish Legal Model in Contemporary American Legal Theory," in *Harvard Law Review* 106. Pp. 813–894.

——. 2000. "The Intervention of American Law in Jewish Divorce: A Pluralist Analysis," in *Israeli Law Review* 34. Pp. 170–210.

Strawson, P. F. 1995. "Some Problems with Translations," in *Law and Critique* 6. Pp. 21–38.

*Sunan Abī Dāwūd*. 1984. Tr. Ahmad Hassan. Lahore: Ashraf Publications.

Surty, Mohammed Ibrahim. 1991. "The Shariʿa Family Law Courts in Britain and the Protection of Women's Rights in Muslim Family Law with Special Reference to the Dissolution of Marriage at the Instance of the Wife," in *Muslim Education Quarterly* 9. Pp. 59–68.

Tabari, A., and N. Yeganeh. 1982. *In the Shadow of Islam: The Women's Movement in Iran*. London: Zed.

Toledano, Henry. 1981. *Judicial Practice and Family Law in Morocco. The Chapter on Marriage from Sijilmāsī's* al-ʿAmal al-muṭlaq. Boulder, Colo.: Social Science Monographs.

Tucker, Judith E. 1998. *In the House of the Law: Gender and Islamic Law in Ottoman Syria and Palestine*. Berkeley: University of California Press.

Tyan, E. 1945. *Le Notariat et le régime de la preuve par écrit dans la pratique du droit musulman*. [Beirut]: Annales de l'Ecole Française de Droit de Beyrouth.

Union of Muslim Organisations. 1983. *Why Islamic Family Law for British Muslims?* London: Union of Muslim Organisations.

Vila, Salvador. 1931. "Abenmoguit. Formulario notarial," in *Anuario de Historia del Derecho Español* 8. Pp. 5–200.

——. 1933. "Un contrato de matrimonio entre musulmanes del siglo XVI," in *Anuario de Historia del Derecho Español* 10. Pp. 186–196.
Vogel, Frank E. and Samuel L. Hayes, III. 1998. *Islamic Law and Finance: Religion, Risk, and Return*. The Hague: Kluwer Law International.
Wadud-Muhsin, Amina. 1992, ²1999. *The Qur'an and Woman*. Kuala Lumpur: Fajar Bakti; rev. edition Oxford: Oxford University Press.
Wakin, Jeanette A. 1972. *The Function of Documents in Islamic Law: The Chapters on Sales from Ṭaḥāwī's Kitāb al-Shurūṭ al-kabīr*. Albany: State University of New York Press.
Walji, Shirin. 1974. "A History of the Ismaili Community in Tanzania." Ph.D. diss., University of Wisconsin.
Walsh, P. G. (ed. and tr.). 2001. Saint Augustine, Bishop of Hippo. *De bono coniugali; De sancta uirginitate*. Oxford: Clarendon Press.
al-Wansharīsī, Aḥmad b. Yaḥyā. 1981–1983. *al-Miʿyār al-muʿrib wa-l-jāmiʿ al-mughrib ʿan fatāwā ʿulamāʾ Ifrīqiya wa-l-Andalus wa-l-Maghrib*. 13 vols. Ed. M. Ḥajjī et al. Rabat: Wizārat al-Awqāf wa-l-shuʿūn al-islāmiyya.
Wiegers, G. A. 1991. "Yça Gidelli (fl. 1450), his Antecedents and Successors: A Historical Study of Islamic Literature in Spanish and Aljamiado." Ph.D. diss., Leiden University.
Wilson, Nicholas. 1999. "Pre-Nuptial Agreements—Ancillary Relief Reform: Response of Judges of the Family Division to Government Proposals," in *Family Law* 29. Pp. 159–163.
Witte, John. 1997. *From Sacrament to Contract: Marriage, Religion, and Law in the Western Tradition*. Louisville, Kentucky: Westminster John Knox Press.
Würth, Anna. 1995. "A *Sanaʿa* Court: The Family and the Ability to Negotiate," in *Islamic Law and Society* 2:3. Pp. 320–340.
Wynn, L. L. 1994. "Nationalism, Sexuality and the Saudi Gazette," in *McGill Journal of Middle Eastern Studies* 1994: 137–156.
——. 1996. "Marriage Contracts and Women's Rights in Saudi Arabia," in Homa Hoodfar (ed.), *Shifting Boundaries in Marriage and Divorce in Muslim Communities*. Montpellier, France: Women Living Under Muslim Laws. Pp. 106–121.
——. 1997. "The Romance of Tahliyya Street: Youth Culture, Commodities and the Use of Public Space in Jiddah," in *Middle East Report* 204. Pp. 30–31.
Yamani, Mai (ed.). 1996. *Feminism and Islam: Legal and Literary Perspectives*. New York: New York University Press.
——. 2000. *Changed Identities: The Challenge of the New Generation in Saudi Arabia*. London: Royal Institute of International Affairs.
Yazbak, Mahmoud. 2002. "Minor Marriages and Khiyār al-Bulūgh in Ottoman Palestine: A Note on Women's Strategies in a Patriarchal Society," in *Islamic Law and Society* 9:3. Pp. 386–409.
al-Zaylaʿī, Fakhr al-Dīn ibn ʿUthmān ibn ʿAlī. 2000. *Tabyīn al-ḥaqāʾiq sharḥ Kanz al-daqāʾiq*. Beirut: Dār al-Kutub al-ʿIlmiyya.
Ziadeh, Farhat. 1957. "Equality (*Kafāʾah*) in the Muslim Law of Marriage," in *American Journal of Comparative Law* 6:4 (1957). Pp. 503–517.
Zomeño, Amalia. 1997. "Kafāʾa in the Maliki School: A Fatwa from Fifteenth-Century Fes," in R. Gleave and Eugenia Kermeli (eds.), *Islamic Law: Theory and Practice*. London: I. B. Tauris. Pp. 87–106.

——. 2000. "Donaciones matrimoniales y transmisión de propiedades inmuebles: estudio del contenido de la *siyaqa* y la *nihla* en al-Andalus," in P. Cressier, M. Fierro and J.-P. Van Staëvel (eds.), *L'Urbanisme dans l'occident musulman au moyen âge. Aspects juridiques*. Madrid: Casa de Velázquez-CSIC. Pp. 75–99.

——. 2000a. *Dote y matrimonio en al-Andalus y el norte de África: Estudios sobre la jurisprudencia islámica medieval*. Madrid: CSIC.

——. 2002. "Abandoned Wives and Their Possibilities for Divorce in al-Andalus: The Evidence of the *Wathā'iq* Works," in R. Deguilhem and M. Marín (eds.), *Writing the Feminine. Women in Arab Sources*. London and New York: I. B. Tauris.

Zornberg, Lisa. 1995. "Beyond the Constitution: Is the New York Get Legislation Good Law," in *Pace Law Review* 15. Pp. 703–786.

# INDEX